From a Photo by Gunn & Stuart, Richmond, Surrey.

Yours with truth and
regard Isabel Burton

PERSONAL NARRATIVE

OF A

PILGRIMAGE

TO

AL-MADINAH & MECCAH

BY

CAPTAIN SIR RICHARD F. BURTON,

K.C.M.G., F.R.G.S., &c., &c., &c.

EDITED BY HIS WIFE,

ISABEL BURTON.

"Our notions of Mecca must be drawn from the Arabians; as no unbeliever is permitted to enter the city, our travellers are silent."—*Gibbon*, chap. 50.

Memorial Edition.

———

IN TWO VOLUMES

VOLUME I.

DOVER PUBLICATIONS, INC.
NEW YORK

Published in Canada by General Publishing Company, Ltd., 30 Lesmill Road, Don Mills, Toronto, Ontario.

Published in the United Kingdom by Constable and Company, Ltd., 10 Orange Street, London WC 2.

This Dover edition, first published in 1964, is an unabridged republication of the Memorial Edition, as published by Tylston and Edwards in 1893.

Standard Book Number: 486-21217-3
Library of Congress Catalog Card Number: 64-18842

Manufactured in the United States of America
Dover Publications, Inc.
180 Varick Street
New York, N.Y. 10014

CONTENTS

OF

THE FIRST VOLUME.

PART I.—AL-MISR.

Contents.

الليل والخيل والبيداءُ تعرِ فنى

والسيفُ والضيفُ و'المقرطاسُ والقلمِ

Dark and the Desert and Destriers me ken,
And the Glaive and the Joust, and Paper and Pen.
Al-Mutanabbi.

LIST OF ILLUSTRATIONS
IN VOLUME I.

———

This Memorial Edition

OF

THE WORKS OF

CAPTAIN SIR RICHARD F. BURTON

IS

DEDICATED

TO

ALL ENGLISH-SPEAKING PEOPLES,

Who respect and honour the name of RICHARD BURTON, the Soldier, Linguist, Scholar, Explorer and Discoverer, Poet, Author, and Benefactor to Science; in recognition of the labours of a long and honourable life, devoted to the Service of his Country, and to the advancement of its Knowledge and of its Literature.

PREFACE

TO

The Memorial Edition.

—

AFTER my beloved husband had passed away from amongst us, after the funeral had taken place, and I had settled in England, I began to think in what way I could render him the most honour. A material Monument to his memory has already been erected by his countrymen in the shape of a handsome contribution to the beautiful Mausoleum-tent in stone and marble to contain his remains; but I also hoped to erect a less material, but more imperishable, Monument to his name, by making this unique hero better known to his countrymen by his Works, which have hitherto not been sufficiently known, not extensively enough published, and issued perhaps at a prohibitive price. Viewing the long list of Works written by him between 1842 and 1890, many of which are still unpublished, I was almost disheartened by the magnitude of the work, until the Publishers, Messrs. Tylston and Edwards, fully appreciating the interest with which the British Public had followed my husband's adventurous career and fearless enterprise, arranged to produce this uniform Memorial Edition at their own expense.

Mr. Leonard Smithers, a man of great literary talent and of indefatigable energy, who admired and collaborated with my husband in the traduction of Latin Classics for two years before he died, has also kindly volunteered to be my working assistant and to join with me in the editing.

My part is to give up all my copyrights, and to search out such papers, annotations, and latest notes and corrections, as will form the most complete work; also to write all the Prefaces, and to give every assistance in my power as Editress.

The Memorial Edition commences with the present "Pilgrimage to Al-Madinah and Meccah," which will be followed at intervals by others of my husband's works. Since this "*Memorial Edition*" was arranged, and the Prospectus issued, I have parted with the Copyright of my husband's famous translation of the "Arabian Nights" to the Publishers, and they are arranging to bring out that work at an early date, and as nearly as possible uniform in appearance with the Memorial Edition.

The ornamentations on the binding are, a figure of my husband in his Arab costume, his monogram in Arabic, and, on the back of the book, the tent which is his tomb.*

Both the publishers and myself have to thank Mr. Smithers for the infinite trouble he has taken in collating the first, second, third and fourth editions of the 'Pilgrimage' with Sir Richard's own original annotated copies. All the lengthy notes and appendices of the first edition have been retained, and these are supplemented by the notes and appendices in the later editions, as well as by the author's MS. notes. He has adopted Sir Richard's latest and

*In this Dover edition, the illustration of Sir Richard Burton in his Arab costume appear as the frontispiece to Volume II. Burton's monogram in Arabic is reproduced on page xxiv, and his tomb at Mortlake appears on the page facing page 1.

most correct orthography of Arabic words, and has passed the sheets through the press. Following my husband's plan in "The Thousand Nights and a Night," he has put the accents on Arabic words only the first time of their appearance, to show *how* they ought to be; thinking it unnecessary to preserve throughout, what is an eyesore to the reader and a distress to the printer. So it is with Arabic books,— the accents are only put for the early student; afterwards, they are left to the practical knowledge of the reader. All the original coloured illustrations of the first edition, and also the wood engravings of the later issues, are reproduced for the first time in *one* uniform edition. The map and plans are fac-similes of those in the latest (fourth) edition. In fact, everything has been done to make this book worthy of its author and of the public's appreciation.*

For those who may not know the import of "A Pilgrimage to Al-Madinah and Meccah," in 1853, they will not take it amiss when I say that there are Holy Shrines of the Moslem world in the far-away Desert, where no white man, European, or Christian, could enter (save as a Moslem), or even approach, without certain death. They are more jealously guarded than the "Holy Grail," and this Work narrates how this Pilgrimage was accomplished. My husband had lived as a Dervish in Sind, which greatly helped him; and he studied every separate thing until he was master of it, even apprenticing himself to a blacksmith to learn how to make horse-shoes and to shoe his own horses. It meant living with his life in his hand, amongst the strangest and wildest companions, adopting their unfamiliar manners, living for nine months in the hottest and most unhealthy climate, upon

*This Dover edition contains black and white reproductions of all the illustrations in the Memorial Edition, but a few of the maps and plans are reproduced in a somewhat smaller format.

xviii *Pilgrimage to Al-Madinah and Meccah.*

repulsive food ; it meant complete and absolute isolation from everything that makes life tolerable, from all civilisation, from all his natural habits ; the brain at high tension, but the mind never wavering from the *rôle* he had adopted ; but he liked it, he was happy in it, he felt at home in it, and in this Book he tells you how he did it, and what he saw.

Sir Richard Burton died at the age of 70, on the 20th October, 1890. During the last 48 years of his life, he lived only for the benefit and for the welfare of England and of his countrymen, and of the Human Race at large. Let us reverently raise up this "Monument," *aere perennius,* to his everlasting memory.

ISABEL BURTON.

May 24, 1893.

PREFACE

TO THE

THIRD EDITION.

———

AFTER a lapse of twenty-five years, a third edition of my Pilgrimage has been called for by the public, to whom I take this opportunity of returning thanks. Messrs. Mullan have chosen the very best opportunity. My two publications concerning the Khedival Expeditions to Midian ("The Gold Mines of Midian," and "The Land of Midian Revisited"), are, as I have stated in the Preface, sequels and continuations of this Pilgrimage from which the adventures forming their subject may be said to date.

The text has been carefully revised, and the "baggage of notes" has been materially lightened.[1] From the Appendix I have removed matter which, though useful to the student, is of scant general interest. The quaint and interesting "Narrative and Voyages of Ludovicus Vertomannus, Gentleman of Rome," need no longer be read in extracts, when the whole has been printed by the Hakluyt Society. (The Travels of Ludovico di Varthema in Egypt, Syria, Arabia Deserta and Arabia Felix, in Persia, India, and Ethiopia, A.D. 1503 to 1508. Translated from the original Italian edition of 1510, with a Preface by John Winter Jones, Esq., F.S.A., and edited,

———

[1] These omitted notes and appendices have all been restored to the present Edition.

with notes and an Introduction, by George Percy Badger, late Government Chaplain in the Presidency of Bombay. London.) On the other hand, I have inserted after the Appendix, with the permission of the author, two highly interesting communications from Dr. Aloys Sprenger, the well-known Orientalist and Arabist, concerning the routes of the Great Caravans. My friend supports his suspicions that an error of direction has been made, and geographers will enjoy the benefit of his conscientious studies, topographical and linguistic.

The truculent attacks made upon pilgrims and Darwayshes call for a few words of notice. Even that learned and amiable philanthropist, the late Dr. John Wilson of Bombay ("Lands of the Bible," vol. ii., p. 302) alludes, in the case of the Spaniard Badia, *alias* Ali Bey al-Abbásí, to the "unjustifiable fanciful disguise of a Mohammedan Pilgrim." The author of the Ruddy Goose Theory ("Voice of Israel from Mount Sinai") and compiler of the "Historical Geography of Arabia" has dealt a foul blow to the memory of Burckhardt, the energetic and inoffensive Swiss traveller, whose name has ever been held in the highest repute. And now the "Government Chaplain" indites (Introduction, p. xxvii.) the following invidious remarks touching the travels of Ludovico di Varthema —the *vir Deo carus*, be it remarked, of the learned and laical Julius Cæsar Scaliger:

"This is not the place to discuss the morality of an act involving the deliberate and voluntary denial of what a man holds to be truth in a matter so sacred as that of Religion. Such a violation of conscience is not justifiable by the end which the renegade (!) may have in view, however abstractedly praiseworthy it may be; and even granting that his demerit should be gauged by the amount of knowledge which he possesses of what is true and what false, the conclusion is inevitable, that nothing short of utter ignorance of the precepts of his faith, or a

conscientious disbelief in them, can fairly relieve the
Christian, who conforms to Islamism without a corres-
ponding persuasion of its verity, of the deserved odium
all honest men attach to apostasy and hypocrisy."

The reply to this tirade is simply, "Judge not; especially when you are ignorant of the case which you are
judging." Perhaps also the writer may ask himself, Is
it right for those to cast stones who dwell in a tenement
not devoid of fragility?

The second attack proceeds from a place whence no
man would reasonably have expected it. The author of
the "Narrative of a Year's Journey through Central and
Eastern Arabia" (vol. i., pp. 258-59) thus expresses his
opinions:—

"Passing oneself off for a wandering Darweesh, as
some European explorers have attempted to do in the
East, is for more reasons than one a very bad plan. It
is unnecessary to dilate on that moral aspect of the proceeding which will always first strike unsophisticated
minds. To feign a religion which the adventurer himself
does not believe, to perform with scrupulous exactitude,
as of the highest and holiest import, practices which he
inwardly ridicules, and which he intends on his return to
hold up to the ridicule of others, to turn for weeks and
months together the most sacred and awful bearings of
man towards his Creator into a deliberate and truthless
mummery, not to mention other and yet darker touches,
—all this seems hardly compatible with the character of
a European gentleman, let alone that of a Christian."

This comes admirably *à propos* from a traveller who,
born a Protestant, of Jewish descent, placed himself "in
connection with," in plain words took the vows of, "the
order of the Jesuits," an order "well-known in the annals
of philanthropic daring"; a popular preacher who de-
claimed openly at Bayrút and elsewhere against his own
nation, till the proceedings of a certain Father Michael

Cohen were made the subject of an official report by
Mr. Consul-General Moore (Bayrut, November 11, 1857);
an Englishman by birth who accepted French protection,
a secret mission, and the "liberality of the present Emperor of the French"; a military officer travelling in the
garb of what he calls a native (Syrian) "quack" with a
comrade who "by a slight but necessary fiction
passed for his brother-in-law[1]"; a gentleman who by
return to Protestantism violated his vows, and a traveller
who was proved by the experiment of Colonel (now Sir
Lewis) Pelly to have brought upon himself all the perils
and adventures that have caused his charming work to
be considered so little worthy of trust.   Truly such attack
argues a sublime daring.   It is the principle of "vieille
coquette, nouvelle dévote"; it is Satan preaching against
Sin.   Both writers certainly lack the "giftie" to see
themselves as others see them.

In noticing these extracts my object is not to defend
myself : I recognize no man's right to interfere between a
human being and his conscience.   But what is there, I
would ask, in the Moslem Pilgrimage so offensive to
Christians—what makes it a subject of "inward ridicule"?
Do they not also venerate Abraham, the Father of the
Faithful?   Did not Locke, and even greater names, hold
Mohammedans to be heterodox Christians, in fact Arians
who, till the end of the fourth century, represented the
mass of North-European Christianity?   Did Mr. Lane
neverconform by praying at a Mosque in Cairo? did he
ever fear to confess it? has he been called an apostate for
so doing?   Did not Father Michael Cohen prove himself
an excellent Moslem at Wahhábi-land?
The fact is, there are honest men who hold that Al-

---

1 The brother-in-law, Barakat J'rayj'ray, has since that time
followed suit: educated at the Jesuit college of Mu'allakah (Libanus)
he has settled as a Greek Catholic priest at the neighbouring town
of Zahleh.

Islam, in its capital tenets, approaches much nearer to the faith of Jesus than do the Pauline and Athanasian modifications which, in this our day, have divided the Indo-European mind into Catholic and Roman, Greek and Russian, Lutheran and Anglican. The disciples of Dr. Daniel Schenkel's school ("A Sketch of the Character of Jesus," Longmans, 1869) will indeed find little difficulty in making this admission. Practically, a visit after Arab Meccah to Angle-Indian Aden, with its " priests after the order of Melchisedeck," suggested to me that the Moslem may be more tolerant, more enlightened, more charitable, than many societies of self-styled Christians.

And why rage so furiously against the "disguise of a wandering Darwaysh?" In what point is the Darwaysh more a mummer or in what does he show more of *bêtise* than the quack? Is the Darwaysh anything but an Oriental Freemason, and are Freemasons less Christians because they pray with Moslems and profess their belief in simple unitarianism?

I have said. And now to conclude.

After my return to Europe, many inquired if I was not the only living European who has found his way to the Head Quarters of the Moslem Faith. I may answer in the affirmative, so far, at least, that when entering the penetralia of Moslem life my Eastern origin was never questioned, and my position was never what *cagots* would describe as *in loco apostatæ*.

On the other hand, any Jew, Christian, or Pagan, after declaring before the Kázi and the Police Authorities at Cairo, or even at Damascus, that he embraces Al-Islam, may perform, without fear of the so-called Mosaic institution, "Al-Sunnah," his pilgrimage in all safety. It might be dangerous to travel down the Desert-line between Meccah and Al-Madinah during times of popular excitement; but the coast route is always safe. To the "new Moslem," however, the old Moslem is rarely well affected; and the former, as a rule, returns home unpleasantly impressed by his experiences.

The Eastern world moves slowly—*eppur si muove.* Half a generation ago steamers were first started to Jeddah: now we hear of a projected railroad from that port to Meccah, the shareholders being all Moslems. And the example of Jerusalem encourages us to hope that long before the end of the century a visit to Meccah will not be more difficult than a trip to Hebron.

Ziyadeh hadd-i-adab!

RICHARD F. BURTON.

London, 31st March, 1879.

الحاج عبد الله

Sir Richard Burton's monogram in Arabic.

PREFACE

TO THE

FIRST EDITION.

The interest just now felt in everything that relates to the East would alone be sufficient to ensure to the author of " El Medinah and Meccah " the favourable consideration of the Reading Public. But when it is borne in mind that since the days of William Pitts of Exeter (A.D. 1678—1688) no European travellers, with the exception of Burckhardt[1] and Lieut. Burton,[2] have been able to send us back an account of their travels there, it cannot be doubted but that the present work will be hailed as a welcome addition to our knowledge of these hitherto mysterious *penetralia* of Mohammedan superstition. In fact, El Madinah may be considered almost a virgin theme ; for as Burckhardt was prostrated by sickness throughout the period of his stay in the Northern Hejaz, he was not able to describe it as satisfactorily or minutely as he did the Southern country,— he could not send a plan of the Mosque, or correct the popular but erroneous ideas which prevail concerning it and the surrounding city.

The reader may question the propriety of introducing

---

1 In 1811.

2 Captain Sadlier is not mentioned, as his Frankish dress prevented his entering the city.

in a work of description, anecdotes which may appear open to the charge of triviality. The author's object, however, seems to be to illustrate the peculiarities of the people—to dramatise, as it were, the dry journal of a journey,—and to preserve the tone of the adventures, together with that local colouring in which mainly consists "*l'education d'un voyage.*" For the same reason, the prayers of the "Visitation" ceremony have been translated at length, despite the danger of inducing tedium; they are an essential part of the subject, and cannot be omitted, nor be represented by "specimens."

The extent of the Appendix requires some explanation. Few but literati are aware of the existence of Lodovico Bartema's naive recital, of the quaint narrative of Jos. Pitts, or of the wild journal of Giovanni Finati. Such extracts have been now made from these writers that the general reader can become acquainted with the adventures and opinions of the different travellers who have visited El Hejaz during a space of 350 years. Thus, with the second volume of Burckhardt's Travels in Arabia, the geographer, curious concerning this portion of the Moslem's Holy Land, possesses all that has as yet been written upon the subject.

The editor, to whom the author in his absence has intrusted his work, had hoped to have completed it by the simultaneous publication of the third volume, containing the pilgrimage to Meccah. The delay, however, in the arrival from India of this portion of the MS. has been such as to induce him at once to publish El Misr and El Medinah. The concluding volume on Meccah is now in the hands of the publisher, and will appear in the Autumn of the present year. Meanwhile the Public will not lose sight of the subject of Arabia. Part of El Hejaz has lately been inspected by M. Charles Didier, an eminent name in French literature, and by the Abbé Hamilton,—persuaded, it is believed, by our author to

visit Taif and Wady Laymum. Though entirely unconnected with the subjects of Meccah and El Medinah, the
account of the Sherif's Court where these gentlemen were
received with distinction, and of the almost unknown
regions about Jebel Kora, will doubtless be welcomed by
the Orientalists and Geographers of Europe.

Mr. Burton is already known by his "History of
Sindh." And as if to mark their sense of the spirit of
observation and daring evinced by him when in that
country, and still more during his late journeyings in
Arabia and East Africa, the Geographical Society,
through their learned Secretary, Dr. Norton Shaw, have
given valuable aid to this work in its progress through
the press, supplying maps where necessary to complete
the illustrations supplied by the author,—who, it will be
perceived, is himself no mean draughtsman.

It was during a residence of many years in India
that Mr. Burton had fitted himself for his late undertaking, by acquiring, through his peculiar aptitude for such
studies, a thorough acquaintance with various dialects of
Arabia and Persia ; and, indeed, his Eastern cast of
features (*vide* Frontispiece, Vol. II.) seemed already to
point him out as the very person of all others best suited
for an expedition like that described in the following
pages.

It will be observed that in writing Arabic, Hindoc-
stannee, Persian, or Turkish words, the author has
generally adopted the system proposed by Sir William
Jones and modified by later Orientalists.[1] But when a
word (like Fatihah for Fát-háh) has been "stamped" by
general popular use, the conversational form has been

---

[1] The orthography of Eastern words has been revised for this
Edition by Mr. Leonard C. Smithers, from Sir R. F. Burton's MS.
corrections, and in accordance with the orthography of Sir Richard's
most recent Oriental Work, "The Book of the Thousand Nights and
a Night."

preferred; and the same, too, may be said of the common corruptions, Cairo, Kadi, &c., which, in any other form, would appear to us pedantic and ridiculous. Still, in the absence of the author, it must be expected that some trifling errors and inaccuraces will have here and there have crept in. In justice to others and himself, the Editor, however, feels bound to acknowledge, with much gratitude, that where such or even greater mistakes have been avoided, it has been mainly due to the continued kindness of an Eastern scholar of more than European reputation,—who has assisted in revising the sheets before finally consigning them to the printer.

Let us hope that the proofs now furnished of untiring energy and capacity for observation and research by our author, as well as his ability to bear fatigue and exposure to the most inclement climate, will induce the Governments of this country and of India to provide him with men and means (evidently all that is required for the purpose) to pursue his adventurous and useful career in other countries equally difficult of access, and, if possible, of still greater interest, than the Eastern shores of the Red Sea.

THOMAS L. WOLLEY.

Hampton Court Palace,
June, 1855.

I DO not parade your name, my dear Colonel, in the van of this volume, after the manner of that acute tactician who stuck a Koran upon his lance in order to win a battle. Believe me it is not my object to use your orthodoxy as a cover to my heresies of sentiment and science, in politics, political economy and—what not ?

But whatever I have done on this occasion,—if I have done any thing,—has been by the assistance of a host of friends, amongst whom you were ever the foremost. And the highest privilege I aim at is this opportunity of publicly acknowledging the multitude of obligations owed to you and to them. Accept, my dear Colonel, this humble return for your kindness, and ever believe me,

The sincerest of your well wishers,

RICHARD F. BURTON.

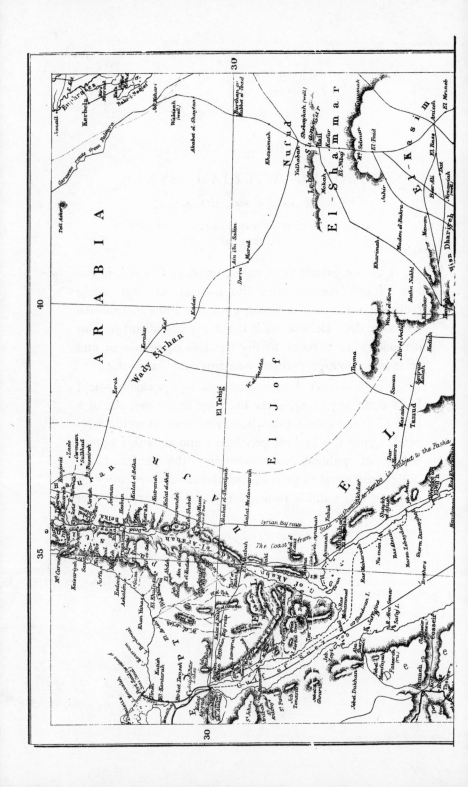

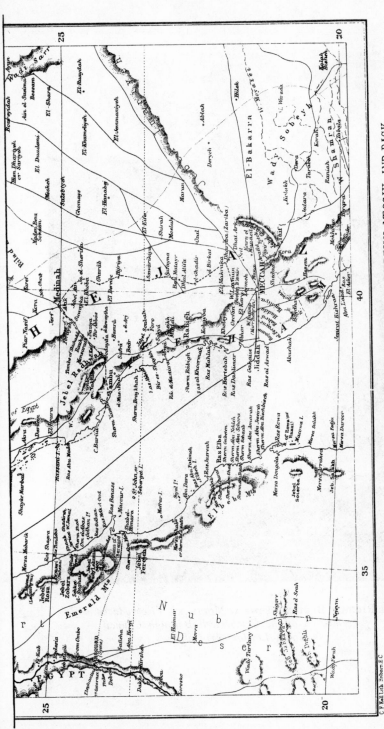

THE ROUTE OF SIR RICHARD F. BURTON, FROM SUEZ TO AL-MADINAH, MECCAH, AND BACK.

Outward Route ———————
Return   ‚‚ ———————

C.F. Kell Lith Holborn E.C.

SIR RICHARD BURTON'S TOMB AT MORTLAKE. *(Reproduced by permission of the Camberwell Borough Council: South London Art Gallery.)*

PART I.

AL-MISR.

CHAPTER I.

TO ALEXANDRIA.

A few Words concerning what induced me to a Pilgrimage.

IN the autumn of 1852, through the medium of my excellent friend, the late General Monteith, I offered my services to the Royal Geographical Society of London, for the purpose of removing that opprobrium to modern adventure, the huge white blot which in our maps still notes the Eastern and the Central regions of Arabia. Sir Roderick I. Murchison, Colonel P. Yorke and Dr. Shaw, a deputation from that distinguished body, with their usual zeal for discovery and readiness to encourage the discoverer, honoured me by warmly supporting, in a personal interview with the then Chairman of the then Court of Directors to the then Honourable East India Company, my application for three years' leave of absence on special duty from India to Maskat. But they were unable to prevail upon the said Chairman, the late Sir James Hogg, who,[1] remembering the fatalities which of late years have befallen sundry soldier-travellers in the East, refused his sanction, alleging as a reason[1]

---

1 "Remembering . . . . reason," *afterwards altered by the author to* "much disliking, if fact must be told, my impolitic habit of telling political truths, (in 1851 I had submitted to the Court of Directors certain remarks upon the subject of Anglo-Indian misrule: I

that the contemplated journey was of too dangerous a
nature. In compensation, however, for the disappointment, I was allowed the additional furlough of a year, in
order to pursue my Arabic studies in lands where the
language is best learned.

What remained for me but to prove, by trial, that
what might be perilous to other travellers was safe to
me? The "experimentum crucis" was a visit to Al-Híjaz,
at once the most difficult and the most dangerous point by
which a European can enter Arabia. I had intended,
had the period of leave originally applied for been granted,
to land at Maskat—a favourable starting-place—and
there to apply myself, slowly and surely, to the task of
spanning the deserts. But now I was to hurry, in the
midst of summer, after a four years' sojourn in Europe,
during which many things Oriental had faded away from
my memory, and—after passing through the ordeal of
Egypt, a country where the police is curious as in
Rome or Milan—to begin with the Moslem's Holy Land,
the jealously guarded and exclusive Harím. However,
being liberally supplied with the means of travel by the
Royal Geographical Society; thoroughly tired of " progress " and of " civilisation ;" curious to see with my eyes
what others are content to " hear with ears," namely,
Moslem inner life in a really Mohammedan country; and
longing, if truth be told, to set foot on that mysterious
spot which no vacation tourist has yet described, measured, sketched and photographed, I resolved to resume
my old character of a Persian wanderer,[1] a " Darwaysh,"
and to make the attempt.

---

need hardly say that the publication was refused with many threats),
and not unwilling to mortify my supporter (his colleague, Colonel
W. Sykes), refused his sanction, alleging as a no-reason," *et seq.*

1 The vagrant, the merchant, and the philosopher, amongst
Orientals, are frequently united in the same person.

The principal object with which I started was this : to cross the unknown Arabian Peninsula, in a direct line from either Al-Madínah to Maskat, or diagonally from Meccah to Makallah on the Indian Ocean. By what "Circumstance, the miscreator" my plans were defeated, the reader will discover in the course of these volumes. The secondary objects were numerous. I was desirous to find out if any market for horses could be opened between Central Arabia and India, where the studs were beginning to excite general dissatisfaction ; to obtain information concerning the Great Eastern wilderness, the vast expanse marked Rub'a al-Khálí (the " Empty Abode ") in our maps ; to inquire into the hydrography of the Hijaz, its water-shed, the disputed slope of the country, and the existence or non-existence of perennial streams ; and finally, to try, by actual observation, the truth of a theory proposed by Colonel W. Sykes, namely, that if tradition be true, in the population of the vast Peninsula there must exist certain physiological differences sufficient to warrant our questioning the common origin of the Arab family. As regards horses, I am satisfied that from the Eastern coast something might be done,—nothing on the Western, where the animals, though thorough-bred, are mere " weeds," of a foolish price and procurable only by chance. Of the Rub'a al-Khali I have heard enough, from credible relators, to conclude that its horrid depths swarm with a large and half-starving population ; that it abounds in Wadys, valleys, gullies and ravines, partially fertilised by intermittent torrents ; and, therefore, that the land is open to the adventurous traveller. Moreover, I am satisfied, that in spite of all geographers, from Ptolemy to Jomard, Arabia, which abounds in *fiumaras*,[1] possesses not

---

1 In a communication made to the Royal Geographical Society, and published in the 24th vol. of the Journal, I have given my reasons for naturalising this word. It will be used in the following pages to

a single perennial stream worthy the name of river;[1] and the testimony of the natives induces me to think, with Wallin, contrary to Ritter and others, that the Peninsula falls instead of rising towards the south. Finally, I have found proof, to be produced in a future part of this publication, for believing in three distinct races. 1. The aborigines of the country, driven like the Bhíls and other autochthonic Indians, into the eastern and south-eastern wilds bordering upon the ocean. 2. A Syrian or Mesopotamian stock, typified by Shem and Joktan, that drove the Indigenæ from the choicest tracts of country ; these invaders still enjoy their conquests, representing the great Arabian people. And 3. An impure Syro-Egyptian clan—we personify it by Ishmael, by his son Nabajoth, and by Edom, (Esau, the son of Isaac) — that populated and still populates the Sinaitic Peninsula. And in most places, even in the heart of Meccah, I met with *débris* of heathenry, proscribed by Mohammed, yet still popular, while the ignorant observers of the old customs assign to them a modern and a rationalistic origin.

I have entitled this account of my summer's tour through Al-Hijaz, a Personal Narrative, and I have laboured to make its nature correspond with its name, simply because " it is the personal that interests mankind." Many may not follow my example ;[2] but some

---

express a " hill water-course, which rolls a torrent after rain, and is either partially or wholly dry during the droughts." It is, in fact, the Indian " Nullah, or Nalá."

1 " In provinciis Arabum, ait Ibn Haukal, nullus dignoscitur fluvius, aut mare quod navigia ferat." This truth has been disputed, but now it is generally acknowledged.

2 A French traveller, the Viscount Escayrac de Lanture, was living at Cairo as a native of the East, and preparing for a pilgrimage when I was similarly engaged. Unfortunately he went to Damascus, where some disturbance compelled him to resume his nationality. The only European I have met with who visited Meccah without

perchance will be curious to see what measures I adopted, in order to appear suddenly as an Eastern upon the stage of Oriental life ; and as the recital may be found useful by future adventurers, I make no apology for the egotistical semblance of the narrative. Those who have felt the want of some " silent friend " to aid them with advice, when it must not be asked, will appreciate what may appear to the uninterested critic mere outpourings of a mind full of self.[1]

On the evening of April 3, 1853, I left London for Southampton. By the advice of a brother officer, Captain (now Colonel) Henry Grindlay, of the Bengal Cavalry,—little thought at that time the adviser or the advised how valuable was the suggestion !—my Eastern dress was called into requisition before leaving town, and all my " impedimenta " were taught to look exceedingly Oriental. Early the next day a " Persian Prince," accompanied by Captain Grindlay, embarked on board the Peninsular and Oriental Company's magnificent screw steamer " Bengal."

---

apostatising, is M. Bertolucci, Swedish Consul at Cairo. This gentleman persuaded the Badawin camel men who were accompanying him to Táif to introduce him in disguise : he naïvely owns that his terror of discovery prevented his making any observations. Dr. George A. Wallin, of Finland, performed the Hajj in 1845 ; but his " somewhat perilous position, and the filthy company of Persians," were effectual obstacles to his taking notes.

1 No one felt the want of this " silent friend " more than myself ; for though Eastern Arabia would not have been strange to me, the Western regions were a terra incognita. Through Dr. Norton Shaw, Secretary to the Royal Geographical Society, I addressed a paper full of questions to Dr. Wallin, professor of Arabic at the University of Helsingfors. But that adventurous traveller and industrious Orientalist was then, as we afterwards heard with sorrow, no more ; so the queries remained unanswered. In these pages I have been careful to solve all the little financial and domestic difficulties, so perplexing to the " freshman," whom circumstances compel to conceal his freshness from the prying eyes of friends.

A fortnight was profitably spent in getting into the train of Oriental manners. For what polite Chesterfield says of the difference between a gentleman and his reverse,—namely, that both perform the same offices of life, but each in a several and widely different way—is notably as applicable to the manners of the Eastern as of the Western man. Look, for instance, at that Indian Moslem drinking a glass of water. With us the operation is simple enough, but his performance includes no fewer than five novelties. In the first place he clutches his tumbler as though it were the throat of a foe ; secondly, he ejaculates, " In the name of Allah the Compassionate, the Merciful !" before wetting his lips ; thirdly, he imbibes the contents, swallowing them, not sipping them as he ought to do, and ending with a satisfied grunt ; fourthly, before setting down the cup, he sighs forth, " Praise be to Allah !"—of which you will understand the full meaning in the Desert ; and, fifthly, he replies, " May Allah make it pleasant to thee !" in answer to his friend's polite " Pleasurably and health !" Also he is careful to avoid the irreligious action of drinking the pure element in a standing position, mindful, however, of the three recognised exceptions, the fluid of the Holy Well Zemzem, water distributed in charity, and that which remains after Wuzu, the lesser ablution. Moreover, in Europe, where both extremities are used indiscriminately, one forgets the exclusive use of the right hand, the manipulation of the rosary, the abuse of the chair,—your genuine Oriental gathers up his legs, looking almost as comfortable in it as a sailor upon the back of a high-trotting horse—the rolling gait with the toes straight to the front, the grave look and the habit of pious ejaculations.

Our voyage over the " summer sea " was eventless. In a steamer of two or three thousand tons you discover the once dreaded, now contemptible, "stormy waters" only by the band—a standing nuisance be it remarked—performing

> " There we lay
> All the day,
> In the Bay of Biscay, O !"

The sight of glorious Trafalgar[1] excites none of the sentiments with which a tedious sail used to invest it. " Gib " is, probably, better known to you, by Théophile Gautier and Eliot Warburton, than the regions about Cornhill; besides which, you anchor under the Rock exactly long enough to land and to breakfast. Malta, too, wears an old familiar face, which bids you order a dinner and superintend the iceing of claret (beginning of Oriental barbarism), instead of galloping about on donkey-back through fiery air in memory of St. Paul and White-Cross Knights. But though our journey might be called monotonous, there was nothing to complain of. The ship was in every way comfortable; the cook, strange to say, was good, and the voyage lasted long enough, and not too long. On the evening of the thirteenth day after our start, the big-trowsered pilot, so lovely in his deformities to western eyes, made his appearance, and the good screw " Bengal " found herself at anchor off the Headland of Clay.[2]

Having been invited to start from the house of a kind friend, John W. Larking, I disembarked with him, and

---

1 " Then came Trafalgar : would that Nelson had known the meaning of that name ! it would have fixed a smile upon his dying lips !" so says the Rider through the Nubian Desert, giving us in a foot note the curious information that " Trafalgar " is an Arabic word, which means the " *Cape of Laurels.*" Trafalgar is nothing but a corruption of Tarf al-Ghárb—the side or skirt of the West ; it being the most occidental point then reached by Arab conquest.

2 In Arabic " Rás al-Tín," the promontory upon which immortal Pharos once stood. It is so called from the argile there found and which supported an old pottery.

rejoiced to see that by dint of a beard and a shaven head
I had succeeded, like the Lord of Geesh, in "misleading
the inquisitive spirit of the populace." The mingled herd
of spectators before whom we passed in review on the
landing-place, hearing an audible "Alhamdolillah"[1] whispered "Muslim!" The infant population spared me the
compliments usually addressed to hatted heads; and when
a little boy, presuming that the occasion might possibly
open the hand of generosity, looked in my face and exclaimed
"Bakhshísh,"[2] he obtained in reply a "Mafísh;"[3] which
convinced the bystanders that the sheep-skin covered a
real sheep. We then mounted a carriage, fought our
way through the donkeys, and in half an hour found ourselves, chibúk in mouth and coffee-cup in hand, seated
on the díwán of my friend Larking's hospitable home.

Wonderful was the contrast between the steamer
and that villa on the Mahmudiyah canal! Startling the
sudden change from presto to adagio life! In thirteen
days we had passed from the clammy grey fog, that at-

---

1 "Praise be to Allah, Lord of the (three) worlds!" a pious
ejaculation, which leaves the lips of the True Believer on all occasions
of concluding actions.

2 "*Bakhshish*," says a modern writer, "is a fee or present which
the Arabs (he here means the Egyptians, who got the word from the
Persians through the Turks,) claim on all occasions for services you
render them, as well as for services they have rendered you. A
doctor visits a patient gratis,—the patient or his servant will ask for a
bakhshish (largesse) ; you employ, pay, clothe, and feed a child—the
father will demand his *bakhshish ;* you may save the life of an Arab,
at the risk of your own, and he will certainly claim a *bakhshish*. This
bakhshish, in fact, is a sort of alms or tribute, which the poor Arab
believes himself entitled to claim from every respectable-looking
person."

3 Mafish, "there is none," equivalent to, "I have left my purse at
home." Nothing takes the Oriental mind so much as a retort alliter-
ative or jingling. An officer in the Bombay army (Colonel Hamerton)
once saved himself from assault and battery by informing a furious
band of natives, that under British rule "*harakat* na hui, *barakat* hui,"
"*blessing* hath there been to you ; *bane* there hath been none."

mosphere of industry which kept us at anchor off the Isle of Wight, through the loveliest air of the Inland Sea, whose sparkling blue and purple haze spread charms even on N. Africa's beldame features, and now we are sitting silent and still, listening to the monotonous melody of the East—the soft night-breeze wandering through starlit skies and tufted trees, with a voice of melancholy meaning.

And this is the Arab's *Kayf.* The savouring of animal existence ; the passive enjoyment of mere sense ; the pleasant languor, the dreamy tranquillity, the airy castle-building, which in Asia stand in lieu of the vigorous, intensive, passionate life of Europe. It is the result of a lively, impressible, excitable nature, and exquisite sensibility of nerve ; it argues a facility for voluptuousness unknown to northern regions, where happiness is placed in the exertion of mental and physical powers ; where *Ernst ist das Leben ;* where niggard earth commands ceaseless sweat of face, and damp chill air demands perpetual excitement, exercise, or change, or adventure, or dissipation, for want of something better. In the East, man wants but rest and shade : upon the banks of a bubbling stream, or under the cool shelter of a perfumed tree, he is perfectly happy, smoking a pipe, or sipping a cup of coffee, or drinking a glass of sherbet, but above all things deranging body and mind as little as possible ; the trouble of conversations, the displeasures of memory, and the vanity of thought being the most unpleasant interruptions to his *Kayf.* No wonder that " Kayf " is a word untranslatable in our mother-tongue ![1]

" Laudabunt alii claram Rhodon aut Mytelenen."

Let others describe the once famous Capital of

---

[1] In a coarser sense " kayf " is applied to all manner of intoxication. Sonnini is not wrong when he says, " the Arabs give the name of Kayf to the voluptuous relaxation, the delicious stupor, produced by the smoking of hemp."

Egypt, this City of Misnomers, whose dry docks are ever
wet, and whose marble fountain is eternally dry, whose
" Cleopatra's Needle "[1] is neither a needle nor Cleopatra's; whose " Pompey's Pillar " never had any earthly
connection with Pompey; and whose Cleopatra's Baths
are, according to veracious travellers, no baths at all.
Yet it is a wonderful place, this " Libyan suburb " of our
day, this outpost of civilisation planted upon the skirts
of barbarism, this Osiris seated side by side with Typhon,
his great old enemy.   Still may be said of it, " it ever
beareth something new[2];" and Alexandria, a threadbare
subject in Bruce's time, is even yet, from its perpetual
changes, a fit field for modern description.[3]

---

1 Cleopatra's Needle is called by the native Ciceroni " Masallat
Firaun," Pharaoh's packing needle. What Solomon, and the Jinnís
and Sikandar zu'l karnain (Alexander of Macedon), are to other
Moslem lands, such is Pharaoh to Egypt, the " Cæsar aut Diabolus "
of the Nile. The ichneumon becomes " Pharaoh's cat,"—even the
French were bitten and named it, le rat de Pharaon; the prickly
pear, " Pharaoh's fig;" the guinea-worm, " Pharaoh's worm;" certain unapproachable sulphur springs, " Pharaoh's bath;" a mausoleum at Petra, " Pharaoh's palace;" the mongrel race now
inhabiting the valley of the Nile is contemptuously named by
Turks and Arabs " Jins Firaun," or "Pharaoh's Breed;" and a foul
kind of vulture (vultur percnopterus, ak baba of the Turks, and ukab
of Sind), " Pharaoh's hen." This abhorrence of Pharaoh is, however, confined to the vulgar and the religious. The philosophers
and mystics of Al-Islam, in their admiration of his impious daring,
make him equal, and even superior, to Moses. Sáhil, a celebrated
Súfi, declares that the secret of the soul (*i.e.*, its emanation) was
first revealed when Pharaoh declared himself a god. And Al-
Ghazáli sees in such temerity nothing but the most noble aspiration
to the divine, innate in the human, spirit. (Dabistán, vol. iii.)

2 Aἐί φερεί τι καίνον. " Quid novi fert Africa ? " said the Romans.
" In the same season Fayoles, tetrarch of Numidia, sent from the
land of Africa to Grangousier, the most hideously great mare that
was ever seen ; for you know well enough how it is said, that ' Africa
always is productive of some new thing.'"

3 Alexandria, moreover, is an interesting place to Moslems, on
account of the prophecy that it will succeed to the honours of Meccah,

The better to blind the inquisitive eyes of servants
and visitors, my friend, Larking, lodged me in an out-
house, where I could revel in the utmost freedom of
life and manners. And although some Armenian Dragoman, a restless spy like all his race, occasionally remarked
voilà un Persan diablement dégagé, none, except those
who were entrusted with the secret, had any idea of the
part I was playing. The domestics, devout Moslems,
pronounced me an 'Ajami,[1] a kind of Mohammedan, not
a good one like themselves, but, still better than nothing.
I lost no time in securing the assistance of a Shaykh,[2]
and plunged once more into the intricacies of the Faith;
revived my recollections of religious ablutions, read the
Koran, and again became an adept in the art of prostration. My leisure hours were employed in visiting the
baths and coffee-houses, in attending the bazars, and in
shopping,—an operation which hereabouts consists of
sitting upon a chapman's counter, smoking, sipping
coffee, and telling your beads the while, to show that you
are not of the slaves for whom time is made; in fact, in
pitting your patience against that of your adversary, the
vendor. I found time for a short excursion to a country
village on the banks of the canal; nor was an opportunity
of seeing " Al-nahl," the " Bee-dance," neglected, for it
would be some months before my eyes might dwell on
such a pleasant spectacle again.

" Delicias videam, Nile jocose, tuas ! "

Careful of graver matters, I attended the mosque,
and visited the venerable localities in which modern
Alexandria abounds. Pilgrimaging Moslems are here

---

when the holy city falls into the hands of the infidel. In its turn
Alexandria will be followed by Kairawan (in the Regency of Tunis) ;
and this by Rashid or Rosetta, which last shall endure to the end of
time.

1 A Persian as opposed to an Arab.

2 A priest, elder, chieftain, language-master, private-tutor, &c., &c.

shown the tomb of Al-nabi Daniyal (Daniel the Prophet), discovered upon a spot where the late Sultan Mahmúd dreamed that he saw an ancient man at prayer.[1] Sikandar al-Rumi, the Moslem Alexander the Great, of course left his bones in the place bearing his name, or, as he ought to have done so, bones have been found for him.   Alexandria also boasts of two celebrated Walís—holy men. One is Mohammed al-Busiri, the author of a poem called Al-Burdah, universally read by the world of Islam, and locally recited at funerals and on other solemn occasions.   The other is Abu Abbas al-Andalúsi, a sage and saint of the first water, at whose tomb prayer is never breathed in vain.

It is not to be supposed that the people of Alexandria could look upon my phials and pill-boxes without a yearning for their contents.   An Indian doctor, too, was a novelty to them; Franks they despised,—but a man who had come so far from East and West ! Then there was something infinitely seducing in the character of a magician, doctor, and fakír, each admirable of itself, thus combined to make " great medicine."   Men, women, and children besieged my door, by which means I could see the people face to face, and especially the fair sex, of which Europeans, generally speaking, know only the worst specimens.   Even respectable natives, after witnessing a performance of " Mandal" and the Magic mirror[2], opined that the stranger was a holy man, gifted

---

1 The Persians place the Prophet's tomb at Susan or Sus, described by Ibn Haukal (p. 76).   The readers of Ibn Batutah may think it strange that the learned and pious traveller in his account of Alexandria (chap. 2.) makes no allusion to the present holy deceased that distinguish the city.   All the saints are now clear forgotten.   For it is the fate of saints, like distinguished sinners, to die twice.

2 The Mandal is that form of Oriental divination which owes its present celebrity in Europe to Mr. Lane.   Both it and the magic mirror are hackneyed subjects, but I have been tempted to a few words concerning them in another part of these volumes.   Meanwhile

with supernatural powers, and knowing everything. One old person sent to offer me his daughter in marriage; he said nothing about dowry,—but I thought proper to decline the honour. And a middle-aged lady proffered me the sum of one hundred piastres, nearly one pound sterling, if I would stay at Alexandria, and superintend the restoration of her blind left eye.

But the reader must not be led to suppose that I acted " Carabin " or " Sangrado " without any knowledge of my trade. From youth I have always been a dabbler in medical and mystical study. Moreover, the practice of physic is comparatively easy amongst dwellers in warm latitudes, uncivilised peoples, where there is not that complication of maladies which troubles more polished nations. And further, what simplifies extremely the treatment of the sick in these parts is the undoubted periodicity of disease, reducing almost all to one type—ague.[1] Many of the complaints of tropical climates, as medical men well know, display palpably intermittent symptoms little known to colder countries ; and speaking from individual experience, I may safely assert that in all cases of suffering, from a wound to ophthalmia, this phenomenon has forced itself upon my notice. So much by way of excuse. I therefore considered myself as well qualified for the work as if I had taken out a *buono per l'estero* diploma at Padua, and not more likely to do active harm than most of the regularly graduated young surgeons who start to "finish" themselves upon the frame of the British soldier.

After a month's hard work at Alexandria, I prepared to assume the character of a wandering Darwaysh; after

---

I request the reader not to set me down as a mere charlatan ; medicine in the East is so essentially united with superstitious practices, that he who would pass for an expert practitioner, must necessarily represent himself an " adept."

1 Hence the origin, I believe, of the Chronothermal System, a discovery which physic owes to my old friend, the late Dr. Samuel Dickson.

reforming my title from "Mirza"[1] to "Shaykh" Abdullah.[2]   A reverend man, whose name I do not care to
quote, some time ago initiated me into his order, the
Kadiriyah, under the high-sounding name of Bismillah-
Shah :[3] and, after a due period of probation, he graciously
elevated me to the proud position of a Murshid,[4] or Master
in the mystic craft.   I was therefore sufficiently well acquainted with the tenets and practices of these Oriental
Freemasons.   No character in the Moslem world is so
proper for disguise as that of the Darwaysh.   It is assumed
by all ranks, ages, and creeds ; by the nobleman who has
been disgraced at court, and by the peasant who is too
idle to till the ground ; by Dives, who is weary of life, and
by Lazarus, who begs his bread from door to door.
Further, the Darwaysh is allowed to ignore ceremony and
politeness, as one who ceases to appear upon the stage of
life ; he may pray or not, marry or remain single as he
pleases, be respectable in cloth of frieze as in cloth of
gold, and no one asks him—the chartered vagabond—

---

1 The Persian " Mister."   In future chapters the reader will see
the uncomfortable consequences of my having appeared in Egypt as
a Persian.   Although I found out the mistake, and worked hard to
correct it, the bad name stuck to me ; bazar reports fly quicker and
hit harder than newspaper paragraphs.

2 Arab Christians sometimes take the name of "Abdullah," servant
of Allah—" which," as a modern traveller observes, " all sects and religions might be equally proud to adopt."   The Moslem Prophet
said, " the names most approved of God are Abdullah, Abd-al-
rahman (Slave of the Compassionate), and such like."

3 " King in-the-name-of-Allah," a kind of Oriental " Praise-God-
Barebones."   When a man appears as a Fakir or Darwaysh, he casts
off, in process of regeneration, together with other worldly sloughs,
his laical name for some brilliant coat of nomenclature rich in religious promise.

4 A Murshid is one allowed to admit Murids or apprentices into
the order.   As the form of the diploma conferred upon this occasion
may be new to many European Orientalists, I have translated it in
Appendix I.

Why he comes here ? or Wherefore he goes there ? He
may wend his way on foot alone, or ride his Arab mare
followed by a dozen servants ; he is equally feared without weapons, as swaggering through the streets armed to
the teeth. The more haughty and offensive he is to the
people, the more they respect him ; a decided advantage
to the traveller of choleric temperament. In the hour of
imminent danger, he has only to become a maniac, and
he is safe ; a madman in the East, like a notably eccentric
character in the West, is allowed to say or do whatever
the spirit directs. Add to this character a little knowledge of medicine, a "moderate skill in magic, and a reputation for caring for nothing but study and books," together with capital sufficient to save you from the chance
of starving, and you appear in the East to peculiar
advantage. The only danger of the "Mystic Path"[1] is,
that the Darwaysh's ragged coat not unfrequently covers
the cut-throat, and, if seized in the society of such a
"brother," you may reluctantly become his companion,
under the stick or on the stake. For be it known, Darwayshes are of two orders, the Sharai, or those who conform to religion, and the Bi-Sharai, or Lútí, whose practices are hinted at by their own tradition that "he we
daurna name" once joined them for a week, but at the
end of that time left them in dismay, and returned to
whence he came.

---

1 The Taríkat or path, which leads, or is supposed to lead, to
Heaven.

CHAPTER II.

I LEAVE ALEXANDRIA.

THE thorough-bred wanderer's idiosyncracy I presume to be a composition of what phrenologists call "inhabitiveness" and "locality" equally and largely developed. After a long and toilsome march, weary of the way, he drops into the nearest place of rest to become the most domestic of men. For a while he smokes the "pipe of permanence"[1] with an infinite zest; he delights in various siestas during the day, relishing withal deep sleep during the dark hours; he enjoys dining at a fixed dinner hour, and he wonders at the demoralisation of the mind which cannot find means of excitement in chit-chat or small talk, in a novel or a newspaper. But soon the passive fit has passed away; again a paroxysm of ennui coming on by slow degrees, Viator loses appetite, he walks about his room all night, he yawns at conversations, and a book acts upon him as a narcotic. The man wants to wander, and he must do so, or he shall die.

After about a month most pleasantly spent at Alexandria, I perceived the approach of the enemy, and as nothing hampered my incomings and outgoings, I surrendered. The world was "all before me," and there was pleasant excitement in plunging single-handed into its chilling depths. My Alexandrian Shaykh, whose heart

---

[1] The long pipe which at home takes the place of the shorter chibúk used on the road.

fell victim to a new "jubbah," which I had given in exchange for his tattered za'abút[1] offered me, in consideration
of a certain monthly stipend, the affections of a brother and
religious refreshment, proposing to send his wife back to
her papa, and to accompany me, in the capacity of private
chaplain to the other side of Káf.[2] I politely accepted
the " Bruderschaft," but many reasons induced me to
decline his society and services. In the first place, he
spoke the detestable Egyptian jargon. Secondly, it was
but prudent to lose the " spoor " between Alexandria and
Suez. And, thirdly, my " brother " had shifting eyes
(symptoms of fickleness), close together (indices of cunning) ; a flat-crowned head, and large ill-fitting lips ; signs
which led me to think lightly of his honesty, firmness,
and courage. Phrenology and physiognomy, be it observed, disappoint you often amongst civilised people, the
proper action of whose brain upon the features is impeded
by the external pressure of education, accident, example, habit, and necessity. But they are tolerably safe
guides when groping your way through the mind of man
in his so-called natural state, a being of impulse, in that
chrysalis condition of mental development which is rather
instinct than reason.

Before my departure, however, there was much to be
done.

The land of the Pharaohs is becoming civilised, and
unpleasantly so : nothing can be more uncomfortable than
its present middle state, between barbarism and the reverse. The prohibition against carrying arms is rigid as
in Italy ; all " violence" is violently denounced ; and be-

---

1 The jubbah is a long outer garment, generally of cloth, worn by
learned and respectable men. The za'abut is a large bag-sleeved black
or brown coloured robe made of home-spun woollen, the garb of the
peasant, the hedge-priest, and the darwaysh.

2 The mountain which encircles the globe, according to the sacred
geography of the Moslems. To "go to Kaf" is equivalent to our "go
to Jericho," or—somewhere else.

heading being deemed cruel, the most atrocious crimes, as well as those small political offences, which in the days of the Mamlúks would have led to a beyship or a bow-string, receive fourfold punishment by deportation to Fayzoghlú, the local Cayenne.   If you order your peasant to be flogged, his friends gather in threatening hundreds at your gates; when you curse your boatman, he complains to your consul; the dragomans afflict you with strange wild notions about honesty ; a Government order prevents you from using vituperative language to the "natives" in general ; and the very donkey boys are becoming cognisant of the right of man to remain unbastinadoed.   Still the old leaven remains behind: here, as elsewhere in the "Morning-land," you cannot hold your own without employing the *voie de fait.*   The passport system, now dying out of Europe, has sprung up, or rather has revived, in Egypt, with peculiar vigour.[1]   Its good effects claim for it our respect ; still we cannot but lament its inconvenience.   By *we,* I mean real Easterns. As strangers—even those whose beards have whitened in the land—know absolutely nothing of what unfortunate natives must endure, I am tempted to subjoin a short

---

1 Sir G. Wilkinson, referring his readers to Strabo, remarks that the "troublesome system of passports seems to have been adopted by the Egyptians at a very early period." Its present rigours, which have lasted since the European troubles in 1848 and 1849, have a two-fold object ; in the first place, to act as a clog upon the dangerous emigrants which Germany, Italy, and Greece have sent out into the world ; and secondly, to confine the subjects of the present Pasha of Egypt to their fatherland and the habit of paying taxes. The enlightened ruler (this was written during the rule of Abbás Pasha) knows his own interests, and never willingly parts with a subject liable to cess, at times objecting even to their obeying pilgrimage law. We, on the other hand, in India, allow a freedom of emigration, in my humble opinion, highly injurious to us. For not only does this exodus thin the population, and tend to impoverish the land, it also serves to bring our rule into disrepute in foreign lands. At another time I shall discuss this subject more fully.

sketch of my adventures in search of a Tazkirah, or passport, at Alexandria.

Through ignorance which might have cost me dear
but for friend Larking's weight with the local authorities,
I had neglected to provide myself with a passport in
England, and it was not without difficulty, involving
much unclean dressing and an unlimited expenditure of
broken English, that I obtained from H. B. M's Consul at
Alexandria a certificate, declaring me to be an Indo-
British subject named Abdullah, by profession a doctor,
aged thirty, and not distinguished—at least so the frequent blanks seemed to denote—by any remarkable conformation of eyes, nose, or cheek. For this I disbursed
a dollar. And here let me record the indignation with
which I did it. That mighty Britain—the mistress of
the seas—the ruler of one-sixth of mankind—should
charge five shillings to pay for the shadow of her protect-
ing wing! That I cannot speak my modernised "*civis sum
Romanus*" without putting my hand into my pocket, in
order that these officers of the Great Queen may not take
too ruinously from a revenue of seventy millions! O the
meanness of our magnificence! the littleness of our greatness!

My new passport would not carry me without the
Zábít or Police Magistrate's counter-signature, said
H.B.M.'s Consul. Next day I went to the Zabit, who referred me to the Muháfiz (Governor) of Alexandria, at
whose gate I had the honour of squatting at least three
hours, till a more compassionate clerk vouchsafed the information that the proper place to apply to was the Diwan
Khárijíyah (the Foreign Office). Thus a second day was
utterly lost. On the morning of the third I started, as
directed, for the Palace, which crowns the Headland of
Clay. It is a huge and couthless shell of building in
parallelogrammic form, containing all kinds of public
offices in glorious confusion, looking with their glaring

white-washed faces upon a central court, where a few leafless wind-wrung trees seem struggling for the breath of life in an eternal atmosphere of clay-dust and sunblaze.[1]

The first person I addressed was a Kawwás[2] or police officer, who, coiled comfortably up in a bit of shade fitting his person like a robe, was in full enjoyment of the Asiatic " Kayf." Having presented the consular certificate and briefly stated the nature of my business, I ventured to inquire what was the right course to pursue for a visá.

They have little respect for Darwayshes, it appears, at Alexandria.

M'adri—" Don't know," growled the man of áuthority, without moving any thing but the quantity of tongue absolutely necessary for articulation.

Now there are three ways of treating Asiatic officials, —by bribe, by bullying, or by bothering them with a dogged perseverance into attending to you and your concerns. The latter is the peculiar province of the poor; moreover, this time I resolved, for other reasons, to be patient. I repeated my question in almost the same words. Ruh ! " Be off," was what I obtained for all reply. But this time the questioned went so far as to open his eyes. Still I stood twirling the paper in my hands, and looking very humble and very persevering, till a loud Ruh ya Kalb ! " Go, O dog !" converted into a responsive curse the little speech I was preparing about

---

1 The glare of Alexandria has become a matter of fable in the East. The stucco employed in overlaying its walls, erected by Zulkarnayn, was so exquisitely tempered and so beautifully polished, that the inhabitants, in order to protect themselves from blindness, were constrained to wear masks.

2 The word literally means "a bowman, an archer," reminding us of "les archers de la Sainte Hermandade," in the most delicious of modern fictions. Some mis-spell the word "Kawas," "Cavass," and so forth !

the brotherhood of Al-Islam and the mutual duties obligatory on true believers. I then turned away slowly and fiercely, for the next thing might have been a cut with the Kurbaj,[1] and, by the hammer of Thor ! British flesh and blood could never have stood *that*.

After which satisfactory scene,—for satisfactory it was in one sense, proving the complete fitness of the Darwaysh's costume,—I tried a dozen other promiscuous sources of information,—policemen, grooms, scribes, donkey-boys, and idlers in general. At length, wearied of patience, I offered a soldier some pinches of tobacco, and promised him an Oriental sixpence if he would manage the business for me. The man was interested by the tobacco and the pence ; he took my hand, and inquiring the while he went along, led me from place to place, till, mounting a grand staircase, I stood in the presence of Abbas Effendi, Naib or deputy to the Governor.

It was a little, whey-faced, black-bearded Turk, coiled up in the usual conglomerate posture upon a calico-covered diwan, at the end of a long, bare, large-windowed room. Without deigning even to nod the head, which hung over his shoulder with transcendent listlessness and affectation of pride, in answer to my saláms and benedictions, he eyed me with wicked eyes, and faintly ejaculated " Min ent[2] ? " Then hearing that I was a Darwaysh and doctor—he must be an Osmanli Voltairean, that little Turk—the official snorted a contemptuous snort. He condescendingly added, however, that the proper source to seek was " Taht," which, meaning simply " below," conveyed to an utter stranger rather imperfect information from a topographical point of view.

At length, however, my soldier guide found out that

---

1 A whip, a cravache of dried and twisted hippopotamus hide, the ferule, horsewhip, and "cat o' nine tails" of Egypt.

2 For "man anta ? " who art thou ?

a room in the custom-house bore the honourable appellation of " Foreign Office." Accordingly I went there, and,
after sitting at least a couple of hours at the bolted door
in the noon-day sun, was told, with a fury which made
me think I had sinned, that the officer in whose charge
the department was, had been presented with an olive
branch in the morning, and consequently that business
was not to be done that day. The angry-faced official
communicated the intelligence to a large group of Anado-
lian, Caramanian, Bosniac, and Roumelian Turks,—
sturdy, undersized, broad-shouldered, bare-legged, splay-
footed, horny-fisted, dark-browed, honest-looking mountaineers, who were lounging about with long pistols and
yataghans stuck in their broad sashes, head-gear composed of immense tarbúshes with proportionate turbands
coiled round them, and bearing two or three suits of substantial clothes, even at this season of the year, upon their
shoulders.

Like myself they had waited some hours, but they
were not so patient under disappointment : they bluntly
told the angry official that he and his master were a pair
of idlers, and the curses that rumbled and gurgled in their
hairy throats as they strode towards the door sounded
like the growling of wild beasts.

Thus was another day truly orientally lost. On the
morrow, however, I obtained permission, in the character
of Dr. Abdullah, to visit any part of Egypt I pleased,
and to retain possession of my dagger and pistols.

And now I must explain what induced me to take
so much trouble about a passport. The home reader
naturally inquires, Why not travel under your English
name ?

For this reason. In the generality of barbarous
countries you must either proceed, like Bruce, preserving
the " dignity of manhood," and carrying matters with a
high hand, or you must worm your way by timidity and

subservience; in fact, by becoming an animal too contemptible for man to let or injure. But to pass through the
Moslem's Holy Land, you must either be a born believer,
or have become one; in the former case you may demean
yourself as you please, in the latter a path is ready prepared for you. My spirit could not bend to own myself
a *Burmá*,[1] a renegade—to be pointed at and shunned
and catechised, an object of suspicion to the many and of
contempt to all. Moreover, it would have obstructed
the aim of my wanderings. The convert is always
watched with Argus eyes, and men do not willingly give
information to a "new Moslem," especially a Frank:
they suspect his conversion to be feigned or forced, look
upon him as a spy, and let him see as little of life as
possible. Firmly as was my heart set upon travelling in
Arabia, by Heaven! I would have given up the dear
project rather than purchase a doubtful and partial success
at such a price. Consequently, I had no choice but to
appear as a born believer, and part of my birthright in
that respectable character was toil and trouble in obtaining a Tazkirah.[2]

Then I had to provide myself with certain necessaries for the way. These were not numerous. The
silver-mounted dressing-bag is here supplied by a rag
containing a Miswák[3] or tooth-stick, a bit of soap and
a comb, wooden, for bone and tortoiseshell are not, religiously speaking, correct. Equally simple was my ward-

---

1 An opprobrious name given by the Turks to their Christian
converts. The word is derived from *burmak*, "to twist, to turn."

2 During my journey, and since my return, some Indian papers
conducted by jocose editors made merry upon an Englishman "turning Turk." Once for all, I beg leave to point above for the facts of
the case; it must serve as a general answer to any pleasant little
fictions which may hereafter appear.

3 A stick of soft wood chewed at one end. It is generally used
throughout the East, where brushes should be avoided, as the natives
always suspect hogs' bristles.

robe ; a change or two of clothing. It is a great mistake to carry too few clothes, and those who travel as Orientals should always have at least one very grand suit for use on critical occasions. Throughout the East a badly dressed man is a pauper, and, as in England, a pauper—unless he belongs to an order having a right to be poor—is a scoundrel. The only article of canteen description was a Zemzemiyah, a goat-skin water-bag, which, especially when new, communicates to its contents a ferruginous aspect and a wholesome, though hardly an attractive, flavour of tanno-gelatine. This was a necessary; to drink out of a tumbler, possibly fresh from pig-eating lips, would have entailed a certain loss of reputation. For bedding and furniture I had a coarse Persian rug— which, besides being couch, acted as chair, table, and oratory—a cotton-stuffed chintz-covered pillow, a blanket in case of cold, and a sheet, which did duty for tent and mosquito curtains in nights of heat.[1]   As shade is a con- venience not always procurable, another necessary was a huge cotton umbrella of Eastern make, brightly yellow, suggesting the idea of an overgrown marigold. I had also a substantial housewife, the gift of a kind relative, Miss Elizabeth Stisted ; it was a roll of canvas, carefully soiled, and garnished with needles and thread, cobblers' wax, buttons, and other such articles. These things were most useful in lands where tailors abound not ; besides which, the sight of a man darning his coat or patching his slippers teems with pleasing ideas of humility. A dagger,[2] a brass inkstand and pen-holder

---

1 Almost all Easterns sleep under a sheet, which becomes a kind of respirator, defending them from the dews and mosquitoes by night and the flies by day. The " rough and ready " traveller will learn to follow the example, remembering that " Nature is founder of Customs in savage countries ;" whereas, amongst the *soi-disant* civilised, Nature has no deadlier enemy than Custom.

2 It is strictly forbidden to carry arms in Egypt. This, however, does not prevent their being as necessary—especially in places like

stuck in the belt, and a mighty rosary, which on occasion
might have been converted into a weapon of offence,
completed my equipment. I must not omit to mention
the proper method of carrying money, which in these
lands should never be entrusted to box or bag. A
common cotton purse secured in a breast pocket (for
Egypt now abounds in that civilised animal, the pick-
pocket[1]), contained silver pieces and small change.[2] My
gold, of which I carried twenty-five sovereigns, and papers,
were committed to a substantial leathern belt of Maghrabi
manufacture, made to be strapped round the waist
under the dress. This is the Asiatic method of concealing valuables, and one more civilised than ours in the
last century, when Roderic Random and his companion
" sewed their money between the lining and the waist-
band of their breeches, except some loose silver for im-

Alexandria, where Greek and Italian ruffians abound—as they ever
were in Rome or Leghorn during the glorious times of Italian
" liberty."

1 In the Azhar Mosque, immediately after Friday service, a fellow
once put his hand into my pocket, which fact alone is ample evidence
of " progress."

2 As a general rule, always produce, when travelling, the minutest
bit of coin. At present, however, small change is dear in Egypt; the
Sarráfs, or money-changers, create the dearth in order to claim a
high agio. The traveller must prepare himself for a most unpleasant
task in learning the different varieties of currency, which appear all
but endless, the result of deficiency in the national circulating medium.
There are, however, few copper coins, the pieces of ten or five faddah
(or parahs), whereas silver and gold abound. As regards the latter
metal, strangers should mistrust all small pieces, Turkish as well as
Egyptian. "The greater part are either cut or cracked, or perhaps
both, and worn down to mere spangles: after taking them, it
will not be possible to pass them without considerable loss."
Above all things, the traveller must be careful never to change
gold except in large towns, where such a display of wealth would not
arouse suspicion or cupidity ; and on no occasion when travelling
even to pronounce the ill-omened word " Kís " (purse). Many have
lost their lives by neglecting these simple precautions.

mediate expense on the road." The great inconvenience
of the belt is its weight, especially where dollars must be
carried, as in Arabia, causing chafes and discomfort at
night. Moreover, it can scarcely be called safe. In
dangerous countries wary travellers will adopt surer
precautions.[1]

A pair of common native Khurjín, or saddle-bags,
contained my wardrobe ; the bed was readily rolled up into
a bundle; and for a medicine chest[2] I bought a pea-
green box with red and yellow flowers, capable of standing falls from a camel twice a day.

---

1 Some prefer a long chain of pure gold divided into links and
covered with leather, so as to resemble the twisted girdle which the
Arab fastens round his waist.   It is a precaution well known to the
wandering knights of old.   Others, again, in very critical situations,
open with a lancet the shoulder, or any other fleshy part of the body,
and insert a precious stone, which does not show in its novel purse.

2 Any " Companion to the Medicine Chest " will give, to those
that require such information, the names of drugs and instruments
necessary for a journey ; but it must be borne in mind that hot countries require double quantities of tonics, and half the allowance of
cathartics necessary in cold climates.   Sonnini, however, is right
when he says of the Egyptian fellahs, that their stomachs, accustomed
to digest bread badly baked, acrid and raw vegetables, and other
green and unwholesome nourishment, require doses fit only for
horses.   Advisable precautions are, in the first place, to avoid, if
travelling as a native, any signs of European manufacture in knives,
scissors, weights, scales and other such articles.   Secondly, glass
bottles are useless : the drugs should be stowed away in tin or wooden
boxes, such as the natives of the country use, and when a phial is
required, it must be fitted into an *étui* of some kind.   By this means,
ground glass stoppers and plentiful cotton stuffing, the most volatile
essences may be carried about without great waste.   After six months
of the driest heat, in Egypt and Arabia, not more than about one-
fourth of my Prussic acid and chloroform had evaporated.   And,
thirdly, if you travel in the East, a few bottles of tincture of canthar-
ides—highly useful as a rubefacient, excitant, et cetera—must never
be omitted.   I made the mistake of buying my drugs in England, and
had the useless trouble of looking after them during the journey.
Both at Alexandria and Cairo they are to be found in abundance,
cheaper than in London, and good enough for all practical purposes.

The next step was to find out when the local steamer would start for Cairo, and accordingly I betook myself to the Transit Office. No vessel was advertised ; I was directed to call every evening till satisfied. At last the fortunate event took place: a "weekly departure," which, by the bye, occurred once every fortnight or so, was in orders for the next day. I hurried to the office, but did not reach it till past noon—the hour of idleness. A little, dark gentleman—Mr. Green—so formed and dressed as exactly to resemble a liver-and-tan bull-terrier, who with his heels on the table was dosing, cigar in mouth, over the last "Galignani," positively refused, after a time,— for at first he would not speak at all,—to let me take my passage till three in the afternoon. I inquired when the boat started, upon which he referred me, as I had spoken bad Italian, to the advertisement. I pleaded inability to read or write, whereupon he testily cried *Alle nove! alle nove !*—at nine! at nine! Still appearing uncertain, I drove him out of his chair, when he rose with a curse and read 8 A.M. An unhappy Eastern, depending upon what he said, would have been precisely one hour too late.

Thus were we lapsing into the real good old East-Indian style of doing business. Thus Anglo-Indicus orders his first clerk to execute some commission ; the senior, having "work" upon his hands, sends a junior ; the junior finds the sun hot, and passes on the word to a "peon;" the "peon" charges a porter with the errand ; and the porter quietly sits or doses in his place, trusting that Fate will bring him out of the scrape, but firmly resolved, though the shattered globe fall, not to stir an inch.

The reader, I must again express a hope, will pardon the length of these descriptions,—my object is to show him how business is carried on in these hot countries. Business generally. For had I been, not Abdullah the Darwaysh, but a rich native merchant, it would have been

the same.   How many complaints of similar treatment
have I heard in different parts of the Eastern world! and
how little can one realise them without having actually
experienced the evil!   For the future I shall never see a
" nigger " squatting away half a dozen mortal hours in a
broiling sun patiently waiting for something or for some
one, without a lively remembrance of my own cooling of
the *calces* at the custom-house of Alexandria.

At length, about the end of May (1853) all was ready.
Not without a feeling of regret I left my little room
among the white myrtle blossoms and the rosy oleander
flowers with the almond smell.   I kissed with humble
ostentation my good host's hand in presence of his servants—he had become somewhat unpleasantly anxious,
of late, to induce in me the true Oriental feeling, by a
slight administration of the bastinado—I bade adieu to
my patients, who now amounted to about fifty, shaking
hands with all meekly and with religious equality of
attention ; and, mounted in a " trap " which looked like a
cross between a wheel-barrow and a dog-cart, drawn by a
kicking, jibbing, and biting mule, I set out for the steamer,
the " Little Asthmatic."

CHAPTER III.

THE NILE STEAMBOAT—THE "LITTLE ASTHMATIC."

In the days of the Pitts we have invariably a " Relation " of Egyptian travellers who embark for a place
called " Roseet " on the " River Nilus." Wanderers of
the Brucean age were wont to record their impressions of
voyage upon land subjects observed between Alexandria
and Cairo. A little later we find every one inditing
rhapsodies about, and descriptions of, his or her Daha-
biyah (barge) on the canal. After this came the steamer.
And after the steamer will come the railroad, which may
disappoint the author tourist, but will be delightful to
that sensible class of men who wish to get over the
greatest extent of ground with the least inconvenience to
themselves and others. Then shall the Mahmudiyah—
ugliest and most wearisome of canals—be given up to
cotton boats and grain barges, and then will note-books
and the headings of chapters clean ignore its existence.

I saw the canal at its worst, when the water was low;
and I have not one syllable to say in its favour. Instead
of thirty hours, we took three mortal days and nights to
reach Cairo, and we grounded with painful regularity four
or five times between sunrise and sunset. In the scenery on
the banks sketchers and describers have left you nought to
see. From Pompey's Pillar to the Maison Carrée, Kariom
and its potteries, Al-Birkah[1] of the night birds, Bastarah

---

1 Villages notorious for the peculiar Egyptian revelry, an undoubted relic of the good old times, when " the most religious of

with the alleys of trees, even unto Atfah, all things are
perfectly familiar to us, and have been so years before
the traveller actually sees them.   The Níl al-Mubárak
itself—the Blessed Nile,—as notably fails too at this season
to arouse enthusiasm.   You see nothing but muddy waters,
dusty banks, a sand mist, a milky sky, and a glaring sun :
you feel nought but a breeze like the blast from a potter's
furnace.   You can only just distinguish through a veil of
reeking vapours the village Shibr Katt from the village
Kafr al-Zayyát, and you steam too far from Wardán
town to enjoy the Timonic satisfaction of enraging its
male population with " Haykal ! ya ibn Haykal ! O
Haykal !—O son of Haykal[1] !" You are nearly wrecked,
as a matter of course, at the Barrage ; and you are certainly
dumbfoundered by the sight of its ugly little Gothic
crenelles.[2]   The Pyramids of Khufa and Kháfrá (Cheops

---

men " revelled at Canopus with an ardent piety in honour of Isis and
Osiris.

  1 " Haykal " was a pleasant fellow, who, having basely abused
the confidence of the fair ones of Wardan, described their charms in
sarcastic verse, and stuck his scroll upon the door of the village
mosque, taking at the same time the wise precaution to change his
lodgings without delay.   The very mention of his name affronts the
brave Wardanenses to the last extent, making them savage as Oxford
bargees.

  2 The Barrage is a handsome bridge,—putting the style of architecture out of consideration,—the work of French engineers, originally projected by Napoleon the First.   It was intended to act as a
dam, raising the waters of the Nile and conducting them to Suez, the
salt lakes, and a variety of other places, through a number of canals,
which, however, have not yet been opened.   Meanwhile, it acts upon
the river's trunk as did the sea of old upon its embouchures, blocking
it up and converting the land around it to the condition of a swamp.
Moreover, it would have cleaned out the bed by means of sluice gates,
forming an artificial increase of current to draw off the deposit ; but
the gates are wanting, so the piers, serving only to raise the soil by
increasing the deposit of silt, collect and detain suspended matter,
which otherwise would not settle.   Briefly, by a trifling expenditure
the Barrage might be made a blessing to Egypt ; in its present state

and Cephren) "rearing their majestic heads above the margin of the Desert," only suggest of remark that they have been remarkably well-sketched; and thus you proceed till with a real feeling of satisfaction you moor alongside of the tumble-down old suburb " Bulak."

To me there was double dulness in the scenery: it seemed to be Sind over again—the same morning mist and noon-tide glare; the same hot wind and heat clouds, and fiery sunset, and evening glow; the same pillars of dust and " devils " of sand sweeping like giants over the plain; the same turbid waters of a broad, shallow stream studded with sand-banks and silt-isles, with crashing earth slips and ruins nodding over a kind of cliff, whose base the stream gnaws with noisy tooth. On the banks, saline ground sparkled and glittered like hoar-frost in the sun; and here and there mud villages, solitary huts, pigeon-towers, or watch turrets, whence little brown boys shouted and slung stones at the birds, peeped out from among bright green patches of palm-tree, tamarisk, and mimosa, of maize, tobacco, and sugar-cane. Beyond the narrow tongue of land on the river banks lay the glaring, yellow Desert, with its low hills and sand slopes, bounded by innumerable pyramids of Nature's architecture. The boats, with their sharp bows, preposterous sterns, and lateen sails, might have belonged to the Indus. So might the chocolate-skinned, blue-robed peasantry; the women carrying progeny on their hips, with the eternal waterpot on their heads; and the men sleeping in the shade or following the plough, to which probably Osiris first put hand. The lower animals, like the higher, were the same; gaunt, mange-stained camels, muddy buffaloes, scurvied donkeys, sneaking jackals, and fox-like dogs. Even the feathered creatures were perfectly familiar to my eye—

---

it is a calamity, an "enormous, cruel wonder," more crushing to the people than were the pyramids and sphinxes of old.

paddy birds, pelicans, giant cranes, kites and wild water-fowl.

I had taken a third-class or deck-passage, whereby the evils of the journey were exasperated. A roasting sun pierced the canvas awning like hot water through a gauze veil, and by night the cold dews fell raw and thick as a Scotch mist. The cooking was abominable, and the dignity of Darwaysh-hood did not allow me to sit at meat with Infidels or to eat the food which they had polluted. So the Pilgrim squatted apart, smoking perpetually, with occasional interruptions to say his prayers and to tell his beads upon the mighty rosary; and he drank the muddy water of the canal out of a leathern bucket, and he munched his bread and garlic[1] with a desperate sanctimoniousness.

The " Little Asthmatic" was densely crowded, and discipline not daring to mark out particular places, the scene on board of her was motley enough. There were two Indian officers, who naturally spoke to none but each other, drank bad tea, and smoked their cigars exclusively

---

1 Those skilled in simples, Eastern as well as Western, praise garlic highly, declaring that it "strengthens the body, prepares the constitution for fatigue, brightens the sight, and, by increasing the digestive power, obviates the ill-effects arising from sudden change of air and water." The traveller inserts it into his dietary in some pleasant form, as " Provence-butter," because he observes that, wherever fever and ague abound, the people, ignorant of cause but observant of effect, make it a common article of food. The old Egyptians highly esteemed this vegetable, which, with onions and leeks, enters into the list of articles so much regretted by the Hebrews (Numbers, xi. 5; Koran, chap. 2). The modern people of the Nile, like the Spaniards, delight in onions, which, as they contain between 25 and 30 per cent. of gluten, are highly nutritive. In Arabia, however, the stranger must use this vegetable sparingly. The city people despise it as the food of a Fellah—a boor. The Wahhabis have a prejudice against onions, leeks, and garlic, because the Prophet disliked their strong smell, and all strict Moslems refuse to eat them immediately before visiting the mosque, or meeting for public prayer.

like Britons. A troop of the Kurd Kawwas,[1] escorting
treasure, was surrounded by a group of noisy Greeks; these
men's gross practical jokes sounding anything but pleasant to the solemn Moslems, whose saddle-bags and
furniture were at every moment in danger of being defiled by abominable drinks and the ejected juices of
tobacco. There was one pretty woman on board, a
Spanish girl, who looked strangely misplaced—a rose in a
field of thistles. Some silent Italians, with noisy inter-
preters, sat staidly upon the benches. It was soon found
out, through the communicative dragoman, that their
business was to buy horses for H. M. of Sardinia : they
were exposed to a volley of questions delivered by a party
of French tradesmen returning to Cairo, but they shielded
themselves and fought shy with Machiavellian dexterity.
Besides these was a German, a "beer-bottle in the morning
and a bottle of beer in the evening," to borrow a simile from
his own nation ; a Syrian merchant, the richest and ugliest of Alexandria; and a few French house-painters going
to decorate the Pasha's palace at Shubrá. These last
were the happiest of our voyagers,—veritable children of
Paris, Montagnards, Voltaireans, and thoroughbred Sans-
Soucis. All day they sat upon deck chattering as only
their lively nation can chatter, indulging in ultra-gallic
maxims, such as " *on ne vieillit jamais à table ;*" now playing écarté for love or nothing, then composing " *des pon-
ches un peu chiques ;*" now reciting adventures of the
category " Mirabolant," then singing, then dancing, then
sleeping, and rising to play, to drink, talk, dance, and sing
again. One chaunted :

> " Je n'ai pas connu mon père
> Ce respectable vieillard.
> Je suis né trois ans trop tard," &c.;

Whilst another trolled out :

> " Qu'est ce que je vois ?
> Un canard en rôbe de chambre !"

---

[1] A policeman; see Chap. I.

They being new comers, free from the western *morgue* so soon caught by Oriental Europeans, were particularly civil to me, even wishing to mix me a strong draught ; but I was not so fortunate with all on board. A large shopkeeper threatened to "*briser*" my "*figure*" for putting my pipe near his pantaloons ; but seeing me finger my dagger curiously, though I did not shift my pipe, he forgot to remember his threat. I had taken charge of a parcel for one M. P——, a student of Coptic, and remitted it to him on board ; of this little service the only acknowledgment was a stare and a petulant inquiry why I had not given it to him before. And one of the Englishmen, half publicly, half privily, as though communing with himself, condemned my organs of vision because I happened· to touch his elbow. He was a man in my own service ; I pardoned him in consideration of the compliment paid to my disguise.

Two fellow-passengers were destined to play an important part in my comedy of Cairo. Just after we had started, a little event afforded us some amusement. On the bank appeared a short, crummy, pursy kind of man, whose efforts to board the steamer were notably ridiculous. With attention divided between the vessel and a carpet-bag carried by his donkey boy, he ran along the sides of the canal, now stumbling into hollows, then climbing heights, then standing shouting upon the projections with the fierce sun upon his back, till everyone thought his breath was completely gone. But no! game to the backbone, he would have perished miserably rather than lose his fare : " patience and perseverance," say the wise, " got a wife for his Reverence." At last he was taken on board, and presently he lay down to sleep. His sooty complexion, lank black hair, features in which appeared *beaucoup de finesse*, that is to say, abundant rascality, an eternal smile and treacherous eyes, his gold[1] ring, dress

---

[1] The stricter sort of Moslems, such as the Arabs, will not wear gold ornaments, which are forbidden by their law.

of showy colours, fleshy stomach, fat legs, round back, and a peculiar manner of frowning and fawning simultaneously, marked him an Indian. When he awoke he introduced himself to me as Miyán Khudábakhsh Námdár, a native of Lahore : he had carried on the trade of a shawl merchant in London and Paris, where he had lived two years, and, after a pilgrimage intended to purge away the sins of civilised lands, he had settled at Cairo.

My second friend, Háji Wali, I will introduce to the reader in a future chapter ; and my two expeditions to Midian have brought him once more into notice.[1]

Long conversations in Persian and Hindústaní abridged the tediousness of the voyage, and when we arrived at Bulak, the polite Khudabakhsh insisted upon my making his house my home. I was unwilling to accept the man's civility, disliking his looks ; but he advanced cogent reasons for changing my mind. His servant cleared my luggage through the custom-house, and a few minutes after our arrival I found myself in his abode near the Azbakíyah Gardens, sitting in a cool Mashrabíyah[2] that gracefully projected over a garden, and sipping the favourite glass of pomegranate syrup.

As the Wakálahs or Caravanserais were at that time full of pilgrims, I remained with Khudabakhsh ten days or a fortnight. But at the end of that time my patience was thoroughly exhausted. My host had become a civilised man, who sat on chairs, who ate with a fork, who talked European politics, and who had learned to admire, if not to understand, liberty—liberal ideas ! and was I not flying from such things ? Besides which, we English have a

---

1 See " The Gold Mines of Midian," and " The Land of Midian (Revisited)," by Sir R. F. Burton.

2 The projecting latticed window, made of wood richly carved, for which Cairo was once so famous. But they are growing out of fashion with young Egypt, disappearing before heating glass and unsightly green blinds.

peculiar national quality, which the Indians, with their characteristic acuteness, soon perceived, and described by an opprobrious name. Observing our solitary habits, that we could not, and would not, sit and talk and sip sherbet and smoke with them, they called us " Jangli "— wild men, fresh caught in the jungle and sent to rule over the land of Hind.[1] Certainly nothing suits us less than perpetual society, an utter want of solitude, when one cannot retire into oneself an instant without being asked some puerile question by a companion, or look into a book without a servant peering over one's shoulder ; when from the hour you rise to the time you rest, you must ever be talking or listening, you must converse yourself to sleep in a public dormitory, and give ear to your companions' snores and mutterings at midnight.[2]

The very essence of Oriental hospitality, however, is this family style of reception, which costs your host neither coin nor trouble. I speak of the rare tracts in which the old barbarous hospitality still lingers. You make one more at his eating tray, and an additional mattress appears in the sleeping-room. When you depart, you leave if you like a little present, merely for a memorial, with your entertainer ; he would be offended if you offered it him openly as a remuneration, and you give

---

1 Caste in India arises from the peculiarly sociable nature of the native mind, for which reason " it is found existing among sects whose creeds are as different and as opposite as those of the Hindú and the Christian." (B. A. Irving's Prize Essay on the Theory and Practice of Caste.) Hence, nothing can be more terrible to a man than expulsion from caste ; the excommunication of our feudal times was not a more dreadful form of living death.

2 With us every man's house is his castle. But caste divides a people into huge families, each member of which has a right to know everything about his " caste-brother," because a whole body might be polluted and degraded by the act of an individual. Hence, there is no such thing as domestic privacy, and no system of espionage devised by rulers could be so complete as that self-imposed by the Hindus.

some trifling sums to the servants. Thus you will be welcome wherever you go. If perchance you are detained perforce in such a situation,—which may easily happen to you, medical man,—you have only to make yourself as disagreeable as possible, by calling for all manner of impossible things. Shame is a passion with Eastern nations. Your host would blush to point out to you the indecorum of your conduct ; and the laws of hospitality oblige him to supply the every want of a guest, even though he be a *détênu.*

But of all Orientals, the most antipathetical companion to an Englishman is, I believe, an East-Indian. Like the fox in the fable, fulsomely flattering at first, he gradually becomes easily friendly, disagreeably familiar, offensively rude, which ends by rousing the " spirit of the British lion." Nothing delights the Hindí so much as an opportunity of safely venting the spleen with which he regards his victors.[1] He will sit in the presence of a

---

1 The Calcutta Review (No. 41), noticing " L'Inde sous la Domination Anglaise," by the Baron Barchou de Penhoën, delivers the following sentiment : " Whoever states, as the Baron B. de P. states and repeats, again and again, that the natives generally entertain a bad opinion of the Europeans generally, states what is decidedly untrue." The reader will observe that I differ as decidedly from the Reviewer's opinion. Popular feeling towards the English in India was " at first one of fear, afterwards of horror : Hindús and Hindís (Moslems) considered the strangers a set of cow-eaters and fire-drinkers, tetræ beluæ ac molossis suis ferociores, who would fight like Iblis, cheat their own fathers, and exchange with the same readiness a broadside of shots and thrusts of boarding-pikes, or a bale of goods and a bag of rupees." (Rev. Mr. Anderson—The English in Western India.) We have risen in a degree above such a low standard of estimation ; still, incredible as it may appear to the Frank himself, it is no less true, that the Frank everywhere in the East is considered a contemptible being, and dangerous withal. As regards Indian opinion concerning our government, my belief is, that in and immediately about the three presidencies, where the people owe everything to and hold everything by our rule, it is most popular.

magistrate, or an officer, the very picture of cringing submissiveness. But after leaving the room, he is as different from his former self as a counsel in court from a counsel at a concert, a sea captain at a club dinner from a sea captain on his quarter-deck. Then he will discover that the English are not brave, nor clever, nor generous, nor civilised, nor anything but surpassing rogues ; that every official takes bribes, that their manners are utterly offensive, and that they are rank infidels. Then he will descant complacently upon the probability of a general Bartholomew's Day in the East, and look forward to the hour when enlightened Young India will arise and drive the " foul invader " from the land.[1] Then he will submit his political opinions nakedly, that India should be wrested from the Company and given to the Queen, or taken from the Queen and given to the French. If the Indian has been a European traveller, so much the worse for you. He has blushed to own,—explaining, however, conquest by bribery,—that 50,000 Englishmen hold 150,000,000 of his compatriots in thrall, and for aught you know, republicanism may have become his idol. He has lost all fear of the white face, and having been accustomed to unburden his mind in

> " The land where, girt by friend or foe,
> A man may say the thing he will,"—

he pursues the same course in other lands where it is exceedingly misplaced. His doctrines of liberty and

---

At the same time I am convinced that in other places the people would most willingly hail any change. And how can we hope it to be otherwise,—we, a nation of strangers, aliens to the country's customs and creed, who, even while resident in India, act the part which absentees do in other lands ? Where, in the history of the world, do we read that such foreign dominion ever made itself loved ?

[1] This was written three years before the Indian Mutiny. I also sent into the Court of Directors a much stronger report—for which I duly suffered.

equality he applies to you personally and practically, by
not rising when you enter or leave the room,—at first
you could scarcely induce him to sit down,—by not offering you his pipe, by turning away when you address him;
in fact, by a variety of similar small affronts which none
knows better to manage skilfully and with almost im-
palpable gradations.   If—and how he prays for it!—an
opportunity of refusing you anything presents itself, he
does it with an air.

> " In rice strength,
> In an Indian manliness,[1]"

say the Arabs.   And the Persians apply the following
pithy tale to their neighbours.   " Brother," said the
leopard to the jackal, " I crave a few of thy cast-off
hairs; I want them for medicine;[2] where can I find
them?"   " Wa'lláhi!" replied the jackal, " I don't exactly
know—I seldom change my coat—I wander about the
hills.   Allah is bounteous,[3] brother! hairs are not so
easily shed."

Woe to the unhappy Englishman, Pasha, or private
soldier, who must serve an Eastern lord!   Worst of all,
if the master be an Indian, who, hating all Europeans,[4]

---

1 In the Arabic "Muruwwat," generosity, the noble part of human
nature, the qualities which make a man.

2 " For medicine," means for an especial purpose, an urgent occasion.

3 " Allah Karím!" said to a beggar when you do not intend to be
bountiful.

4 Read an account of Típú Sáhib's treatment of his French employés.   If Rangít Singh behaved better to his European officers, it
was only on account of his paramount fear and hatred of the British.
The Panjábi story of the old lion's death is amusing enough, contrasted with that Anglomania of which so much has been said and
written.   When the Sikh king, they declare, heard of our success in
Afghánistán—he had allowed us a passage through his dominions, as
ingress into a deadly trap—his spirits (metaphorically and literally)
failed him; he had not the heart to drink, he sickened and he died.

adds an especial spite to Oriental coarseness, treachery, and tyranny. Even the experiment of associating with them is almost too hard to bear. But a useful deduction may be drawn from such observations ; and as few have had greater experience than myself, I venture to express my opinion with confidence, however unpopular or unfashionable it may be.

I am convinced that the natives of India cannot respect a European who mixes with them familiarly, or especially who imitates their customs, manners, and dress. The tight pantaloons, the authoritative voice, the pococurante manner, and the broken Hindustani impose upon them—have a weight which learning and honesty, which wit and courage, have not. This is to them the master's attitude : they bend to it like those Scythian slaves that faced the sword but fled from the horsewhip. Such would never be the case amongst a brave people, the Afghán for instance; and for the same reason it is not so, we read, with "White Plume," the North American Indian. " The free trapper combines in the eye of an Indian (American) girl, all that is dashing and heroic in a warrior of her own race, whose gait and garb and bravery he emulates, with all that is gallant and glorious in the white man." There is but one cause for this phenomenon ; the " imbelles Indi " are still, with few exceptions,[1] a cowardly and slavish people, who would raise themselves by depreciating those superior to them in the scale of creation. The Afghans and American aborigines, being chivalrous races, rather exaggerate the valour of their foes, because by so doing they exalt their own.[2]

---

1 The Rájputs, for instance, "whose land has ever been the focus of Indian chivalry, and the home of Indian heroes."

2 As my support against the possible, or rather the probable, imputation of "extreme opinions," I hold up the honoured name of the late Sir Henry Elliot (Preface to the Biographical Index to the Historians of Mohammedan India). " These idle

CHAPTER IV.

LIFE IN THE WAKALAH.

THE " Wakálah," as the Caravanserai or Khán is called in Egypt, combines the offices of hotel, lodging-house, and store. It is at Cairo, as at Constantinople, a massive pile of buildings surrounding a quadrangular " Hosh " or court-yard. On the ground-floor are rooms like caverns for merchandise, and shops of different kinds —tailors, cobblers, bakers, tobacconists, fruiterers, and others. A roofless gallery or a covered verandah, into which all the apartments open, runs round the first and sometimes the second story : the latter, however, is usually exposed to the sun and wind. The accommodations consist of sets of two or three rooms, generally an inner one and an outer; the latter contains a hearth for cooking, a bathing-place, and similar necessaries. The stair-cases are high, narrow, and exceedingly dirty; dark at night, and often in bad repair; a goat or donkey is tethered upon the different landings ; here and there a fresh skin is stretched in process of tanning, and the smell reminds the veteran traveller of those closets in the old French

vapourers (bombastic Bábús, and other such political ranters), should learn that the sacred spark of patriotism is exotic here, and can never fall on a mine that can explode ; for history will show them that certain peculiarities of physical, as well as moral organi-sation, neither to be strengthened by diet nor improved by educa-tion, have hitherto prevented their ever attempting a national inde-pendence ; which will continue to exist to them but as a name, and as an offscouring of college declamations."

inns where cat used to be prepared for playing the part
of jugged hare. The interior is unfurnished ; even the
pegs upon which clothes are hung have been pulled down
for fire-wood : the walls are bare but for stains, thick
cobwebs depend in festoons from the blackened rafters of
the ceiling, and the stone floor would disgrace a civilised
prison : the windows are huge apertures carefully barred
with wood or iron, and in rare places show remains of
glass or paper pasted over the framework. In the court-
yard the poorer sort of travellers consort with tethered
beasts of burden, beggars howl, and slaves lie basking
and scratching themselves upon mountainous heaps of
cotton bales and other merchandise.

This is not a tempting picture, yet is the Wakalah a
most amusing place, presenting a succession of scenes
which would delight lovers of the Dutch school—a rich
exemplification of the grotesque, and what is called by
artists the " dirty picturesque."

I could find no room in the Wakalah Khan Khalíl,
the Long's, or Meurice's of native Cairo ; I was therefore
obliged to put up with the Jamáliyah, a Greek quarter,
swarming with drunken Christians, and therefore about
as fashionable as Oxford Street or Covent Garden.
Even for this I had to wait a week. The pilgrims were
flocking to Cairo, and to none other would the prudent
hotel keepers open their doors, for the following sufficient
reasons. When you enter a Wakalah, the first thing you
have to do is to pay a small sum, varying from two to
five shillings, for the Miftáh (the key). This is generally
equivalent to a month's rent ; so the sooner you leave the
house the better for it. I was obliged to call myself a
Turkish pilgrim in order to get possession of two most
comfortless rooms, which I afterwards learned were celebrated for making travellers ill ; and I had to pay eighteen
piastres for the key and eighteen ditto per mensem for

rent, besides five piastres to the man who swept and washed the place. So that for this month my house-hire amounted to nearly four pence a day.

But I was fortunate enough in choosing the Jama-liyah Wakalah, for I found a friend there. On board the steamer a fellow-voyager, seeing me sitting alone and therefore as he conceived in discomfort, placed himself by my side and opened a hot fire of kind inquiries. He was a man about forty-five, of middle size, with a large round head closely shaven, a bull-neck, limbs sturdy as a Saxon's, a thin red beard, and handsome features beaming with benevolence. A curious dry humour he had, delighting in " quizzing," but in so quiet, solemn, and quaint a way that before you knew him you could scarcely divine his drift.

" Thank Allah, we carry a doctor ! " said my friend more than once, with apparent fervour of gratitude, after he had discovered my profession. I was fairly taken in by the pious ejaculation, and some days elapsed before the drift of his remark became apparent.

" You doctors," he explained, when we were more intimate, " what do you do ? A man goes to you for ophthalmia : it is a purge, a blister, and a drop in the eye ! Is it for fever ? well ! a purge and kinákíná (quinine). For dysentery ? a purge and extract of opium. Wa'llahi ! I am as good a physician as the best of you," he would add with a broad grin, " if I only knew the Dirham-birhams,[1]—drams and drachms,—and a few break-jaw Arabic names of diseases."

Haji Wali[2] therefore emphatically advised me to

---

1 The second is an imitative word, called in Arabic grammar Tábi'a, as " Zayd Bayd," " Zayd and others ; " so used, it denotes contempt for drachms and similar parts of drug-craft.

2 This familiar abbreviation of Wali al-Dín was the name assumed by the enterprising traveller, Dr. Wallin.

make bread by honestly teaching languages. " We are
doctor-ridden," said he, and I found it was the case.

When we lived under the same roof, the Haji and I
became fast friends. During the day we called on each
other frequently, we dined together, and passed the
evening in a Mosque, or some other place of public pas-
time. Coyly at first, but less guardedly as we grew
bolder, we smoked the forbidden weed " Hashísh,[1]" conversing lengthily the while about that world of which I
had seen so much. Originally from Russia, he also had
been a traveller, and in his wanderings he had cast off most
of the prejudices of his people. " I believe in Allah and
his Prophet, and in nothing else," was his sturdy creed;
he rejected alchemy, jinnis and magicians, and truly he
had a most unoriental distaste for tales of wonder. When
I entered the Wakalah, he constituted himself my cicerone,
and especially guarded me against the cheating of tradesmen. By his advice I laid aside the Darwaysh's gown, the
large blue pantaloons, and the short shirt; in fact all connection with Persia and the Persians. " If you persist in
being an 'Ajami," said the Haji, "you will get yourself into
trouble; in Egypt you will be cursed; in Arabia you will
be beaten because you are a heretic; you will pay the
treble of what other travellers do, and if you fall sick you
may die by the roadside." After long deliberation about

---

1 By the Indians called Bhang, the Persians Bang, the Hottentots
Dakhá, and the natives of Barbary Fasúkh. Even the Siberians, we
are told, intoxicate themselves by the vapour of this seed thrown
upon red-hot stones. Egypt surpasses all other nations in the
variety of compounds into which this fascinating drug enters, and
will one day probably supply the Western world with " Indian hemp,"
when its solid merits are duly appreciated. At present in Europe it
is chiefly confined, as cognac and opium used to be, to the apothe-
cary's shelves. Some adventurous individuals at Paris, after the
perusal of Monte Christo, attempted an " orgie " in one of the cafés,
but with poor success.

the choice of nations, I became a "Pathán.[1]" Born in India of Afghan parents, who had settled in the country, educated at Rangoon, and sent out to wander, as men of that race frequently are, from early youth, I was well guarded against the danger of detection by a fellow-countryman. To support the character requires a knowledge of Persian, Hindustani and Arabic, all of which I knew sufficiently well to pass muster; any trifling inaccuracy was charged upon my long residence at Rangoon. This was an important step; the first question at the shop, on the camel, and in the Mosque, is "What is thy name?" the second, "Whence comest thou?" This is not generally impertinent, or intended to be annoying; if, however, you see any evil intention in the questioner, you may rather roughly ask him, "What may be his maternal parent's name?"—equivalent to enquiring, *Anglicè*, in what church his mother was married,—and escape your difficulties under cover of the storm. But this is rarely necessary. I assumed the polite, pliant manners of an Indian physician, and the dress of a small Effendi (or gentleman), still, however, representing myself to be a Darwaysh, and frequenting the places where Darwayshes congregate. "What business," asked the Haji, "have those reverend men with politics or statistics, or any of the information which you are collecting? Call yourself a religious wanderer if you like, and let those who ask the object of your peregrinations know that you are under a vow to visit all the holy places in Al-Islam. Thus you will persuade them that you are a

---

1 The Indian name of an Afghan, supposed to be a corruption of the Arabic Fat'hán (a conqueror), or a derivation from the Hindustani *paithna*, to penetrate (into the hostile ranks). It is an honourable term in Arabia, where "Khurásani" (a native of Khorasan), leads men to suspect a Persian, and the other generic appellation of the Afghan tribes "Sulaymáni," a descendant from Solomon, reminds the people of their proverb, "Sulaymáni hárámi!"—"the Afghans are ruffians!"

man of rank under a cloud, and you will receive much
more civility than perhaps you deserve," concluded my
friend with a dry laugh. The remark proved his sagacity;
and after ample experience I had not to repent having
been guided by his advice.

Haji Wali, by profession a merchant at Alexandria,
had accompanied Khudabakhsh, the Indian, to Cairo on
law-business. He soon explained his affairs to me, and
as his case brought out certain Oriental peculiarities in a
striking light, with his permission I offer a few of its
details.

My friend was defendant in a suit instituted against
him in H.B.M.'s Consular Court, Cairo, by one Mohammed
Sháfi'a, a scoundrel of the first water. This man lived,
and lived well, by setting up in business at places where
his name was not known; he enticed the unwary by
artful displays of capital; and, after succeeding in
getting credit, he changed residence, carrying off all he
could lay hands upon. But swindling is a profession
of personal danger in uncivilised countries, where law
punishes pauper debtors by a short imprisonment;
and where the cheated prefer to gratify their revenge
by the cudgel or the knife. So Mohammed Shafi'a,
after a few narrow escapes, hit upon a prime ex-
pedient. Though known to be a native of Bokhara—he
actually signed himself so in his letters, and his appearance at once bespoke his origin,—he determined to protect
himself by a British passport. Our officials are sometimes careless enough in distributing these documents,
and by so doing they expose themselves to a certain loss
of reputation at Eastern courts[1]; still Mohammed Shafi'a

---

1 For the simple reason that no Eastern power confers such an
obligation except for value received. In old times, when official
honour was not so rigorous as it is now, the creditors of Eastern
powers and principalities would present high sums to British Resi-
dents and others for the privilege of being enrolled in the list of their

found some difficulties in effecting his fraud. To recount all his Reynardisms would weary the reader ; suffice it to say that by proper management of the subalterns in the consulate, he succeeded without ruining himself. Armed with this new defence, he started boldly for Jeddah on the Arabian coast. Having entered into partnership with Haji Wali, whose confidence he had won by prayers, fastings, and pilgrimages, he openly trafficked in slaves, sending them to Alexandria for sale, and writing with matchless impudence to his correspondent that he would dispose of them in person, but for fear of losing his British passport and protection.

Presently an unlucky adventure embroiled this worthy British subject with Faraj Yúsuf, the principal merchant of Jeddah, and also an English protégé. Fearing so powerful an adversary, Mohammed Shafi'a packed up his spoils and departed for Egypt. Presently he quarrels with his former partner, thinking him a soft man, and claims from him a debt of £165. He supports his pretensions by a document and four witnesses, who are ready to swear that the receipt in question was "signed, sealed, and delivered" by Haji Wali. The latter adduces his books to show that accounts have been settled, and can prove that the witnesses in question are paupers, therefore, not legal ; moreover, that each has received from the plaintiff two dollars, the price of perjury.

---

subjects or servants. This they made profitable ; for their claims, however exorbitant, when backed by a name of fear, were certain to be admitted, unless the Resident's conscience would allow of his being persuaded by weightier arguments of a similar nature to abandon his protégé. It is almost needless to remark that nothing of the kind can occur in the present day, and at the same time that throughout the Eastern world it is firmly believed that such things are of daily occurrence. Ill fame descends to distant generations ; whilst good deeds, if they blossom, as we are told, in the dust, are at least as short-lived as they are sweet.

Now had such a suit been carried into a Turkish court of justice, it would very sensibly have been settled by the bastinado, for Haji Wali was a respectable merchant, and Mohammed Shafi'a a notorious swindler. But the latter was a British subject, which notably influenced the question. The more to annoy his adversary, he went up to Cairo, and began proceedings there, hoping by this acute step to receive part payment of his demand.

Arrived at Cairo, Mohammed Shafi'a applied himself stoutly to the task of bribing all who could be useful to him, distributing shawls and piastres with great generosity. He secured the services of an efficient lawyer ; and, determining to enlist heaven itself in his cause, he passed the Ramazán ostentatiously; he fasted, and he slaughtered sheep to feed the poor.

Meanwhile Haji Wali, a simple truth-telling man, who could never master the rudiments of that art which teaches man to blow hot and to blow cold with the same breath, had been persuaded to visit Cairo by Khudabakhsh, the wily Indian, who promised to introduce him to influential persons, and to receive him in his house till he could provide himself with a lodging at the Wakalah. But Mohammed Shafi'a, who had once been in partnership with the Indian, and who possibly knew more than was fit to meet the public ear, found this out ; and, partly by begging, partly by bullying, persuaded Khudabakhsh to transfer the influential introductions to himself. Then the Hakím[1] Abdullah—your humble servant—appears upon the scene : he has travelled in Feringistán, he has seen many men and their cities, he becomes an intimate and an adviser of the Haji, and he finds out evil passages in Mohammed Shafi'a's life. Upon which Khudabakhsh ashamed, or rather afraid of his duplicity, collects his Indian friends. The Hakim Abdullah draws up a peti-

---

[1] A doctor, a learned man ; not to be confounded with Hákim, a ruler.

tion addressed to Mr. Walne (H.B.M's Consul) by the Indian merchants and others resident at Cairo, informing him of Mohammed Shafi'a's birth, character, and occupation as a vendor of slaves, offering proof of all assertions, and praying him for the sake of their good name to take away his passport. And all the Indians affix their seals to this paper. Then Mohammed Shafi'a threatens to waylay and to beat the Haji. The Haji, not loud or hectoringly, but with a composed smile, advises his friends to hold him off.

One would suppose that such a document would have elicited some inquiry.

But Haji Wali was a Persian protégé, and proceedings between the Consulates had commenced before the petition was presented. The pseudo-British subject, having been acknowledged as a real one, must be supported. Consuls, like kings, may err, but must not own to error No notice was taken of the Indian petition; worse still, no inquiry into the slave-affair was set on foot[1]; and it was discovered that the passport having been granted by a Consul-General could not with official etiquette be resumed by a Consul.[2]

---

1 It may be as well to remark that our slave laws require reform throughout the East, their severity, like Draco's Code, defeating their purpose. In Egypt, for instance, they require modification. Constitute the offence a misdemeanour, not a felony, inflict a fine (say £100), half of which should be given to the informer, and make the imprisonment either a short one, or, what would be better still, let it be done away with, except in cases of non-payment; and finally, let the Consul or some other magistrate residing at the place have power to inflict the penalty of the law, instead of being obliged, as at present, to transmit offenders to Malta for trial. As the law now stands, our officials are unwilling to carry its rigours into effect; they therefore easily lend an ear to the standard excuse—ignorance—in order to have an opportunity of decently dismissing a man, with a warning not to do it again.

2 Yet at the time there was at Alexandria an acting Consul-General, to whom the case could with strict propriety have been referred.

Thus matters were destined to proceed as they began. Mohammed Shafi'a had offered 5,000 piastres to the Persian Consul's interpreter; this of course was refused, but still somehow or other all the Haji's affairs seemed to go wrong. His statements were mistranslated, his accounts were misunderstood, and the suit was allowed to drag on to a suspicious length. When I left Cairo in July, Haji Wali had been kept away nearly two months from his business and family, though both parties—for the plaintiff's purse was rapidly thinning—appeared eager to settle the difference by arbitration : when I returned from Arabia in October, matters were almost *in statu quo antè*, and when I started for India in January, the proceedings had not closed.

Such is a brief history, but too common, of a case in which the subject of an Eastern state has to contend against British influence. It is doubtless a point of honour to defend our protégés from injustice, but the higher principle should rest upon the base of common honesty. The worst part of such a case is, that the injured party has no redress.

"Fiat *in*justitia, ruat cœlum,"

is the motto of his "natural protectors," who would violate every law to gratify the false pride of a petty English official. And, saving the rare exceptions where rank or wealth command consideration, with what face, to use the native phrase, would a hapless Turk appeal to the higher powers, our ministers or our Parliament ?

After lodging myself in the Wakalah, my first object was to make a certain stir in the world. In Europe your travelling doctor advertises the loss of a diamond ring, the gift of a Russian autocrat ; or he monopolises a whole column in a newspaper, feeing perhaps a title for the use of a signature; the large brass plate, the gold-headed cane, the rattling chariot, and the summons from the sermon complete the work. Here, there is no such Royal

Road to medical fame. You must begin by sitting with
the porter, who is sure to have blear eyes, into which you
drop a little nitrate of silver, whilst you instil into his ear
the pleasing intelligence that you never take a fee from the
poor. He recovers; his report of you spreads far and
wide, crowding your doors with paupers. They come to
you as though you were their servant, and when cured
they turn their backs upon you for ever. Hence it is that
European doctors generally complain of ingratitude on
the part of their Oriental patients. It is true that if you
save a man's life, he naturally asks you for the means of
preserving it. Moreover, in none of the Eastern languages with which I am acquainted is there a single term
conveying the meaning of our "gratitude," and none
but Germans[1] have ideas unexplainable by words. But
you must not condemn this absence of a virtue without considering the cause. An Oriental deems that he
has the right to your surplus. "Daily bread is divided"
(by heaven), he asserts, and eating yours, he considers it
his own. Thus it is with other things. He is thankful to Allah for the gifts of the Creator, but he has a claim
to the good offices of a fellow-creature. In rendering him
a service you have but done your duty, and he would not
pay you so poor a compliment as to praise you for the
act. He leaves you, his benefactor, with a short prayer
for the length of your days. "Thank you," being expressed by "Allah increase thy weal!" or the selfish wish
that your shadow (with which you protect him and his
fellows) may never be less. And this is probably the last
you hear of him.

There is a discomfort in such proceedings, a reason-

---

1 Johann Gottlieb Fichte expressly declares that the scope of his
system has never been explained by words, and that it even admits
not of being so explained. To make his opinions intelligible, he
would express them by a system of figures, each of which must have
a known and positive value.

able, a metaphysical coldness, uglily contrasting in
theory with the genial warmth which a little more heart
would infuse into them.   In theory, I say, not in practice.
Human nature feels kindness is displayed to return it in
kind.   But Easterns do not carry out the idea of such
obligations as we do.   What can be more troublesome
than, when you have obliged a man, to run the gauntlet
of his and his family's thanksgivings, to find yourself
become a master from being a friend, a great man when
you were an equal ; not to be contradicted, where shortly
before every one gave his opinion freely?   You must
be unamiable if these considerations deter you from bene-
fiting your friend; yet, I humbly opine, you still may fear
his gratefulness.

   To resume.   When the mob has raised you to fame,
patients of a better class will slowly appear on the scene.
After some coquetting about "etiquette," whether you
are to visit them, or they are to call upon you, they make
up their minds to see you, and to judge with their eyes
whether you are to be trusted or not ; whilst you, on your
side, set out with the determination that they shall at
once cross the Rubicon,—in less classical phrase, swallow
your drug.   If you visit the house, you insist upon the
patient's servants attending you; he must also provide and pay an ass for your conveyance, no matter if it
be only to the other side of the street.   Your confidential
man accompanies you, primed for replies to the "fifty
searching questions" of the "servants' hall."   You are
lifted off the saddle tenderly, as nurses dismount their
charges, when you arrive at the gate ; and you waddle up-
stairs with dignity.   Arrived at the sick room, you salute
those present with a general "Peace be upon you!" to
which they respond, "And upon thee be the peace and the
mercy of Allah, and his blessing!"   To the invalid you
say, "There is nothing the matter, please Allah, except
the health;" to which the proper answer—for here every

sign of ceremony has its countersign[1]—is, " May Allah give thee health !" Then you sit down, and acknowledge the presence of the company by raising your right hand to your lips and forehead, bowing the while circularly; each individual returns the civility by a similar gesture. Then inquiry about the state of your health ensues. Then you are asked what refreshment you will take: you studiously mention something not likely to be in the house, but at last you rough it with a pipe and a cup of coffee. Then you proceed to the patient, who extends his wrist, and asks you what his complaint is. Then you examine his tongue, you feel his pulse, you look learned, and—he is talking all the time—after hearing a detailed list of all his ailments, you gravely discover them, taking for the same as much praise to yourself as does the practising phrenologist for a similar simple exercise of the reasoning faculties. The disease, to be respectable, must invariably be connected with one of the four temperaments, or the four elements, or the " humours of Hippocrates." Cure is easy, but it will take time, and you, the doctor, require attention ; any little rudeness it is in your power to punish by an alteration in the pill, or the powder, and, so unknown is professional honour, that none will brave your displeasure. If you would pass for a native practitioner, you must finally proceed to the most uncomfortable part of your visit, bargaining for fees. Nothing more effectually arouses suspicion than disinterestedness in a doctor. I once cured a rich Hazramaut merchant of rheumatism, and neglected to make him pay for treatment ; he carried off one of my coffee cups, and was unceasingly wondering where I came from. So I made him produce five piastres, a shilling, which he threw upon the carpet, cursing Indian avarice. " You will bring on

---

1 M. C. de Perceval (Arabic Grammar), and Lane (Mod. Egyptians, Chapter 8 *et passim*), give specimens.

another illness," said my friend, the Haji, when he heard
of it.   Properly speaking, the fee for a visit to a respectable man is 20 piastres, but with the rich patient you
begin by making a bargain.   He complains, for instance,
of dysentery and sciatica.   You demand £10 for the dysentery, and £20 for the sciatica.   But you will rarely get
it.   The Eastern pays a doctor's bill as an Oirishman does
his "rint," making a grievance of it.   Your patient will
show indisputable signs of convalescence : he will laugh
and jest half the day; but the moment you appear,
groans and a lengthened visage, and pretended complaints, welcome you.   Then your way is to throw out
some such hint as

"The world is a carcass, and they who seek it are dogs."

And you refuse to treat the second disorder, which conduct may bring the refractory one to his senses.   "Dat
Galenus opes," however, is a Western apothegm : the
utmost "Jálínús" can do for you here is to provide you
with the necessaries and comforts of life.   Whatever you
prescribe must be solid and material, and if you accompany it with something painful, such as rubbing to
scarification with a horse-brush, so much the better.
Easterns, like our peasants in Europe, wish the doctor to
"give them the value of their money."   Besides which,
rough measures act beneficially upon their imagination.
So the Hakim of the King of Persia cured fevers by the
bastinado ; patients are beneficially baked in a bread-
oven at Bághdád; and an Egyptian at Alexandria, whose
quartan resisted the strongest appliances of European
physic, was effectually healed by the actual cautery, which
a certain Arab Shaykh applied to the crown of his head.
When you administer with your own hand the remedy—
half-a-dozen huge bread pills, dipped in a solution of aloes
or cinnamon water, flavoured with assafœtida, which in
the case of the dyspeptic rich often suffice, if they will but

diet themselves—you are careful to say, " In the name of
Allah, the Compassionate, the Merciful." And after the
patient has been dosed, " Praise be to Allah, the Curer,
the Healer ;" you then call for pen, ink, and paper, and
write some such prescription as this :

" A.[1]

" In the name of Allah, the Compassionate, the Merciful,
and blessings and peace be upon our Lord the Apostle, and his
family, and his companions one and all! But afterwards let
him take bees-honey and cinnamon and album græcum, of each
half a part, and of ginger a whole part, which let him pound
and mix with the honey, and form boluses, each bolus the weight
of a Miskál, and of it let him use every day a Miskal on the
saliva.[2] Verily its effects are wonderful. And let him abstain
from flesh, fish, vegetables, sweetmeats, flatulent food, acids
of all descriptions, as well as the major ablution, and live in
perfect quiet. So shall he be cured by the help of the King,
the Healer.[3] And The Peace.[4] "

The diet, I need scarcely say, should be rigorous ;
nothing has tended more to bring the European system of
medicine into contempt among Orientals than our inatten-
tion to this branch of the therapeutic art. When an
Hindi or a Hindu " takes medicine," he prepares himself
for it by diet and rest two or three days before adhibition,
and as gradually, after the dose, he relapses into his usual
habits; if he break through the régime it is concluded
that fatal results must ensue. The ancient Egyptians
we learn from Herodotus devoted a certain number of
days in each month to the use of alteratives, and the

---

1 A monogram generally placed at the head of writings. It is
the initial letter of "Allah," and the first of the alphabet, used from
time immemorial to denote the origin of creation. " I am Alpha and
Omega, the first and the last."

2 "Alà-rik," that is to say, fasting—the first thing in the
morning.

3 The Almighty. 4 W'as-salám, *i.e.* adieu.

period was consecutive, doubtless in order to graduate the
strength of the medicine. The Persians, when under
salivation, shut themselves up in a warm room, never un-
dress, and so carefully guard against cold that they even
drink tepid water. When the Afghan princes find it necessary to employ Chob-Chini, (the Jin-seng,[1] or China

---

1 From M. Huc we learn that Jin-seng is the most considerable
article of Manchurian commerce, and that throughout China there is
no chemist's shop unprovided with more or less of it. He adds :
" The Chinese report marvels of the Jin-seng, and no doubt it is for
Chinese organisation a tonic of very great effect for old and weak
persons ; but its nature is too heating, the Chinese physicians admit,
for the European temperament, already in their opinion too hot.
The price is enormous, and doubtless its dearness contributes with a
people like the Chinese to raise its celebrity so high. The rich and
the Mandarins probably use it only because it is above the reach of
other people, and out of pure ostentation." It is the principal tonic
used throughout Central Asia, and was well known in Europe when
Sarsaparilla arose to dispute with it the palm of popularity. In India,
Persia, and Afghanistan, it is called chob-chini,—the " Chinese
wood." The preparations are in two forms, 1. Sufúf, or powder ;
2. Kahwah, or decoction. The former is compound of Radix China
Orient, with gum mastich and sugar-candy, equal parts ; about a
dram of this compound is taken once a day, early in the morning.
For the decoction one ounce of fine parings is boiled for a quarter of
an hour in a quart of water. When the liquid assumes a red colour
it is taken off the fire and left to cool. Furthermore, there are two
methods of adhibiting the chob-chini : 1. Band ; 2. Kholá. The
first is when the patient confines himself to a garden, listening to
music, enjoying the breeze, the song of birds, and the bubbling of
a flowing stream. He avoids everything likely to trouble and annoy
him ; he will not even open a letter, and the doctor forbids anyone
to contradict him. Some grandees in central Asia will go through
a course of forty days in every second year ; it reminds one of
Epicurus' style of treatment,—the downy bed, the garlands of flowers,
the good wine, and the beautiful singing girl, and is doubtless at least
as efficacious in curing as the sweet relaxation of Gräfenberg or
Malvern. So says Socrates, according to the Anatomist of Melancholy,

root so celebrated as a purifier, tonic, and aphrodisiac) they choose the spring season ; they remove to a garden, where flowers and trees and bubbling streams soothe their senses ; they carefully avoid fatigue and trouble of all kinds, and will not even hear a letter read, lest it should contain bad news.

When the prescription is written out, you affix an impression of your ring seal to the beginning and to the end of it, that no one may be able to add to or take from its contents. And when you send medicine to a patient of rank, who is sure to have enemies, you adopt some similar precaution against the box or the bottle being opened. One of the Pashas whom I attended,—a brave soldier who had been a favourite with Mohammed Alí, and therefore was degraded by his successor,—kept an impression of my ring in wax, to compare with that upon the phials. Men have not forgotten how frequently, in former times, those who became obnoxious to the State were seized with sudden and fatal cramps in the stomach. In the case of the doctor it is common prudence to adopt these precautions, as all evil consequences would be charged upon him, and he would be exposed to the family's revenge.

Cairo, though abounding in medical practitioners, can still support more ; but to thrive they must be Indians, Chinese, or Maghrabis. The Egyptians are thoroughly disgusted with European treatment, which is here about as efficacious as in India—that is to say, not at all. But they are ignorant of the medicine of Hind, and therefore great is its name ; deservedly perhaps, for skill in simples and dietetics. Besides which the Indian

---

" Oculum non curabis sine toto capite,
  Nec caput sine toto corpore,
  Nec totum corpus sine animo."
The " Khola " signifies that you take the tonic without other precautions than the avoiding acids, salt, and pepper, and choosing summer time, as cold is supposed to induce rheumatism.

may deal in charms and spells,—things to which the lati-
tude gives such force that even Europeans learn to put
faith in them.   The traveller who, on the banks of the
Seine, scoffs at Sights and Sounds, Table-turning and
Spirit-rapping, sees in the wilds of Tartary and Thibet a
something supernatural and diabolical in the bungling
Sie-fa of the *Bokte*.[1]   Some sensible men, who pass for
philosophers among their friends, have been caught by
the incantations of the turbanded and bearded Cairo magician.   In our West African colonies the phrase "growing
black" was applied to colonists, who, after a term of
residence, became thoroughly imbued with the superstitions of the land.   And there are not wanting old Anglo-
Indians, intelligent men, that place firm trust in tales and
tenets too puerile even for the Hindus to believe.   As a
" Hindi" I could use animal magnetism, taking care,
however, to give the science a specious supernatural appearance.   Haji Wali, who, professing positive scepticism,
showed the greatest interest in the subject as a curiosity,
advised me not to practise pure mesmerism ; otherwise,
that I should infallibly become a " Companion of Devils."
" You must call this an Indian secret," said my friend,
" for it is clear that you are no Mashaikh,[2] and people will
ask, where are your drugs, and what business have you
with charms ?"   It is useless to say that I followed his
counsel; yet patients would consider themselves my

---

1 Certain Lamas who, we learn from M. Huc, perform famous
Sie-fa, or supernaturalisms, such as cutting open the abdomen, licking
red-hot irons, making incisions in various parts of the body, which
an instant afterwards leave no trace behind, &c., &c.   The devil may
" have a great deal to do with the matter " in Tartary, for all I know ;
but I can assure M. Huc, that the Rufá'i Darwayshes in India and the
Sa'adiyah at Cairo perform exactly the same feats.   Their jugglery,
seen through the smoke of incense, and amidst the enthusiasm of a
crowd, is tolerably dexterous, and no more.

2 A holy man.   The word has a singular signification in a plural
form, " *honoris causâ.*"

Muríds (disciples), and delighted in kissing the hand of the Sáhib Nafas[1] or minor saint.

The Haji repaid me for my docility by vaunting me everywhere as the very phœnix of physicians. My first successes were in the Wakalah ; opposite to me there lived an Arab slave dealer, whose Abyssinians constantly fell sick. A tender race, they suffer when first transported to Egypt from many complaints, especially consumption, dysentery and varicose veins. I succeeded in curing one girl. As she was worth at least fifteen pounds, the gratitude of her owner was great, and I had to dose half a dozen others in order to cure them of the pernicious and price-lowering habit of snoring. Living in rooms opposite these slave girls, and seeing them at all hours of the day and night, I had frequent opportunities of studying them. They were average specimens of the steatopygous Abyssinian breed, broad-shouldered, thin-flanked, fine-limbed, and with haunches of a prodigious size. None of them had handsome features, but the short curly hair that stands on end being concealed under a kerchief, there was something pretty in the brow, eyes, and upper part of the nose, coarse and sensual in the pendent lips, large jowl and projecting mouth, whilst the whole had a combination of piquancy with sweetness. Their style of flirtation was peculiar.

" How beautiful thou art, O Maryam !—what eyes ! —what—"

---

1 A title literally meaning the " Master of Breath," one who can cure ailments, physical as well as spiritual, by breathing upon them— a practice well known to mesmerists. The reader will allow me to observe, (in self-defence, otherwise he might look suspiciously upon so credulous a narrator), that when speaking of animal magnetism, as a thing established, I allude to the lower phenomena, rejecting the discussion of all disputed points, as the existence of a magnetic Aura, and of all its unintelligibilities—Prevision, Levitation, Introvision, and other divisions of Clairvoyance.

" Then why,"—would respond the lady—" don't you buy me ?"

" We are of one faith—of one creed—formed to form each other's happiness."

" Then why don't you buy me ?"

" Conceive, O Maryam, the blessing of two hearts—"

" Then why don't you buy me ?"

and so on. Most effectual gag to Cupid's eloquence ! Yet was not the plain-spoken Maryam's reply without its moral. How often is it our fate, in the West as in the East, to see in bright eyes and to hear from rosy lips an implied, if not an expressed, " Why don't you buy me ?" or, worse still, " Why *can't* you buy me ?"

All I required in return for my services from the slave-dealer, whose brutal countenance and manners were truly repugnant, was to take me about the town, and explain to me certain mysteries in his craft, which knowledge might be useful in time to come. Little did he suspect who his interrogator was, and freely in his unsuspiciousness he entered upon the subject of slave hunting in the Somali country, and Zanzibar, of all things the most interesting to me. I have, however, nothing new to report concerning the present state of bondsmen in Egypt. England has already learned that slaves are not necessarily the most wretched and degraded of men. Some have been bold enough to tell the British public that, in the generality of Oriental countries,[1] the serf fares far

---

1 In the generality, not in all. Nothing, for instance, can be more disgraceful to human nature than the state of prædial slavery, or serfs attached to the glebe, when Malabar was under the dominion of the "mild Hindu." And as a rule in the East it is only the domestic slaves who taste the sweets of slavery. Yet there is truth in Sonnini's terrible remark : " The severe treatment under which the slaves languish in the West Indies is the shameful prerogative of civilisation, and is unknown to those nations among whom barbarism is reported to hold sway." (Travels in Upper and Lower Egypt, vol. ii.)

better than the servant, or indeed than the poorer orders of freemen. " The laws of Mahomet enjoin his followers to treat slaves with the greatest mildness, and the Moslems are in general scrupulous observers of the Apostle's recommendation. Slaves are considered members of the family, and in houses where free servants are also kept, they seldom do any other work than filling the pipes, presenting the coffee, accompanying their master when going out, rubbing his feet when he takes his nap in the afternoon, and driving away the flies from him. When a slave is not satisfied, he can legally compel his master to sell him. He has no care for food, lodging, clothes and washing, and has no taxes to pay; he is exempt from military service and soccage, and in spite of his bondage is freer than the freest Fellah in Egypt.[1]" This is, I believe, a true statement, but of course it in nowise affects the question of slavery in the abstract. A certain amount of reputation was the consequence of curing the Abyssinian girls: my friend Haji Wali carefully told the news to all the town, and before fifteen days were over, I found myself obliged to decline extending a practice which threatened me with fame.

Servants are most troublesome things to all Englishmen in Egypt, but especially to one travelling as a respectable native, and therefore expected to have slaves. After much deliberation, I resolved to take a Berberi,[2]

---

1 The author has forgotten to mention one of the principal advantages of slaves, namely, the prospect of arriving at the highest rank of the empire. The Pasha of the Syrian caravan with which I travelled to Damascus, had been the slave of a slave, and he is but a solitary instance of cases perpetually occuring in all Moslem lands. " *C'est un homme de bonne famille,*" said a Turkish officer in Egypt, " *il a été acheté.*"

2 A " Barbarian " from Nubia and Upper Egypt. Some authorities, Mr. Lane for instance, attribute the good reputation of these people to their superior cunning. Sonnini says, " they are intelligent and handy servants, but knaves." Others believe in them. As far as I

and accordingly summoned a Shaykh—there is a Shaykh
for everything down to thieves in "the East," (in
Egypt since the days of Diodorus Siculus), and made
known my want. The list of *sine quâ nons* was necessarily
rather an extensive one,—good health and a readiness to
travel anywhere, a little skill in cooking, sewing and
washing, willingness to fight, and a habit of regular
prayers. After a day's delay the Shaykh brought me a
specimen of his choosing, a broad-shouldered, bandy-
legged fellow, with the usual bull-dog expression of the
Berberis, in his case rendered doubly expressive by the
drooping of an eyelid—an accident brought about with
acrid juice in order to avoid conscription. He responded
sturdily to all my questions. Some Egyptian donkey
boys and men were making a noise in the room at the
time, and the calm ferocity with which he ejected them
commanded my approval. When a needle, thread, and
an unhemmed napkin were handed to him, he sat down,
held the edge of the cloth between his big toe and its
neighbour, and finished the work in quite a superior style.
Walking out, he armed himself with a Kurbaj, which he
used, now lightly, then heavily, upon all laden animals,
biped and quadruped, that came in the way. His conduct proving equally satisfactory in the kitchen, after
getting security from him, and having his name registered
by the Shaykh,[1] I closed with him for eighty piastres a

---

could find out, they were generally esteemed more honest than the
Egyptians, and they certainly possess a certain sense of honour un-
known to their northern brethren. "Berberi" is a term of respect;
"Masri" (corrupted from Misri) in the mouth of a Badawi or an
Arab of Arabia is a reproach. "He shall be called an Egyptian,"
means "he shall belong to a degraded race."

[1] Who becomes responsible, and must pay for any theft his protégé may commit. Berberis, being generally "les Suisses" of respectable establishments, are expected to be honest. But I can assert from
experience that, as a native, you will never recover the value of a
stolen article without having recourse to the police. For his valuable

month. But Ali the Berberi and I were destined to part.
Before a fortnight he stabbed his fellow servant—a Surat
lad, who wishing to return home forced his services upon
me—and for this trick he received, with his dismissal, 400
blows on the feet by order of the Zabit, or police magistrate. After this failure I tried a number of servants, Egyptians, Sa'ídís,[1] and clean and unclean eating[2] Berberis.
Recommended by different Shaykhs, all had some fatal
defect ; one cheated recklessly, another robbed me, a third
drank, a fourth was always in scrapes for infringing the
Julian edict, and the last, a long-legged Nubian, after
remaining two days in the house, dismissed me for ex-

---

security, the Shaykh demands a small fee (7 or 8 piastres), which,
despite the urgent remonstrances of protector and protégé, you
deduct from the latter's wages. The question of pay is a momentous
one ; too much always spoils a good servant, too little leaves you
without one. An Egyptian of the middle class would pay his Berberi
about 40 piastres a month, besides board, lodging, some small perquisites, and presents on certain occasions. This, however, will not
induce a man to travel, especially to cross the sea.

1 A man from the Sa'íd or Upper Egypt.

2 A favourite way of annoying the Berberis is to repeat the saying, " we have eaten the clean, we have eaten the unclean,"—meaning,
that they are by no means cunning in the difference between right
and wrong, pure and impure. I will relate the origin of the saying,
as I heard it differently, from Mansfield Parkyns, (Life in Abyssinia,
chap. 31.) A Berberi, said my informant, had been carefully fattening
a fine sheep for a feast, when his cottage was burned by an accident.
In the ashes he found roasted meat, which looked tempting to a hungry
man : he called his neighbours, and all sat down to make merry over
the mishap; presently they came to the head, which proved to be
that of a dog, some enemy having doubtless stolen the sheep and put
the impure animal in its place. Whereupon, sadly perplexed, all the
Berberis went to their priest, and dolefully related the circumstance,
expecting absolution, as the offence was involuntary. " You have
eaten filth," said the man of Allah. " Well," replied the Berberis,
falling upon him with their fists, " filth or not, we have eaten it."
The Berberi, I must remark, is the " Paddy " of this part of the
world, celebrated for bulls and blunders.

pressing a determination to travel by sea from Suez to Yambu'. I kept one man ; he complained that he was worked to death : two—they did nothing but fight ; and three—they left me, as Mr. Elwes said of old, to serve myself. At last, thoroughly tired of Egyptian domestics, and one servant being really sufficient for comfort, as well as suitable to my assumed rank, I determined to keep only the Indian boy. He had all the defects of his na-tion ; a brave at Cairo, he was an arrant coward at Al-Madinah ; the Badawin despised him heartily for his effeminacy in making his camel kneel to dismount, and he could not keep his hands from picking and stealing. But the choice had its advantages : his swarthy skin and chubby features made the Arabs always call him an Abys-sinian slave, which, as it favoured my disguise, I did not care to contradict ; he served well, he was amenable to discipline, and being completely dependent upon me, he was therefore less likely to watch and especially to prate about my proceedings. As master and man we performed the pilgrimage together ; but, on my return to Egypt after the pilgrimage, Shaykh (become Haji) Núr, finding me to be a Sáhib,[1] changed for the worse. He would not work, and reserved all his energy for the purpose of pil-fering, which he practised so audaciously upon my friends, as well as upon myself, that he could not be kept in the house.

Perhaps the reader may be curious to see the neces-sary expenses of a bachelor residing at Cairo. He must observe, however, in the following list that I was not a strict economist, and, besides that, I was a stranger in the country: inhabitants and old settlers would live as well for little more than two-thirds the sum.

---

1 The generic name given by Indians to English officials.

IV.—Life in the Wakalah.

	Piastres.	Faddah.
House rent at 18 piastres per mensem - - - 0		24
Servant at 80 piastres per do. - - - 2		26
Breakfast for self and servant. { 10 eggs - - - - - 0		5
Coffee - - - - - 0		10
Water melon (now 5 piastres) - 1		0
Two rolls of bread - - - 0		10
Dinner. { 2 lbs. of meat - - - - 2		20
Two rolls of bread - - - 0		10
Vegetables - - - - 0		20
Rice - - - - - - 0		5
Oil and clarified butter - - 1		0
Sundries. { A skin of Nile water - - - 1		0
Tobacco[1] - - - - - 1		0
Hammám (hot bath) - - - 3		20

Total - 12   50

Equal to about two shillings and sixpence.

---

[1] There are four kinds of tobacco smoked in Egypt. The first and best is the well-known Latakia, generally called " Jabali," either from a small seaport town about three hours' journey south of Latakia, or more probably because grown on the hills near the ancient Laodicea. Pure, it is known by its blackish colour, fine shredding, absence of stalk, and an undescribable odour, to me resembling that of creosote; the leaf, too, is small, so that when made into cigars it must be covered over with a slip of the yellow Turkish tobacco called Báfrá. Except at the highest houses unadulterated Latakia is not to be had in Cairo. Yet, mixed as it is, no other growth exceeds it in flavour and fragrance. Miss Martineau smoked it, we are told, without inconvenience, and it differs from our Shag, Bird's-eye, and Returns, in degree, as does Château Margeau from a bottle of cheap strong Spanish wine. To bring out its flavour, the connoisseur smokes it in long pipes of cherry, jasmine, maple, or rosewood, and these require a servant skilled in the arts of cleaning and filling them. The best Jabali at Cairo costs about seven piastres the pound ; after which a small sum must be paid to the Farram or chopper, who prepares it for use.

2nd. Súri (Tyrian), or Shámi, or Suryáni, grown in Syria, an inferior growth, of a lighter colour than Latakia, and with a greenish tinge ; when cut, its value is about three piastres per pound. Some smokers mix this leaf with Jabali, which, to my taste, spoils the flavour of the latter without improving the former. The strongest kind, called

In these days who at Cairo without a Shaykh ? I thought it right to conform to popular custom, and accordingly, after having secured a servant, my efforts were directed to finding a teacher; the pretext being that as an Indian doctor I wanted to read Arabic works on medicine, as well as to perfect myself in divinity and pronunciation.[1] My theological studies were in the Sháfe'í school for two reasons : in the first place, it is the least rigorous of the Four Orthodox, and, secondly, it most resembles the Shi'ah heresy, with which long intercourse

Koráni or Jabayl, is generally used for cigarettes; it costs, when of first-rate quality, about five piastres per pound.

3rd. Tumbak, or Persian tobacco, called Hijazi, because imported from the Hijaz, where everybody smokes it, and supposed to come from Shíráz, Kázerún, and other celebrated places in Persia. It is all but impossible to buy this article unadulterated, except from the caravans returning after the pilgrimage. The Egyptians mix it with native growths, which ruins its flavour and gives it an acridity that "catches the throat," whereas good tumbak never yet made a man cough. Yet the taste of this tobacco, even when second-rate, is so fascinating to some smokers that they will use no other. To be used it should be wetted and squeezed, and it is invariably inhaled through water into the lungs: almost every town has its favourite description of pipe, and these are of all kinds, from the pauper's rough cocoa-nut mounted with two reeds, to the prince's golden bowl set with the finest stones. Tumbak is cheap, costing about four piastres a pound, but large quantities of it are used.

4th. Hummi, as the word signifies, a "hot" variety of the tumbak, grown in Al-Yaman and other countries. It is placed in the tile on the búri or cocoa-nut pipe, unwetted, and has a very acrid flavour. Being supposed to produce intoxication, or rather a swimming in the head, hummi gives its votaries a bad name : respectable men would answer "no" with rage if asked whether they are smoking it, and when a fellow tells you that he has seen better days, but that now he smokes Hummi in a buri, you understand him that his misfortunes have affected either his brain or his morality. Hence it is that this tobacco is never put into pipes intended for smoking the other kinds. The price of Hummi is about five piastres per pound.

[1] A study essential to the learned, as in some particular portions of the Koran a mispronunciation becomes a sin.

with Persians had made me familiar.[1] My choice of doctrine, however, confirmed those around me in their conviction that I was a rank heretic, for the 'Ajami, taught by his religion to conceal offensive tenets[2] in lands where the open expression would be dangerous, always represents himself to be a Shafe'i. This, together with the original mistake of appearing publicly at Alexandria as a " Mirza" in a Persian dress, caused me infinite small annoyance at Cairo, in spite of all precautions and contrivances. And throughout my journey, even in Arabia, though I drew my knife every time an offensive hint was thrown out, the ill-fame clung to me like the shirt of Nessus.

It was not long before I happened to hit upon a proper teacher, in the person of Shaykh Mohammed al-Attár, or the "Druggist." He had known prosperity, having once been a Khatíb (preacher) in one of Mohammed Ali's mosques. But His Highness the late Pasha had dismissed him, which disastrous event, with its subsequent train of misfortunes, he dates from the melancholy day when he took to himself a wife. He talks of her abroad as a stern and rigid master dealing with a naughty slave, though, by the look that accompanies his rhodomontade, I am convinced that at home he is the very model of " managed men." His dismissal was the reason that compelled him to fall back upon the trade of a druggist, the refuge for the once wealthy, though now destitute, Sages of Egypt.

His little shop in the Jamaliyah Quarter is a perfect gem of Nilotic queerness. A hole, about five feet long

---

1 The Shafe'i, to quote but one point of similarity, abuse Yazid, the Syrian tyrant, who caused the death of the Imám Husayn : this expression of indignation is forbidden by the Hanafi doctors, who rigidly order their disciples to " judge not."

2 A systematic concealment of doctrine, and profession of popular tenets, technically called by the Shi'ahs " Takíyah :" the literal meaning of the word is " fear," or " caution."

and six deep, pierced in the wall of some house, it is
divided into two compartments separated by a thin par-
tition of wood, and communicating by a kind of arch cut
in the boards. The inner box, germ of a back parlour,
acts as store-room, as the pile of empty old baskets tossed
in dusty confusion upon the dirty floor shows. In the
front is displayed the stock in trade, a matting full of
Persian tobacco and pipe-bowls of red clay, a palm-leaf
bag containing vile coffee and large lumps of coarse,
whity-brown sugar wrapped up in browner paper. On
the shelves and ledges are rows of well-thumbed wooden
boxes, labelled with the greatest carelessness, pepper for
rhubarb, arsenic for Tafl, or wash-clay, and sulphate of
iron where sal-ammoniac should be. There is also a
square case containing, under lock and key, small change
and some choice articles of commerce, damaged perfumes, bad antimony for the eyes, and pernicious rouge.
And dangling close above it is a rusty pair of scales, ill
poised enough for Egyptian Themis herself to use. To
hooks over the shop-front are suspended reeds for pipes,
tallow candles, dirty wax tapers and cigarette paper ;
instead of plate-glass windows and brass-handled doors,
a ragged net keeps away the flies when the master is in,
and the thieves when he goes out to recite in the Hasanayn Mosque his daily chapter " Yá Sín.[1]" A wooden
shutter which closes down at night-time, and by day two
palm-stick stools intensely dirty and full of fleas, occupying
the place of the Mastabah or earthen bench,[2] which accom-
modated purchasers, complete the furniture of my preceptor's establishment.

---

1 One of the most esteemed chapters of the Koran, frequently
recited as a Wazífah or daily task by religious Moslems in Egypt.

2 The Mastabah here is a long earthen bench plastered over with
clay, and raised about two feet from the ground, so as to bring the
purchaser's head to a level with the shop. Mohammed Ali ordered
the people to remove them, as they narrowed the streets ; their place
is now supplied by " Kafas," cages or stools of wicker-work.

There he sits, or rather lies (for verily I believe he
sleeps through three-fourths of the day), a thin old man
about fifty-eight,[1] with features once handsome and regular; a sallow face, shaven head, deeply wrinkled cheeks,
eyes hopelessly bleared, and a rough grey beard ignorant
of oil and comb. His turband, though large, is brown
with wear; his coat and small-clothes display many a
hole; and, though his face and hands must be frequently
washed preparatory to devotion, still they have the quality
of looking always unclean. It is wonderful how fierce
and gruff he is to the little boys and girls who flock to
him grasping farthings for pepper and sugar. On such
occasions I sit admiring to see him, when forced to exertion, wheel about on his place, making a pivot of that
portion of our organisation which mainly distinguishes
our species from the other families of the Simiadæ, to
reach some distant drawer, or to pull down a case from
its accustomed shelf. How does he manage to say his
prayers, to kneel and to prostrate himself upon that two
feet of ragged rug, scarcely sufficient for a British infant
to lie upon? He hopelessly owns that he knows nothing
of his craft, and the seats before his shop are seldom
occupied. His great pleasure appears to be when the
Haji and I sit by him a few minutes in the evening,
bringing with us pipes, which he assists us to smoke,
and ordering coffee, which he insists upon sweetening
with a lump of sugar from his little store. There we
make him talk and laugh, and occasionally quote a few
lines strongly savouring of the jovial: we provoke him
to long stories about the love borne him in his student-
days by the great and holy Shaykh Abd al-Rahmán, and
the antipathy with which he was regarded by the equally

1 A great age in Lower Egypt, where but few reach the 12th
lustre. Even the ancients observed that the old Egyptians, despite
their attention to diet and physic, were the most short-lived, and the
Britons, despite their barbarism, the longest lived of men.

great and holy Shakh Nasr al-Dín, his memorable single imprisonment for contumacy,[1] and the temperate but effective lecture, beginning with " O almost entirely destitute of shame !" delivered on that occasion in presence of other under-graduates by the Right Reverend principal of his college. Then we consult him upon matters of doctrine, and quiz him tenderly about his powers of dormition, and flatter him, or rather his age, with such phrases as, " The water from thy hand is of the Waters of Zemzem;" or, " We have sought thee to deserve the Blessings of the Wise upon our undertakings." Sometimes, with interested motives it must be owned, we induce him to accompany us to the Hammám,[2] where he insists upon paying the smallest sum, quarrelling with everything and

---

1 This is the " imposition " of Oxford and Cambridge.

2 The Hammam, or hot bath, being a kind of religious establishment, is one of the class of things—so uncomfortably numerous in Eastern countries—left *'ala júd'ak,* " to thy generosity." Consequently, you are pretty sure to have something disagreeable there, which you would vainly attempt to avoid by liberality. The best way to deal with all such extortioners, with the Láwingi (undresser) of a Cairo Hammam, or the " jarvey " of a London Hansom, is to find out the fare, and never to go beyond it—never to be generous. The Hammam has been too often noticed to bear another description : one point, however, connected with it I must be allowed to notice. Mr. Lane (Modern Egyptians) asserts that a Moslem should not pray nor recite the Koran in it, as the bath is believed to be a favourite resort of Jinnis (or genii). On the contrary, it is the custom of some sects to recite a Ruk'atayn (two-bow) prayer immediately after religious ablution in the hot cistern. This, however, is *makrúh,* or improper without being sinful, to the followers of Abú Hanífah. As a general rule, throughout Al-Islam, the *Farz* (obligatory) prayers may be recited everywhere, no matter how impure the place may be : but those belonging to the classes *sunnat* (traditionary) and *nafilah* (supererogatory) are *makruh,* though not actually unlawful, in certain localities. I venture this remark on account of the extreme accuracy of the work referred to. A wonderful contrast to the generality of Oriental books, it amply deserves a revision in the rare places requiring care.

everybody, and giving the greatest trouble. We are generally his only visitors ; acquaintances he appears to have few, and no friends ; he must have had them once, for he was rich, but is not so now, so they have fallen away from the poor old man.

When the Shaykh Mohammed sits with me, or I climb up into his little shop for the purpose of receiving a lesson from him, he is quite at his ease, reading when he likes, or making me read, and generally beginning each lecture with some such preamble as this[1] :—

" *Aywá! aywa! aywa!*[2]"—Even so, even so, even so ! we take refuge with Allah from Satan the Stoned ! In the name of Allah, the Compassionate, the Merciful, and the Blessings of Allah upon our Lord Mohammed, and his Family and his Companions one and all ! Thus saith the author, may Almighty Allah have mercy upon him ! ' Section I. of chapter two, upon the orders of prayer,' &c."

He becomes fiercely sarcastic when I differ from him in opinion, especially upon a point of grammar, or the theology over which his beard has grown grey.

" Subhán' Allah ! (Allah be glorified ![3]) What words are these ? If thou be right, enlarge thy turband,[4]" (*i.e.*, set up as a learned man), " and throw away thy

---

1 Europeans so seldom see the regular old Shaykh, whose place is now taken by polite young men educated in England or France, that this scene may be new even to those who have studied of late years on the banks of the Nile.

2 This word is often used to signify simply " yes." It is corrupted from Ay wa'lláhi, " Yes, by Allah." In pure Arabic " ay " or " I " is synonymous with our " yes " or " ay " ; and " Allah " in those countries enters somehow into every other phrase.

3 This is, of course, ironical : " Allah be praised for creating such a prodigy of learning as thou art !"

4 The larger the turband the greater are the individual's pretensions to religious knowledge and respectability of demeanour. This is the custom in Egypt, Turkey, Persia, and many other parts of the Moslem world.

drugs, for verily it is better to quicken men's souls than to destroy their bodies, O Abdullah !"

Oriental-like, he revels in giving good counsel.

" Thou art always writing, O my brave !¹" (this is said on the few occasions when I venture to make a note in my book), " what evil habit is this ? Surely thou hast learned it in the lands of the Frank. Repent !"

He loathes my giving medical advice gratis.

" Thou hast two servants to feed, O my son ! The doctors of Egypt never write A, B, without a reward. Wherefore art thou ashamed ? Better go and sit upon the mountain² at once " (*i.e.*, go to the desert), " and say thy prayers day and night !"

And finally, he is prodigal of preaching upon the subject of household expenses.

" Thy servant did write down two pounds of flesh yesterday ! What words are these, O he ?³ Dost thou never say, ' Guard us, Allah, from the sin of extravagance ?' "

He delights also in abruptly interrupting a serious subject when it begins to weigh upon his spirits. For instance,

" Now the waters of ablution being of seven different kinds, it results that——hast thou a wife ?—No ?—Then verily thou must buy thee a female slave, O youth ! This conduct is not right, and men will say of thee —— Repentance : I take refuge with Allah⁴ —— ' of a truth his mouth watereth for the spouses of other Moslems.' "

---

1 *Ya gad'a*, as the Egyptians pronounce it, is used exactly like the " mon brave " of France, and our " my good man."

2 The " mountain " in Egypt and Arabia is what the " jungle " is in India. When informed that " you come from the mountain," you understand that you are considered a mere clodhopper : when asserting that you will " sit upon the mountain," you hint to your hearers an intention of turning anchorite or magician.

3 *Ya hú*, a common interpellative, not, perhaps, of the politest description.

4 A religious formula used when compelled to mention anything abominable or polluting to the lips of a pious man.

But sometimes he nods over a difficult passage under my very eyes, or he reads it over a dozen times in the wantonness of idleness, or he takes what school-boys call a long " shot " most shamelessly at the signification. When this happens I lose my temper, and raise my voice, and shout, " Verily there is no power nor might save in Allah, the High, the Great !" Then he looks at me, and with passing meekness whispers—

" Fear Allah, O man !"

CHAPTER V.

THE RAMAZAN.

THIS year the Ramazán befell in June, and a fearful infliction was that " blessed month," making the Moslem unhealthy and unamiable. For the space of sixteen consecutive hours and a quarter, we were forbidden to eat, drink, smoke, snuff, and even to swallow our saliva designedly. I say forbidden, for although the highest orders of Turks,—the class is popularly described as

" Turco fino
Mangia porco è beve vino,"—

may break the ordinance in strict privacy, popular opinion would condemn any open infraction of it with uncommon severity. In this, as in most human things, how many are there who hold that

" Pécher en secret n'est pas pécher,
Ce n'est que l'éclat qui fait le crime " ?

The middle and lower ranks observe the duties of the season, however arduous, with exceeding zeal : of all who suffered severely from such total abstinence, I found but one patient who would eat even to save his life. And among the vulgar, sinners who habitually drink when they should pray, will fast and perform their devotions through the Ramazan.

Like the Italian, the Anglo-Catholic, and the Greek fasts, the chief effect of the " blessed month " upon True Believers is to darken their tempers into positive gloom.

Their voices, never of the softest, acquire, especially after noon, a terribly harsh and creaking tone. The men curse one another [1] and beat the women. The women slap and abuse the children, and these in their turn cruelly entreat, and use bad language to, the dogs and cats. You can scarcely spend ten minutes in any populous part of the city without hearing some violent dispute. The " Karakún," or station-houses, are filled with lords who have administered an undue dose of chastisement to their ladies, and with ladies who have scratched, bitten, and otherwise injured the bodies of their lords. The Mosques are crowded with a sulky, grumbling population, making themselves offensive to one another on earth whilst working their way to heaven ; and in the shade, under the outer walls, the little boys who have been expelled the church attempt to forget their miseries in spiritless play. In the bazars and streets, pale long-drawn faces, looking for the most part intolerably cross, catch your eye, and at this season a stranger will sometimes meet with positive incivility. A shopkeeper, for instance, usually says when he rejects an insufficient offer, " Yaftah Allah,"—" Allah opens.[2]" During the Ramazan, he will grumble about the bore of Ghashím, or " Johnny raws," and gruffly tell you not to stand there wasting his time. But as a rule the shops are either shut or destitute of shopmen, merchants will not purchase, and students will not study. In fine,

---

1 Of course all quarrelling, abuse, and evil words are strictly forbidden to the Moslem during Ramazan. If one believer insult another, the latter should repeat " I am fasting " three times before venturing himself to reply. Such is the wise law. But human nature in Egypt, as elsewhere, is always ready to sacrifice the spirit to the letter, rigidly to obey the physical part of an ordinance, and to cast away the moral, as if it were the husk and not the kernel.

2 Allah opens (the door of daily bread) is a polite way of informing a man that you and he are not likely to do business ; in other words, that you are not in want of his money.

the Ramazan, for many classes, is one-twelfth of the year wantonly thrown away.

The following is the routine of a fast day. About half an hour after midnight, the gun sounds its warning to faithful men that it is time to prepare for the " Sahúr," (early breakfast) or morning meal. My servant then wakes me, if I have slept; brings water for ablution, spreads the Sufrah [1] (or leather cloth) ; and places before me certain remnants of the evening's meal. It is some time before the stomach becomes accustomed to such hours, but in matters of appetite, habit is everything, and for health's sake one should strive to eat as plentifully as possible. Then sounds the Salám, or Blessings on the Prophet,[2] an introduction to the Call of Morning Prayer. Smoking sundry pipes with tenderness, as if taking leave of a friend ; and until the second gun, fired at about half-past two A.M., gives the Imsák,[2]—the order to abstain from food,—I wait the Azán,[3] which in this month is called somewhat earlier than usual. Then, after a ceremony termed the Níyat[4] (purpose) of fasting, I say my

---

1 The Sufrah is a piece of leather well tanned, and generally of a yellow colour, bordered with black. It is circular, has a few small pouches for knives or spoons, and, by means of a thong run through rings in the periphery, can be readily converted into a bag for carrying provisions on a journey. Figuratively it is used for the meal itself. " Sufrah házir " means that dinner is upon the table.

2 The Salam at this hour of the morning is confined to the devotions of Ramazan. The curious reader may consult Lane's Modern Egyptians, chap. 25, for a long and accurate interpretation of these words.

3 The summons to prayer.

4 In the Mohammedan church every act of devotion must be preceded by what is called its Niyat, or purpose. This intention must be either mentally conceived, or, as the more general rule is, audibly expressed. For instance, the worshipper will begin with " I purpose to pray the four-bows of mid-day prayer to Allah the Almighty," and then he will proceed to the act of worship. Moslems of the Shafe'i faith must perform the Niyat of fasting every night

prayers, and prepare for repose.[1] At 7 A.M. the labours
of the day begin for the working classes of society;
the rich spend the night in revelling, and rest in down
from dawn till noon.

The first thing on rising is to perform the Wuzu, or
lesser ablution, which invariably follows sleep in a reclining position; without this it would be improper to
pray, to enter the Mosques, to approach a religious man,
or to touch the Koran. A few pauper patients usually
visit me at this hour, report the phenomena of their complaints,—which they do, by the bye, with unpleasant
minuteness of detail,—and receive fresh instructions. At
9 A.M. Shaykh Mohammed enters, with " lecture " written
upon his wrinkled brow; or I pick him up on the way,
and proceed straight to the Mosque Al-Azhar. After
three hours' hard reading, with little interruption from
bystanders—this is long vacation, most of the students
being at home—comes the call to mid-day prayer. The
founder of Al-Islam ordained but few devotions for the
morning, which is the business part of the Eastern day;
but during the afternoon and evening they succeed one
another rapidly, and their length increases. It is then
time to visit my rich patients, and afterwards, by way of
accustoming myself to the sun, to wander among the
bookshops for an hour or two, or simply to idle in the
street. At 3 P.M. I return home, recite the afternoon
prayers, and re-apply myself to study.

This is the worst part of the day. In Egypt the
summer nights and mornings are, generally speaking,

---

for the ensuing day; the Málikis, on the other hand, " purpose "
abstinence but once for the thirty days of Ramazan. Lane tells a
pleasant tale of a thief in the Mosque saying, " I purpose (before
prayer) to carry off this nice pair of new shoes ! "

1 Many go to sleep immediately after the Imsak, or about a
quarter of an hour before the dawn prayer, and do not perform their
morning devotions till they awake. But this is not, strictly speaking,
correct.

pleasant, but the forenoons are sultry, and the afternoons are serious. A wind wafting the fine dust and furnace-heat of the desert blows over the city; the ground returns with interest the showers of caloric from above, and not a cloud or a vapour breaks the dreary expanse of splendour on high. There being no such comforts as Indian tatties, and few but the wealthiest houses boasting glass windows, the interior of your room is somewhat more fiery than the street. Weakened with fasting, the body feels the heat trebly, and the disordered stomach almost affects the brain. Every minute is counted with morbid fixity of idea as it passes on towards the blessed sunset, especially by those whose terrible lot is manual labour at such a season. A few try to forget their afternoon miseries in slumber, but most people take the Kaylúlah, or Siesta, shortly after the meridian, holding it unwholesome to sleep late in the day.

As the Maghrib, the sunset hour, approaches—and how slowly it comes !—the town seems to recover from a trance. People flock to the windows and balconies, in order to watch the moment of their release. Some pray, others tell their beads; while others, gathering together in groups or paying visits, exert themselves to while away the lagging time.

O Gladness ! at length it sounds, that gun from the citadel. Simultaneously rises the sweet cry of the Mu'ezzin, calling men to prayer, and the second cannon booms from the Abbásíyah Palace,[1]—" Al Fitár ! Al

---

1 When the late Pasha of Egypt (H.H. Abbás Hilmí) came to power, he built a large pile of palace close outside the walls of Cairo, on the direction of Suez, and induced his courtiers to follow his example. This was done readily enough, for Asiatics, like Europeans, enjoy the fine air of the desert after the rank atmosphere of towns and cities. If the successor of His Highness does not follow the usual Oriental method of wiping away all vestiges of the predecessor, except his grave, there will be, at no distant period, a second Cairo on the site of the Abbasiyah.

Fitar !" fast-breaking ! fast-breaking ! shout the people,
and a hum of joy rises from the silent city. Your acute
ears waste not a moment in conveying the delightful
intelligence to your parched tongue, empty stomach, and
languid limbs. You exhaust a pot full of water, no
matter its size. You clap hurried hands[1] for a pipe ; you
order coffee ; and provided with these comforts, you sit
down, and calmly contemplate the coming pleasures of
the evening.

Poor men eat heartily at once. The rich break their
fast with a light meal,—a little bread and fruit, fresh or
dry, especially water-melon, sweetmeats, or such digestible
dishes as " Muhallabah,"—a thin jelly of milk, starch,
and rice-flour. They then smoke a pipe, drink a cup of
coffee or a glass of sherbet, and recite the evening prayers ;
for the devotions of this hour are delicate things, and
while smoking a first pipe after sixteen hours' abstinence,
time easily slips away. Then they sit down to the
Fatúr (breakfast), *the* meal of the twenty-four hours, and
eat plentifully, if they would avoid illness.

There are many ways of spending a Ramazan evening. The Egyptians have a proverb, like ours of the
Salernitan school :

---

1 One of our wants is a history of the bell and its succedanai.
Strict Moslems have an aversion to all modifications of this instrument, striking clocks, gongs, &c., because they were considered by
the Prophet peculiar to the devotions of Christians. He, therefore,
instituted the Azan, or call to prayer, and his followers still clap their
hands when we should ring for a servant. The symbolical meaning
of the bell, as shown in the sistrum of Isis, seems to be the movement and mixture of the elements, which is denoted by clattering
noise. " Hence," observes a learned antiquary, " the ringing of
bells and clattering of plates of metal were used in all lustraఁions,
sacrifices, &c." We find them amongst the Jews, worn by the high
priest ; the Greeks attached them to images of Priapus, and the
Buddhists of Thibet still use them in their worship, as do the
Catholics of Rome when elevating the Host.

" After Al-Ghadá rest, if it be but for two moments :
   After Al-Ashá [1] walk, if it be but two steps."

The streets are now crowded with a good-humoured
throng of strollers ; the many bent on pleasure, the few
wending their way to Mosque, where the Imam recites
" Taráwíh " prayers.[2] They saunter about, the accustomed pipe in hand, shopping, for the stalls are open till
a late hour ; or they sit in crowds at the coffee-house
entrance, smoking Shíshas,[3] (water-pipes), chatting, and
listening to story-tellers, singers and itinerant preachers.
Here a bare-footed girl trills and quavers, accompanied by
a noisy tambourine and a " scrannel pipe " of abominable
discordance, in honour of a perverse saint whose corpse
insisted upon being buried inside some respectable man's
dwelling-house.[4] The scene reminds you strongly of the
Sonneurs of Brittany and the *Zampognari* from the Abruz-
zian Highlands bagpiping before the Madonna. There
a tall, gaunt Maghrabi displays upon a square yard of

---

1 Al-Ghada is the early dinner : Al-Asha, the supper, eaten
shortly after sunset. (See Lane's Modern Egyptians, Chap. 5.)

2 Extra prayers repeated in the month of Ramazan, (Lane,
Chap. 25, " Tarawih.") They take about an hour, consisting of 23
prostrations, with the Salam (or blessing on the Prophet) after every
second prostration.

3 The Shisha, or Egyptian and Syrian water-pipe, is too well
known to require any description. It is filled with a kind of tobacco
called Tumbak, for which see Chap. 4 of this Volume.

4 Strangers often wonder to see a kind of cemetery let into a
dwelling-house in a crowded street. The reason is, that some obstinate saint has insisted upon being buried there, by the simple process
of weighing so heavily in his bier, that the bearers have been obliged
to place him on the pavement. Of course, no good Moslem would
object to have his ground floor occupied by the corpse of a holy man.
The reader will not forget, that in Europe statues have the whims
which dead bodies exhibit in Egypt. So, according to the Abbé
Marche, the little statue of Our Lady, lately found in the forest of
Pennacom, " became, notwithstanding her small size, heavy as a
mountain, and would not consent to be removed by any one but the
chaplain of the chateau."

dirty paper certain lines and blots, supposed to represent the venerable Ka'abah, and collects coppers to defray the expenses of his pilgrimage. A steady stream of loungers sets through the principal thoroughfares towards the Azbakiyah Gardens, which skirt the Frank quarter ; there they sit in the moonlight, listening to Greek and Turkish bands, or making merry with cakes, toasted grains, coffee, sugared-drinks, and the broad pleasantries of Kara Gyúz[1] (the local Punch and Judy). Here the scene is less thoroughly Oriental than within the city; but the appearance of Frank dress amongst the varieties of Eastern costume, the moon-lit sky, and the light mist hanging over the deep shade of the Acacia trees—whose rich scented yellow-white blossoms are popularly compared to the old Pasha's beard[2]—make it passing picturesque. And the traveller from the far East remarks with wonder the presence of certain ladies, whose only mark of modesty is the Burká, or face-veil : upon this laxity the police looks with lenient eyes, inasmuch as, until very lately, it paid a respectable tax to the state.[3]

Returning to the Moslem quarter, you are bewildered

---

1 Europeans compare " Kara Gyuz " to our Chinese shadows. He is the Turkish "Punch," and his pleasantries may remind the traveller of what he has read concerning the Mines and Fescennine performances of the Romans. On more than one occasion, Kara Gyuz has been reported to the police for scandalously jibing and deriding consuls, Frank merchants, and even Turkish dignitaries.

2 Mohammed Ali drained and planted the Azbakiyah, which, before his day, was covered with water and mud long after the inundation had ceased. The Egyptians extract a perfume, an aphrodisiac, which they call " Fitnah," from this kind of Acacia.

3 All " Agapemones " are at this time suppressed, by order of His Highness (Abbas Pasha), whose august mother occasionally insisted upon banishing whole colleges of Ambubaiæ to Upper Egypt. As might be expected, this proceeding had a most injurious effect upon the morals of society. I was once at Cairo during the ruler's absence on a tour up to the Nile ; his departure was the signal for the general celebration of Cotyttia.

by its variety of sounds. Everyone talks, and talking
here is always in extremes, either in a whisper, or in a
scream ; gesticulation excites the lungs, and strangers
cannot persuade themselves that men so converse without
being or becoming furious. All the street cries, too, are
in the soprano key. " In thy protection ! in thy protection !" shouts a Fellah peasant to a sentinel, who is flogging
him towards the station-house, followed by a tail of
women, screaming, " Yá Gháratí—yá Dahwatí—yá Has-
ratí—yá Nidáma tí—O my calamity ! O my shame !"
The boys have elected a Pasha, whom they are conducting in procession, with wisps of straw for Mash'als, or
cressets, and outrunners, all huzzaing with ten-schoolboy
power. " O thy right ! O thy left ! O thy face ! O thy
heel ! O thy back, thy back !" cries the panting footman,
who, huge torch on shoulder, runs before the grandee's
carriage ; " Bless the Prophet and get out of the way !"
" O Allah bless him !" respond the good Moslems, some
shrinking up to the walls to avoid the stick, others rushing across the road, so as to give themselves every chance
of being knocked down. The donkey boy beats his ass
with a heavy palm-cudgel,—he fears no treadmill here,—
cursing him at the top of his voice for a " pander," a
" Jew," a " Christian," and a " son of the One-eyed,
whose portion is Eternal Punishment." " O chick pease !
O pips !" sings the vendor of parched grains, rattling the
unsavoury load in his basket. " Out of the way, and
say, ' There is one God,' " pants the industrious water-
carrier, laden with a skin, fit burden for a buffalo.
" Sweet-water, and gladden thy soul, O lemonade !" pipes
the seller of that luxury, clanging his brass cups together.
Then come the beggars, intensely Oriental. " My supper
is in Allah's hands, my supper is in Allah's hands ! whatever thou givest, that will go with thee !" chaunts the
old vagrant, whose wallet perhaps contains more provision than the basket of many a respectable shopkeeper.

" Na'al abúk[1]—rucse thy father—O brother of a naughty
sister !'" is the response of some petulant Greek to the
touch of the old man's staff. " The grave is darkness,
and good deeds are its lamp !" sing the blind women,
rapping two sticks together : " upon Allah ! upon Allah !
O daughter!" cry the bystanders, when the obstinate
" bint "[2] (daughter) of sixty years seizes their hands, and
will not let go without extorting a farthing. " Bring the
sweet " (*i.e.* fire), " and take the full,"[3] (*i.e.,* empty cup),
euphuistically cry the long-moustached, fierce-browed
Arnauts to the coffee-house keeper, who stands by them
charmed by the rhyming *repartee* that flows so readily
from their lips.

" Han*ien*," may it be pleasant to thee ![4] is the signal
for encounter.

---

1 For *La'an abúk*, curse thy father. So in Europe pious men have
sworn *per diem*, instead of *per Deum*, and " drat " acts for something
stronger.

2 A daughter, a girl. In Egypt, every woman expects to be
addressed as " O lady !" " O female-pilgrim !" " O bride !" or, " O
daughter !" even though she be on the wrong side of fifty. In Syria
and in Arabia, you may say " y'al mara !" (O woman) ; but if you
attempt it near the Nile, the answer of the offended fair one will be
" may Allah cut out thy heart !" or, " the *woman*, please Allah, in
thine eye !" And if you want a violent quarrel, " y'al agúz !" (O old
woman !) pronounced drawlingly,—y'al ago-o-ooz,—is sure to satisfy
you. On the plains of Sorrento, in my day, it was always customary,
when speaking to a peasant girl, to call her " bella fé," (beautiful
woman), whilst the worst of insults was " vecchiarella." So the
Spanish Calesero, under the most trying circumstances, calls his
mule " Vieja, rivieja," (old, very old). Age, it appears, is as unpopular
in Southern Europe as in Egypt.

3 " Fire " is called the "" sweet " by euphuism, as to name it
directly would be ill-omened. So in the Moslem law, flame and water
being the instruments of Allah's wrath, are forbidden to be used by
temporal rulers. The " full " means an empty coffee cup, as we say
in India *Mez barhúo* (" increase the table,") when ordering a servant
to remove the dishes.

4 Or " pleasurably and health" : Hanien is a word taken from the

" Thou drinkest for *ten*," replies the other, instead of returning the usual religious salutation.

" I am the cock and thou art the *hen!*" is the rejoinder,—a tart one.

" Nay, I am the thick one and thou art the *thin!*" resumes the first speaker, and so on till they come to equivoques which will not bear a literal English translation.

And sometimes, high above the hubbub, rises the melodious voice of the blind mu'ezzin, who, from his balcony in the beetling tower rings forth, " Hie ye to devotion! Hie ye to salvation." And (at morning-prayer time) he adds : " Devotion is better than sleep! Devotion is better than sleep!" Then good Moslems piously stand up, and mutter, previous to prayer, " Here am I at Thy call, O Allah! here am I at Thy call!"

Sometimes I walked with my friend to the citadel, and sat upon a high wall, one of the outworks of Mohammed Ali's Mosque, enjoying a view which, seen by night, when the summer moon is near the full, has a charm no power of language can embody. Or escaping from " stifled Cairo's filth,[1]" we passed, through the Gate of Victory, into the wilderness beyond the City of the Dead.[2] Seated upon some mound of ruins, we inhaled

Koran.   The proper answer to this is " May Allah cause thee to have pleasure!" Hanná-kumú'llah, not " Allah yahanník!" which I have heard abominably perverted by Arnaut and other ruffians.

1 This in these days must be said comparatively : Ibráhím Pasha's order, that every housekeeper should keep the space before his house properly swept and cleaned, has made Cairo the least filthy city in the East.

2 Here lies the Swiss Burckhardt, who enjoyed a wonderful immunity from censure, until a certain pseudo-orientalist of the present day seized the opportunity of using the " unscrupulous traveller's" information, and of abusing his memory.   Some years ago, the sum of £20 (I am informed) was collected, in order to raise a fitting monument over the discoverer of Petra's humble grave

the fine air of the Desert, inspiriting as a cordial, when star-light and dew-mists diversified a scene, which, by day, is one broad sea of yellow loam with billows of chalk rock, thinly covered by a film-like spray of sand surging and floating in the fiery wind. There, within a mile of crowded life, all is desolate ; the town walls seem crumbling to decay, the hovels are tenantless, and the paths untrodden; behind you lies the Wild, before you, the thousand tomb-stones, ghastly in their whiteness ; while beyond them the tall dark forms of the Mamluk Soldans' towers rise from the low and hollow ground like the spirits of kings guarding ghostly subjects in the Shadowy Realm. Nor less weird than the scene are the sounds !—the hyæna's laugh, the howl of the wild dog, and the screech of the low-flying owl. Or we spent the evening at some Takíyah[1] (Darwayshes' Oratory), generally preferring that called the " Gulshani," near the Muayyid Mosque outside the Mutawallí's saintly door. There is nothing attractive in its appearance. You mount a flight of ragged steps, and enter a low verandah enclosing an open stuccoed terrace, where stands the holy man's domed tomb : the two stories contain small dark rooms in which the Darwayshes dwell, and the ground-floor doors open into the

---

Some objection, however, was started, because Moslems are supposed to claim Burckhardt as one of their own saints. Only hear the Egyptian account of his death ! After returning from Al-Hijaz, he taught Tajwíd (Koran chaunting) in the Azhar Mosque, where the learned, suspecting him to be at heart an infidel, examined his person, and found the formula of the Mohammedan faith written in token of abhorrence upon the soles of his feet. Thereupon, the principal of the Mosque, in a transport of holy indignation, did decapitate him with one blow of the sword. It only remains to be observed, that nothing can be more ridiculous than the popular belief, except it be our hesitating to offend the prejudices of such believers.

1 A Takiyah is a place where Darwayshes have rooms, and perform their devotions.

verandah.   During the fast-month, Zikrs[1] are rarely performed in the Takiyahs: the inmates pray there in con-
gregations, or they sit conversing upon benches in the
shade.   And a curious medley of men they are, composed
of the choicest vagabonds from every nation of Al-Islam.
Beyond this I must not describe the Takiyah or the
doings there, for the " path " of the Darwaysh may not
be trodden by feet profane.

Curious to see something of my old friends the Persians, I called with Haji Wali upon one Mirza Husayn,
who by virtue of his dignity as " Sháhbandar[2] " (he calls
himself " Consul-General "), ranks with the dozen little
quasi-diplomatic kings of Cairo.   He suspends over his
lofty gate a sign-board in which the Lion and the Sun
(Irán's proud ensign) are by some Egyptian limner's art
metamorphosed into a preternatural tabby cat grasping
a scimitar, with the jolly fat face of a " gay " young lady,
curls and all complete, resting fondly upon her pet's concave back.   This high dignitary's reception room was a
court-yard *sub dio :* fronting the door were benches and
cushions composing the Sadr or high place, with the
parallel rows of Diwans spread down the less dignified
sides, and a line of naked boards, the lowest seats, ranged
along the door-wall.   In the middle stood three little
tables supporting three huge lanterns—as is their size so
is the owner's dignity—each of which contained three of
the largest spermaceti candles.

The Haji and I entering took our seats upon the
side benches with humility, and exchanged salutations
with the great man on the Sadr.   When the Darbar or
levee was full, in stalked the Mirza, and all arose as he
calmly divested himself of his shoes; and with all due

---

1 Certain forms of worship peculiar to Darwayshes.   For a
description see Lane (Modern Egyptians, ch. 24).

2 Shahbandar, Harbour-King, is here equivalent to our "Consul."

solemnity ascended his proper cushion. He is a short, thin man about thirty-five, with regular features and the usual preposterous lamb-skin cap and beard, two peaked black cones at least four feet in length, measured from the tips, resting on a slender basement of pale yellow face. After a quarter of an hour of ceremonies, polite mutterings and low bendings with the right hand on the left breast, the Mirza's pipe was handed to him first, in token of his dignity—at Teheran he was probably an under-clerk in some government office. In due time we were all served with Kaliúns[1] (Persian hookahs) and coffee by the servants, who made royal *congés* whenever they passed the great man ; and more than once the janissary, in dignity of belt and crooked sabre, entered the court to quicken our awe.

The conversation was the usual Oriental thing. It is, for instance, understood that you have seen strange things in strange lands.

" Voyaging—is—victory," quotes the Mirza ; the quotation is a hackneyed one, but it steps forth majestic as to pause and emphasis.

" Verily," you reply with equal ponderousness of pronunciation and novelty of citation, " in leaving home one learns life, yet a journey is a bit of Jahannam."

Or if you are a physician the " *lieu commun* " will be,

" Little-learn'd doctors the body destroy :
Little-learn'd parsons the soul destroy."

To which you will make answer, if you would pass for a man of *belles lettres*, by the well-known lines,

" Of a truth, the physician hath power with drugs,
Which, long as the patient hath life, may relieve him ;
But the tale of our days being duly told,
The doctor is daft, and his drugs deceive him."

After sitting there with dignity, like the rest of the guests, I took my leave, delighted with the truly Persian

1 Written " Ghalayún."

" apparatus " of the scene. The Mirza, having no salary,
lives by fees extorted from his subjects, who pay rather
than lack protection ; and his dragoman for a counter-fee
will sell their interests shamelessly. He is a hidalgo of
blue blood in pride, pompousness and poverty. There is
not a sheet of writing-paper in the " Consulate "—when
they want one a farthing is sent to the grocer's—yet the
Consul drives out in an old carriage with four outriders,
two tall-capped men preceding and two following the
crazy vehicle. And the Egyptians laugh heartily at this
display, being accustomed by Mohammed Ali to consider
all such parade obsolete.

About half-an-hour before midnight sounds the Abrár[1]
or call to prayer, at which time the latest wanderers
return home to prepare for the Sahur, their dawn meal.
You are careful on the way to address each sentinel with
a " Peace be upon thee !" especially if you have no
lantern, otherwise you may chance to sleep in the guard-
house. And, *chemin faisant*, you cannot but stop to gaze
at streets as little like what civilised Europe understands
by that name as is an Egyptian temple to the new Houses
of Parliament.

There are certain scenes, cannily termed " Ken-
speckle," which print themselves upon Memory, and
which endure as long as Memory lasts,—a thunder-cloud
bursting upon the Alps, a night of stormy darkness off
the Cape, an African tornado, and, perhaps, most awful
of all, a solitary journey over the sandy Desert.

Of this class is a stroll through the thoroughfares
of old Cairo by night. All is squalor in the brilliancy of
noon-day. In darkness you see nothing but a silhouette.
When, however, the moon is high in the heavens, and
the summer stars rain light upon God's world, there is
something not of earth in the view. A glimpse at the

---

[1] See Lane (Modern Egyptians, chap. 24).

strip of pale blue sky above scarcely reveals three ells
of breadth : in many places the interval is less : here
the copings meet, and there the outriggings of the houses
seem to interlace. Now they are parted by a pencil of
snowy sheen, then by a flood of silvery splendour ; while
under the projecting cornices and the huge hanging
balcony-windows of fantastic wood-work, supported by
gigantic brackets and corbels, and under deep verandahs,
and gateways, vast enough for Behemoth to pass through,
and in blind wynds and long cul-de-sacs, lie patches of thick
darkness, made visible by the dimmest of oil lamps. The
arch is a favourite feature : in one place you see it a
mere skeleton-rib opening into some huge deserted hall ;
in another the ogre is full of fretted stone and wood
carved like lace-work. Not a line is straight, the tall
dead walls of the Mosques slope over their massy but-
tresses, and the thin minarets seem about to fall across
your path. The cornices project crookedly from the
houses, while the great gables stand merely by force of
cohesion. And that the Line of Beauty may not be
wanting, the graceful bending form of the palm, on
whose topmost feathers, quivering in the cool night
breeze, the moonbeam glistens, springs from a gloomy
mound, or from the darkness of a mass of houses almost
level with the ground. Briefly, the whole view is so
strange, so fantastic, so ghostly, that it seems preposterous to imagine that in such places human beings like
ourselves can be born, and live through life, and carry out
the command " increase and multiply," and die.

CHAPTER VI.

THE MOSQUE.

When the Byzantine Christians, after overthrowing the temples of Paganism, meditated re-building and re-modelling them, poverty of invention and artistic impotence reduced them to group the spoils in a heterogeneous mass.[1] The sea-ports of Egypt and the plains and mountains of Syria abounding in pillars of granite, syenite and precious marbles, in Pharaonic, Grecian, and Roman statuary, and in all manner of structural ornaments, the architects were at no loss for material. Their Syncretism, the result of chance and precipitancy, of extravagance and incuriousness, fell under eyes too ignorant to be hurt by the hybrid irregularity : it was perpetuated in the so-called Saracenic style, a plagiarism from the Byzantine,[2] and it was reiterated in the Gothic, an offshoot from the Saracenic.[3] This fact accounts in the Gothic style for its manifold incongruities of architecture, and for the phenomenon,—not solely attributable to the buildings

---

1 In the capitals of the columns, for instance.

2 This direct derivation is readily detected in the Mosques at Old Cairo.

3 The roof supported by arches resting on pillars, was unknown to classic antiquity, and in the earliest ages of Al-Islam, the cloisters were neither arched nor domed. A modern writer justly observes, " A compound of arcade and colonnade was suggested to the architects of the Middle Ages by the command that ancient buildings gave them of marble columns."

having been erected piecemeal,—of its most classic period being that of its greatest irregularity.

Such " architectural lawlessness," such disregard for symmetry,—the result, I believe, of an imperfect " amalgamation and enrichment,"—may doubtless be defended upon the grounds both of cause and of effect. Architecture is of the imitative arts, and Nature, the Myriomorphous, everywhere delighting in variety, appears to abhor nothing so much as perfect similarity and precise uniformity. To copy her exactly we must therefore seek that general analogy compatible with individual variety ; in fact, we should avoid the over-display of order and regularity. And again, it may be asserted that, however incongruous these disorderly forms may appear to the conventional eye, we find it easy to surmount our first antipathy. Perhaps we end in admiring them the more, as we love those faces in which irregularity of feature is compensated for by diversity and piquancy of expression.

There is nothing, I believe, new in the Arab Mosque ; it is an unconscious revival of the forms used from the earliest ages to denote by symbolism the worship of the generative and the creative gods. The reader will excuse me if I only glance at a subject of which the investigation would require a volume, and which, discussed at greater length, would be out of place in such a narrative as this.

The first Mosque in Al-Islam was erected by Mohammed at Kubá, near Al-Madinah : shortly afterwards, when he entered Meccah as a conqueror, he destroyed the three hundred and sixty idols of the Arab Pantheon, and thus purified that venerable building from its abominations. He had probably observed in Syrian Bostra the two forms appropriated by the Christians to their places of worship, the cross and the parallelogramic Basilica ; he therefore preferred for the prayers of the "Saving Faith" a square,—some authors say, with, others without, a cloister. At length in the reign of Al-Walíd (A.H. 90) the cupola, the niche, and the minaret made their appearance; and what is called the Saracenic style became for ever the order of the Moslem world.

The Hindus I believe to have been the first who symbolised by an equilateral triangle their peculiar cult, the Yoni-Linga : in their temple architecture, it became either a conoid or a perfect pyramid. Egypt denoted it by the obelisk, peculiar to that country; and the form appeared in different parts of the world : thus in England it was a mere upright stone, and in Ireland a round tower. This we might expect to see. D'Hancarville and Brotier have successfully traced the worship itself, in its different modifications, to all people : the symbol would therefore be found everywhere. The old Arab minaret is a plain cylindrical or polygonal tower, without balcony or stages, widely different from the Turkish, modern Egyptian, and Hijazi combinations of tube and prism, happily compared by a French traveller to "*une chandelle coiffée d'un éteignoir.*" And finally the ancient minaret, made solid as all Gothic architecture is, and provided with a belfry, became the spire and steeple of our ancestors.

From time immemorial, in hot and rainy lands, a hypæthral court, either round or square, surrounded by a covered portico, was used for the double purpose of church and mart,—a place where God and Mammon were worshipped turn by turn. In some places we find rings of stones, like the Persian Pyrœtheia; in others, circular concave buildings representing the vault of heaven, where Fire, the divine symbol, was worshipped; and in Arabia, columnar aisles, which, surmounted by the splendid blue vault, resemble the palm-grove. The Greeks adopted this idea in the fanes of Creator Bacchus; and at Pozzuoli, near Naples, it may be seen in the building vulgarly called the Temple of Serapis. It was equally well known to the Kelts: in some places the Temenos was a circle, in others a quadrangle. And such to the present day is the Mosque of Al-Islam.

Even the Riwák or porches surrounding the area in the Mosque are revivals of older forms. " The range of square buildings which enclose the temple of Serapis are not, properly speaking, parts of the fane, but apartments of the priests, places for victims, and sacred utensils, and chapels dedicated to subordinate deities, introduced by a more complicated and corrupt worship, and probably unknown to the founders of the original edifice." The cloisters in the Mosque became cells, used as lecture rooms, and stores for books bequeathed to the college. They are unequal, because some are required to be of larger, others to be of smaller, dimensions. The same reason causes difference of size when the building is distributed into four hyposteles opening upon the area: the porch in the direction of the Ka'abah, where worshippers mostly congregate, demands greater depth than the other three. The wings were not unfrequently made unequal, either from want of building materials, or because the same extent of accommodation was not required in both. The columns were of different substances; some of handsome marble, others of rough stone meanly plastered over, with dissimilar capitals, vulgarly cut shafts of various sizes; here with a pediment, there without, now turned upside down, then joined together by halves in the centre, and almost invariably nescient of intercolumnar rule. This is the result of Byzantine syncretism, carelessly and ignorantly grafted upon Arab ideas of the natural and the sublime. Loving and admiring the great, or rather the big in plan,[1] they care

---

1 " The Oriental mind," says a clever writer on Indian subjects, " has achieved everything save real greatness of aim and execution." That the Arab mind always aimed, and still aims, at the physically great is sufficiently evident. Nothing affords the Meccans greater

little for the execution of mere details, and they have not
the acumen to discern the effect which clumsy workman-
ship, crooked lines, and visible joints,—parts apparently
insignificant,—exercise upon the whole of an edifice.
Their use of colours was a false taste, commonly
displayed by mankind in their religious houses, and
statues of the gods. The Hindus paint their pagodas,
inside and outside ; and rub vermilion, in token of honour,
over their deities. The Persian Colossi of Kaiomars and
his consort on the Balkh road and the Sphinx of Egypt,
as well as the temples of the Nile, still show traces of
artificial complexion. The fanes in classic Greece have
been dyed. In the Forum Romanum, one of the finest
buildings, still bears stains of the Tyrian purple. And
to mention no other instances, in the churches and
belfries of Modern Italy, we see alternate bands of
white and black material so disposed as to give them
the appearance of giant zebras. The origin of " Arabesque " ornament must be referred to one of the
principles of Al-Islam. The Moslem, forbidden by his
law to decorate his Mosque with statuary and pictures,[1]
supplied their place with quotations from the Koran, and
inscriptions, " plastic metaphysics," of marvellous per-

---

pride than the vast size of their temple.　Nothing is more humiliating
to the people of Al-Madinah than the comparative smallness of their
Mosque.　Still, with a few exceptions, Arab greatness is the vulgar
great, not the grand.

[1] That is to say, imitations of the human form.　All the doctors
of Al-Islam, however, differ on this head : some absolutely forbidding
any delineation of what has life, under pain of being cast into hell ;
others permitting pictures even of the bodies, though not of the
faces, of men.　The Arabs are the strictest of Misiconists ; yet even
they allow plans and pictures of the Holy Shrines.　Other nations
are comparatively lax.　The Alhambra abounds in paintings and fres-
coes.　The Persians never object to depict in books and on walls the
battles of Rustam, and the Turks preserve in the Seraglio treasury
of Constantinople portraits, by Greeks and other artists, of their
Sultans in regular succession.

plexity. His alphabet lent itself to the purpose, and hence probably arose that almost inconceivable variety of lace-like fretwork, of incrustations, of Arabesques, and of geometric flowers, in which his eye delights to lose itself.[1]

The Meccan Mosque became a model to the world of Al-Islam, and the nations that embraced the new faith copied the consecrated building, as religiously as Christendom produced imitations of the Holy Sepulchre.[2] The Mosque of Omar at Jerusalem, of Amrú at Babylon on the Nile, and of Taylún at Cairo were erected, with some trifling improvements, such as arched cloisters and inscribed cornices, upon the plan of the Ka'abah. From Egypt and Palestine the ichnography spread far and wide. It was modified, as might be expected, by national taste; what in Arabia was simple and elegant became highly ornate in Spain,[3] florid in Turkey, sturdy in Syria, and effeminate in India. Still divergence of detail had not, even after the lapse of twelve centuries, materially altered the fundamental form.

---

1 This is at least a purer taste than that of our Gothic architects, who ornamented their cathedrals with statuary so inappropriate as to suggest to the antiquary remains of the worship of the Hellespontine god.

2 At Bruges, Bologna, (St. Stefano), and Nürnberg, there are, if I recollect right, imitations of the Holy Sepulchre, although the " palmer " might not detect the resemblance at first sight. That in the Church of Jerusalem at Bruges was built by a merchant, who travelled three times to Palestine in order to ensure correctness, and totally failed. " Arab art," says a writer in the " Athenæum," " sprang from the Koran, as the Gothic did from the Bible." He should have remembered, that Arab art, in its present shape, was borrowed by Al-Walid from the Greeks, and, perhaps, in part from the Persians and the Hindus, but that the model buildings existed at Meccah, and in Al-Yaman, centuries before the people had " luxurious shawls and weavings of Cashmere " to suggest mural decoration.

3 See Théophile Gautier's admirable description of the Mosque at Cordova.

Perhaps no Eastern city affords more numerous or more accessible specimens of Mosque architecture than Cairo. Between 300 and 400 places of worship ;[1] some stately piles, others ruinous hovels, many new, more decaying and earthquake-shaken, with minarets that rival in obliquity the Pisan monster, are open to the traveller's inspection. And Europeans by following the advice of their hotel-keeper have penetrated, and can penetrate, into any one they please.[2] If architecture be really what I believe it to be, the highest expression of a people's artistic feeling,—highest because it includes all others,— to compare the several styles of the different epochs, to observe how each monarch building his own Mosque, and calling it by his own name, identified the manner of the monument with himself, and to trace the gradual decadence of art through one thousand two hundred years, down to the present day, must be a work of no ordinary interest to Orientalists. The limits of my plan, however, compel me to place only the heads of the argument before the reader. May I be allowed to express a hope that it will induce some learned traveller to investigate a subject in every way worthy his attention ?

The desecrated Jámi' Taylún (ninth century) is simple and massive, yet elegant, and in some of its details peculiar.[3] One of the four colonnades[4] still remains un-

---

1 Joseph Pitts, of Exeter, declares that Cairo contained in his day (A.D. 1678-93) 5 or 6000 Mosques, public and private ; at the same time he corrects Mr. Collins, who enumerated 6000 public, and 20,000 particular buildings, and M. de Thevenot, who (Part I. p. 129), supplied the city with 23,000 !

2 In Niebuhr's time, a Christian passing one of the very holy buildings on foot was liable to be seized and circumcised. All Mosques may now be entered with certain precautions. When at Cairo, I heard occasionally of a Frank being spat at and insulted, but the instances were rare.

3 The " Handbook " contains the story current among the learned concerning the remarkable shape of the minaret.

4 The columns support pointed arches, which, therefore, were

occupied by paupers to show the original magnificence of the building ; the other porches are walled up, and inhabited. In the centre of a quadrangle about 100 paces square is a domed building springing from a square which occupies the proper place of the Ka'abah. This " Jami'[1] " Cathedral is interesting as a point of comparison. If it be an exact copy of the Meccan temple as it stood in A.D. 879, it shows that the latter has greatly altered in this our modern day.

Next in date to the Taylun Mosque is that of the Sultan al-Hákim, third Caliph of the Fatimites, and founder of the Druze mysteries. The minarets are remarkable in shape, as well as size : they are unprovided with the usual outer gallery, they are based upon a cube of masonry, and they are pierced above with apertures apparently meaningless. A learned Cairene informed me that these spires were devised by the eccentric monarch to disperse, like large censers, fragrant smoke over the city during the hours of prayer. The Azhar and Hasanayn[2] Mosques are simple and artless piles, celebrated for sanctity, but remarkable for nothing save ugliness. Few buildings, however, are statelier in appear-

---

known at Cairo 200 years before they were introduced into England. By the discoveries of M. Mariette, it is now ascertained that the Egyptians were perfectly acquainted with the round arch and keystone at a period antecedent to the architectural existence of Greece.

1 A " Jami' " is a place where people assemble to pray—a house of public worship. A " Masjid " is any place of prayer, private or public. From " Masjid " we derive our " Mosque " : its changes on the road to Europe are almost as remarkable as that described in the satiric lines,—

> " Alfana vient d'equus, sans doute,
> Mais il faut avouer aussi,
> Qu en venant de la jusqu'ici
> Il a bien changé sur la route."

2 So called, because supposed to contain relics of Hasan and

ance, or give a nobler idea of both founder and architect than that which bears Sultan Hasan's name. The stranger stands awe-struck before walls high towering without a single break, a hypæthral court severe in masculine beauty, a gateway that might suit the palace of the Titans, and a lofty minaret of massive grandeur. This Mosque (finished about A.D. 1363), with its fortress aspect, owns no more relationship to the efforts of a later age than does Canterbury Cathedral to an Anglo-Indian " Gothic." For dignified beauty and refined taste, the Mosque and tomb of Káid Bey and the other Mamluk kings are admirable. Even in their present state, picturesqueness presides over decay, and the traveller has seldom seen aught more striking than the rich light of the stained glass pouring through the first shades of evening upon the marble floor.

The modern Mosques must be visited to see Egyptian architecture in its decline and fall. That of Sittná Zaynab (our Lady Zaynab), founded by Murád Bey, the Mamluk, and interrupted by the French invasion, shows, even in its completion, some lingering traces of taste. But nothing can be more offensive than the building which every tourist flogs donkey in his hurry to see—old Mohammed Ali's " Folly " in the citadel. Its Greek architect has toiled to caricature a Mosque to emulate the glories of our English " Oriental Pavilion." Outside, as Monckton Milnes sings,

" The shining minarets, thin and high,"

are so thin, so high above the lumpy domes, that they

Husayn, the martyred grandsons of Mohammed. The tradition is little credited, and the Persians ostentatiously avoid visiting the place. "You are the first 'Ajami that ever said the Fatihah at this holy spot," quoth the Mujáwir, or guardian of the tomb, after compelling me, almost by force, to repeat the formula, which he recited with the prospect of a few piastres.

look like the spindles of crouching crones, and are placed
in full sight of Sultan Hasan the Giant, so as to derive
all the disadvantages of the contrast. Is the pointed
arch forgotten by man, that this hapless building should
be disgraced by large and small parallelograms of glass
and wood,[1] so placed and so formed as to give its
exterior the appearance of a European theatre *coiffé* with
Oriental cupolas ? Outside as well as inside, money has
been lavished upon alabaster full of flaws ; round the
bases of pillars run gilt bands ; in places the walls are
painted with streaks to resemble marble, and the wood-
work is overlaid with tinsel gold. After a glance at these
abominations, one cannot be surprised to hear the old
men of Egypt lament that, in spite of European education, and of prizes encouraging geometry and architecture,
modern art offers a melancholy contrast to antiquity. It
is said that H. H. Abbas Pasha proposes to erect for
himself a Mosque that shall far surpass the boast of the
last generation. I venture to hope that his architect
will light the " sacred fire " from Sultan Hasan's, not
from Mohammed Ali's, Turco-Grecian splendours. The
former is like the genuine Osmanli of past ages, fierce,
cold, with a stalwart frame, index of a strong mind—
there was a sullen grandeur about the man. The latter
is the pert and puny modern Turk in pantaloons, frock
coat and Fez, ill-dressed, ill-conditioned, and ill-bred, body
and soul.

---

1 This is becoming the fashion for young Egyptians, who will
readily receive a pair of common green *persiennes* in exchange for fine
old windows of elaborately carved wood. They are as sensible in a
variety of other small matters. Natives of a hot climate generally
wear slippers of red and yellow leather, because they are cool and
comfortable : on the banks of the Nile, the old chaussure is gradually
yielding to black shoes, which blister the feet with heat, but are
European, and, therefore, *bon ton*. It must, however, be confessed
that the fine old carved wood-work of the windows was removed
because it was found to be dangerous in cases of fire.

We will now enter the Mosque Al-Azhar. At the dwarf wooden railing we take off our slippers, hold them in the left hand, sole to sole, that no dirt may fall from them, and cross the threshold with the right foot, ejaculating Bismillah, &c. Next we repair to the Mayza'ah, or large tank, for ablution, without which it is unlawful to appear in the House of Allah. We then seek some proper place for devotion, place our slippers on some other object in front of us to warn the lounger, and perform a two-bow prayer in honour of the Mosque.[1] This done, we may wander about, and inspect the several objects of curiosity.

The moon shines splendidly upon a vast open court, paved with stones which are polished like glass by the feet of the Faithful. There is darkness in the body of the building, a large oblong hall, at least twice too lengthy for its height, supported by a forest of pillars, thin, poor-looking, crooked marble columns, planted avenue-like, upon torn and dirty matting. A few oil lamps shed doubtful light over scanty groups, who are debating some point of grammar, or are listening to the words of wisdom that fall from the mouth of a Wá'iz.[2] Presently they will leave the hypostyle, and throw themselves upon the flags of the quadrangle, where they may enjoy the open air and avoid some fleas. It is now " long vacation ": so the holy building has become a kind of Caravanserai for tra-

---

1 Irreligious men neglect this act of propriety. There are many in Egypt who will habitually transgress one of the fundamental orders of their faith, namely, never to pray when in a state of religious impurity. In popular *Argot,*' prayer without ablution is called Salát Mamlúkíyah, or " slaves' prayers," because such men perform their devotions only in order to avoid the master's staff. Others will touch the Koran when impure, a circumstance which highly disgusts Indian Moslems.

2 An " adviser," or " lecturer,"—any learned man who, generally in the months of Ramazan and Muharram, after the Friday service and sermon, delivers a discourse upon the principles of Al-Islam.

vellers ; perhaps a score of nations meet in it ; there is
a confusion of tongues, and the din at times is deafening.
Around the court runs a tolerably well-built colonnade,
whose entablature is garnished with crimson arabesques,
and in the inner wall are pierced apartments, now closed
with plank doors. Of the Riwak, as the porches are
called, the Azhar contains twenty-four, one for each recognised nation in Al-Islam, and of these fifteen are still
open to students.[1] Inside them we find nothing but
matting and a pile of large dingy wooden boxes, which
once contained the college library ; they are now, generally
speaking, empty.[2]

There is nothing worth seeing in the cluster of little
dark chambers that form the remainder of the Azhar.
Even the Záwiyat al-Umyán (or the Blind men's Oratory),
a place where so many " town and gown rows " have
emanated, is rendered interesting only by the fanaticism
of its inmates, and the certainty that, if recognised in this

---

1 Amongst them is a foundation for Jáwi scholars. Some of our
authors, by a curious mistake, have confounded Moslem Jawa (by
the Egyptians pronounced Gáwa), with " Goa," the Christian colony
of the Portuguese.

2 Cairo was once celebrated for its magnificent collections of
books. Besides private libraries, each large Mosque had its biblio-
theca, every MS. of which was marked with the word " Wakf "
(entailed bequest), or " Wukifa l'Illahi Ta'álá " (bequeathed to God
Almighty). But Cairo has now for years supplied other countries
with books, and the decay of religious zeal has encouraged the
unprincipled to steal and sell MSS. marked with the warning words.
The Hijaz, in particular, has been inundated with books from Egypt.
Cairo has still some large libraries, but most of them are private
property, and the proprietors will not readily lend or give access to
their treasures. The principal opportunity of buying books is during the month Ramazan, when they are publicly sold in the Azhar
Mosque. The Orientalist will, however, meet with many disappoint-
ments ; besides the difficulty of discovering good works, he will find
in the booksellers, scribes, *et hoc genus omne*, a finished race of scoundrels.

sanctum, we shall run the gauntlet under the staves of
its proprietors, the angry blind.

The Azhar is the grand collegiate Mosque of this
city,—the Christ Church, in fact, of Cairo,—once celebrated throughout the world of Al-Islam. It was built,
I was told, originally in poor style by one Jauhar al-
Káid,[1] originally the slave of a Moorish merchant, in
consequence of a dream that ordered him to "erect a
place whence the light of science should shine upon
Al-Islam."

It gradually increased by "Wakf[2]" (entailed bequests) of lands, money, and books ; and pious rulers
made a point of adding to its size and wealth. Of late
years it has considerably declined, the result of sequestra-
tions, and of the diminished esteem in which the purely
religious sciences are now held in the land of Egypt.[3]
Yet it is calculated that between 2000 and 3000 students
of all nations and ages receive instruction here gratis.

1 Lane (Mod. Egyptians) has rectified Baron von Hammer-
Purgstall's mistake concerning the word "Azhar" ; our English
Orientalist translates it the "splendid Mosque." I would venture to
add, that the epithet must be understood in a spiritual and not in a
material sense. Wilkinson attributes the erection of the building to
Jauhar al-Kaid, general under Al-Moaz, about A.D. 970. Wilson
ascribes it partly to Al-Moaz the Fatimite (A.D. 973), partly to his
general and successor, Al-Hakim (?).

2 Wakf, property become mortmain. My friend Yacoub Artin
declares that the whole Nile Valley has parcel by parcel been made
Wakf at some time or other, and then retaken.

3 If I may venture to judge, after the experience of a few
months, there is now a re-action in favour of the old system.
Mohammed Ali managed to make his preparatory, polytechnic, and
other schools, thoroughly distasteful to the people, and mothers
blinded their children, to prevent their being devoted for life to
infidel studies. The printing-press, contrasting in hideousness with
the beauty of the written character, and the contemptible Arabic
style of the various works translated by order of government from
the European languages, have placed arms in the hands of the
orthodox party.

Each one is provided with bread, in a quantity determined by the amount of endowment, at the Riwak set apart for his nation,[1] with some article of clothing on festival days, and a few piastres once a year. The professors, who are about 150 in number, may not take fees from their pupils ; some lecture on account of the religious merit of the action, others to gain the high title of " Teacher in Al Azhar.[2]" Six officials receive stipends from the government,—the Shaykh al-Jami' or dean, the Shaykh al-Sakká, who regulates the provision of water for ablution, and others that may be called heads of departments.

The following is the course of study in the Azhar. The school-boy of four or five years' standing has been taught, by a liberal application of the maxim " the Green Rod is of the Trees of Paradise," to chant the Koran without understanding it, the elementary rules of arithmetic, and, if he is destined to be a learned man, the art of writing.[3] He then registers his name in Al-Azhar, and applies

1 Finding the Indian Riwak closed, and hearing that an endowment still belonged to it, I called twice upon the Shaykh or Dean, wishing to claim the stipend as a precedent. But I failed in finding him at home, and was obliged to start hurriedly for Suez. The Indians now generally study in the Sulaymániyah, or Afghan College.

2 As the attending of lectures is not compulsory, the result is that the lecturer is always worth listening to. May I commend this consideration to our college reformers at home? In my day, men were compelled to waste—notoriously to waste—an hour or two every morning, for the purpose of putting a few pounds sterling into the pocket of some droning Don.

3 The would-be calligrapher must go to a Constantinople Khwájah (schoolmaster), and after writing about two hours a day regularly through a year or two, he will become, if he has the necessary disposition, a skilful penman. This acquirement is but little valued in the present day, as almost nothing is to be gained by it. The Turks particularly excel in the ornamental character called " Suls." I have seen some Korans beautifully written ; and the late Pasha gave an impetus to this branch of industry, by forbidding, under the

himself to the branches of study most cultivated in Al-Islam, namely Nahw (syntax), Fikh (the law), Hadís (the traditions of the Prophet), and Tafsír, or Exposition of the Koran.

The young Egyptian reads at the same time Sarf, or Inflexion, and Nahw (syntax). But as Arabic is his mother-tongue, he is not required to study the former so deeply as are the Turks, the Persians, and the Indians. If he desire, however, to be a proficient, he must carefully peruse five books in Sarf,[1] and six in Nahw.[2]

---

plea of religious scruples, the importation of the incorrect Korans cheaply lithographed by the Persians at Bombay. The Persians surpass the Turks in all but the Suls writing. Of late years, the Pashas of Cairo have employed a gentleman from Khorasan, whose travelling name is " Mirza Sanglákh" to decorate their Mosques with inscriptions. I was favoured with a specimen of his art, and do not hesitate to rank him the first of his age, and second to none amongst the ancients but those Raphaels of calligraphy, Mír of Shíráz, and Rahmán of Herát. The Egyptians and Arabs, generally speaking, write a coarse and clumsy hand, and, as usual in the East, the higher the rank of the writer is, the worse his scrawl becomes.

1 The popular volumes are, 1. Al-Amsilah, showing the simple conjugation of the triliteral verb ; 2. Bisí'a, the work of some un-known author, explaining the formation of the verb into increased infinities, the quadrilateral verb, &c. ; 3. The Maksú'a, a well-known book written by the great Imam Abu' Hanífah ; 4. The "Izzí," an explanatory treatise, the work of a Turk, "Izzat Effendi." And lastly, the Maráh of Ahmad al-Sa'údi. These five tracts are bound together in a little volume, printed at the government establishment. Al-Amsilah is explained in Turkish, to teach boys the art of "parsing "; Egyptians generally confine themselves in Al-Sarf to the Izzi, and the Lámiyat al-Af'ál of the grammarian Ibn Málik.

2 First, the well-known "Ajrumiyah " (printed by M. Vaucelle), and its commentary, Al-Kafrawi. Thirdly, the Alfíyah (Thousand Distichs) of Ibn Malik, written in verse for mnemonic purposes, but thereby rendered so difficult as to require the lengthy commentary of Al-Ashmúmi. The fifth is the well-known work called the Katr al-Nidá (the Dew Drop), celebrated from Cairo to Kábul ; and last of all the "Azhari."

Master of grammar, our student now applies himself to its proper end and purpose, Divinity. Of the four schools those of Abu Hanifah and Al-Shafe'i are most common in Cairo; the followers of Ibn Malik abound only in Southern Egypt and the Berberah country, and the Hanbali is almost unknown. The theologian begins with what is called a Matn or text, a short, dry, and often obscure treatise, a mere string of precepts; in fact, the skeleton of the subject. This he learns by repeated perusal, till he can quote almost every passage *literatim*. He then passes to its "Sharh," or commentary, generally the work of some other savant, who explains the difficulty of the text, amplifies its Laconicisms, enters into exceptional cases, and deals with principles and reasons, as well as with mere precept. A difficult work will sometimes require "Háshiyah," or "marginal notes"; but this aid has a bad name :—

> "Who readeth with note,
> But learneth by rote,"

says a popular doggrel. The reason is, that the student's reasoning powers being little exercised, he learns to depend upon the *dixit* of a master rather than to think for himself. It also leads to the neglect of another practice, highly advocated by the Eastern pedagogue.

> "The lecture is one.
> The dispute (upon the subject of the lecture) is one thousand."

In order to become a Fakíh, or divine of distinguished fame, the follower of Abu Hanifah must peruse about ten volumes,[1] some of huge size, written in a diffuse style;

---

1 I know little of the Hanafi school; but the name of the following popular works were given to me by men upon whose learning I could depend. The book first read is the text, called Maráh al-Faláh, containing about twenty pages, and its commentary, which is about six times longer. Then comes the Matn al-Kanz, a brief text of from 35 to 40 pages, followed by three long Sharh. The shortest of these, "Al-Tái," contains 500 pages; the next, "Mullá Miskín," at least 900; and the "Sharh Ayní" nearly 2000. To these succeeds the Text

the Shafe'i's reading is not quite so extensive.[1] Theology is much studied, because it leads directly to the gaining of daily bread, as priest or tutor; and other scientific pursuits are neglected for the opposite reason.

The theologian in Egypt, as in other parts of Al-Islam, must have a superficial knowledge of the Prophet's traditions. Of these there are eight well known collections,[2] but only the first three are generally read.

School-boys are instructed, almost when in their infancy, to intone the Koran; at the university they are

---

" Al-Durar," the work of the celebrated Khusraw, (200 pages), with a large commentary by the same author; and last is the Matn Tanwír Al-Absár, containing about 500 pages, and its Sharh, a work upwards of four times the size. Many of these books may be found—especially when the MS. is an old one—with Hashiyah, or marginal notes, but most men write them for themselves, so that there is no generally used collection. The above-mentioned are the works containing a full course of theological study; it is rare, however, to find a man who reads beyond the " Al-Kanz," with the shortest of its commentaries, the " Al-Tai."

1 He begins with a little text called, after the name of its author, Abu Shujá'a of Isfáhán, and proceeds to its commentary, a book of about 250 pages, by Ibn Kásim of Ghazzah (Gaza). There is another Sharh, nearly four times larger than this, " Al-Khatib "; it is seldom read. Then comes Al-Tahrír, the work of Zakaríyá al-Ansári,—a celebrated divine buried in the Mosque of Al-Shafe'i,—and its commentary by the same author, a goodly MS. of 600 pages. Most students here cry: " Enough!" The ambitious pass on to Al-Minhaj and its commentary, (1600 pages). Nor need they stop at this point. A man may addle his brains over Moslem theology, as upon Aristotle's schoolmen, till his eyesight fails him—both subjects are all but interminable.

2 The three best known are the Arbain al-Nawawi, and the Sahihayn—" the two (universally acknowledged to be) trustworthy,"— by Al-Muslim and Al-Bokhári, celebrated divines. The others are Al-Jami' al-Saghír, " the smaller collection," so called to distinguish it from a rarer book, Al-Jami' al-Kabír, the " greater collection "; both are the work of Al-Siyúti. The full course concludes with Al-Shifá, Shamáil, and the labours of Kázi Ayyáz.

taught a more exact system of chanting. The style called " Hafs" is most common in Egypt, as it is indeed throughout the Moslem world. And after learning to read the holy volume, some savans are ambitious enough to wish to understand it : under these circumstances they must dive into the 'Ilm al-Tafsír,[1] or the Exegesis of the Koran.

Our student is now a perfect Fakih or Mullá.[2] But

---

1 Two Tafsirs are known all over the modern world. The smaller one is called Jaláláni (" the two Jaláls," *i.e.* the joint work of Jalal al-Siyuti and Jalal al-Mahalli), and fills two stout volumes octavo. The larger is the Exposition of Al-Bayzáwi, which is supposed to contain the whole subject. Some few divines read Al-Kházin.

2 To conclude the list of Moslem studies, not purely religious.

Al-Mantik (or logic) is little valued ; it is read when judged advisable, after Al-Nahw, from which it flows, and before Ma'ání Bayán (rhetoric) to which it leads. In Egypt, students are generally directed to fortify their memories, and give themselves a logical turn of mind, by application to Al-Jabr (algebra). The only logical works known are the Isághúji (the εἰσαγωγή of Porphyry), Al-Shamsiyah, the book Al-Sullam, with its Sharh Al-Akhzari, and, lastly, Kází Mír. Equally neglected are the Tawáríkh (history) and the Hikmat (or philosophy), once so ardently cultivated by Moslem savans ; indeed, it is now all but impossible to get books upon these subjects. For upwards of six weeks, I ransacked the stalls and the bazar, in order to find some one of the multitudinous annals of Al-Hijaz, without seeing for sale anything but the fourth volume of a large biographical work called al-Akd al-Samín fi Tárikh al-Balad al-Amín.

The 'Ilm al-'Arúz, or Prosody, is not among the Arabs, as with us, a chapter hung on to the tail of grammar. It is a long and difficult study, prosecuted only by those who wish to distinguish themselves in " Arabiyat,"—the poetry and the eloquence of the ancient and modern Arabs. The poems generally studied, with the aid of commentaries, which impress every verse upon the memory, are the Búrdah and the Hamzíyah, well-known odes by Mohammed of Abúsír. They abound in obsolete words, and are useful at funerals, as on other solemn occasions. The Bánat Su'ádí, by Ka'ab al-Ahbár (or Akhbár), a companion of the Apostle, and the Diwan 'Umar ibn Fáriz, a celebrated mystic, are also learned compositions. Few attempt the bulky volume of Al-Mutanabbí—though many

the poor fellow has no scholarship or fellowship—no easy
tutorship—no fat living to look forward to. After wasting

---

place it open upon the sofa,—fewer still the tenebrous compositions
of Al-Haríri; nor do the modern Egyptians admire those fragments
of ancient Arab poets, which seem so sweetly simple to the European
ear. The change of faith has altered the national taste to such an
extent, that the decent bard must now sing of woman in the masculine gender. For which reason, a host of modern poetasters can
attract the public ear, which is deaf to the voices of the " Golden
Song."

In the exact sciences, the Egyptian Moslems, a backward race
according to European estimation, are far superior to the Persians
and the Moslems of India. Some of them become tolerable arith-
meticians, though very inferior to the Coptic Christians ; they have
good and simple treatises on algebra, and still display some of their
ancestors' facility in the acquisition of geometry. The 'Ilm al-
Míkát, or " Calendar-calculating," was at one time publicly taught
in the Azhar ; the printing-press has doomed that study to death.

The natural sciences find but scant favour on the banks of the
Nile. Astronomy is still astrology, geography a heap of names, and
natural history a mass of fables. Alchemy, geomancy, and sum-
moning of fiends, are pet pursuits ; but the former has so bad a name,
that even amongst friends it is always alluded to as,'Ilm al-Káf,—the
"science of K," so called from the initial letter of the word "Kímiyá."
Of the state of. therapeutics I have already treated at length.

Aided by the finest of ears, and flexible organs of articulation,
the Egyptian appears to possess many of the elements of a good
linguist. The stranger wonders to hear a Cairene donkey-boy
shouting sentences in three or four European dialects, with a pronunciation as pure as his own. How far this people succeed in
higher branches of language, my scanty experience does not enable
me to determine. But even for students of Arabic, nothing can be
more imperfect than those useful implements, Vocabularies and Dictionaries. The Cairenes have, it is true, the Kámús of Fayrúzábádí,
but it has never been printed in Egypt ; it is therefore rare, and when
found, lost pages and clerical errors combined with the intrinsic difficulty of the style, exemplify the saying of Golius, that the most learned
Orientalist must act the part of a diviner, before he can perform that
of interpreter. They have another Lexicon, the Siháh, and an
abbreviation of the same, the Siháh al-Saghír (or the lesser), both of
them liable to the same objections as the Kamus. For the benefit
of the numerous students of Turkish and Persian, short grammars

seven years, or twice seven years, over his studies, and reading till his brain is dizzy, his digestion gone, and his eyes half blind, he must either starve upon college alms, or squat, like my old Shaykh Mohammed, in a druggist's shop, or become pedagogue and preacher in some country place, on the pay of £8 per annum. With such prospects it is wonderful how the Azhar can present any attractions; but the southern man is essentially an idler, and many become Olemá, like Capuchins, in order to do nothing. A favoured few rise to the degree of Mudarris (professors), and thence emerge Kázís and Muftís. This is another inducement to matriculate; every undergraduate having an eye upon the Kazi-ship, with as much chance of obtaining it as the country *parocco* has of becoming a cardinal. Others again devote themselves to laical pursuits, degenerate into Wakíls (lawyers), or seek their fortunes as Kátibs—public or private accountants.

To conclude this part of the subject, I cannot agree with Dr. Bowring when he harshly says, upon the subject of Moslem education: "The instruction given by the Doctors of the Law in the religious schools, for the formation of the Mohammedan priesthood, is of the most worthless character."[1] His opinion is equally open to

---

and vocabularies have been printed at a cheap price, but the former are upon the model of Arabic, a language essentially different in formation, and the latter are mere strings of words.

As a specimen of the state of periodical literature, I may quote the history of the "Bulak Independent," as Europeans facetiously call it. When Mohammed Ali, determining to have an "organ," directed an officer to be editor of a weekly paper, the officer replied, that no one would read it, and consequently that no one would pay for it. The Pasha remedied this by an order that a subscription should be struck off from the pay of all employés, European and Egyptian, whose salary amounted to a certain sum. Upon which the editor accepted the task, but being paid before his work was published, he of course never supplied his subscribers with their copies.

[1] Would not a superficial, hasty, and somewhat prejudiced

objection with that of those who depreciate the law itself because it deals rather in precepts than in principle, in ceremonies and ordinances rather than in ethics and æsthetics. Both are what Eastern faiths and Eastern training have ever been,—both are eminently adapted for the Oriental mind. When the people learn to appreciate ethics, and to understand psychics and æsthetics, the demand will create a supply. Meanwhile they leave transcendentalism to their poets and philosophers, and they busy themselves with preparing for heaven by practising the only part of their faith now intelligible to them—the Material.

It is not to be supposed that a nation in this stage of civilisation could be so fervently devout as the Egyptians are, without the bad leaven of bigotry. The same tongue which is employed in blessing Allah, is, it is conceived, doing its work equally well in cursing Allah's enemies. Wherefore the Káfir is denounced by every sex, age, class, and condition, by the man of the world,[1] as by the boy at school; and out of, as well as in, the Mosque. If you ask your friend who is the person with a black turband, he replies,

" A Christian.   Allah make his Countenance cold !"

If you inquire of your servant, who are the people singing in the next house, it is ten to one that his answer will be,

" Jews.   May their lot be Jahannam !"

It appears unintelligible, still it is not less true, that Egyptians who have lived as servants under European roofs for years, retain the liveliest loathing for the manners

---

Egyptian or Persian say exactly the same thing about the systems of Christ Church and Trinity College ?

1 And when the man of the world, as sometimes happens, professes to see no difference in the forms of faith, or whispers that his residence in Europe has made him friendly to the Christian religion, you will be justified in concluding his opinions to be latitudinarian.

and customs of their masters. Few Franks, save those who have mixed with the Egyptians in Oriental disguise, are aware of their repugnance to, and contempt for, Europeans—so well is the feeling veiled under the garb of innate politeness, and so great is their reserve when conversing with those of strange religions. I had a good opportunity of ascertaining the truth when the first rumour of a Russian war arose. Almost every able-bodied man spoke of hastening to the Jihád,—a crusade, or holy war,— and the only thing that looked like apprehension was the too eager depreciation of their foes. All seemed delighted with the idea of French co-operation, for, somehow or other, the Frenchman is everywhere popular. When speaking of England, they were not equally easy : heads were rolled, pious sentences were ejaculated, and finally out came the old Eastern cry, "Of a truth they are Shaytáns, those English.[1]" The Austrians are despised, because the East knows nothing of them since the days when Osmanli hosts threatened the gates of Vienna. The Greeks are hated as clever scoundrels, ever ready to do Al-Islam a mischief. The Maltese, the greatest of cowards off their own ground, are regarded with a profound contempt : these are the protégés which bring the British nation into disrepute at Cairo. And Italians are known chiefly as "*istruttori*" and "*distruttori*"[2]—doctors, druggists, and pedagogues.

Yet Egyptian human nature is, like human nature everywhere, contradictory. Hating and despising Europeans, they still long for European rule. This people ad-

---

1 I know only one class in Egypt favourable to the English,—the donkey boys,—and they found our claim to the possession of the country upon a base scarcely admissible by those skilled in casuistry, namely, that we hire more asses than any other nation.

2 The story is, that Mohammed Ali used to offer his flocks of foreigners their choice of two professions,—"destruction," that is to say, physic, or "instruction."

mire an iron-handed and lion-hearted despotism; they hate a timid and a grinding tyranny.[1] Of all foreigners, they would prefer the French yoke,—a circumstance which I attribute to the diplomatic skill and national dignity of our neighbours across the Channel.[2] But whatever European nation secures Egypt will win a treasure. Moated on the north and south by seas, with a glacis of impassable deserts to the eastward and westward, capable of supporting an army of 180,000 men, of paying a

---

1 Of this instances abound. Lately an order was issued to tax the villages of the Badawin settled upon the edge of the Western desert, who, even in Mohammed Ali's time, were allowed to live free of assessment. The Aulád 'Ali, inhabitants of a little village near the Pyramids, refused to pay, and turned out with their matchlocks, defying the Pasha. The government then insisted upon their leaving their houses, and living under hair-cloth like Badawin, since they claimed the privileges of Badawin. The sturdy fellows at once pitched their tents, and when I returned to Cairo (in December, 1853), they had deserted their village. I could offer a score of such cases, proving the present debased condition of Egypt.

2 At Constantinople the French were the first to break through the shameful degradation to which the ambassadors of infidel powers were bribed, by 300 or 400 rations a day, to submit. M. de Saint Priest refused to give up his sword. General Sebastiani insisted upon wearing his military boots; and the Republican Aubert Dubajet rejected the dinner, and the rich dress, with which " the naked and hungry barbarian who ventured to rub his brow upon the Sublime Porte," was fed and clothed before being admitted to the presence, saying that the ambassadors of France wanted neither this nor that. At Cairo, M. Sabatier, the French Consul-general, has had the merit of doing away with some customs prejudicial to the dignity of his nation. The next English envoy will, if anxious so to distinguish himself, have an excellent opportunity. It is usual, after the first audience, for the Pasha to send, *in token of honour*, a sorry steed to the new comer. This custom is a mere relic of the days when Mohammed the Second threatened to stable his charger in St. Peter's, and when a ride through the streets of Cairo exposed the Inspector-general Tott, and his suite, to lapidation and an "*avanie*." To send a good horse is to imply degradation, but to offer a bad one is a positive insult.

heavy tribute, and yet able to show a considerable surplus of revenue, this country in western hands will command India, and by a ship-canal between Pelusium and
Suez would open the whole of Eastern Africa.[1]

There is no longer much to fear from the fanaticism
of the people, and a little prudence would suffice to com-
.mand the interests of the Mosque.[2] The chiefs of corporations,[3] in the present state of popular feeling, would offer

---

1 As this canal has become a question of national interest, its
advisability is surrounded with all the circumstance of unsupported
assertion and bold denial. The English want a railroad, which would
confine the use of Egypt to themselves. The French desire a canal
that would admit the hardy cruisers of the Mediterranean into the
Red Sea. The cosmopolite will hope that both projects may be
carried out. Even in the seventh century Omar forbade Amru to cut
the Isthmus of Suez for fear of opening Arabia to Christian vessels.
As regards the feasibility of the ship-canal, I heard M. Linant de
Bellefonds—the best authority upon all such subjects in Egypt—expressly assert, after levelling and surveying the line, that he should
have no difficulty in making it. The canal is now a fact. As late
as April, 1864, Lord Palmerston informed the House of Commons
that labourers might be more usefully employed in cultivating cotton
than in " digging a canal through a sandy desert, and in making two
harbours in deep mud and shallow water." It is, however, understood that the Premier was the only one of his Cabinet who took
this view. Mr. Robert Stephenson, C.E., certainly regretted before
his death the opinion which he had been induced to express by
desire.

2 There are at present about eighteen influential Shaykhs at
Cairo, too fanatic to listen to reason. These it would be necessary to
banish. Good information about what goes on in each Mosque, especially on Fridays, when the priests preach to the people, and a guard
of honour placed at the gates of the Kazi, the three Muftis, and the
Shaykh of the Azhar, are simple precautions sufficient to keep the
Olema in order.

3 These Rákaiz Al-'Usab, as they are called, are the most influential part of the immense mass of dark intrigue which Cairo, like
most Oriental cities, conceals beneath the light surface. They generally appear in the ostensible state of barbers and dyers. Secretly,
they preside over their different factions, and form a kind of small

even less difficulty to an invader or a foreign ruler than the Olema.   Briefly, Egypt is the most tempting prize which the East holds out to the ambition of Europe, not excepted even the Golden Horn.

Vehm.   The French used to pay these men, but Napoleon, detecting them in stirring up the people, whilst appearing to maintain public tranquillity, shot eighteen or twenty (about half their number), and thereby improved the conduct of the rest.   They are to be managed, as Sir Charles Napier governed Sind,—by keeping a watchful eye upon them, a free administration of military law, disarming the population, and forbidding large bodies of men to assemble.

CHAPTER VII.

PREPARATIONS TO QUIT CAIRO.

AT length the slow "month of blessings" passed away. We rejoiced like Romans finishing their Quaresima, when a salvo of artillery from the citadel announced the end of our Lenten woes. On the last day of Ramazan all gave alms to the poor, at the rate of a piastre and a half for each member of the household—slave, servant, and master. The next day, first of the three composing the Bayram or Íd[1] (the Lesser Festival), we arose before dawn, performed our ablutions, and repaired to the Mosque, to recite the peculiar prayer of the season, and to hear the sermon which bade us be "merry and wise." After which we ate and drank heartily; then, with pipes and tobacco-pouches in hand, we sauntered out to enjoy the contemplation of smiling faces and street scenery.

The favourite resort on this occasion is the large cemetery beyond the Bab al-Nasr[2]—that stern, old, massive gateway which opens upon the Suez road. There we found a scene of jollity. Tents and ambulant coffee-houses were full of men equipped in their—*anglicè*

---

1 Festival. It lasts the three first days of Shawwál, the month immediately following Ramazan, and therefore, among Moslems, corresponds with our Paschal holidays, which succeed Lent. It is called the " Lesser Festival," the " Greater " being in Zú'l Hijjah, the pilgrimage-month.

2 In Chap. V. of this Volume, I have mentioned this cemetery as Burckhardt's last resting-place.

—"Sunday best," listening to singers and musicians, smoking, chatting, and looking at jugglers, buffoons, snake-charmers, Darwayshes, ape-leaders, and dancing boys habited in women's attire. Eating-stalls and lolli-pop-shops, booths full of playthings, and sheds for lemonade and syrups, lined the roads, and disputed with swings and merry-go-rounds the regards of the little Moslems and Moslemahs. The chief item of the crowd, fair Cairenes, carried in their hands huge palm branches, intending to ornament therewith the tombs of parents and friends. Yet, even on this solemn occasion, there is, they say, not a little flirtation and love-making; parties of policemen are posted, with orders to interrupt all such irregularities, with a long cane; but their vigilance is notoriously unequal to the task. I could not help ob-serving that frequent pairs, doubtless cousins or other relations, wandered to unusual distances among the sand-hills, and that sometimes the confusion of a dis-tant bastinado struck the ear. These trifles did not, however, by any means interfere with the general joy. Every one wore something new; most people were in the fresh suits of finery intended to last through the year; and so strong is personal vanity in the breasts of Orientals, men and women, young and old, that from Cairo to Calcutta it would be difficult to find a sad heart under a handsome coat. The men swaggered, the women minced their steps, rolled their eyes, and were eternally arranging, and coquetting with their head-veils. The little boys strutting about foully abused any one of their number who might have a richer suit than his neigh-bours. And the little girls ogled every one in the ecstacy of conceit, and glanced contemptuously at other little girls their rivals.

Weary of the country, the Haji and I wandered about the city, paying visits, which at this time are like new-year calls in continental Europe. I can describe the operation of calling in Egypt only as the discussion of pipes and coffee in one place, and of coffee and pipes in another. But on this occasion, whenever we meet a friend we throw ourselves upon each other's breast, placing right arms over left shoulders, and *vice versâ*, squeezing like wrestlers, with intermittent hugs, then laying cheek to cheek delicately, at the same time making the loud noise of many kisses in the air.[1] The compliment of the season is, "Kull'ám antum bil khayr" —"Every year may you be well!"—in fact, our "Many happy returns of the day!" After this come abundant good wishes, and kindly prophecies; and from a "religious person" a blessing, and a short prayer. To complete the resemblance between a Moslem and a Christian festival, we have dishes of the day, fish, Shurayk, the cross-bun, and a peculiarly indigestible cake, called in Egypt Kahk,[2] the plum-pudding of Al-Islam.

This year's Íd was made gloomy, comparatively speaking, by the state of politics. Report of war with Russia, with France, with England, who was going to land three million men at Suez, and with Infideldom in general, rang through Egypt, and the city of Mars[3] became unusually martial. The government armouries, arsenals, and manufactories, were crowded with kidnapped workmen. Those who purposed a pilgrimage feared forcible detention. Wherever men gathered together, in the Mosques, for instance, or the coffee-houses, the police

1 You are bound also to meet even your enemies in the most friendly way—for which mortification you afterwards hate them more cordially than before.

2 Persian.

3 With due deference to the many of a different opinion, I believe "Káhirah" (corrupted through the Italian into Cairo) to mean, not the "victorious," but the "City of Káhir," or Mars the Planet. It was so called because, as Richardson has informed the world, it was founded in A.D. 968 by one Jauhar, a Dalmatian renegade before mentioned, when the warlike planet was in the ascendant.

closed the doors, and made forcible capture of the able-
bodied. This proceeding, almost as barbarous as our
impressment law, filled the main streets with detach-
ments of squalid-looking wretches, marching to be made
soldiers, with collars round their necks and irons on their
wrists. The dismal impression of the scene was deepened
by crowds of women, who, habited in mourning, and scattering dust and mud over their rent garments, followed
their sons, brothers, and husbands, with cries and shrieks.
The death-wail is a peculiar way of cheering on the
patriot departing *pro patriâ mori*, and the origin of the
custom is characteristic of the people. The principal
public amusements allowed to Oriental women are those
that come under the general name of "Fantasia,"—
birth-feasts, marriage festivals, and funerals. And the
early campaigns of Mohammed Ali's family in Syria,
and Al-Hijaz having, in many cases, deprived the be-
reaved of their sex-right to "keen" for the dead, they have
now determined not to waste the opportunity, but to
revel in the luxury of woe at the live man's wake.[1]

Another cloud hung over Cairo. Rumours of con-
spiracy were afloat. The Jews and Christians,—here as
ready to take alarm as the English in Italy,—trembled at
the fancied preparations for insurrection, massacre, and
plunder. And even the Moslems whispered that some
hundred desperadoes had resolved to fire the city, beginning with the bankers' quarter, and to spoil the wealthy
Egyptians. Of course H.H. Abbas Pasha was absent
at the time, and, even had he been at Cairo, his presence
would have been of little use: the ruler can do nothing

---

1 "There were no weeping women; no neighbours came in to sit
down in the ashes, as they might have done had the soldier died at
home; there was no Nubian dance for the dead, no Egyptian song of
the women lauding the memory of the deceased, and beseeching him
to tell why he had left them alone in the world to weep."—(Letter
from Widdin, March 25, 1854, describing a Turkish soldier's funeral.)

towards restoring confidence to a panic-stricken Oriental nation.

At the end of the Íd, as a counter-irritant to political excitement, the police magistrates began to bully the people. There is a standing order in the chief cities of Egypt, that all who stir abroad after dark without a lantern shall pass the night in the station-house.[1] But at Cairo, in certain quarters, the Azbakiyah[2] for instance, a little laxity is usually allowed. Before I left the capital the licence was withdrawn, and the sudden strictness caused many ludicrous scenes.

If by chance you (clad in Oriental garb) had sent on your lantern to a friend's house by your servant, and had leisurely followed it five minutes after the hour of eight, you were sure to be met, stopped, collared, questioned, and captured by the patrol. You probably punched three or four of them, but found the dozen too strong for you. Held tightly by the sleeves, skirts, and collar of your wide outer garment, you were hurried away on a plane of about nine inches above the ground, your feet mostly treading the air. You were dragged along with a rapidity which scarcely permitted you to answer strings of questions concerning your name, nation, dwelling, faith, profession, and self in general,—especially concerning the present state of your purse. If you lent an ear to the voice of the charmer that began by asking a crown to release you, and gradually came down to two-pence halfpenny, you fell into a simple trap ; the butt-end of a musket applied *à posteriori*, immediately after the transfer of property, convicted you of wilful waste. But if, more sensibly, you pretended to have forgotten your purse, you

1 Captain Haines wisely introduced the custom into Aden. I wonder that it is not made universal in the cities of India, where so much iniquity is perpetrated under the shadow of night.

2 The reason being that respectable Europeans, and the passengers by the Overland Mail, live and lodge in this quarter.

were reviled, and dragged with increased violence of shaking to the office of the Zabit, or police magistrate. You were spun through the large archway leading to the court, every fellow in uniform giving you, as you passed, a Kafá, " cuff," on the back of the neck. Despite your rage, you were forced up the stairs to a long gallery full of people in a predicament like your own. Again your name, nation,—I suppose you to be masquerading,—offence, and other particulars were asked, and carefully noted in a folio by a ferocious-looking clerk. If you knew no better, you were summarily thrust into the Hásil or condemned cell, to pass the night with pickpockets or ruffians, pell-mell. But if an adept in such matters, you insisted upon being conducted before the " Pasha of the Night," and, the clerk fearing to refuse, you were hurried to the great man's office, hoping for justice, and dealing out ideal vengeance to your captors,—the patrol. Here you found the dignitary sitting with pen, ink, and paper before him, and pipe and coffee-cup in hand, upon a wide Diwan of dingy chintz, in a large dimly-lit room, with two guards by his side, and a semi-circle of recent seizures vociferating before him. When your turn came, you were carefully collared, and led up to the presence, as if even at that awful moment you were mutinously and murderously disposed. The Pasha, looking at you with a vicious sneer, turned up his nose, ejaculated " 'Ajami," and prescribed the bastinado. You observed that the mere fact of being a Persian did not give mankind a right to capture, imprison, and punish you ; you declared moreover that you were no Persian, but an Indian under British protection. The Pasha, a man accustomed to obedience, then stared at you, to frighten you, and you, we will suppose, stared at him, till, with an oath, he turned to the patrol, and asked them your offence. They all simultaneously swore—by Allah !—that you had been found without a lantern, dead-drunk, beating respectable people, breaking into houses, invading and robbing harims. You openly told the Pasha that they were eating abominations; upon which he directed one of his guards to smell your breath,—the charge of drunkenness being tangible. The fellow, a comrade of your capturers, advanced his nose to your lips; as might be expected, cried " Kikh," contorted his countenance, and answered, by the beard of " Effendiná[1]" that he perceived a pestilent odour of distilled waters. This announcement probably elicited a grim grin from the " Pasha of the Night," who loves Curaçoa, and who is not indifferent to the charms of Cognac. Then by his favour, for you improved the occasion, you were allowed to spend the hours of darkness on a wooden bench, in the adjacent long gallery, together with certain little parasites, for which polite language has no name.[2] In the morning the janissary of your Consulate was sent for: he came, and claimed you; you were led off criminally; again you gave your name and address, and if your offence was merely sending on your lantern, you were dismissed with advice to be more careful in future. And assuredly your first step was towards the Hammam.

But if, on the other hand, you had declared yourself a European, you would either have been dismissed at once, or sent to your Consul, who is here judge, jury, and jailor. Egyptian authority has of late years lost half its prestige. When Mr. Lane first settled at Cairo, all Europeans accused of aggression against Moslems were, he tells us, surrendered to the Turkish magistrates. Now, the native powers have no jurisdiction over strangers,

---

1 " Our lord," *i. e.* H.H. the Pasha. " Kikh " is an interjection noting disapproval, or disgust,—" Fie!" or " Ugh!"

2 Shortly after the Ramazan of 1853, the Consul, I am told, obtained an order that British subjects should be sent directly from the police office, at all hours of the night, to the Consulate. This was a most sensible measure.

nor can the police enter their houses. If the West would raise the character of its Eastern co-religionists, it will be forced to push the system a point further, and to allow all *bonâ-fide* Christian subjects to register their names at the different Consulates whose protection they might prefer. This is what Russia has so " unwarrantably and outrageously" attempted. We confine ourselves to a lesser injustice, which deprives Eastern states of their right as independent Powers to arrest, and to judge foreigners, who for interest or convenience settle in their dominions. But we still shudder at the right of arrogating any such claim over the born lieges of Oriental Powers. What, however, would be the result were Great Britain to authorise her sons resident at Paris, or Florence, to refuse attendance at a French or an Italian court of justice, and to demand that the police should never force the doors of an English subject ?   I commend this consideration to all those who " stickle for abstract rights " when the interest and progress of others are concerned, and who become somewhat latitudinarian and concrete in cases where their own welfare and aggrandisement are at stake.

Besides patients, I made some pleasant acquaintances at Cairo. Antun Zananire, a young Syrian of considerable attainments as a linguist, paid me the compliment of permitting me to see the fair face of his " Harím." Mr. Hatchadur Nury, an Armenian gentleman, well known in Bombay, amongst other acts of kindness, introduced me to one of his compatriots, Khwajah Yúsuf, whose advice was most useful to me. The Khwajah had wandered far and wide, picking up everywhere some scrap of strange knowledge, and his history was a romance. Expelled from Cairo for a youthful peccadillo, he started upon his travels, qualified himself for sanctity at Meccah and Al-Madinah, became a religious beggar at Baghdad, studied French at Paris, and finally settled down as a professor of languages,[1] under an amnesty, at Cairo. In his house I saw an Armenian marriage. The occasion was memorable : after the gloom and sameness of Moslem society, nothing could be more gladdening than the unveiled face of a pretty woman. Some of the guests were undeniably charming brunettes, with the blackest possible locks, and the brightest conceivable eyes. Only one pretty girl wore the national costume ;[2] yet they all smoked chibuks and sat upon the Diwans, and, as they entered the room, they kissed with a sweet simplicity the hands of the priest, and of the other old gentlemen present.

Among the number of my acquaintances was a Meccan boy, Mohammed al-Basyúni, from whom I bought the pilgrim-garb called "Al-Ihram" and the Kafan or shroud, with which the Moslem usually starts upon such a journey as mine. He, being in his way homewards after a visit to Constantinople, was most anxious to accompany me in the character of a "companion." But he had travelled too much to suit me ; he had visited India, he had seen Englishmen, and he had lived with the "Nawáb Bálú" of Surat. Moreover, he showed signs of over-wisdom. He had been a regular visitor, till I cured one of his friends of an ophthalmia, after which

---

1 Most Eastern nations, owing to their fine ear for sounds, are quick at picking up languages ; but the Armenian is here, what the Russian is in the West, the *facile princeps* of conversational linguists. I have frequently heard them speak with the purest accent, and admirable phraseology, besides their mother tongue, Turkish, Arabic, Persian, and Hindustani, nor do they evince less aptitude for acquiring the Occidental languages.

2 It has been too frequently treated of, to leave room for a fresh description. Though pretty and picturesque, it is open to the reproach of Moslem dressing, namely, that the in-door toilette admits of a display of bust, and is generally so scanty and flimsy that it is unfit to meet the eye of a stranger. This, probably the effect of secluding women, has now become a cause for concealing them.

he gave me his address at Meccah, and was seen no more.   Haji Wali described him and his party to be " Nás jarrár " (extractors), and certainly he had not misjudged them.   But the sequel will prove how *der Mensch denkt und Gott lenkt;* and as the boy, Mohammed, eventually did become my companion throughout the Pilgrimage, I will place him before the reader as summarily as possible.

He is a beardless youth, of about eighteen, chocolate-brown, with high features, and a bold profile; his bony and decided Meccan cast of face is lit up by the peculiar Egyptian eye, which seems to descend from generation to generation.[1]   His figure is short and broad, with a tendency to be obese, the result of a strong stomach and the power of sleeping at discretion.   He can read a little, write his name, and is uncommonly clever at a bargain.   Meccah had taught him to speak excellent Arabic, to understand the literary dialect, to be eloquent in abuse, and to be profound at Prayer and Pilgrimage.   Constantinople had given him a taste for Anacreontic singing, and female society of the questionable kind, a love of strong waters,—the hypocrite looked positively scandalised when I first suggested the subject, —and an off-hand latitudinarian mode of dealing with serious subjects in general.   I found him to be the youngest son of a widow, whose doting fondness had moulded his disposition; he was selfish and affectionate, as spoiled children usually are, volatile, easily offended and as easily pacified (the Oriental), coveting other men's goods, and profuse of his own (the Arab), with a matchless intrepidity of countenance (the traveller), brazen lunged, not more than half brave, exceedingly astute, with an acute sense of honour, especially where his

---

1 He was from the banks of the Nile, as his cognomen, al-Basyuni proves, but his family, I was told, had been settled for three or four generations at Meccah.

relations were concerned (the individual). I have seen him in a fit of fury because some one cursed his father; and he and I nearly parted because on one occasion I applied to him an epithet which, etymologically considered, might be exceedingly insulting to a high-minded brother, but which in popular *parlance* signifies nothing. This "*point d'honneur*" was the boy Mohammed's strong point.

During the Ramazan I laid in my stores for the journey. These consisted of tea, coffee, loaf-sugar, rice, dates, biscuit, oil, vinegar, tobacco, lanterns, and cooking pots, a small bell-shaped tent, costing twelve shillings, and three water-skins for the Desert.[1] The provisions were placed in a " Kafas " or hamper artistically made of palm sticks, and in a huge Sahhárah, or wooden box, about three feet each way, covered with leather or skin, and provided with a small lid fitting into the top.[2] The

---

1 Almost all the articles of food were so far useful, that they served every one of the party at least as much as they did their owner. My friends drank my coffee, smoked my tobacco, and ate my rice. I bought better tea at Meccah than at Cairo, and found as good sugar there. It would have been wiser to lay in a small stock merely for the voyage to Yambu', in which case there might have been more economy. But I followed the advice of those interested in setting me wrong. Turks and Egyptians always go pilgrimaging with a large outfit, as notably as the East-Indian cadet of the present day, and your outfitter at Cairo, as well as Cornhill, is sure to supply you with a variety of superfluities. The tent was useful to me; so were the water-skins, which I preferred to barrels, as being more portable, and less liable to leak. Good skins cost about a dollar each; they should be bought new and always kept half full of water.

2 This shape secures the lid, which otherwise, on account of the weight of the box, would infallibly be torn off, or burst open. Like the Kafas, the Sahharah should be well padlocked, and if the owner be a saving man, he does not entrust his keys to a servant. I gave away my Kafas at Yambu', because it had been crushed during the sea-voyage, and I was obliged to leave the Sahharah at Al-Madinah, as my Badawi camel-shaykh positively refused to carry it to Meccah, so that both these articles were well nigh useless to me. The Kafas

former, together with my green box containing medicines, and saddle-bags full of clothes, hung on one side of the camel, a counterpoise to the big Sahharah on the other flank ; the Badawin, like muleteers, always requiring a balance of weight. On the top of the load was placed transversely a Shibríyah or cot, on which Shaykh Nur squatted like a large crow.   This worthy had strutted out into the streets armed with a pair of horse-pistols and a sword almost as long as himself.   No sooner did the mischievous boys of Cairo—they are as bad as the *gamins* of Paris and London—catch sight of him than they began to scream with laughter at the sight of the " Hindi (Indian) in arms," till, like a vagrant owl pursued by a flight of larks, he ran back into the Caravanserai.

Having spent all my ready money at Cairo, I was obliged to renew the supply.   My native acquaintances advised me to take at least eighty pounds sterling, and considering the expense of outfit for Desert travelling, the sum did not appear excessive.   I should have found some difficulty in raising the money had it not been for the kindness of a friend at Alexandria, John Thurburn, now, I regret to say, no more, and Mr. Sam Shepheard, then of Shepheard's Hotel, Cairo, presently a landed proprietor near Rugby, and now also gone.   My Indians scrutinised the diminutive square of paper [1] — the

---

cost four shillings, and the Sahharah about twelve.   When these large boxes are really strong and good, they are worth about a pound sterling each.

[1] At my final interview with the committee of the Royal Geographical Society, one member, Sir Woodbine Parish, advised an order to be made out on the Society's bankers ;   another, Sir Roderick Murchison, kindly offered to give me one on his own, Coutts & Co. ; but I, having more experience in Oriental travelling, begged only to be furnished with a diminutive piece of paper, permitting me to draw upon the Society.   It was at once given by Dr. Shaw, the Secretary, and it proved of much use eventually.   It was purposely made as small as possible, in order to fit into a talisman case.   But the traveller must

letter of credit—as a raven may sometimes be seen peering, with head askance, into the interior of a suspected marrow-bone. "Can this be a *bonâ-fide* draft?" they mentally inquired. And finally they offered, politely, to write to England for me, to draw the money, and to forward it in a sealed bag directed "Al-Madinah." I need scarcely say that such a style of transmission would, in the case of precious metals, have left no possible chance of its safe arrival. When the difficulty was overcome, I bought fifty pounds' worth of German dollars (Maria Theresas), and invested the rest in English and Turkish sovereigns.[1] The gold I myself carried; part of the silver I sewed up in Shaykh Nur's leather waistbelt, and part was packed in the boxes, for this reason,—when Badawin begin plundering a respectable man, if they find a certain amount of ready money in his baggage, they do not search his person. If they find none they proceed to a bodily inspection, and if his waist-belt be empty they are rather disposed to rip open his stomach, in the belief that he must have some peculiarly ingenious way of secreting valuables. Having passed through this trouble I immediately fell into another. My hardly-earned Alexandrian passport required a double visá, one at the Police office, the other at the Consul's. After returning to Egypt, I found it was the practice of travellers

---

bear in mind, that if his letters of credit be addressed to Orientals, the sheet of paper should always be large, and grand-looking. These people have no faith in notes,—commercial, epistolary, or diplomatic.

1 Before leaving Cairo, I bought English sovereigns for 112, and sold them in Arabia for 122 piastres. "Abú Tákahs," (pataks, or Spanish pillar-dollars), as they are called in Al-Hijaz, cost me 24 piastres, and in the Holy City were worth 28. The "Sinku" (French five franc piece) is bought for 22 piastres in Egypt, and sells at 24 in Arabia. The silver Majídi costs 20 at Cairo, and is worth 22 in the Red Sea, and finally I gained 3 piastres upon the gold "Ghází" of 19. Such was the rate of exchange in 1853. It varies, however, perpetually, and in 1863 may be totally different.

who required any civility from Dr. Walne, then the English official at Cairo, to enter the " Presence " furnished with an order from the Foreign Office.

I had neglected the precaution, and had ample reason to regret having done so. Failing at the British Consulate, and unwilling to leave Cairo without being " *en règle*,"—the Egyptians warned me that Suez was a place of obstacles to pilgrims,[1]—I was obliged to look elsewhere for protection. My friend Haji Wali was the first consulted ; after a long discussion he offered to take me to his Consul, the Persian, and to find out for what sum I could become a temporary subject of the Shah. We went to the sign of the " Lion and the Sun," and we found the dragoman,[2] a subtle Syrian Christian, who,

---

1 The reason of this will be explained in a future chapter.

2 The Consular dragoman is one of the greatest abuses I know. The tribe is, for the most part, Levantine and Christian, and its connections are extensive. The father will perhaps be interpreter to the English, the son to the French Consulate. By this means the most privy affairs will become known to every member of the department, except the head, and eventually to that best of spy-trainers, the Turkish government. This explains how a subordinate, whose pay is £200 per annum, and who spends double that sum, can afford, after twelve or thirteen years' service, to purchase a house for £2,000 and to furnish it for as much more. Besides which, the condition, the ideas, and the very nature of these dragomans are completely Oriental. The most timid and cringing of men, they dare not take the proper tone with a government to which, in case of the expulsion of a Consul, they and their families would become subject. And their prepossessions are utterly Oriental. Hanna Massara, dragoman to the Consul-General at Cairo, in my presence and before others, advocated the secret murder of a Moslem girl who had fled with a Greek, on the grounds that an adulteress must always be put to death, either publicly or under the rose. Yet this man is an " old and tried servant " of the State. Such evils might be in part mitigated by employing English youths, of whom an ample supply, if there were any demand, would soon be forthcoming. This measure has been advocated by the best authorities, but without success. Most probably, the reason of the neglect is the difficulty how to begin, or where to end, the Augean labour of Consular reform.

after a rigid inquiry into the state of my purse (my country was no consideration at all[1]), introduced me to the Great Man. I have described this personage once already, and he merits not a second notice. The interview was truly ludicrous. He treated us with exceeding *hauteur*, motioned me to sit almost out of hearing, and after rolling his head in profound silence for nearly a quarter of an hour, vouchsafed the information that though my father *might* be a Shírázi, and my mother an Afghan, he had not the honour of my acquaintance. His companion, a large old Persian with Polyphemean eyebrows and a mulberry beard, put some gruff and discouraging questions. I quoted the verses

" He is a man who benefits his fellow men,
   Not he who says ' why?' and ' wherefore?' and ' how much?' "

upon which an imperious wave of the arm directed me to return to the dragoman, who had the effrontery to ask me four pounds sterling for a Persian passport. I offered one. He derided my offer, and I went away perplexed. On my return to Cairo some months afterwards, he sent to say that had he known me as an Englishman, I should have had the document gratis,—a civility for which he was duly thanked.

At last my Shaykh Mohammed hit upon *the* plan. " Thou art," said he, " an Afghan ; I will fetch hither the principal of the Afghan college at the Azhar, and he, if

---

1 In a previous chapter I have alluded to the species of protection formerly common in the East. Europe, it is to be feared, is not yet immaculate in this respect, and men say that were a list of " protected " furnished by the different Consulates at Cairo, it would be a curious document. As no one, Egyptian or foreigner, would, if he could possibly help it, be subject to the Egyptian government, large sums might be raised by the simple process of naturalising strangers. At the Persian Consulate 110 dollars—the century for the Consul, and the decade for his dragoman—have been paid for protection. A stern fact this for those who advocate the self-government of the childish East.

thou make it worth his while," (this in a whisper) " will be thy friend." The case was looking desperate ; my preceptor was urged to lose no time.

Presently Shaykh Mohammed returned in company with the principal, a little, thin, ragged-bearded, one-eyed, hare-lipped divine, dressed in very dirty clothes, of nondescript cut. Born at Maskat of Afghan parents, and brought up at Meccah, he was a kind of cosmopolite, speaking five languages fluently, and full of reminiscences of toil and travel. He refused pipes and coffee, professing to be ascetically disposed : but he ate more than half my dinner, to reassure me, I presume, should I have been fearful that abstinence might injure his health. We then chatted in sundry tongues. I offered certain presents of books, which were rejected (such articles being valueless), and the Shaykh Abd al-Wahháb having expressed his satisfaction at my account of myself, told me to call for him at the Azhar Mosque next Morning.

Accordingly at six P.M. Shaykh Mohammed and Abdullah Khan,[1]—the latter equipped in a gigantic sprigged-muslin turband, so as to pass for a student of theology,—repaired to Al-Azhar. Passing through the open quadrangle, we entered the large hall which forms the body of the Mosque. In the northern wall was a dwarf door, leading by breakneck stairs to a pigeon-hole, the study of the learned Afghan Shaykh. We found him ensconced behind piles of musty and greasy manuscripts, surrounded by scholars and scribes, with whom he was cheapening books. He had not much business to transact ; but long before he was ready, the stifling atmosphere drove us out of the study, and we repaired to the hall. Presently the Shaykh joined us, and we all rode on to the citadel, and waited in a Mosque till the office hour struck. When the doors were opened we went into the

---

1 Khan is a title assumed in India and other countries by all Afghans, and Pathans, their descendants, simple as well as gentle.

"Diwan," and sat patiently till the Shaykh found an opportunity of putting in a word. The officials were two in number; one an old invalid, very thin and sickly-looking, dressed in the Turco-European style, whose hand was being severely kissed by a troop of religious beggars, to whom he had done some small favours; the other was a stout young clerk, whose duty it was to engross, and not to have his hand kissed.

My name and other essentials were required, and no objections were offered, for who holier than the Shaykh Abd al-Wahháb ibn Yúnus al-Sulaymáni? The clerk filled up a printed paper in the Turkish language, apparently borrowed from the European method for spoiling the traveller; certified me, upon the Shaykh's security, to be one Abdullah, the son of Yúsuf (Joseph), originally from Kábul, described my person, and, in exchange for five piastres, handed me the document. I received it with joy.

With bows, and benedictions, and many wishes that Allah might make it the officials' fate to become pilgrims, we left the office, and returned towards Al-Azhar. When we had nearly reached the Mosque, Shaykh Mohammed lagged behind, and made the sign. I drew near the Afghan, and asked for his hand. He took the hint, and muttering, "It is no matter!"—"It is not necessary!"—"By Allah it is not required!" extended his fingers, and brought the "*musculus guineorum*" to bear upon three dollars.

Poor man! I believe it was his necessity that consented to be paid for the doing a common act of Moslem charity; he had a wife and children, and the calling of an Alim [1] is no longer worth much in Egypt.

My departure from Cairo was hastened by an accident. I lost my reputation by a little misfortune that happened in this wise.

---

[1] A theologian, a learned man.

At Haji Wali's room in the Caravanserai, I met a Yuzbáshi, or captain of Albanian Irregulars, who was in Egypt on leave from Al-Hijaz. He was a tall, bony, and broad-shouldered mountaineer, about forty years old, with the large *bombé* brow, the fierce eyes, thin lips, lean jaws, and peaky chin of his race. His mustachios were enormously long and tapering, and the rest of his face, like his head, was close shaven. His *Fustan*[1] was none of the cleanest ; nor was the red cap, which he wore rakishly pulled over his frowning forehead, quite free from stains. Not permitted to carry the favourite pistols, he contented himself with sticking his right hand in the empty belt, and stalking about the house with a most military mien. Yet he was as little of a bully as carpet knight, that same Ali Ághá ; his body showed many a grisly scar, and one of his shin bones had been broken by a Turkish bullet, when he was playing tricks on the Albanian hills,—an accident inducing a limp, which he attempted to conceal by a heavy swagger. When he spoke, his voice was affectedly gruff ; he had a sad knack of sneering, and I never saw him thoroughly sober.

Our acquaintance began with a kind of storm, which blew over, and left fine weather. I was showing Haji Wali my pistols with Damascene barrels when Ali Agha entered the room. He sat down before me with a grin, which said intelligibly enough, " What business have *you* with weapons ?"—snatched the arm out of my hand, and began to inspect it as a *connoisseur*. Not admiring this procedure, I wrenched it away from him, and, addressing myself to Haji Wali, proceeded quietly with my dissertation. The captain of Irregulars and I then looked at each other. He cocked his cap on one side, in token of excited pugnacity. I twirled my moustachios to display a kindred emotion. Had he been armed, and in Al-Hijaz,

---

1 The stiff, white, plaited kilt worn by Albanians.

we should have fought it out at once, for the Arnauts are
"*terribili colla pistola,*" as the Italians say, meaning that
upon the least provocation they pull out a horse-pistol,
and fire it in the face of friend or foe. Of course, the only
way under these circumstances is to anticipate them; but
even this desperate prevention seldom saves a stranger,
as whenever there is danger, these men go about in
pairs. I never met with a more reckless brood. Upon
the line of march Albanian troops are not allowed
ammunition; for otherwise there would be half a dozen
duels a day. When they quarrel over their cups, it is
the fashion for each man to draw a pistol, and to place it
against his opponent's breast. The weapons being kept
accurately clean, seldom miss fire, and if one combatant
draw trigger before the other, he would immediately be
shot down by the bystanders.[1] In Egypt these men,—
who are used as Irregulars, and are often quartered upon
the hapless villagers, when unable or unwilling to pay
taxes,—were the terror of the population. On many
occasions they have quarrelled with foreigners, and insulted European women. In Al-Hijaz their recklessness
awes even the Badawin. The townspeople say of them
that, "tripe-sellers, and bath-servants, at Stambul, they
become Pharaohs (tyrants, ruffians,) in Arabia." At
Jeddah the Arnauts have amused themselves with firing
at the English Consul, Mr. Ogilvie, when he walked upon
his terrace. And this man-shooting appears a favourite
sport with them: at Cairo numerous stories illustrate the
sang froid with which they used to knock over the camel-
drivers, if any one dared to ride past their barracks.
The Albanians vaunt their skill in using weapons, and
their pretensions impose upon Arabs as well as Egyptians;
yet I have never found them wonderful with any arm

---

[1] Those curious about the manners of these desperadoes may
consult the pages of Giovanni Finati (Murray, London, 1830), and I
will be answerable that he exaggerates nothing.

(the pistol alone excepted); and our officers, who have visited their native hills, speak of them as tolerable but by no means first-rate rifle shots.

The captain of Irregulars being unhappily debarred the pleasure of shooting me, after looking fierce for a time, rose, and walked majestically out of the room. A day or two afterwards, he called upon me civilly enough, sat down, drank a cup of coffee, smoked a pipe, and began to converse. But as he knew about a hundred Arabic words, and I as many Turkish, our conversation was carried on under difficulties. Presently he asked me in a whisper for " 'Araki."[1] I replied that there was none in the house, which induced a sneer and an ejaculation sounding like " Himár," (ass,) the slang synonym amongst fast Moslems for water-drinker. After rising to depart, he seized me waggishly, with an eye to a trial of strength. Thinking that an Indian doctor and a temperance man would not be very dangerous, he exposed himself to what is professionally termed a " cross-buttock," and had his " nut " come in contact with the stone floor instead of my bed, he might not have drunk for many a day. The fall had a good effect upon his temper. He jumped up,

---

1 Vulgarly Ráki, the cognac of Egypt and Turkey. Generically the word means any spirit ; specifically, it is applied to that extracted from dates, or dried grapes. The latter is more expensive than the former, and costs from 5 to 7 piastres the bottle. It whitens the water like Eau de Cologne, and being considered a stomachic, is patronised by Europeans as much as by Asiatics. In the Azbakiyah gardens at Cairo, the traveller is astonished by perpetual " shouts " for " Sciroppo di gomma," as if all the Western population was afflicted with sore throat. The reason is that spirituous liquors in a Moslem land must not be sold in places of public resort ; so the infidel asks for a " syrup of gum," and obtains a " dram " of 'Araki. The favourite way of drinking it, is to swallow it neat, and to wash it down with a mouthful of cold water. Taken in this way it acts like the " petit verre d'absinthe." Egyptian women delight in it, and Eastern topers of all classes and sexes prefer it to brandy and cognac, the smell of which, being strange, is offensive to them.

patted my head, called for another pipe, and sat down to show me his wounds, and to boast of his exploits. I could not help remarking a ring of English gold, with a bezel of bloodstone, sitting strangely upon his coarse, sun-stained hand. He declared that it had been snatched by him from a Konsúl (Consul) at Jeddah, and he volubly related, in a mixture of Albanian, Turkish, and Arabic, the history of his acquisition. He begged me to supply him with a little poison that " would not lie," for the purpose of quieting a troublesome enemy, and he carefully stowed away in his pouch five grains of calomel, which I gave him for that laudable purpose. Before taking leave he pressed me strongly to go and drink with him; I refused to do so during the day, but, wishing to see how these men sacrifice to Bacchus, promised compliance that night. About nine o'clock, when the Caravanserai was quiet, I took a pipe, and a tobacco-pouch,[1] stuck my dagger in my belt, and slipped into Ali Agha's room. He was sitting on a bed spread upon the ground: in front of him stood four wax candles (all Orientals hate drinking in any but a bright light), and a tray containing a basin of stuff like soup maigre, a dish of cold stewed meat, and two bowls of Salátah,[2] sliced cucumber, and curds. The "materials" peeped out of an iron pot filled with water; one was a long, thin, white-glass flask of 'Araki, the other a bottle of some strong

---

1 When Egyptians of the middle classes call upon one another, the visitor always carries with him his tobacco-pouch, which he hands to the servant, who fills his pipe.

2 The "Salatah" is made as follows. Take a cucumber, pare, slice and place it in a plate, sprinkling it over with salt. After a few minutes, season it abundantly with pepper, and put it in a bowl containing some peppercorns, and about a pint of curds. When the dish is properly mixed, a live coal is placed upon the top of the compound to make it bind, as the Arabs say. It is considered a cooling dish, and is esteemed by the abstemious, as well as by the toper.

perfume. Both were wrapped up in wet rags, the usual refrigerator.

Ali Agha welcomed me politely, and seeing me admire the preparations, bade me beware how I suspected an Albanian of not knowing how to drink; he made me sit by him on the bed, threw his dagger to a handy distance, signalled me to do the same, and prepared to begin the bout. Taking up a little tumbler, in shape like those from which French postilions used to drink *la goutte*, he inspected it narrowly, wiped out the interior with his forefinger, filled it to the brim, and offered it to his guest[1] with a bow. I received it with a low salam, swallowed its contents at once, turned it upside down in proof of fair play, replaced it upon the floor, with a jaunty movement of the arm, somewhat like a pugilist delivering a "rounder," bowed again, and requested him to help himself. The same ceremony followed on his part. Immediately after each glass,—and rapidly the cup went about,—we swallowed a draught of water, and ate a spoonful of the meat or the Salatah in order to cool our palates. Then we re-applied ourselves to our pipes, emitting huge puffs, a sign of being "fast" men, and looked facetiously at each other,—drinking being considered by Moslems a funny and pleasant sort of sin.

The Albanian captain was at least half seas over when we began the bout, yet he continued to fill and to drain without showing the least progress towards ebriety. I in vain for a time expected the *bad-masti* (as the Persians call it,) the horse play, and the gross facetiæ, which gene-

---

1 These Albanians are at most half Asiatic as regards manner. In the East generally, the host drinks of the cup, and dips his hand into the dish before his guest, for the same reason that the master of the house precedes his visitor over the threshold. Both actions denote that no treachery is intended, and to reverse them, as amongst us, would be a gross breach of custom, likely to excite the liveliest suspicions.

rally accompany southern and eastern tipsiness. Ali Agha, indeed, occasionally took up the bottle of perfume, filled the palm of his right hand, and dashed it in my face : I followed his example, but our pleasantries went no further.

Presently my companion started a grand project, namely, that I should entice the respectable Haji Wali into the room, where we might force him to drink. The idea was facetious ; it was making a Bow-street magistrate polk at a casino. I started up to fetch the Haji ; and when I returned with him Ali Agha was found in a new stage of "freshness." He had stuck a green-leaved twig upright in the floor, and had so turned over a gugglet of water, that its contents trickled slowly, in a tiny stream under the verdure ; whilst he was sitting before it mentally gazing, with an outward show of grim Quixotic tenderness, upon the shady trees and the cool rills of his fatherland. Possibly he had peopled the place with " young barbarians at play ;" for verily I thought that a tear " which had no business there " was glistening in his stony eye.

The appearance of Haji Wali suddenly changed the scene. Ali Agha jumped up, seized the visitor by the shoulder, compelled him to sit down, and, ecstasied by the old man's horror at the scene, filled a tumbler, and with the usual grotesque grimaces insisted upon its being drunk off. Haji Wali stoutly refused ; then Ali Agha put it to his own lips, and drained it, with a hurt feeling and reproachful aspect. We made our unconvivial friend smoke a few puffs, and then we returned to the charge. In vain the Haji protested that throughout life he had avoided the deadly sin ; in vain he promised to drink with us to-morrow,—in vain he quoted the Koran, and alternately coaxed, and threatened us with the police. We were inexorable. At last the Haji started upon his feet, and rushed away, regardless of any thing but escape, leaving his Tarbush, his slippers, and his pipe, in the hands of the enemy. The host did not dare to pursue his recreant guest beyond the door, but returning he carefully sprinkled the polluting liquid on the cap, pipe, and shoes, and called the Haji an ass in every tongue he knew.

Then we applied ourselves to supper, and dispatched the soup, the stew, and the Salatah. A few tumblers and pipes were exhausted to obviate indigestion, when Ali Agha arose majestically, and said that he required a troop of dancing girls to gladden his eyes with a ballet.

I represented that such persons are no longer admitted into Caravanserais.[1] He inquired, with calm ferocity, "who hath forbidden it?" I replied "the Pasha;" upon which Ali Agha quietly removed his cap, brushed it with his dexter fore-arm, fitted it on his forehead, raking forwards, twisted his mustachios to the sharp point of a single hair, shouldered his pipe, and moved towards the door, vowing that he would make the Pasha himself come, and dance before us.

I foresaw a brawl, and felt thankful that my boon companion had forgotten his dagger. Prudence whispered me to return to my room, to bolt the door, and to go to bed, but conscience suggested that it would be unfair to abandon the Albanian in his present helpless state. I followed him into the outer gallery, pulling him, and begging him, as a despairing wife might urge a drunken husband, to return home. And he, like the British husband, being greatly irritated by the unjovial advice, instantly belaboured with his pipe-stick [2] the first person

---

1 Formerly these places, like the coffee-houses, were crowded with bad characters. Of late years the latter have been refused admittance, but it would be as easy to bar the door to gnats and flies. They appear as "foot-pages," as washerwomen, as beggars; in fact, they evade the law with ingenuity and impunity.

2 Isma'íl Pasha was murdered by Malik Nimr, chief of Shendy,

he met in the gallery, and sent him flying down the stairs with fearful shouts of "O Egyptians! O ye accursed! O genus of Pharaoh! O race of dogs! O Egyptians!"

He then burst open a door with his shoulder, and reeled into a room where two aged dames were placidly reposing by the side of their spouses, who were basket-makers. They immediately awoke, seeing a stranger, and, hearing his foul words, they retorted with a hot volley of vituperation.

Put to flight by the old women's tongues, Ali Agha, in spite of all my endeavours, reeled down the stairs, and fell upon the sleeping form of the night porter, whose blood he vowed to drink—the Oriental form of threatening " spiflication." Happily for the assaulted, the Agha's servant, a sturdy Albanian lad, was lying on a mat in the doorway close by. Roused by the tumult, he jumped up, and found the captain in a state of fury. Apparently the man was used to the master's mood. Without delay he told us all to assist, and we lending a helping hand, half dragged and half carried the Albanian to his room. Yet even in this ignoble plight, he shouted with all the force of his lungs the old war-cry, "O Egyptians! O race of dogs! I have dishonoured all Sikandariyah—all Kahirah—all Suways.[1]" And in this vaunting frame of mind he was put to bed. No Welsh undergraduate at Oxford, under similar circumstances, ever gave more trouble.

" You had better start on your pilgrimage at once,"

---

for striking him with a chibuk across the face. Travellers would do well to remember, that in these lands the pipe-stick and the slipper disgrace a man, whereas a whip or a rod would not do so. The probable reason of this is, that the two articles of domestic use are applied slightingly, not seriously, to the purposes of punishment.

1 *Anglicè*, Alexandria, Cairo, and Suez,—an extensive field of operations.

said Haji Wali, meeting me the next morning with a
" goguenard " smile.

He was right. Throughout the Caravanserai nothing
was talked of for nearly a week but the wickedness of the
captain of Albanian Irregulars, and the hypocrisy of the
staid Indian doctor. Thus it was, gentle reader, that I lost
my reputation of being a " serious person " at Cairo.
And all I have to show for it is the personal experience
of an Albanian drinking-bout.

I wasted but little time in taking leave of my friends,
telling them, by way of precaution, that my destination
was Meccah *viâ* Jeddah, and firmly determining, if possible, to make Al-Madinah *viâ* Yambu'. " Conceal,"
says the Arab's proverb, " Thy Tenets, thy Treasure, and
thy Travelling."

CHAPTER VIII.

FROM CAIRO TO SUEZ.

SHAYKH NASSÁR, a Badawi of Túr (Mount Sinai,) being on his way homewards, agreed to let me have two dromedaries for the sum of fifty piastres, or about ten shillings, each.[1] Being desirous to set out with a certain display of respectability, I accepted these terms : a man of humble pretensions would have travelled with a single animal, and a camel-man running behind him. But, besides ostentation, I wanted my attendant to be mounted, that we might make a forced march in order to ascertain how much a four years' life of European effeminacy had impaired my powers of endurance. The reader may believe the assertion that there are few better tests than an eighty-four mile ride in mid-summer, on a bad wooden saddle, borne by a worse dromedary, across the Suez Desert. Even the Squire famed for being copper-sheeted might not have disdained a trial of the kind.

I started my Indian boy and heavy luggage for Suez two days before the end of the Íd,—laden camels generally taking fifty-five or sixty hours to do the journey, and I spent the intermediate time with Haji Wali. He advised me to mount about 3 P.M., so that I might arrive at Suez on the evening of the next day, and assisted me

---

[1] The proper hire of a return dromedary from Cairo to Suez is forty piastres. But every man is charged in proportion to his rank, and Europeans generally pay about double.

in making due preparations of water, tobacco, and provisions.   Early on the morning of departure the Afghan
Shaykh came to the Caravanserai, and breakfasted with
us, " because Allah willed it."   After a copious meal
he bestowed upon me a stately benediction, and would
have embraced me, but I humbly bent over his hand :
sad to relate, immediately that his back was turned,
Haji Wali raised his forefinger to a right angle with
the palm (chaff), and burst into a shout of irreverent
laughter.   At three o'clock Nassar, the Badawi, came to
announce that the dromedaries were saddled.   I dressed
myself, sticking a pistol in my belt, and passing the crimson silk cord of the " Hamáil " or pocket Koran over my
shoulder, in token of being a pilgrim.   Then distributing
a few trifling presents to friends and servants, and accompanied by the Shaykh Mohammed and Haji Wali, I descended the stairs with an important gait. In the courtyard
squatted the camels, (dromedaries they could not be called,)
and I found that a second driver was going to accompany
us.   I objected to this, as the extra Badawi would, of
course, expect to be fed by me ; but Nassar swore that the
man was his brother, and as you rarely gain by small
disputes with these people, he was allowed to have his
own way.

Then came the preparatory leave-takings.   Haji
Wali embraced me heartily, and so did my poor old Shaykh,
who, despite his decrepitude and my objections, insisted
upon accompanying me to the city gate.   I mounted the
camel, crossed my legs before the pommel—stirrups
are not used in Egypt[1]—and, preceding .my friend, de-

---

1 The tender traveller had better provide himself with a pair of
stirrups, but he will often find, when on camel back, that his legs
are more numbed by hanging down, than by the Arab way of
crossing them before and beneath the pommel.   He must, however,
be careful to inspect his saddle, and, should bars of wood not suit
him, to have them covered with stuffed leather.   And again, for my

scended the street leading towards the Desert. As we emerged from the huge gateway of the Caravanserai all the bystanders, except only the porter, who believed me to be a Persian, and had seen me with the drunken captain, exclaimed, "Allah bless thee, Y'al-Hájj,[1] and restore thee to thy country and thy friends!" And passing through the Bab al-Nasr, where I addressed the salutation of peace to the sentry, and to the officer commanding the guard, both gave me God-speed with great cordiality[2]—the pilgrim's blessing in Asia, like the old woman's in Europe, being supposed to possess peculiar efficacy. Outside the gate my friends took a final leave of me, and I will not deny having felt a tightening of heart as their honest faces and forms faded in the distance.

But Shaykh Nassar switches his camel's shoulder, and appears inclined to take the lead. This is a trial of manliness. There is no time for emotion. Not a moment can be spared, even for a retrospect. I kick my dromedary, who steps out into a jog-trot. The Badawin with a loud ringing laugh attempt to give me the go-by. I resist, and we continue like children till the camels are at their speed, though we have eighty-four miles before us, and above us an atmosphere like a furnace blast. The road is deserted at this hour, otherwise grave Moslem

---

part, I would prefer riding a camel with a nose-ring,—Mongol and Sindian fashion,—to holding him, as the Egyptians do, with a halter, or to guiding him,—Wahhábiwise,—with a stick.

1 "O pilgrim!" The Egyptians write the word Hájj, and pronounce Hagg. In Persia, India, and Turkey, it becomes Háji. These are mere varieties of form, derived from one and the same Arabic root.

2 The Egyptians and Arabs will not address "Salam" to an infidel; the Moslems of India have no such objection. This, on the banks of the Nile, is the revival of an old prejudice. Alexander of Alexandria, in his circular letter, describes the Arian heretics as "men whom it is not lawful to salute, or to bid God-speed."

travellers would have believed the police to be nearer than convenient to us.

Presently we drew rein, and exchanged our pace for one more seasonable, whilst the sun began to tell on man and beast. High raised as we were above the ground, the reflected heat struck us sensibly, and the glare of a macadamized road added a few extra degrees of caloric.[1] The Badawin, to refresh themselves, prepare to smoke. They fill my chibuk, light it with a flint and steel, and cotton dipped in a solution of gunpowder, and pass it over to me.[2] After a few puffs I return it to them, and they use it turn by turn. Then they begin to while away the tedium of the road by asking questions, which *passe-temps* is not easily exhausted; for they are never satisfied till they know as much of you as you do of yourself. They next resort to talking about victuals; for with this hungry race, food, as a topic of conversation, takes the place of money in happier lands. And lastly, even this engrossing subject being exhausted for the moment,

1 It is Prince Pückler Muskau, if I recollect rightly, who mentions that in his case a pair of dark spectacles produced a marked difference of apparent temperature, whilst travelling over the sultry sand of the Desert. I have often remarked the same phenomenon. The Arabs, doubtless for some reason of the kind, always draw their head-kerchiefs, like hoods, far over their brows, and cover up their mouths, even when the sun and wind are behind them. Inhabitants of the Desert are to be recognised by the net-work of wrinkles traced in the skin round the orbits, the result of half-closing their eyelids; but this is done to temper the intensity of the light.

2 Their own pipe-tubes were of coarse wood, in shape somewhat resembling the German porcelain pipe. The bowl was of soft stone, apparently steatite, which, when fresh, is easily fashioned with a knife. In Arabia the Badawin, and even the townspeople, use on journeys an earthen tube from five to six inches shorter than the English "clay," thicker in the tube, with a large bowl, and coloured yellowish-red. It contains a handful of tobacco, and the smoker emits puffs like a chimney. In some of these articles the bowl forms a rectangle with the tube; in others, the whole is an unbroken curve, like the old Turkish Meerschaum.

they take refuge in singing ; and, monotonous and droning as it is, their *Modinha* has yet an artless plaintiveness,
which admirably suits the singer and the scenery.   If
you listen to the words, you will surely hear allusions
to bright verdure, cool shades, bubbling rills, or something which hereabouts man hath not, and yet which his
soul desires.

And now while Nassar and his brother are chaunting
a duet,—the refrain being,

       " W'al arz mablúl bi matar,"
       " And the earth wet with rain,"—

I must crave leave to say a few words, despite the trite-
ness of the subject, about the modern Sinaitic race of
Arabs.

Besides the tribes occupying the northern parts of
the peninsula, five chief clans are enumerated by Burckhardt.[1] Nassar, and other authorities at Suez, divided
them into six, namely :—

1. Karashi, who, like the Gara in Eastern Arabia,
claim an apocryphal origin from the great Koraysh tribe.

2. Sálihi, the principal family of the Sinaitic Badawin.

3. Árimí : according to Burckhardt this clan is merely
a sub-family of the Sawálihahs.

4. Sa'ídi. Burckhardt calls them Walad Sa'íd and
derives them also from the Sawalihahs.

5. Aliki ; and lastly, the

6. Muzaynah, generally pronounced M'zaynah. This
clan claims to be an off-shoot from the great Juhaynah tribe
inhabiting the coasts and inner barrens about Yambu'.
According to oral tradition, five persons, the ancestors
of the present Muzaynah race, were forced by a blood-
feud to fly their native country. They landed at the
Shurúm,[2] or creek-ports, and have now spread them-

---

1 See Wallin's papers, published in the Journals of the Royal
Geographical Society.

2 Shurum, (plural of Sharm, a creek), a word prefixed to the
proper names of three small ports in the Sinaitic peninsula.

selves over the Eastern parts of the so-called "Sinaitic" peninsula. In Al-Hijaz the Muzaynah is an old and noble tribe. It produced Ka'ab al-Ahbar, the celebrated poet, to whom Mohammed gave the cloak which the Ottomans believe to have been taken by Sultan Salím from Egypt, and to have been converted under the name of Khirkah Sharíf, into the national Oriflamme.

There are some interesting ethnographical points about these Sinaitic clans—interesting at least to those who would trace the genealogy of the great Arabian family. Any one who knows the Badawin can see that the Muzaynah are pure blood. Their brows are broad, their faces narrow, their features regular, and their eyes of a moderate size; whereas the other Tawarah[1] (Sinaitic) clans are as palpably Egyptian. They have preserved that roundness of face which may still be seen in the Sphinx as in the modern Copt, and their eyes have that peculiar size, shape, and look, which the old Egyptian painters attempted to express by giving to the profile, the form of the full, organ. Upon this feature, so characteristic of the Nilotic race, I would lay great stress. No traveller familiar with the true Egyptian eye,—long, almond-shaped, deeply fringed, slightly raised at the outer corner and dipping in front like the Chinese,[2]—can ever mistake it. It is to be seen in half-castes, and, as I have before remarked, families originally from the banks of the Nile, but settled for generations in the Holy Land of Al-Hijaz, retain the peculiarity.

I therefore believe the Turi Badawin to be an impure

---

1 Tawarah, plural of Túri, an inhabitant of Túr or Sinai.

2 This feature did not escape the practised eye of Denon. " Eyes long, almond-shaped, half shut, and languishing, and turned up at the outer corner, as if habitually fatigued by the light and heat of the sun ; cheeks round, &c.," (*Voyage en Egypt*). The learned Frenchman's description of the ancient Egyptians applies in most points to the Turi Badawin.

race, Syro-Egyptian,[1] whereas their neighbour the Hijázi is the pure Syrian or Mesopotamian.

A wonderful change has taken place in the Tawarah tribes, whilome pourtrayed by Sir John Mandeville as "folke fulle of alle evylle condiciouns." Niebuhr notes the trouble they gave him, and their perpetual hankering for both murder and pillage. Even in the late Mohammed Ali's early reign, no governor of Suez dared to flog, or to lay hands upon, a Turi, whatever offence he might have committed within the walls of the town. Now the Wild Man's sword is taken from him, before he is allowed to enter the gates,[2] and my old acquaintance, Ja'afar Bey, would think no more of belabouring a Badawi than of flogging a Fellah.[3] Such is the result of

1 " And he" (Ishmael) "dwelt in the wilderness of Paran," (Wady Firán ?) "and his mother took him a wife, out of the land of Egypt," (Gen. xxi. 21). I wonder that some geographers have attempted to identify Massa, the son of Ishmael, (Gen. xxv. 14), with Meccah, when in verse 18 of the same chapter we read, " And they" (the twelve princes, sons of Ishmael) *"dwelt from Havilah unto Shur."* This asserts, as clearly as language can, that the posterity of, or the race typified by, Ishmael,—the Syro-Egyptian,—occupied only the northern parts of the peninsula. Their *habitat* is not even included in Arabia by those writers who bound the country on the north by an imaginary line drawn from Ras Mohammed to the mouths of the Euphrates. The late Dr. J. Wilson ("Lands of the Bible"), repeated by Eliot Warburton ("Crescent and Cross"), lays stress upon the Tawarah tradition, that they are Benú Isrá'íl converted to Al-Islam, considering it a fulfilment of the prophecy, "that a remnant of Israel shall dwell in Edom." With due deference to so illustrious an Orientalist and Biblical scholar as was Dr. Wilson, I believe that most modern Moslems, being ignorant that Jacob was the first called " prince with God," apply the term Benu-Isra'il to all the posterity of Abraham, not to Jews only.

2 In 1879 the Gates of Suez are a thing of the past; and it is not easy to find where they formerly stood.

3 In the mouth of a Turk, no epithet is more contemptuous than that of " Felláh ibn Felláh,"—"boor, son of a boor !" The Osmanlis have, as usual, a semi-religious tradition to account for the superiority of their nation over the Egyptians. When the learned doctor, Abú

Mohammed Ali's vigorous policy, and such the effects of even semi-civilisation, when its influence is brought to bear direct upon barbarism.

To conclude this subject, the Tawarah still retain many characteristics of the Badawi race. The most good-humoured and sociable of men, they delight in a jest, and may readily be managed by kindness and courtesy. Yet they are passionate, nice upon points of honour, revengeful, and easily offended, where their peculiar pre-judices are misunderstood. I have always found them pleasant companions, and deserving of respect, for their hearts are good, and their courage is beyond a doubt. Those travellers who complain of their insolence and extortion may have been either ignorant of their language or offensive to them by assumption of superiority, —in the Desert man meets man,—or physically unfitted to acquire their esteem.

We journeyed on till near sunset through the wilderness without ennui. It is strange how the mind can be amused by scenery that presents so few objects to occupy it. But in such a country every slight modifica-tion of form or colour rivets observation : the senses are sharpened, and the perceptive faculties, prone to sleep over a confused mass of natural objects, act vigorously when excited by the capability of embracing each detail. Moreover, Desert views are eminently suggestive ; they

Abdullah Mohammed bin Idris al-Shafe'i, returned from Meccah to the banks of the Nile, he mounted, it is said, a donkey belonging to one of the *Asinarii* of Bulak. Arriving at the Caravanserai, he gave the man ample fare, whereupon the Egyptian, putting forth his hand, and saying "hát" (give !) called for more. The doctor doubled the fee ; still the double was demanded. At last the divine's purse was exhausted, and the proprietor of the donkey waxed insolent. A wandering Turk seeing this, took all the money from the Egyptian, paid him his due, solemnly kicked him, and returned the rest to Al-Shafe'i, who asked him his name—" Osmán "—and his nation—the " Osmanli,"—blessed him, and prophesied to his countrymen supremacy over the Fellahs and donkey boys of Egypt.

appeal to the Future, not to the Past : they arouse because they are by no means memorial. To the solitary way- farer there is an interest in the Wilderness unknown to Cape seas and Alpine glaciers, and even to the rolling Prairie,—the effect of continued excitement on the mind, stimulating its powers to their pitch. Above, through a sky terrible in its stainless beauty, and the splendours of a pitiless blinding glare, the Samún[1] caresses you like a lion with flaming breath. Around lie drifted sand-heaps, upon which each puff of wind leaves its trace in solid waves, flayed rocks, the very skeletons of mountains, and hard unbroken plains, over which he who rides is spurred by the idea that the bursting of a water-skin, or the pricking of a camel's hoof, would be a certain death of torture,—a haggard land infested with wild beasts, and wilder men,—a region whose very fountains murmur the warning words " Drink and away ! " What can be more exciting ? what more sublime ? Man's heart bounds in his breast at the thought of measuring his puny force with Nature's might, and of emerging triumphant from the trial. This explains the Arab's pro- verb, " Voyaging is victory." In the Desert, even more than upon the ocean, there is present death : hardship is there, and piracies, and shipwreck, solitary, not in crowds, where, as the Persians say, " Death is a Festival"; —and this sense of danger, never absent, invests the scene of travel with an interest not its own.

Let the traveller who suspects exaggeration leave the Suez road for an hour or two, and gallop northwards over the sands : in the drear silence, the solitude, and the fantastic desolation of the place, he will feel what the Desert may be.

And then the Oases,[2] and little lines of fertility—

---

1 From Samm, the poison-wind. Vulgar and most erroneously called the Simoon.

2 Hugh Murray derives this word from the Egyptian, and quoting

how soft and how beautiful !—even though the Wady al-
Ward (the Vale of Flowers) be the name of some stern
flat upon which a handful of wild shrubs blossom while
struggling through a cold season's ephemeral existence.
In such circumstances the mind is influenced through the
body. Though your mouth glows, and your skin is
parched, yet you feel no languor, the effect of humid
heat; your lungs are lightened, your sight brightens,
your memory recovers its tone, and your spirits become
exuberant; your fancy and imagination are powerfully
aroused, and the wildness and sublimity of the scenes
around you stir up all the energies of your soul—whether
for exertion, danger, or strife. Your *morale* improves; you
become frank and cordial, hospitable and single-minded :
the hypocritical politeness and the slavery of civilisation are left behind you in the city. Your senses are
quickened : they require no stimulants but air and exercise,—in the Desert spirituous liquors excite only disgust.
There is a keen enjoyment in mere animal existence.
The sharp appetite disposes of the most indigestible food ;

Strabo and Abulfeda makes it synonymous with Auasis and Hyasis. I
believe it to be a mere corruption of the Arabic Wády (وادى) or Wah.
Nothing can be more incorrect than the vulgar idea of an Arabian
Oasis, except it be the popular conception of an Arabian Desert.
One reads of "isles of the sandy sea," but one never sees them.
The real "Wady" is, generally speaking, a rocky valley bisected by
the bed of a mountain torrent, dry during the hot season. In such
places the Badawin love to encamp, because they find food and
drink,—water being always procurable by digging. When the supply
is perennial, the Wady becomes the site of a village. The Desert is
as unaptly compared to a "sandy sea." Most of the wilds of Arabia
resemble the tract between Suez and Cairo ; only the former are of
primary formation, whereas the others are of a later date. Sand-
heaps are found in every Desert, but sand-plains are a local feature,
not the general face of the country. The Wilderness, east of the Nile,
is mostly a hard dry earth, which requires only a monsoon to become
highly productive : even where silicious sand covers the plain, the
waters of a torrent, depositing *humus* or vegetable mould, bind the
particles together, and fit it for the reception of seed.

the sand is softer than a bed of down, and the purity of
the air suddenly puts to flight a dire cohort of diseases.
Hence it is that both sexes, and every age, the most
material as well as the most imaginative of minds, the
tamest citizen, the parson, the old maid, the peaceful
student, the spoiled child of civilisation, all feel their
hearts dilate, and their pulses beat strong, as they look
down from their dromedaries upon the glorious Desert.
Where do we hear of a traveller being disappointed by
it ? It is another illustration of the ancient truth that
Nature returns to man, however unworthily he has treated
her. And believe me, when once your tastes have conformed to the tranquillity of such travel, you will suffer
real pain in returning to the turmoil of civilisation. You
will anticipate the bustle and the confusion of artificial
life, its luxury and its false pleasures, with repugnance.
Depressed in spirits, you will for a time after your return
feel incapable of mental or bodily exertion. The air of
cities will suffocate you, and the care-worn and cadaverous
countenances of citizens will haunt you like a vision of
judgment.[1]

As the black shadow mounted in the Eastern sky,[2] I
turned off the road, and was suddenly saluted by a figure
rising from a little hollow with an " As' Salamu 'alaykum "
of truly Arab sound.[3] I looked at the speaker for a
moment without recognising him. He then advanced
with voluble expressions of joy, invited me to sup, seized

---

1 The intelligent reader will easily understand that I am speaking
of the Desert in the temperate season, not during the summer heats,
when the whole is one vast furnace, nor in winter, when the Sarsar
wind cuts like an Italian Tramontana.

2 This, as a general rule in Al-Islam, is a sign that the Maghrib
or evening prayer must not be delayed. The Shafe'i school performs
its devotions immediately after the sun has disappeared.

3 This salutation of peace is so differently pronounced by every
Eastern nation that the observing traveller will easily make of it a
shibboleth.

my camel's halter without waiting for an answer,
" nakh'd ¹ " it (*i.e.* forced it to kneel), led me hurriedly to
a carpet spread in a sandy hollow, pulled off my slippers,
gave me cold water for ablution, told me that he had
mistaken me at a distance for a " Sheríf " (or Prince) of
the Arabs, but was delighted to find himself in error ; and
urged me to hurry over ablution, otherwise that night
would come on before we could say our prayers.   It was
Mohammed al-Basyuni, the Meccan boy of whom I had
bought my pilgrim-garb at Cairo.   There I had refused
his companionship, but here for reasons of his own—one
of them was an utter want of money,—he would take no
excuse.   When he prayed, he stood behind me,² thereby
proving pliancy of conscience, for he suspected me from
the first of being at least a heretic.

After prayer he lighted a pipe, and immediately
placed the snake-like tube in my hand ; this is an argument which the tired traveller can rarely resist.   He then
began to rummage my saddle-bags ; he drew forth stores
of provisions, rolls, water-melons, boiled eggs, and dates,
and whilst lighting the fire and boiling the coffee, he managed to distribute his own stock, which was neither plentiful
nor first-rate, to the camel-men.   Shaykh Nassar and
his brother looked aghast at this movement, but the boy
was inexorable.   They tried a few rough hints, which he
noticed by singing a Hindustani couplet that asserts the
impropriety of anointing rats' heads with jasmine oil.
They suspected abuse, and waxed cross ; he acknowledged this by deriding them.   " I have heard of Nasrs
and Násirs and Mansúrs, but may Allah spare me the

---

1 To "nakh" in vulgar, as in classical, Arabic is to gurgle "Ikh!
ikh!" in the bottom of one's throat till the camel kneels down.   We
have no English word for this proceeding ; but Anglo-Oriental travellers are rapidly naturalising the "nakh."

2 There are many qualifications necessary for an Imam—a leader
of prayer ; the first condition, of course, is orthodoxy.

mortification of a Nassar !" said the boy, relying upon
my support. And I urged him on, wanting to see how
the city Arab treats the countryman. He then took my
tobacco-pouch from the angry Badawin, and in a stage-
whisper reproved me for entrusting it to such thieves ;
insisting, at the same time, upon drinking all the coffee,
so that the poor guides had to prepare some for themselves. He improved every opportunity of making mischief. " We have eaten. water-melon !" cried Nassar,
patting its receptacle in token of repletion. " Dost thou
hear, my lord, how they grumble ?—the impudent
ruffians !" remarked Mohammed—" *We have eaten water-
melon !* that is to say, we ought to have eaten meat !"
The Badawin, completely out of temper, told him not to
trust himself among their hills. He seized a sword, and
began capering about after the fashion of the East-Indian
school of arms, and boasted that he would attack single-
handed the whole clan, which elicited an ironical " Allah !
Allah !" from the hearers.

After an hour most amusingly spent in this way, I
arose, and insisted upon mounting, much to the dissatisfaction of my guides, who wished to sleep there. Shaykh
Nassar and his brother had reckoned upon living gratis,
for at least three days, judging it improbable that a
soft Effendi would hurry himself. When they saw the
fair vision dissolve, they began to finesse : they induced
the camel-man, who ran by the side of Mohammed's dromedary, to precede the animal—a favourite manœuvre to
prevent overspeed. Ordered to fall back, the man pleaded
fatigue, and inability to walk. The boy Mohammed immediately asked if I had any objection to dismount one
of my guides, and to let his weary attendant ride for an
hour or so. I at once assented, and the Badawin obeyed
me with ominous grumblings. When we resumed our
march the melancholy Arabs had no song left in them ;
whereas Mohammed chaunted vociferously, and quoted

bad Hindustani and worse Persian till silence was forcibly imposed upon him. The camel-men lagged behind, in order to prevent my dromedary advancing too fast, and the boy's guide, after dismounting, would stride along in front of us, under pretext of showing the way. And so we jogged on, now walking, then trotting, till the dromedaries began to grunt with fatigue, and the Arabs clamoured for a halt.

At midnight we reached the Central Station, and lay down under its walls to take a little rest. The dews fell heavily, wetting the sheets that covered us; but who cares for such trifles in the Desert ? The moon shone bright;[1] the breeze blew coolly, and the jackal sang a lullaby which lost no time in inducing the soundest sleep. As the Wolf's Tail[2] showed in the heavens we arose. Grey mists floating over the hills northwards gave the Dár al-Baydá,[3] the Pasha's Palace, the look of some old feudal castle. There was a haze in the atmosphere, which beautified even the face of Desolation. The swift flying Katá[4] sprang in noisy coveys from the road, and a stray gazelle paced daintily over the stony plain. As we passed by the Pilgrims' tree, I

1 " The sun shall not smite thee by day, nor the moon by night," (Psalm cxxi. 6). Easterns still believe firmly in the evil effects of moonlight upon the human frame,—from Sind to Abyssinia, the traveller will hear tales of wonder concerning it.

2 The Dum i Gurg, or wolf's tail, is the Persian name for the first brushes of grey light which appear as forerunners of dawn.

3 Dar al-Bayda is a palace belonging to H.H. Abbas Pasha. This " white house " was formerly called the " red house,"—I believe from the colour of its windows,—but the name was changed, as being not particularly good-omened.

4 The Tetrao Kata or sand-grouse, (Pterocles melanogaster ; in Sind called the rock pigeon), is a fast-flying bird, not unlike a grey partridge whilst upon the wing. When, therefore, Shanfara boasts " The ash-coloured Katas can only drink my leavings, after hastening all night to slake their thirst in the morning," it is a hyperbole to express exceeding swiftness.

added another rag to its coat of tatters.[1] We then invoked the aid of the holy saint Al-Dakrúri[2] from his cream-coloured abode, mounted our camels, and resumed the march in real earnest. The dawn passed away in its delicious coolness, and sultry morning came on. Then day glared in its fierceness, and the noontide sun made the plain glow with terrible heat. Still we pressed onwards.

At 3 P.M. we turned off the road into a dry water-course, which is not far from No. 13 Station. The sand was dotted with the dried-up leaves of the Datura, and strongly perfumed by "Shih," a kind of Absinthe (*Artemisia*),[3] the sweetest herb of the Desert. A Mimosa was there, and although its shade at this season is little better than

---

1 I have already, when writing upon the subject of Sind, alluded to this system as prevalent throughout Al-Islam, and professed, like Mr. Lane, ignorance of its origin and object. In Huc's travels, we are told that the Tartars worship mountain spirits by raising an "Obo,"—dry branches hung with bones and strips of cloth, and planted in enormous heaps of stones. Park, also, in Western Africa, conformed to the example of his companions, in adding a charm or shred of cloth on a tree (at the entrance of the Wilderness), which was completely covered with these guardian symbols. And, finally, the Tárikh Tabari mentions it as a practice of the Pagan Arabs, and talks of evil spirits residing in the date-tree. May not, then, the practice in Al-Islam be one of the many débris of fetish-worship which entered into the heterogeneous formation of the Saving Faith? Some believe that the Prophet permitted the practice, and explain the peculiar name of the expedition called Zát al-Riká'a (place of shreds of cloth), by supposing it to be a term for a tree to which the Moslems hung their *ex-voto* rags.

2 The saint lies under a little white-washed dome, springing from a square of low walls—a form of sepulchre now common to Al-Hijaz, Egypt, and the shores and islands of the Red Sea. As regards his name my informants told me it was that of a Hijazi Shaykh. The subject is by no means interesting; but the exact traveller will find the word written Takroore, and otherwise explained by Sir Gardner Wilkinson.

3 Called by the Arabs Shih (شيح), which the dictionaries translate "wormwood of Pontus." We find Wallin in his works speaking of *Ferashat al-shih*, or wormwood carpets.

a cocoa tree's,[1] the Badawin would not neglect it. We lay down upon the sand, to rest among a party of Maghrabi pilgrims travelling to Suez. These wretches, who were about a dozen in number, appeared to be of the lowest class; their garments consisted of a Búrnus-cloak and a pair of sandals; their sole weapon a long knife, and their only stock a bag of dry provisions. Each had his large wooden bowl, but none carried water with him. It was impossible to help pitying their state, nor could I eat, seeing them hungry, thirsty, and way-worn. So Nassar served out about a pint of water and a little bread to each man. Then they asked for more. None was to be had, so they cried out that money would do as well. I had determined upon being generous to the extent of a few pence. Custom, as well as inclination, was in favour of the act; but when the alms became a demand, and the demand was backed by fierce looks and a derisive sneer, and a kind of reference to their knives, gentle Charity took the alarm and fled. My pistols kept them at bay, for they were only making an attempt to intimidate, and, though I took the precaution of sitting apart from them, there was no real danger. The Suez road, by the wise regulations of Mohammed Ali, has become as safe to European travellers as that between Hampstead and Highgate; and even Easterns have little to fear but what their fears create. My Indian servant was full of the dangers he had run, but I did not believe in them. I afterwards heard that the place where the Maghrabis attempted to frighten what they thought a timid Turk was notorious for plunder and murder. Here the spurs of two opposite hills almost meet upon the plain, a favourable ground for Badawi ambuscade. Of the Magh-

---

1 We are told in verse of "a cocoa's feathery shade," and *sous l'ombre d'un cocotier.* But to realise the prose picture, let the home reader, choosing some sultry August day, fasten a large fan to a long pole, and enjoy himself under it.

rabis I shall have more to say when relating my voyage in the Pilgrim Ship : they were the only travellers from whom we experienced the least annoyance. Numerous parties of Turks, Arabs, and Afghans, and a few East-Indians[1] were on the same errand as ourselves. All, as we passed them, welcomed us with the friendly saluta-tion that becomes men engaged in a labour of religion.

About half an hour before sunset, I turned off the road leftwards ; and, under pretext of watering the drome-daries, rode up to inspect the fort Al-'Ajrúdi.[2] It is a quadrangle with round towers at the gateway and at the corners, newly built of stone and mortar ; the material is already full of crevices, and would not stand before a twelve-pounder. Without guns or gunners, it is occupied by about a dozen Fellahs, who act as hereditary "Ghafírs," (guardians) ; they were expecting at that time to be reinforced by a party of Báshi Buzuks— Irregulars from Cairo. The people of the country were determined that an English fleet would soon appear in the Red Sea, and this fort is by them ridiculously con-sidered the key of Suez. As usual in these Vauban-

---

1 On a subsequent occasion, I met a party of Panjábís, who had walked from Meccah to Cairo in search of " Abú Tabílah," (General Avitabile), whom report had led to the banks of the Nile. Some were young, others had white beards—all were weary and wayworn ; but the saddest sight was an old woman, so decrepit that she could scarcely walk. The poor fellows were travelling on foot, carrying their wallets, with a few pence in their pockets, utterly ignorant of route and road, and actually determined in this plight to make Lahore by Baghdad, Búshír, and Káráchí. Such—so incredible—is Indian improvidence !

2 Upon this word Cacography has done her worst—" Haji Rood " may serve for a specimen. My informants told me that Al-'Ajrudi is the name of a Hijazi Shaykh whose mortal remains repose under a little dome near the fort. This, if it be true, completely nullifies the efforts of Etymology to discern in it a distinct allusion to "the over-throw of Pharaoh's chariots, whose Hebrew appellation, ' Ageloot,' bears some resemblance to this modern name."

lacking lands, the well supplying the stronghold is in a detached and distant building, which can be approached by an enemy with the greatest security. Over the gateway was an ancient inscription reversed; the water was brackish, and of bad quality.[1]

We resumed our way: Suez now stood near. In the blue distance rose the castellated peaks of Jabal Rahah and the wide sand-tracts over which lies the land-route to Al-Hijaz. Before us the sight ever dear to English eyes,—a strip of sea gloriously azure, with a gallant steamer walking the waters. On the right-hand side the broad slopes of Jabal Mukattam, a range of hills which flanks the road all the way from Cairo. It was at this hour a spectacle not easily to be forgotten. The near range of chalk and sandstone wore a russet suit, gilt where the last rays of the sun seamed it with light, and the deep folds were shaded with the richest purple; whilst the background of the higher hills, Jabal Tawari, generally known as Abú Daráj (the Father of Steps), was sky-blue streaked with the lightest plum colour. We drew up at a small building called Bir Suways (Well of Suez); and, under pretext of watering the cattle, I sat for half an hour admiring the charms of the Desert. The eye never tires of such loveliness of hue, and the memory of the hideousness of this range, when a sun in front exposed each gaunt and barren feature, supplied the evening view with another element of attraction.

It was already night when we passed through the tumbling six-windowed gateway of Suez; and still remained the task of finding my servant and effects. After

---

1 The only sweet water in Suez is brought on camel back from the Nile, across the Desert. The "Bir Suez" is fit for beasts only; the 'Uyún Músa (Moses' Wells) on the Eastern side, and that below Abu Daraj, on the Western shore of the Suez Gulf, are but little better. The want of sweet water is the reason why no Hammam is found at Suez.

wandering in and out of every Wakalah in the village, during which peregrination the boy Mohammed proved himself so useful that I determined at all risks to make him my companion, we accidentally heard that a Hindi had taken lodgings at a hostelry bearing the name of Jirjís al-Zahr.[1] On arriving there our satisfaction was diminished by the intelligence that the same Hindi, after locking the door, had gone out with his friends to a ship in the harbour; in fact, that he had made all preparations for running away. I dismounted, and tried to persuade the porter to break open the wooden bolt, but he absolutely refused, and threatened the police. Meanwhile Mohammed had found a party of friends, men of Al-Madinah, returning to the pilgrimage after a begging tour through Egypt and Turkey. The meeting was characterised by vociferous inquiries, loud guffaws and warm embraces. I was invited to share their supper and their dormitory,—an uncovered platform projecting from the gallery over the square court below,—but I had neither appetite nor spirits enough to be sociable. The porter, after much persuasion, showed me an empty room, in which I spread my carpet. That was a sad night. My eighty-four mile ride had made every bone ache; I had lost epidermis, and the sun had seared every portion of skin exposed to it. So, lamenting my degeneracy and the ill effects of four years' domicile in Europe, and equally disquieted in mind about the fate of my goods and chattels, I fell into an uncomfortable sleep.

---

1 The " George ": so called after its owner, a Copt, Consular Agent for Belgium. There are 36 Caravanserais at Suez, 33 small ones for merchandise, and 3 for travellers; of these the best is that of Sayyid Háshim. The pilgrim, however, must not expect much comfort or convenience, even at Sayyid Hashim's.

CHAPTER IX.

SUEZ.

EARLY on the morning after my arrival, I arose, and consulted my new acquaintances about the means of recovering the missing property. They unanimously advised a visit to the governor, whom, however, they described to be a " Kalb ibn kalb," (dog, son of a dog,) who never returned Moslems' salutations, and who thought all men dirt to be trodden under foot by the Turks. The boy Mohammed showed his *savoir faire* by extracting from his huge Sahará-box a fine embroidered cap, and a grand peach-coloured coat, with which I was instantly invested; he dressed himself with similar magnificence, and we then set out to the " palace."

Ja'afar Bey,—he has since been deposed,—then occupied the position of judge, officer commanding, collector of customs, and magistrate of Suez. He was a Mir-liwá, or brigadier-general, and had some reputation as a soldier, together with a slight tincture of European science and language. The large old Turk received me most superciliously, disdained all return of salam, and, fixing upon me two little eyes like gimlets, demanded my business. I stated that one Shaykh Nur, my Hindi servant, had played me false ; therefore I required permission to break into the room supposed to contain my effects. He asked my profession. I replied the medical. This led him to inquire if I had any medicine for the eyes, and

being answered in the affirmative, he sent a messenger
with me to enforce obedience on the part of the porter.
The obnoxious measure was, however, unnecessary. As
we entered the Caravanserai, there appeared at the door
the black face of Shaykh Nur, looking, though accompanied by sundry fellow-countrymen, uncommonly as if
he merited and expected the bamboo. He had, by his
own account, been seduced into the festivities of a coal-
hulk, manned by Lascars, and the vehemence of his self-
accusation saved him from the chastisement which I had
determined to administer.

I must now briefly describe the party of Meccah and
Madinah men into which fate threw me : their names will
so frequently appear in the following pages, that a few
words about their natures will not be misplaced.

First of all comes Omar Effendi,—so called in honour,
—a Dághistáni or East-Circassian, the grandson of a
Hanafi Mufti at Al-Madinah, and the son of a Shaykh
Rakb, an officer whose duty it is to lead dromedary-cara-
vans. He sits upon his cot, a small, short, plump body,
of yellow complexion and bilious temperament, grey-eyed,
soft-featured, and utterly beardless,—which affects his
feelings,—he looks fifteen, and he owns to twenty-eight.
His manners are those of a student ; he dresses respectably, prays regularly, hates the fair sex, like an Arab,
whose affections and aversions are always in extremes ; is
" serious," has a mild demeanour, an humble gait, and a
soft, slow voice. When roused he becomes furious as a
Bengal tiger. His parents have urged him to marry, and
he, like Kamar al-Zamán, has informed his father that he is
" a person of great age, but little sense." Urged moreover
by a melancholy turn of mind, and the want of leisure
for study at Al-Madinah, he fled the paternal domicile,
and entered himself a pauper Tálib 'ilm (student) in the
Azhar Mosque. His disconsolate friends and afflicted
relations sent a confidential man to fetch him home, by

force should it be necessary ; he has yielded, and is now awaiting the first opportunity of travelling gratis, if possible, to Al-Madinah.

That confidential man is a negro-servant, called Sa'ad, notorious in his native city as Al-Jinni, the Demon. Born and bred a slave in Omar Effendi's family, he obtained manumission, became a soldier in Al-Hijaz, was dissatisfied with pay perpetually in arrears, turned merchant, and wandered far and wide, to Russia, to Gibraltar, and to Baghdad. He is the pure African, noisily merry at one moment, at another silently sulky; affectionate and abusive, brave and boastful, reckless and crafty, exceedingly quarrelsome, and unscrupulous to the last degree. The bright side of his character is his love and respect for the young master, Omar Effendi; yet even him he will scold in a paroxysm of fury, and steal from him whatever he can lay his hands on. He is generous with his goods, but is ever borrowing and never paying money; he dresses like a beggar, with the dirtiest Tarbush upon his tufty poll, and only a cotton shirt over his sooty skin ; whilst his two boxes are full of handsome apparel for himself and the three ladies, his wives, at Al-Madinah. He knows no fear but for those boxes. Frequently during our search for a vessel he forced himself into Ja'afar Bey's presence, and there he demeaned himself so impudently, that we expected to see him lamed by the bastinado; his forwardness, however, only amused the dignitary. He wanders all day about the bazar, talking about freight and passage, for he has resolved, cost what it will, to travel free, and, with doggedness like his, he must succeed.

Shaykh Hámid al-Sammán derives his cognomen, the " Clarified-Butter-Seller," from a celebrated saint and Sufi of the Kádiriyah order, who left a long line of holy descendants at Al-Madinah. This Shaykh squats upon a box full of presents for the "daughter of his paternal uncle" (his wife), a perfect specimen of the town Arab. His poll is crowned with a rough Shúshah or tuft of hair[1]; his face is of a dirty brown, his little *goatee* straggles untrimmed; his feet are bare, and his only garment is an exceedingly unclean ochre-coloured blouse, tucked into a leathern girdle beneath it. He will not pray, because he is unwilling to take pure clothes out of his box; but he smokes when he can get other people's tobacco, and groans between the whiffs, conjugating the verb all day, for he is of active mind. He can pick out his letters, and he keeps in his bosom a little dog's-eared MS. full of serious romances and silly prayers, old and exceedingly ill written; this he will draw forth at times, peep into for a moment, devoutly kiss, and restore to its proper place with the veneration of the vulgar for a book. He can sing all manner of songs, slaughter a sheep with dexterity, deliver a grand call to prayer, shave, cook, fight; and he excels in the science of vituperation : like Sa'ad, he never performs his devotions, except

---

1 When travelling, the Shushah is allowed to spread over the greatest portion of the scalp, to act as a protection against the sun ; and the hair being shaved off about two inches all round the head, leaves a large circular patch. Nothing can be uglier than such tonsure, and it is contrary to the strict law of the Apostle, who ordered a clean shave, or a general growth of the hair. The Arab, however, knows by experience, that though habitual exposure of the scalp to a burning sun may harden the skull, it seldom fails to damage its precious contents. He, therefore, wears a Shushah during his wanderings, and removes it on his return home. Abu Hanifah, if I am rightly informed, wrote a treatise advocating the growth of a long lock of hair on the Násiyah, or crown of the head, lest the decapitated Moslem's mouth or beard be exposed to defilement by an impure hand. This would justify the comparing it to the "chivalry-lock," by which the American brave facilitates the removal of his own scalp. But I am at a loss to discover the origin of our old idea, that the "angel of death will, on the last day, bear all true believers, by this important tuft of hair on the crown, to Paradise." Probably this office has been attributed to the Shushah by the ignorance of the West.

when necessary to " keep up appearances," and though
he has sworn to perish before he forgets his vow to the
" daughter of his uncle," I shrewdly suspect he is no
better than he should be. His brow crumples at the
word wine, but there is quite another expression about
the region of the mouth ; Stambul, where he has lived
some months, without learning ten words of Turkish, is
a notable place for displacing prejudice. And finally, he
has not more than a piastre or two in his pocket, for he
has squandered the large presents given to him at Cairo
and Constantinople by noble ladies, to whom he acted as
master of the ceremonies at the tomb of the Apostle.

Stretched on a carpet, smoking a Persian Kaliun
all day, lies Sálih Shakkar, a Turk on the father's, and
an Arab on the mother's side, born at Al-Madinah. This
lanky youth may be sixteen years old, but he has the
ideas of forty-six ; he is thoroughly greedy, selfish, and un-
generous; coldly supercilious as a Turk, and energetically
avaricious as an Arab. He prays more often, and dresses
more respectably, than the descendant of the Clarified-
Butter-Seller ; he affects the Constantinople style of
toilette, and his light yellow complexion makes people consider him a " superior person." We were intimate
enough on the road, when he borrowed from me a little
money. But at Al-Madinah he cut me pitilessly, as a
" town man " does a continental acquaintance accidentally
met in Hyde Park ; and of course he tried, though in vain,
to evade repaying his debt. He had a tincture of letters,
and appeared to have studied critically the subject of
" largesse." " The Generous is Allah's friend, aye, though
he be a Sinner, and the Miser is Allah's Foe, aye, though
he be a Saint," was a venerable saying always in his
mouth. He also informed me that Pharaoh, although
the quintessence of impiety, is mentioned by name in the
Koran, by reason of his liberality ; whereas Nimrod,
another monster of iniquity, is only alluded to, because

he was a stingy tyrant. It is almost needless to declare
that Salih Shakkar was, as the East-Indians say, a very
"fly-sucker.[1]" There were two other men of Al-Madinah
in the Wakalah Jirgis ; but I omit description, as we left
them, they being penniless, at Suez. One of them, Mohammed Shiklibhá, I afterwards met at Meccah, and
seldom have I seen a more honest and warm-hearted
fellow. When we were embarking at Suez, he fell upon
Hamid's bosom, and both of them wept bitterly, at the
prospect of parting even for a few days.

All the individuals above mentioned lost no time in
opening the question of a loan. It was a lesson in
Oriental metaphysics to see their condition. They had a
twelve days' voyage, and a four days' journey before
them ; boxes to carry, custom-houses to face, and
stomachs to fill ; yet the whole party could scarcely, I
believe, muster two dollars of ready money. Their boxes
were full of valuables, arms, clothes, pipes, slippers,
sweetmeats, and other " notions " ; but nothing short of
starvation would have induced them to pledge the smallest
article.

Foreseeing that their company would be an advantage, I hearkened favourably to the honeyed request
for a few crowns. The boy Mohammed obtained six
dollars ; Hamid about five pounds, as I intended to
make his house at Al-Madinah my home ; Omar Effendi
three dollars ; Sa'ad the Demon two—I gave the money to
him at Yambu',—and Salih Shakkar fifty piastres. But
since in these lands, as a rule, no one ever lends coins,
or, borrowing, ever returns them, I took care to exact
service from the first, to take two rich coats from the
second, a handsome pipe from the third, a " bálá " or
yataghan from the fourth, and from the fifth an imitation
Cashmere shawl. After which, we sat down and drew

---

1 " Makhí-chús," equivalent to our " skin-flint."

out the agreement. It was favourable to me : I lent them Egyptian money, and bargained for repayment in the currency of Al-Hijaz, thereby gaining the exchange, which is sometimes sixteen per cent. This was done, not so much for the sake of profit, as with the view of becoming a Hátim,[1] by a " never mind " on settling day. My companions having received these small sums, became affectionate and eloquent in my praise : they asked me to make one of their number at meals for the future, over-whelmed me with questions, insisted upon a present of sweetmeats, detected in me a great man under a cloud,— perhaps my claims to being a Darwaysh assisted them to this discovery,—and declared that I should perforce be their guest at Meccah and Al-Madinah. On all occasions precedence was forced upon me ; my opinion was the first consulted, and no project was settled without my con-currence : briefly, Abdullah the Darwaysh suddenly found himself a person of consequence. This elevation led me into an imprudence which might have cost me dear ; aroused the only suspicion about me ever expressed during the summer's tour. My friends had looked at my clothes, overhauled my medicine chest, and criticised my pistols ; they sneered at my copper-cased watch,[2] and remembered having seen a compass at Constantinople. Therefore I imagined they would think little about a sextant. This was a mistake. The boy Mohammed, I

---

1 A well-known Arab chieftain, whose name has come to stand for generosity itself.

2 This being an indispensable instrument for measuring distances, I had it divested of gold case, and provided with a facing carefully stained and figured with Arabic numerals. In countries where few can judge of a watch by its works, it is as well to secure its safety by making the exterior look as mean as possible. The watches worn by respectable people in Al-Hijaz are almost always old silver pieces, of the turnip shape, with hunting cases and an outer *étui* of thick leather. Mostly they are of Swiss or German manufacture, and they find their way into Arabia *viâ* Constantinople and Cairo.

afterwards learned,[1] waited only my leaving the room to declare that the would-be Haji was one of the Infidels from India, and a council sat to discuss the case. Fortunately for me, Omar Effendi had looked over a letter which I had written to Haji Wali that morning, and he had at various times received categorical replies to certain questions in high theology. He felt himself justified in declaring, *ex cathedrâ*, the boy Mohammed's position perfectly untenable. And Shaykh Hamid, who looked forward to being my host, guide, and debtor in general, and probably cared scantily for catechism or creed, swore that the light of Al-Islam was upon my countenance, and, consequently, that the boy Mohammed was a pauper, a "fakir," an owl, a cut-off one,[2] a stranger, and a Wahhabi (heretic), for daring to impugn the faith of a brother believer.[3] The scene ended with a general abuse of the acute youth, who was told on all sides that he had no shame, and was directed to "fear Allah." I was struck with the expression of my friends' countenances when they saw the sextant, and, determining with a sigh to

---

1 On my return to Cairo, Omar Effendi, whom I met accidentally in the streets, related the story to me. I never owned having played a part, to avoid shocking his prejudices; and though he must have suspected me,—for the general report was, that an Englishman, disguised as a Persian, had performed the pilgrimage, measured the country, and sketched the buildings,—he had the gentlemanly feeling never to allude to the past. We parted, when I went to India, on the best of terms.

2 Munkati'a—one cut off (from the pleasures and comforts of life). In Al-Hijaz, as in England, any allusion to poverty is highly offensive.

3 The Koran expressly forbids a Moslem to discredit the word of any man who professes his belief in the Saving Faith. The greatest offence of the Wahhabis is their habit of designating all Moslems that belong to any but their own sect by the opprobrious name of Kafirs or infidels. This, however, is only the Koranic precept; in practice a much less trustful spirit prevails.

leave it behind, I prayed five times a day for nearly a
week.

We all agreed not to lose an hour in securing places
on board some vessel bound for Yambu'; and my companions, hearing that my passport as a British Indian
was scarcely *en règle*, earnestly advised me to have it
signed by the governor without delay, whilst they occupied
themselves about the harbour. They warned me that if
I displayed the Turkish Tazkirah given me at the citadel
of Cairo, I should infallibly be ordered to await the caravan, and lose their society and friendship. Pilgrims
arriving at Alexandria, be it known to the reader, are
divided into bodies, and distributed by means of passports
to the three great roads, namely, Suez, Kusayr (Cosseir),
and the Hajj route by land round the Gulf of al-'Akabah.
After the division has once been made, government turns
a deaf ear to the representations of individuals. The Bey
of Suez has an order to obstruct pilgrims as much as
possible till the end of the season, when they are hurried
down that way, lest they should arrive at Meccah too
late.[1] As most of the Egyptian high officials have boats,
which sail up the Nile laden with pilgrims and return
freighted with corn, the government naturally does its
utmost to force the delays and discomforts of this line
upon strangers.[2] And as those who travel by the Hajj
route must spend money in the Egyptian territories at
least fifteen days longer than they would if allowed to

---

1 Towards the end of the season, poor pilgrims are forwarded
gratis, by order of government. But, to make such liberality as
inexpensive as possible, the Pasha compels ship-owners to carry one
pilgrim per 9 ardebs (about 5 bushels each), in small, and 1 per 11 in
large vessels.

2 I was informed by a Prussian gentleman, holding an official
appointment under His Highness the Pasha, at Cairo, that 300,000
ardebs of grain were annually exported from Kusayr to Jeddah.
The rest is brought down the Nile for consumption in Lower Egypt,
.and export to Europe.

embark at once from Suez, the Bey very properly
assists them in the former and obstructs them in the
latter case. Knowing these facts, I felt that a difficulty
was at hand. The first thing was to take Shaykh Nur's
passport, which was *en règle*, and my own, which was not,
to the Bey for signature. He turned the papers over and
over, as if unable to read them, and raised false hopes
high by referring me to his clerk. The under-official at
once saw the irregularity of the document, asked me why
it had not been visé at Cairo, swore that under such
circumstances nothing would induce the Bey to let me
proceed ; and, when I tried persuasion, waxed insolent.
I feared that it would be necessary to travel *via* Cosseir,
for which there was scarcely time, or to transfer myself
on camel-back to the harbour of Tur, and there to await
the chance of finding a place in some half-filled vessel to
Al-Hijaz,—which would have been relying upon an accident. My last hope at Suez was to obtain assistance
from Mr. West, then H.B.M.'s Vice-Consul, and since
made Consul. I therefore took the boy Mohammed with
me, choosing him on purpose, and excusing the step to
my companions by concocting an artful fable about my
having been, in Afghanistan, a benefactor to the British
nation. We proceeded to the Consulate. Mr. West, who
had been told by imprudent Augustus Bernal to expect
me, saw through the disguise, despite jargon assumed to
satisfy official scruples, and nothing could be kinder than
the part he took. His clerk was directed to place himself
in communication with the Bey's factotum ; and, when objections to signing the Alexandrian Tazkirah were offered,
the Vice-Consul said that he would, at his own risk, give
me a fresh passport as a British subject from Suez to
Arabia. His firmness prevailed : on the second day,
the documents were returned to me in a satisfactory
state. I take a pleasure in owning this obligation to
Mr. West : in the course of my wanderings, I have often

received from him open-hearted hospitality and the most friendly attentions.

Whilst these passport difficulties were being solved, the rest of the party was as busy in settling about passage and passage-money. The peculiar rules of the port of Suez require a few words of explanation.[1] " About thirty-five years ago " (*i.e.* about 1818 A.D.), "the shipowners proposed to the then government, with the view of keeping up freight, a Farzah, or system of rotation. It might be supposed that the Pasha, whose object notoriously was to retain all monoplies in his own hands, would have refused his sanction to such a measure. But it so happened in those days that all the court had ships at Suez : Ibrahim Pasha alone owned four or five. Consequently, they expected to share profits with the merchants, and thus to be compensated for the want of port-dues. From that time forward all the vessels in the harbour were registered, and ordered to sail in rotation. This arrangement benefits the owner of the craft 'en départ,' giving him in his turn a temporary monopoly, with the advantage of a full market ; and freight is so high that a single trip often clears off the expense of building and the risk of losing the ship—a sensible *succedaneum* for insurance companies. On the contrary, the public must always be a loser by the 'Farzah.' Two of a trade do not agree elsewhere ; but at Suez even the Christian and the Moslem shipowner are bound by a fraternal tie, in the shape of this rotation system. It injures the general merchant and the Red Sea trader, not only by

---

1 The account here offered to the reader was kindly supplied to me by Henry Levick, Esq. (late Vice-Consul, and afterwards Postmaster at Suez), and it may be depended upon, as coming from a resident of 16 years' standing. All the passages marked with inverted commas are extracts from a letter with which that gentleman favoured me. The information is obsolete now, but it may be interesting as a specimen of the things that were.

perpetuating high freight,[1] but also by causing at one period of the year a break in the routine of sales and in the supplies of goods for the great Jeddah market.[2] At this moment (Nov. 1853), the vessel to which the turn belongs happens to be a large one ; there is a deficiency of export to Al-Hijaz,—her owner will of course wait any length of time for a full cargo ; consequently no vessel with merchandise has left Suez for the last seventy-two days. Those who have bought goods for the Jeddah market at three months' credit will therefore have to meet their acceptances for merchandise still warehoused at the Egyptian port. This strange contrast to free-trade principle is another proof that protection benefits only one party, the protected, while it is detrimental to the interests of the other party, the public." To these remarks of Mr. Levick's, I have only to add that the government supports the Farzah with all the energy of protectionists. A letter from Mr. (now Sir) John Drummond Hay was insufficient to induce the Bey of Suez to break through the rule of rotation in favour of certain princes from Morocco. The recommendations of Lord Stratford de Redcliffe met with no better fate ; and all Mr. West's good will could not pro-

---

1 The rate of freight is at present (1853) about forty shillings per ton—very near the same paid by the P. and O. Company for coals carried from Newcastle *via* the Cape to Suez. Were the " Farzah" abolished, freight to Jeddah would speedily fall to 15 or 16 shillings per ton. Passengers from Suez to Jeddah are sometimes charged as much as 6 or even 8 dollars for standing room—personal baggage forming another pretext for extortion—and the higher orders of pilgrims, occupying a small portion of the cabin, pay about 12 dollars. These first and second class fares would speedily be reduced, by abolishing protection, to 3 and 6 dollars. Note to Second Edition.— The " Farzah," I may here observe, has been abolished by Sa'id Pasha since the publication of these lines : the effects of "free trade" are exactly what were predicted by Mr. Levick.

2 The principal trade from Suez is to Jeddah, Kusayr supplying Yambu'. The latter place, however, imports from Suez wheat, beans, cheese, biscuit, and other provisions for return pilgrims.

cure me a vessel out of her turn.[1] We were forced to
rely upon our own exertions, and the activity of Sa'ad
the Demon. This worthy, after sundry delays and differences, mostly caused by his own determination to travel
gratis, and to make us pay too much, finally closed with
the owner of the "Golden Thread.[2]" He took places for
us upon the poop,—the most eligible part of the vessel at
this season of the year ; he premised that we should not
be very comfortable, as we were to be crowded with
Maghrabi pilgrims, but that "Allah makes all things
easy !" Though not penetrated with the conviction that
this would happen in our case, I paid for two deck
passages eighteen Riyals[3] (dollars), and my companions
seven each, whilst Sa'ad secretly entered himself as an able
seaman. Mohammed Shiklibha we were obliged to leave
behind, as he could not, or might not afford the expense,
and none of us might afford it for him. Had I known
him to be the honest, true-hearted fellow he was—his
kindness at Meccah quite won my heart—I should not
have grudged the small charity.

---

1 My friends were strenuous in their exertions for me to make
interest with Mr. West. In the first place, we should have paid less
for the whole of a privileged vessel, than we did for our wretched
quarters on the deck of the pilgrim-ship ; and, secondly, we might
have touched at any port we pleased, so as to do a little business in
the way of commerce.

2 Afterwards called by Sir R. F. Burton the "Golden Wire."
—ED.

3 For the "Sath," or poop, the sum paid by each was seven
Riyals. I was, therefore, notably cheated by Sa'ad the Demon. The
unhappy women in the "Kamrah," or cabin, bought suffocation at
the rate of 6 dollars each, as I was afterwards informed, and the
third class, in the "Taht," or amidships and forward, contributed
from 3 to 5 Riyals. But, as usual on these occasions, there was no
prix fixe ; every man was either overcharged or undercharged,
according to his means or his necessities. We had to purchase our
own water, but the ship was to supply us with fuel for cooking. We
paid nothing extra for luggage, and we carried an old Maghrabi
woman gratis for good luck.

Nothing more comfortless than our days and nights in the "George" Inn. The ragged walls of our rooms were clammy with dirt, the smoky rafters foul with cobwebs, and the floor, bestrewed with kit, in terrible confusion, was black with hosts of cockroaches, ants, and flies. Pigeons nestled on the shelf, cooing amatory ditties the live-long day, and cats like tigers crawled through a hole in the door, making night hideous with their caterwaulings. Now a curious goat, then an inquisitive jackass, would walk stealthily into the room, remark that it was tenanted, and retreat with dignified demeanour, and the mosquitos sang Io Pæans over our prostrate forms throughout the twenty-four hours. I spare the reader the enumeration of the other Egyptian plagues that infested the place. After the first day's trial, we determined to spend the hours of light in the passages, lying upon our boxes or rugs, smoking, wrangling, and inspecting one another's chests. The latter occupation was a fertile source of disputes, for nothing was more common than for a friend to seize an article belonging to another, and to swear by the Apostle's beard that he admired it, and, therefore, would not return it. The boy Mohammed and Shaykh Nur, who had been intimates the first day, differed in opinion on the second, and on the third came to pushing each other against the wall. Sometimes we went into the Bazar, a shady street flanked with poor little shops, or we sat in the coffee-house,[1] drinking hot saltish water tinged with burnt bean, or we prayed in one of three tumble-down old Mosques, or we squatted upon the pier, lamenting the want of Hammams, and bathing in the tepid sea.[2] I presently came to the conclusion that

---

1 We were still at Suez, where we could do as we pleased. But respectable Arabs in their own country, unlike Egyptians, are seldom to be seen in the places of public resort. "Go to the coffee-house and sing there!" is a reproach sometimes addressed to those who have a habit of humming in decent society.

2 It was only my prestige as physician that persuaded my friend

Suez as a "watering-place" is duller even than Dover. The only society we found, excepting an occasional visitor, was that of a party of Egyptian women, who with their husbands and families occupied some rooms adjoining ours. At first they were fierce, and used bad language, when the boy Mohammed and I,—whilst Omar Effendi was engaged in prayer, and the rest were wandering about the town,—ventured to linger in the cool passage, where they congregated, or to address a facetious phrase to them. But hearing that I was a Hákim-bashi—for fame had promoted me to the rank of a " Physician General " at Suez —all discovered some ailments. They began prudently with requesting me to display the effects of my drugs by dosing myself, but they ended submissively by swallowing the nauseous compounds. To this succeeded a primitive form of flirtation, which mainly consisted of the demand direct. The most charming of the party was one Fattúmah[1], a plump-personed dame, fast verging upon her thirtieth year, fond of a little flattery, and possessing, like all her people, a most voluble tongue. The refrain of every conversation was " Marry me, O Fattumah ! O daughter ! O female pilgrim !" In vain the lady would reply, with a coquettish movement of the sides, a toss of the head, and a flirting manipulation of her head-veil,

to join me in these bathings. As a general rule, the Western Arabs avoid cold water, from a belief that it causes fever. When Mr. C. Cole, H.B.M.'s Vice-Consul, arrived at Jeddah, the people of the place, seeing that he kept up his Indian habits, advised him strongly to drop them. He refused ; but unhappily he soon caught a fever, which confirmed them all in their belief. When Arabs wish to cool the skin after a journey, they wash with a kind of fuller's earth called " Tafl," or with a thin paste of henna, and then anoint the body with oil or butter.

[1] An incrementative form of the name " Fátimah," very common in Egypt. Fatimah would mean a " weaner "—Fattúmah, a " great weaner." By the same barbarism Khadíjah becomes " Khaddúgah"; Amínah, "Ammúnah"; and Nafísah, "Naffúsah," on the banks of the Nile.

" I am mated, O young man !"—it was agreed that she, being a person of polyandrous propensities, could support the weight of at least three matrimonial engagements. Sometimes the entrance of the male Fellahs[1] interrupted these little discussions, but people of our respectability and nation were not to be imposed upon by such husbands. In their presence we only varied the style of conversation — inquiring the amount of "Mahr," or marriage settlement, deriding the cheapness of womanhood in Egypt, and requiring to be furnished on the spot with brides at the rate of ten shillings a head.[2] More often the amiable Fattumah—the fair sex in this country, though passing frail, have the best tempers in the world— would laugh at our impertinences. Sometimes vexed by our imitating her Egyptian accent, mimicking her gestures, and depreciating her country-women,[3] she would wax wroth, and order us to be gone, and stretch out her forefinger—a sign that she wished to put out our eyes, or adjure Allah to cut the hearts out of our bosoms. Then

---

1 The palmy days of the Egyptian husband, when he might use the stick, the sword, or the sack with impunity, are, in civilised places at least, now gone by. The wife has only to complain to the Kazi, or to the governor, and she is certain of redress. This is right in the abstract, but in practice it acts badly. The fair sex is so unruly in this country, that strong measures are necessary to coerce it, and in the arts of deceit men have here little or no chance against women.

2 The amount of settlement being, among Moslems as among Christians, the test of a bride's value,—moral and physical,—it will readily be understood that our demand was more facetious than complimentary.

3 The term Misriyah (an Egyptian woman) means in Al-Hijaz and the countries about it, a depraved character. Even the men own unwillingly to being Egyptians, for the free-born never forget that the banks of the Nile have for centuries been ruled by the slaves of slaves. " He shall be called an Egyptian," is a denunciation which has been strikingly fulfilled, though the country be no longer the " basest of kingdoms."

the " Marry me, O Fattumah, O daughter, O female
pilgrim!" would give way to Y'al Ago-o-oz! (O old woman
and decrepit !) "O daughter of sixty sires, and fit only to
carry wood to market !"—whereupon would burst a storm
of wrath, at the tail of which all of us, like children,
starting upon our feet, rushed out of one another's way.
But—" *qui se dispute, s'adore*"—when we again met all
would be forgotten, and the old tale be told over *de novo*.
This was the amusement of the day. At night we men,
assembling upon the little terrace, drank tea, recited
stories, read books, talked of our travels, and indulged
in various pleasantries. The great joke was the boy
Mohammed's abusing all his companions to their faces
in Hindustani, which none but Shaykh Nur and I could
understand; the others, however, guessed his intention,
and revenged themselves by retorts of the style un-
courteous in the purest Hijazi.

I proceed to offer a few more extracts from Mr.
Levick's letter about Suez and the Suezians. "It appears
that the number of pilgrims who pass through Suez to
Meccah has of late been steadily on the decrease. When
I first came here (in 1838) the pilgrims who annually embarked at this port amounted to between 10,000 and
12,000, the shipping was more numerous, and the merchants were more affluent.[1] I have ascertained from a
special register kept in the government archives that in
the Moslem year 1268 (A.D. 1851-52) the exact number
that passed through was 4893."

" In 1269 A. H. (A.D. 1852-53) it had shrunk to 3136.
The natives assign the falling off to various causes, which

---

[1] In those days merchants depended solely upon the native trade
and the passage of pilgrims. The pecuniary advantage attending
what is called the Overland transit benefits chiefly the lowest orders,
camel-men, sailors, porters, and others of the same class. Sixteen
years ago the hire of a boat from the harbour to the roadstead was a
piastre and a half : now it is at least five.

I attribute chiefly to the indirect effect of ˙European civilisation upon the Moslem powers immediately in contact with it. The heterogeneous mass of pilgrims is composed of people of all classes, colours, and costumes. One sees among them, not only the natives of countries contiguous to Egypt, but also a large proportion of Central Asians from Bokhara, Persia, Circassia, Turkey, and the Crimea, who prefer this route by way of Constantinople to the difficult, expensive and dangerous caravan-line through the Desert from Damascus and Baghdad. The West sends us Moors, Algerines, and Tunisians, and Inner Africa a mass of sable Takrouri,[1] and others from Bornou, the Sudán,[2] Ghadamah near the Niger, and Jabarti from the Habash.[3]"

"The Suez ship-builders are an influential body of men, originally Candiots and Alexandrians. When Mohammed Ali fitted out his fleet for the Hijaz war, he transported a number of Greeks to Suez, and the children now exercise their fathers' craft. There are at present three great builders at this place. Their principal diffi-

---

1 This word, says Mansfield Parkyns (Life in Abyssinia), is applied to the wandering *pilgrim* from Dárfúr, Dár Borghú, Bayárimah, Fellatah, and Western Africa. He mentions, however, a tribe called "Tokrouri," settled in Abyssinia near Nimr's country, but he does not appear to know that the ancient Arab settlement in Western Africa, "Al-Takrúr," (Sakatu ?) which has handed down its name to a large posterity of small kingdoms, will be found in Al-Idrisi (1. climate, 1. section,) ; but I do not agree with the learned translator in writing the word "Tokrour." Burckhardt often alludes in his benevolent way to the "respectable and industrious Tekrourys." I shall have occasion to mention them at a future time.

2 The Sudan (Blackland) in Arabia is applied to Upper Nubia, Senaar, Kordofan, and the parts adjacent.

3 Not only in Ghíz, but also in Arabic, the mother of Ghiz, the word "Habash," whence our "Abyssinians," means a rabble, a mixture of people. Abyssinian Moslems are called by the Arabs "Jabarti."

culty is the want of material. Teak comes from India[1]
viâ Jeddah, and Venetian boards, owing to the expense of
camel-transport, are a hundred per cent. dearer here than
at Alexandria. Trieste and Turkey supply spars, and
Jeddah canvas : the sail-makers are Suez men, and the
crews a mongrel mixture of Arabs and Egyptians; the
Rais, or captain, being almost invariably, if the vessel be
a large one, a Yambu' man. There are two kinds of
craft, distinguished from each other by tonnage, not by
build. The Baghlah[2] (buggalow), is a vessel above fifty
tons burden, the Sambúk (a classical term) from fifteen to
fifty. The shipowner bribes the Amir al-Bahr, or port-
captain, and the Nazir al-Safayn, or the captain commanding the government vessels, to rate his ship as high
as possible; if he pay the price, he will be allowed nine
ardebs to the ton.[3] The number of ships belonging to
the port of Suez amounts to 92 ; they vary from 25 to
250 tons. The departures in A.H. 1269 (1852 and 1853)
were 38, so that each vessel, after returning from a trip,
is laid up for about two years. Throughout the passage
of the pilgrims,—that is to say, during four months,—the
departures average twice a week ; during the remainder
of the year from six to ten vessels may leave the port.
The homeward trade is carried on principally in Jeddah
bottoms, which are allowed to convey goods to Suez,
but not to take in return cargo there : they must not
interfere with, nor may they partake in any way of the
benefits of the rotation system.[4]"

1 There is no such thing as a tree, except the date, the tamarisk,
and the mimosa on the western shores of the Red Sea.

2 This word, which in Arabic is the feminine form of " Baghl,"
a mule, is in Egypt, as in India, pronounced and written by foreigners
"buggalow." Some worthy Anglo-Indians have further corrupted it
to " bungalow."

3 " The ardeb, like most measures in this country of commercial
confusion, varies greatly according to the grain for which it is used.
As a general rule, it may be assumed at 300 lbs."

4 Return Arab boats, at any but the pilgrim season, with little

" During the present year the imports were contained in 41,395 packages, the exports in 15,988. Specie makes up in some manner for this preponderance of imports : a sum of from £30,000 to £40,000, in crown, or Maria Theresa, dollars annually leaves Egypt for Arabia, Abyssinia, and other parts of Africa. I value the imports at about £350,000 ; the export trade to Jeddah at £300,000 per annum. The former consists principally of coffee and gum-arabic ; of these there were respectively 17,460 and 15,132 bales, the aggregate value of each article being from £75,000 to £80,000, and the total amount £160,000. In the previous year the imports were contained in 36,840 packages, the exports in 13,498 : of the staple articles—coffee and gum-arabic — they were respectively 15,499 and 14,129 bales, each bale being valued at about £5. Next in importance comes wax from Al-Yaman and the Hijaz, mother-of-pearl[1] from the Red Sea, sent to England in rough, pepper from Malabar, cloves brought by Moslem pilgrims from Java, Borneo, and Singapore,[2] cherry pipe-sticks from Persia and Bussora, and Persian or Surat 'Timbak' (tobacco). These I value at £20,000 per annum. There were also (A.D. 1853) of cloves 708 packages, and of Malabar pepper 948 : the cost of these two might be £7,000. Minor articles of exportation are,—general spiceries (ginger, car-

---

difficulty obtain permission to carry passengers, but not cargo. Two gentlemen, in whose pleasant society I once travelled from Cairo to Suez,—M. Charles Didier and the Abbé Hamilton,—paid the small sum of 1000 piastres, (say £10) for the whole of a moderate sized " Sambuk " returning to Jeddah.

1 Mother-of-pearl is taken to Jerusàlem, and there made into chaplets, saints' figures, and crucifixes for Christian pilgrims. At Meccah it is worked into rosaries for the Hajis. In Europe, cabinet and ornamental work cause a considerable demand for it. Some good pearls are procurable in the Red Sea. I have seen a drop of fair size and colour sold for seven dollars.

2 I was told at Meccah that the pilgrimage is attended by about 2000 natives of Java and the adjoining islands.

damoms, &c.); Eastern perfumes, such as aloes-wood, attar of rose, attar of pink and others; tamarinds from India and Al-Yaman, Banca tin, hides supplied by the nomade Badawin, senna leaves from Al-Yaman and the Hijaz, and blue chequered cotton Malayahs (women's mantillas), manufactured in southern Arabia. The total value of these smaller imports may be £20,000 per annum."

" The exports chiefly consist of English and native ' grey domestics,' bleached Madipilams, Paisley lappets, and muslins for turbands; the remainder being Manchester prints, antimony, Syrian soap, iron in bars, and common ironmongery, Venetian or Trieste beads, used as ornaments in Arabia and Abyssinia, writing paper, Tarbushes, Papushes (slippers), and other minor articles of dress and ornament."

" The average annual temperature of the year at Suez is 67° Fahrenheit. The extremes of heat and cold are found in January and August; during the former month the thermometer ranges from a minimum of 38° to a maximum of 68°; during the latter the variation extends from 68° to 102°, or even to 104°, when the heat becomes oppressive. Departures from these extremes are rare. I never remember to have seen the thermometer rise above 108° during the severest Khamsin, or to have sunk below 34° in the rawest wintry wind. Violent storms come up from the south in March. Rain is very variable[1]:

---

[1] The following popular puerilities will serve to show how fond barbarians are of explaining the natural by the supernatural. The Moslems of Egypt thus account for the absence of St. Swithin from their drought-stricken lands. When Jacob lost his Benjamin, he cursed the land of Misraim, declaring that it should know no rain ; Joseph on the other hand blessed it, asserting that it should never want water. So the Sind Hindus believe that Hiranyakasipu, the demon-tyrant of Multan, finding Magha-Raja (the Cloud King) troublesome in his dominions, bound him with chains, and only released him upon his oath not to trouble the Unhappy Valley with his presence.

sometimes three years have passed without a shower, whereas in 1841 torrents poured for nine successive days, deluging the town, and causing many buildings to fall."

" The population of Suez now numbers about 4,800. As usual in Mohammedan countries no census is taken here. Some therefore estimate the population at 6,000. Sixteen years ago it was supposed to be under 3,000. After that time it rapidly increased till 1850, when a fatal attack of cholera reduced it to about half its previous number. The average mortality is about twelve a month.[1] The endemic diseases are fevers of typhoid and inter-mittent types in spring, when strong northerly winds cause the waters of the bay to recede,[2] and leave a miasma-breeding swamp exposed to the rays of the sun. In the months of October and November febrile attacks are violent ; ophthalmia more so. The eye-disease is not so general here as at Cairo, but the symptoms are more acute ; in some years it becomes a virulent epidemic, which ends either in total blindness or in a partial opacity of the cornea, inducing dimness of vision, and a permanent weakness of the eyes. In one month three of my acquaintances lost their sight. Dysenteries are also common, and so are bad boils, or rather ulcers. The cold season is not unwholesome, and at this period the

---

I would suggest to those Egyptian travellers who believe that the fall of rain has been materially increased at Cairo of late, by plantations of trees, to turn over the volumes of their predecesors ; they will find almost every one complaining of the discomforts of rain. In Sind it appears certain that during the last few years there has been at times almost a monsoon ; this novel phenomenon the natives attribute to the presence of their conquerors, concerning whom it cannot be said that they have wooded the country to any extent.

1 This may appear a large mortality ; but at Alexandria it is said the population is renewed every fourteen years.

2 During these North winds the sandy bar is exposed, and allows men to cross, which may explain the passage of the Israelites, for those who do not believe the Legend to be a Myth. Similarly at Jed-dah, the bars are covered during the South and bare during the North winds.

pure air of the Desert restores and invigorates the heat-wasted frame."

" The walls, gates, and defences of Suez are in a ruinous state, being no longer wanted to keep out the Sinaitic Badawin. The houses are about 500 in number, but many of the natives prefer occupying the upper stories of the Wakalahs, the rooms on the ground floor serving for stores to certain merchandise, wood, dates, cotton, &c. The Suezians live well, and their bazar is abundantly stocked with meat and clarified butter brought from Sinai, and fowls, corn, and vegetables from the Sharkiyah province; fruit is supplied by Cairo as well as by the Sharkiyah, and wheat conveyed down the Nile in flood to the capital is carried on camel-back across the Desert. At sunrise they eat the Fatur, or breakfast, which in summer consists of a ' fatirah,' a kind of muffin, or of bread and treacle. In winter it is more substantial, being generally a mixture of lentils and rice,[1] with clarified butter poured over it, and a ' kitchen ' of pickled lime or stewed onions. At this season they greatly enjoy the ' fúl mudammas ' (boiled horse-beans),[2] eaten with an abundance of linseed oil, into which they steep bits of bread. The beans form, with carbon-generating matter, a highly nutritive diet, which, if the stomach can digest it,—the pulse is never shelled,—gives great strength. About the middle of the day comes ' Al-Ghada,' a light dinner of wheaten bread, with dates, onions or cheese : in the hot season melons and cool-

---

[1] This mixture, called in India Kichhri, has become common in Al-Hijaz as well as at Suez. " Al-Kajari " is the corruption, which denotes its foreign origin, and renders its name pronounceable to Arabs.

[2] Beans, an abomination to the ancient Egyptians, who were forbidden even to sow them, may now be called the common " kitchen " of the country. The Badawin, who believe in nothing but flesh, milk, and dates, deride the bean-eaters, but they do not consider the food so disgusting as onions.

ing fruits are preferred, especially by those who have
to face the sun. ' Al-Asha,' or supper, is served about
half an hour after sunset ; at this meal all but the poorest
classes eat meat. Their favourite flesh, as usual in this
part of the world, is mutton; beef and goat are little
prized.[1]"

The people of Suez are a finer and fairer race
than the Cairenes. The former have more the appearance of Arabs : their dress is more picturesque, their
eyes are carefully darkened with Kohl, and they wear
sandals, not slippers. They are, according to all accounts,
a turbulent and somewhat fanatic set, fond of quarrels,
and slightly addicted to "pronunciamentos." The general
programme of one of these latter diversions is said
to be as follows. The boys will first be sent by their
fathers about the town in a disorderly mob, and ordered
to cry out "Long live the Sultan!" with its usual sequel,
"Death to the Infidels!" The Infidels, Christians or
others, must hear and may happen to resent this ; or
possibly the governor, foreseeing a disturbance, orders an
ingenuous youth or two to be imprisoned, or to be caned
by the police. Whereupon some person, rendered influential by wealth or religious reputation, publicly
complains that the Christians are all in all, and that in
these evil days Al-Islam is going to destruction. On this
occasion the speaker conducts himself with such insolence,
that the governor perforce consigns him to confinement,
which exasperates the populace still more. Secret meet-
ings are now convened, and in them the chiefs of
corporations assume a prominent position. If the
disturbance be intended by its main-spring to subside
quietly, the conspirators are allowed to take their own
way ; they will drink copiously, become lions about
midnight, and recover their hare-hearts before noon next

---

1 Here concludes Mr. Levick's letter. For the following observations, I alone am answerable.

day. But if mischief be intended, a case of bloodshed is
brought about, and then nothing can arrest the torrent
of popular rage.[1] The Egyptian, with all his good
humour, merriment, and nonchalance, is notorious for
doggedness, when, as the popular phrase is, his "blood is
up." And this, indeed, is his chief merit as a soldier.
He has a certain mechanical dexterity in the use of arms,
and an Egyptian regiment will fire a volley as correctly
as a battalion at Chobham. But when the head, and
not the hands, is required, he notably fails. The reason
of his superiority in the field is his peculiar stubborness,
and this, together with his powers of digestion and of
enduring hardship on the line of march, is the quality
that makes him terrible to his old conqueror, the Turk.[2]

---

1 The government takes care to prevent bloodshed in the towns
by disarming the country people, and by positively forbidding the
carrying of weapons. Moreover, with a wise severity, it punishes all
parties concerned in a quarrel, where blood is drawn, with a heavy
fine and the bastinado *de rigueur*. Hence it is never safe, except as a
European, to strike a man, and the Egyptians generally confine themselves to collaring and pushing each other against the walls. Even in
the case of receiving gross abuse, you cannot notice it as you would
elsewhere. You must take two witnesses,—respectable men,—and
prove the offence before the Zabit, who alone can punish the offender.

2 NOTE TO THIRD (1873) EDITION.—I revisited Suez in September, 1869, and found it altered for the better. The population had
risen from 6,000 to 20,000. The tumble-down gateway was still there,
but of the old houses—including the "George Inn," whose front had
been repaired—I recognised only four, and they looked mean by the
side of the fine new buildings. In a few years ancient Suez will be
no more. The bazars are not so full of filth and flies, now that
pilgrims pass straight through and hardly even encamp. The sweet
water Canal renders a Hammam possible ; coffee is no longer hot
saltish water, and presently irrigation will cover with fields and
gardens the desert plain extending to the feet of Jabal Atakah. The
noble works of the Canal Maritime, which should in justice be called
the "Lesseps Canal," shall soon transform Clysma into a modern
and civilised city. The railway station, close to the hotel, the new
British hospital, the noisy Greek casino, the Frankish shops, the

puffing steamers, and the ringing of morning bells, gave me a novel impression. Even the climate has been changed by filling up the Timsch Lakes. Briefly, the *hat* is now at home in Suez.

NOTE TO FOURTH (1879) EDITION.—The forecast in the last paragraph has not been fulfilled. I again visited Suez in 1877-78, and found that it had been ruined by the Canal leaving it out of line. In fact, another Suez is growing up about the " New Docks," while the old town is falling to pieces. For this and other Egyptian matters, see " The Gold Mines of Midian " (by Sir Richard Burton).

CHAPTER X.

THE PILGRIM SHIP.

THE larger craft anchor some three or four miles from the Suez pier, so that it is necessary to drop down in a skiff or shore-boat.

Immense was the confusion at the eventful hour of our departure. Suppose us gathered upon the beach, on the morning of a fiery July day, carefully watching our hurriedly-packed goods and chattels, surrounded by a mob of idlers, who are not too proud to pick up waifs and strays; whilst pilgrims are rushing about apparently mad; and friends are weeping, acquaintances are vociferating adieux; boatmen are demanding fees, shopmen are claiming debts; women are shrieking and talking with inconceivable power, and children are crying,—in short, for an hour or so we stand in the thick of a human storm. To confound confusion, the boatmen have moored their skiff half a dozen yards away from the shore, lest the porters should be unable to make more than double their fare from the Hajis. Again the Turkish women make a hideous noise, as they are carried off struggling vainly in brawny arms; the children howl because their mothers howl; and the men scold and swear, because in such scenes none may be silent. The moment we had embarked, each individual found that he or she had missed something of vital importance,—a pipe, a child, a box, or a water-melon; and naturally all the servants were in the bazars, when they should have been in the boat. Briefly, despite the rage of the sailors, who feared being too late for a second trip, we stood for some time on the beach before putting off.

From the shore we poled to the little pier, where sat the Bey in person to perform a final examination of our passports. Several were detected without the necessary document. Some were bastinadoed, others were peremptorily ordered back to Cairo, and the rest were allowed to proceed. At about 10 A.M. (6th July) we hoisted sail, and ran down the channel leading to the roadstead. On our way we had a specimen of what we might expect from our fellow-passengers, the Maghrabi.[1] A boat crowded with these

---

1 Men of the Maghrab, or Western Africa; the vulgar plural is Maghrabin, generally written " Mogrebyn." May not the singular form of this word have given rise to the Latin " Maurus," by elision of the Ghayn, to Italians an unpronounceable consonant? From Maurus comes the Portuguese " Moro," and our " Moor." When Vasco de Gama reached Calicut, he found there a tribe of Arab colonists, who in religion and in language were the same as the people of Northern Africa,—for this reason he called them " Moors." This was explained long ago by Vincent (Periplus, lib. 3), and lately by Prichard (Natural History of Man). I repeat it because it has been my fate to hear, at a meeting of a learned society in London, a gentleman declare, that in Eastern Africa he found a people calling *themselves* Moors. Maghrabin—Westerns,—then would be opposed to Sharkiyin, Easterns, the origin of our " Saracen." From Gibbon downwards many have discussed the history of this word; but few expected in the nineteenth century to see a writer on Eastern subjects assert, with Sir John Mandeville, that these people " properly, ben clept Sarrazins of Sarra." The learned M. Jomard, who never takes such original views of things, asks a curious question :—" Mais comment un son aussi distinct que le Chine ش aurait-il pu se confondre avec le Syn س et, pour un mot aussi connu que charq ; comment aurait-on pu se tromper à l'omission des points ?" Simply because the word Saracens came to us through the Greeks (Ptolemy uses it), who have no such sound as sh in their language, and through the Italian which, hostile to the harsh sibilants of Oriental dialects, generally melts sh down into s. So the historical word Hashshásh-iyún—hemp-drinker,—civilised by the Italians into " assassino,"

ruffians ran alongside of us, and, before we could organise a defence, about a score of them poured into our vessel. They carried things too with a high hand, laughed at us, and seemed quite ready to fight. My Indian boy, who happened to let slip the word " Muarras," narrowly escaped a blow with a palm stick, which would have felled a camel. They outnumbered us, and they were armed ; so that, on this occasion, we were obliged to put up with their insolence.

Our Pilgrim Ship, the Silk al-Zahab, or the " Golden Wire," was a Sambuk, of about 400 ardebs (fifty tons), with narrow, wedge-like bows, a clean water-line, a sharp keel, and undecked, except upon the poop, which was high enough to act as a sail in a gale of wind.   She carried two masts, raking imminently forwards, the main being considerably larger than the mizzen ; the former was provided with a huge triangular latine, very deep in the tack, but the second sail was unaccountably wanting. She had no means of reefing, no compass, no log, no sounding lines, no spare ropes, nor even the suspicion of a chart : in her box-like cabin and ribbed hold there was something which savoured of close connection between her model and that of the Indian Toni,[1] or " dug-out."

became, as all know, an expression of European use. But if any one adverse to " etymological fancies " objects to my deriving Maurus from " Maghrab," let him remember Johnson's successfully tracing the course of the metamorphosis of " dies " into " jour." An even more peculiar change we may discover in the word " elephant." " Pilu " in Sanscrit, became " pil " in old Persian, which ignores short final vowels; " fil," and, with the article, " Al-fil," in Arabic, which supplies the place of p (an unknown letter to it), by f ; and elephas in Greek, which is fond of adding " as " to Arabic words, as in the cases of Aretas (Haris) and Obodas (Obayd). " A name," says Humboldt, " often becoming a historical monument, and the etymological analysis of language, however it may be divided, is attended by valuable results."

1 The Toni or Indian canoe is the hollowed-out trunk of a tree,—near Bombay generally a mango. It must have been the first

Such, probably, were the craft which carried old Sesostris across the Red Sea to Deir ; such were the cruisers which once every three years left Ezion-Geber for Tarshish ; such the transports of which 130 were required to convey Ælius Gallus, with his 10,000 men. " Bakhshish " was the last as well as the first odious sound I heard in Egypt. The owner of the shore-boat would not allow us to climb the sides of our vessel before paying him his fare, and when we did so, he asked for Bakhshish. If Easterns would only imitate the example of Europeans,—I never yet saw an Englishman give Bakhshish to a soul,—the nuisance would soon be done away with. But on this occasion all my companions complied with the request, and at times it is unpleasant to be singular. The first look at the interior of our vessel showed a hopeless sight ; Ali Murad, the greedy owner, had promised to take sixty passengers in the hold, but had stretched the number to ninety-seven. Piles of boxes and luggage in every shape and form filled the ship from stem to stern, and a torrent of Hajis were pouring over the sides like ants into the East-Indian sugar-basin. The poop, too, where we had taken our places, was covered with goods, and a number of pilgrims had established themselves there by might, not by right.

Presently, to our satisfaction, appeared Sa'ad the Demon, equipped as an able seaman, and looking most unlike the proprietor of two large boxes full of valuable merchandise. This energetic individual instantly prepared for action. With our little party to back him, he speedily cleared the poop of intruders and their stuff by the simple process of pushing or rather throwing them off it into the pit below. We then settled down as comfortably as we could ; three Syrians, a married Turk with his wife and family, the Rais or captain of the vessel,

---

step in advance from that simplest form of naval architecture, the " Catamaran " of Madras and Aden.

with a portion of his crew, and our seven selves, composing a total of eighteen human beings, upon a space
certainly not exceeding ten feet by eight.   The cabin—a
miserable box about the size of the poop, and three feet
high—was stuffed, like the hold of a slave ship, with
fifteen wretches, children and women, and the other
ninety-seven were disposed upon the luggage or squatted
on the bulwarks.   Having some experience in such
matters, and being favoured by fortune, I found a spare
bed-frame slung to the ship's side; and giving a dollar
to its owner, a sailor—who flattered himself that, because
it was his, he would sleep upon it,—I instantly appropriated it, preferring any hardship outside, to the condition
of a packed herring inside, the place of torment.

Our Maghrabis were fine-looking animals from the
deserts about Tripoli and Tunis; so savage that, but a
few weeks ago, they had gazed at the cock-boat, and
wondered how long it would be growing to the size
of the ship that was to take them to Alexandria.
Most of them were sturdy young fellows, round-headed,
broad-shouldered, tall and large-limbed, with frowning
eyes, and voices in a perpetual roar.   Their manners were
rude, and their faces full of fierce contempt or insolent
familiarity.   A few old men were there, with countenances
expressive of intense ferocity; women as savage and full
of fight as men; and handsome boys with shrill voices,
and hands always upon their daggers.   The women were
mere bundles of dirty white rags.   The males were clad
in "Burnus"—brown or striped woollen cloaks with
hoods; they had neither turband nor tarbush, trusting to
their thick curly hair or to the prodigious hardness of
their scalps as a defence against the sun; and there was
not a slipper nor a shoe amongst the party.   Of course
all were 'armed; but, fortunately for us, none had anything more formidable than a cut-and-thrust dagger about
ten inches long.   These Maghrabis travel in hordes under

a leader who obtains the temporary title of " Maula,"—
the master. He has generally performed a pilgrimage or
two, and has collected a stock of superficial information
which secures for him the respect of his followers, and
the profound contempt of the heaven-made Ciceroni of
Meccah and Al-Madinah. No people endure greater
hardships when upon the pilgrimage than these Africans,
who trust almost entirely to alms and to other such dis-
pensations of Providence. It is not therefore to be
wondered at that they rob whenever an opportunity presents itself. Several cases of theft occurred on board the
" Golden Wire"; and as such plunderers seldom allow
themselves to be baulked by insufficient defence, they are
accused, perhaps deservedly, of having committed some
revolting murders.

The first thing to be done after gaining standing-
room was to fight for greater comfort; and never a
Holyhead packet in the olden time showed a finer scene
of pugnacity than did our pilgrim ship. A few Turks,
ragged old men from Anatolia and Caramania, were
mixed up with the Maghrabis, and the former began the
war by contemptuously elbowing and scolding their wild
neighbours. The Maghrabis, under their leader, " Maula
Ali," a burly savage, in whom I detected a ridiculous
resemblance to the Rev. Charles Delafosse, an old and
well-remembered schoolmaster, retorted so willingly that
in a few minutes nothing was to be seen but a confused
mass of humanity, each item indiscriminately punching
and pulling, scratching and biting, butting and trampling,
with cries of rage, and all the accompaniments of a proper
fray, whatever was obnoxious to such operations. One
of our party on the poop, a Syrian, somewhat incautiously
leapt down to aid his countrymen by restoring order.
He sank immediately below the surface of the living
mass : and when we fished him out, his forehead was cut
open, half his beard had disappeared, and a fine sharp set

of teeth belonging to some Maghrabi had left their mark
in the calf of his leg. The enemy showed no love of fair
play, and never appeared contented unless five or six of
them were setting upon a single man. This made matters
worse. The weaker of course drew their daggers, and a
few bad wounds were soon given and received. In a few
minutes five men were completely disabled, and the victors
began to dread the consequences of their victory.

Then the fighting stopped, and, as many could not
find places, it was agreed that a deputation should wait
upon Ali Murad, the owner, to inform him of the crowded
state of the vessel. After keeping us in expectation at
least three hours, he appeared in a row-boat, preserving
a respectful distance, and informed us that any one who
pleased might quit the ship and take back his fare.
This left the case exactly as it was before; none would
abandon his party to go on shore: so Ali Murad rowed
off towards Suez, giving us a parting injunction to be
good, and not fight; to trust in Allah, and that Allah
would make all things easy to us. His departure was the
signal for a second fray, which in its accidents differed a
little from the first. During the previous disturbance we
kept our places with weapons in our hands. This time
we were summoned by the Maghrabis to relieve their
difficulties, by taking about half a dozen of them on the
poop. Sa'ad the Demon at once rose with an oath, and
threw amongst us a bundle of " Nabbút "—goodly ashen
staves six feet long, thick as a man's wrist, well greased,
and tried in many a rough bout. He shouted to us
" Defend yourselves if you don't wish to be the meat of
the Maghrabis ! " and to the enemy—" Dogs and sons of
dogs ! now shall you see what the children of the Arab
are." " I am Omar of Daghistan ! " " I am Abdullah
the son of Joseph ! " " I am Sa'ad the Demon ! " we exclaimed, " renowning it " by this display of name and
patronymic. To do our enemies justice, they showed no

sign of flinching ; they swarmed towards the poop like angry hornets, and encouraged each other with cries of " Allaho akbar ! " But we had a vantage-ground about four feet above them, and their palm-sticks and short daggers could do nothing against our terrible quarter-staves. In vain the " Jacquerie," tried to scale the poop and to overpower us by numbers ; their courage only secured them more broken heads.

At first I began to lay on load with *main morte*, really fearing to kill some one with such a weapon ; but it soon became evident that the Maghrabis' heads and shoulders could bear and did require the utmost exertion of strength. Presently a thought struck me. A large earthen jar full of drinking water,[1]—in its heavy frame of wood the weight might have been 100 lbs.,—stood upon the edge of the poop, and the thick of the fray took place beneath. Seeing an opportunity, I crept up to the jar, and, without attracting attention, rolled it down by a smart push with the shoulder upon the swarm of assailants. The fall caused a shriller shriek to rise above the ordinary din, for heads, limbs, and bodies were sorely bruised by the weight, scratched by the broken potsherds, and wetted by the sudden discharge. A fear that something worse might be coming made the Maghrabis slink off towards the end of the vessel. After a few minutes, we, sitting in grave silence, received a deputation of individuals in whity-brown Burnus, spotted and striped with what Mephistopheles calls a " curious juice." They solicited peace, which we granted upon the condition that they would pledge themselves to keep it. Our heads, shoulders, and hands were penitentially kissed, and presently the fellows returned to bind up their hurts in dirty

---

1 In these vessels each traveller, unless a previous bargain be made, is expected to provide his own water and firewood. The best way, however, is, when the old wooden box called a tank is sound, to pay the captain for providing water, and to keep the key.

rags. We owed this victory entirely to our own exertions, and the meek Omar was by far the fiercest of the party. Our Rais, as we afterwards learned, was an old fool who could do nothing but call for the Fátihah,[1] claim Bakhshish at every place where we moored for the night, and spend his leisure hours in the " Caccia del Mediterraneo." Our crew consisted of half a dozen Egyptian lads, who, not being able to defend themselves, were periodically chastised by the Maghrabis, especially when any attempt was made to cook, to fetch water, or to prepare a pipe.[2]

At length, about 3 P.M. on the 6th July, 1853, we shook out the sail, and, as it bellied in the favourable wind, we recited the Fatihah with upraised hands which we afterwards drew down our faces.[3] As the " Golden Wire " started from her place, I could not help casting one wistful look upon the British flag floating over the Consulate. But the momentary regret was stifled by the heart-bounding which prospects of an adventure excite, and by the real pleasure of leaving Egypt. I had lived there a stranger in the land, and a hapless life it had been : in the streets every man's face, as he looked upon the Persian, was the face of a foe. Whenever I came in contact with the native officials,[4] insolence marked the

---

1 The " opener "—the first chapter of the Koran, which Moslems recite as Christians do the Lord's Prayer ; it is also used on occasions of danger, the beginnings of journeys, to bind contracts, &c.

2 These Maghrabis, like the Somalis, the Wahhabis of the desert, and certain other barbarous races, unaccustomed to tobacco, appeared to hate the smell of a pipe.

3 The hands are raised in order to catch the blessing that is supposed to descend from heaven upon the devotee ; and the meaning of drawing the palms down the face is symbolically to transfer the benediction to every part of the body.

4 As is the case under all despotic governments, nothing can be more intentionally offensive than the official manners of a superior to his inferior in Egypt. The Indians charge their European fellow-subjects with insolence of demeanour and coarseness of language.

event ; and the circumstance of living within hail of my fellow-countrymen, and yet finding it impossible to enjoy their society, still throws a gloom over the memory of my first sojourn in Egypt.

The ships of the Red Sea—infamous region of rocks, reefs, and shoals—cruise along the coast by day, and at night lay-to in the first cove they find ; they do not sail when it blows hard, and as in winter time the weather is often stormy and the light of day does not last long, the voyage is intolerably slow.[1] At sunset we stayed our adventurous course ; and, still within sight of Suez, com-fortably anchored under the lee of Jabal Atakah, the " Mountain of Deliverance,[2]" the butt-end of Jabal Joshí. We were now on classic waters. The Eastern shore was dotted with the little grove of palm-trees which clusters around the Uyun Musa, or Moses' Wells ; and on the west, between two towering ridges, lay the mouth of the valley (Bádiyah, or Wady Tawarik, or Wady Musa) down which, according to Father Sicard,[3] the Israelites fled to

---

As far as my experience goes, our roughness and brusquerie are mere politeness compared with what passes between Easterns. At the same time it must be owned that I have seen the worst of it.

1 It was far safer and more expeditious in Al-Adrisi's day (A.D. 1154), when the captain used to sit on the poop " furnished with numerous and useful instruments " ; when he " sounded the shallows, and by his knowledge of the depths could direct the helmsman where to steer."

2 In the East it is usual, when commencing a voyage or a journey, to make a short day's work, in order to be at a convenient distance for returning, in case of any essential article having been forgotten.

3 A Jesuit missionary who visited the place in A.D. 1720, and described it in a well-known volume. As every eminent author, however, monopolises a " crossing," and since the head of the Suez creek, as is shown by its old watermark, has materially changed within no very distant period, it is no wonder that the question is still *sub judice*, and that there it will remain most probably till the end of time. The Christians have two equally favourite lines : the Mos-lems patronise one so impossible, that it has had attractions enough

the Sea of Sedge.[1] The view was by no means deficient
in a sort of barbarous splendour. Verdure there was none,
but under the violet and orange tints of the sky the chalky
rocks became heaps of topazes, and the brown-burnt
ridges masses of amethyst. The rising mists, here silvery
white, there deeply rosy, and the bright blue of the
waves,[2] lining long strips of golden sand, compensated for
the want of softness by a semblance of savage gorgeous-
ness.

Next morning (7th July), before the cerulean hue had
vanished from the hills, we set sail. It was not long before
we came to a proper sense of our position. The box containing my store of provisions, and, worse still, my
opium, was at the bottom of the hold, perfectly unapproachable ; we had, therefore, the pleasure of breaking our fast on " Mare's skin,"[3] and a species of biscuit,
hard as a stone and quite as tasteless. During the day,
whilst insufferable splendour reigned above, the dashing
of the waters below kept my nest in a state of perpetual
drench. At night rose a cold, bright moon, with dews
falling so thick and clammy that the skin felt as though
it would never be dry again. It is, also, by no means pleas-

---

to fix their choice.   It extends from Zafaran Point to Hammam
Bluffs, ten miles of deep water.

1 The Hebrew name of this part of the Red Sea. In a communication lately made to the Royal Geographical Society, I gave my
reasons for believing that the Greeks borrowed their Erythræan Sea
from the Arabic " Sea of Himyar."

2 Most travellers remark that they have never seen a brighter
blue than that of the Red Sea. It was the observation of an early
age that " the Rede Sea is not more rede than any other sea, but in
some place thereof is the gravelle rede, and therefore men clepen it
the Rede Sea."

3 Jild al-Faras (or Kamar al-Din), a composition of apricot paste,
dried, spread out, and folded into sheets, exactly resembling the
article after which it is named. Turks and Arabs use it when travelling ; they dissolve it in water, and eat it as a relish with bread or
biscuit.

ant to sleep upon a broken cot about four feet long by two broad, with the certainty that a false movement would throw you overboard, and a conviction that if you do fall from a Sambuk under sail, no mortal power can save you. And as under all circumstances in the East, dozing is one's chief occupation, the reader will understand that the want of it left me in utter, utter idleness.

The gale was light that day, and the sunbeams were fire ; our crew preferred crouching in the shade of the sail to taking advantage of what wind there was. In spite of our impatience we made but little way : near evening time we anchored on a tongue of sand, about two miles distant from the well-known and picturesque heights called by the Arabs Hammam Faraún,[1] which

> —" like giants stand
> To sentinel enchanted land."

The strip of coarse quartz and sandstone gravel is obviously the offspring of some mountain torrent ; it stretches southwards, being probably disposed in that direction by the currents of the sea as they receive the deposit. The distance of the " Hammam Bluffs " prevented my visiting them, which circumstance I regretted the less as they have been described by pens equal to the task.

That evening we enjoyed ourselves upon clean sand, whose surface, drifted by the wind into small yellow waves, was easily converted by a little digging and heaping up, into the coolest and most comfortable of couches. Indeed, after the canescent heat of the day, and the tossing of our ill-conditioned vessel, we should have been contented with lodgings far less luxurious. Fuel was readily collected, and while some bathed, others

---

1 " Pharaoh's hot baths," which in our maps are called " Hummum Bluffs." They are truly " enchanted land " in Moslem fable : a volume would scarcely contain the legends that have been told and written about them. (See Note 1, p. 10, ante.)

erected a hearth—three large stones and a hole open to leeward—lit the fire and put the pot on to boil. Shaykh Nur had fortunately a line; we had been successful in fishing; a little rice also had been bought; with this boiled, and rock-cod broiled upon the charcoal, we made a dinner that caused every one to forget the sore grievance of "Mare's skin" and stone-hard biscuit. A few Maghrabis had ventured on shore, the Rais having terrified the others by threatening them with those "bogies," the Badawin—and they offered us Kuskusu[1] in exchange for fish. As evening fell, we determined, before sleeping, to work upon their "morale" as effectually as we had attacked their physique. Shaykh Hamid stood up and indulged them with the Azan, or call to prayers, pronounced after the fashion of Al-Madinah.[2] They performed their devotions in lines ranged behind us as a token of respect, and when worship was over we were questioned about the Holy City till we grew tired of answering. Again our heads and shoulders, our hands and knees,[3] were kissed, but this time in devotion, not in penitence. My companions could scarcely understand half the rugged words which the Maghrabis used,[4] as their dialect was fresh from the

---

1 One of the numerous species of what the Italians generally call "Pasta." The material is wheaten or barley flour rolled into small round grains. In Barbary it is cooked by steaming, and served up with hard boiled eggs and mutton, sprinkled with red pepper. These Badawi Maghrabis merely boiled it.

2 The Azan is differently pronounced, though similarly worded by every orthodox nation in Al-Islam.

3 The usual way of kissing the knee is to place the finger tips upon it, and then to raise them to the mouth. It is an action denoting great humility, and the condescending superior who is not an immediate master returns the compliment in the same way.

4 The Maghrabi dialect is known to be the harshest and most guttural form of Arabic. It owes this unenviable superiority to its frequency of "Sukun," or the quiescence of one or more consonants;—"K'lab," for instance, for "Kilab," and "'Msik" for "Amsik."

distant Desert. Still we succeeded in making ourselves intelligible to them, vaunting our dignity as the Sons of the Prophet, and the sanctity of our land which should protect its children from every description of fraud and violence. We benignantly promised to be their guides at Al-Madinah, and the boy Mohammed would conduct their devotions at Meccah, always provided that they repented their past misdeeds, avoided any repetition of the same, and promised to perform the duties of good and faithful pilgrims. Presently the Rais joined our party, and the usual story-telling began. The old man knew the name of each hill, and had a legend for every nook and corner in sight. He dwelt at length upon the life of Abu Zulaymah, the patron saint of these seas, whose little tomb stands at no great distance from our bivouac place, and told us how he sits watching over the safety of pious mariners in a cave among the neighbouring rocks, and sipping his coffee, which is brought in a raw state from Meccah by green birds, and prepared in the usual way by the hands of ministering angels. He showed us the spot where the terrible king of Egypt, when close upon the heels of the children of Israel, was whelmed in the " hell of waters,[1] " and he warned us that next day our way would be through breakers, and reefs, and dangerous currents, over whose troubled depths, since that awful day, the Ifrít of the storm has never ceased to flap his sable wing. The wincing of the hearers proved that the shaft of the old man's words was sharp ; but as night was advancing, we unrolled our rugs, and fell asleep upon the sand, all of us happy, for we had fed and drunk, and

---

Thus it is that vowels, the soft and liquid part of language, disappear, leaving in their place a barbarous sounding mass of consonants.

1 Burckhardt mentions the Arab legend that the spirits of the drowned Egyptians may be seen moving at the bottom of the sea, and Finati adds that they are ever busy recruiting their numbers with shipwrecked mariners.

—the *homo sapiens* is a hopeful animal—we made sure that
on the morrow the Ifrit would be merciful, and allow us
to eat fresh dates at the harbour of Tur.

Fair visions of dates doomed to the Limbo of things
which should have been! The grey dawn (8th July) looked
down upon us in difficulties. The water is deep near this
coast; we had anchored at high tide close to the shore, and
the ebb had left us high and dry. When this fact became
apparent, a storm was upon the point of breaking. The
Maghrabis, but for our interference, would have bastinadoed the Rais, who, they said with some reason,
ought to have known better. When this phase of feeling
passed away, they applied themselves to physical efforts.
All except the women and children, who stood on the
shore encouraging their relatives with shrill quaverings,
threw themselves into the water; some pushed, others
applied their shoulders to the vessel's side, and all used
their lungs with might and main. But the "Golden
Wire" was firmly fixed, and their exertions were too irregular. Muscular force failed, upon which they changed
their tactics. At the suggestion of their "Maula," they
prepared to burn incense in honour of the Shaykh Abu
Zulaymah. The material not being forthcoming, they
used coffee, which perhaps accounts for the shortcomings
of that holy man. After this the Rais remembered that
their previous exertions had not begun under the auspices
of the Fatihah. Therefore they prayed, and then re-
applied themselves to work. Still they failed. Finally,
each man called aloud upon his own particular saint or
spiritual guide, and rushed forward as if he alone sufficed
for the exploit. Shaykh Hamid unwisely quoted the
name, and begged the assistance, of his great ancestor,
the "Clarified-Butter-Seller"; the obdurate "Golden
Wire" was not moved, and Hamid retired in momentary
confusion.

It was now about nine A.M., and the water had risen

considerably. My morning had been passed in watching
the influx of the tide, and the grotesque efforts of the
Maghrabis. When the vessel showed some symptoms of
unsteadiness, I arose, walked gravely up to her, ranged
the pilgrims around her with their shoulders to the sides,
and told them to heave with might when they heard
me invoke the revered name of my patron saint. I raised
my hands and voice ; " Ya Piran Pir ! Ya Abd al-Kadir
Jilani¹ " was the signal. Each Maghrabi worked like an
Atlas, the " Golden Wire " canted half over, and, sliding
heavily through the sand, once more floated off into deep
water. This was generally voted a minor miracle, and
the Effendi was respected—for a day or two.

The wind was fair, but we had all to re-embark, an
operation which went on till noon. After starting I remarked the natural cause which gives this Birkat Faraun—
" Pharaoh's Bay,"—a bad name. Here the gulf narrows ;
and the winds, which rush down the clefts and valleys of
the lofty mountains on the Eastern and Western shores,
meeting tides and counter-currents, cause a perpetual
commotion. That day the foam-tipped waves repeatedly
washed over my cot, by no means diminishing its discomforts. In the evening, or rather late in the afternoon,
we anchored, to our infinite disgust, under a ridge of
rocks, behind which lies the plain of Tur. The Rais
deterred all from going on shore by terrible stories about
the Badawin that haunt the place, besides which there
was no sand to sleep upon. We remained, therefore, on
board that night ; and, making sail early the next morning,
we threaded through reefs and sand-banks about noon
into the intricate and dangerous entrance of Tur.

Nothing can be meaner than the present appearance
of the old Phœnician colony, although its position as a

---

¹ I thus called upon a celebrated Sufi or mystic, whom many
East-Indian Moslems reverence as the Arabs do their Prophet. In
Appendix I the curious reader will find Abd al-Kadir again mentioned.

harbour, and its plentiful supply of fruit and fresh water, make it one of the most frequented places on the coast. The only remains of any antiquity—except the wells—are the fortifications which the Portuguese erected to keep out the Badawin. The little town lies upon a plain that stretches with a gradual rise from the sea to the lofty mountain-axis of the Sinaitic group. The country around reminded me strongly of maritime Sind; a flat of clay and sand, clothed with sparse turfs of Salsolæ, and bearing strong signs of a (geologically speaking) recent origin. The town is inhabited principally by Greek and other Christians,[1] who live by selling water and provisions to ships. A fleecy cloud hung lightly over the majestic head of Jabal Tur, about eventide, and the outlines of the giant hills stood " picked out " from the clear blue sky. Our Rais, weather-wise man, warned us that these were indications of a gale, and that, in case of rough weather, he did not intend to leave Tur. I was not sorry to hear this. We had passed a pleasant day, drinking sweet water, and eating the dates, grapes, and pomegranates, which the people of the place carry down to the beach for the benefit of hungry pilgrims. Besides which, there were various sights to see, and with these we might profitably spend the morrow. We therefore pitched the tent upon the sand, and busied ourselves with

---

1 Those people are descendants of Syrians and Greeks that fled from Candia, Scios, the Ionian Islands, and Palestine to escape the persecutions of the Turks. They now wear the Arab dress, and speak the language of the country, but they are easily to be distinguished from the Moslems by the expression of their countenances and sometimes by their blue eyes and light hair. There are also a few families calling themselves Jabaliyah, or mountaineers. Originally they were 100 households, sent by Justinian to serve the convent of St. Catherine, and to defend it against the Berbers. Sultan Kansuh al-Ghori, called by European writers Campson Gaury, the Mamluk King of Egypt, in A.D. 1501, admitted these people into the Moslem community on condition of their continuing the menial service they had afforded to the monks.

extricating a box of provisions: the labour was rendered lighter by the absence of the Maghrabis, some of whom were wandering about the beach, whilst others had gone off to fill their bags with fresh water. We found their surliness insufferable; even when we were passing from poop to forecastle, landing or boarding, they grumbled forth their dissatisfaction.

Our Rais was not mistaken in his prediction. The fleecy cloud on Tur's tops had given true warning. When morning (9th July) broke, we found the wind strong, and the sea white with foam. Most of us thought lightly of these terrors, but our valorous captain swore that he dared not for his life cross in such a storm the mouth of ill-omened Akabah. We breakfasted, therefore, and afterwards set out to visit Moses' Hot Baths, mounted on wretched donkeys with pack-saddles, ignorant of stirrups, and without tails, whilst we ourselves suffered generally from boils, which, as usual upon a journey, make their appearance in localities the most inconvenient. Our road lay northward across the plain towards a long narrow strip of date ground, surrounded by a ruinous mud wall. After a ride of two or three miles, we entered the gardens, and came suddenly upon the Hammam. It is a prim little Cockney bungalow, built by Abbas Pasha of Egypt for his own accommodation; glaringly whitewashed, and garnished with diwans and calico curtains of a gorgeous hue. The guardian had been warned of our visit, and was present to supply us with bathing-cloths and other necessaries. One by one we entered the cistern, which is now in an inner room. The water is about four feet deep, warm in winter, cool in summer, of a saltish-bitter taste, but celebrated for its invigorating qualities, when applied externally. On one side of the calcareous rock, near the ground, is the hole opened for the spring by Moses' rod, which must have been like the " mast of some tall

Ammiral[1]"; and near it are the marks of Moses' nails—deep indentations in the stone, which were probably left there by some extinct Saurian. Our Cicerone informed us that formerly the finger-marks existed, and that they were long enough for a man to lie in. The same functionary attributed the sanitary properties of the spring to the blessings of the Prophet, and, when asked why Moses had not made sweet water to flow, informed us that the Great Lawgiver had intended the spring for bathing in, not for drinking. We sat with him, eating the small yellow dates of Tur, which are delicious, melting like honey in the mouth, and leaving a surpassing *arrière goût*. After finishing sundry pipes and cups of coffee, we gave the bath-man a few piastres, and, mounting our donkeys, started eastward for the Bir Musa,[2] which we reached in half an hour. It is a fine old work, built round and domed over with roughly squared stones, very like what may be seen in some rustic parts of Southern England. The sides of the pit were so rugged that a man could climb down them, and at the bottom was a pool of water, sweet and abundant. We had intended to stay there, and to dine *al fresco*, but the hated faces of our companions, the Maghrabis, meeting us at the entrance, nipped that project in the bud. Accordingly we retired from the burning

---

1 Adam's forehead (says the Tarikh Tabari) brushed the skies, but this height being inconvenient, the Lord abridged it to 100 cubits. The Moslems firmly believe in Anakim. Josephus informs us that Moses was of "divine form and great tallness"; the Arabs specify his stature,—300 cubits. They have, moreover, found his grave in some parts of the country S.E, of the Dead Sea, and make cups of a kind of bitumen called "Moses' Stones." This people *nescit ignorare*—it *will* know everything.

2 "Moses' Well." I have no argument except the untrustworthy traditions of the Badawin, either for or against this having been the identical well near which Moses sat when he fled from the face of Pharaoh to the land of Midian. One thing is certain, namely, that in this part of Arabia, as also at Aden, the wells are of a very ancient date.

sun to a neighbouring coffee-house—a shed of palm leaves kept by a Tur man, and there, seated on mats, we demolished the contents of our basket. Whilst we were eating, some Badawin came in and joined us, when invited so to do. They were poorly dressed, and all armed with knives and cheap sabres, hanging to leathern bandoleers: in language and demeanour they showed few remains of their old ferocity. As late as Mohammed Ali's time these people were noted wreckers, and formerly they were dreaded pirates: now they are lions with their fangs and claws drawn.

In the even, when we returned to our tent, a Syrian, one of our party on the poop, came out to meet us with the information that several large vessels had arrived from Suez, comparatively speaking, empty, and that the captain of one of them would land us at Yambu' for three dollars a head. The proposal was tempting. But presently it became apparent that my companions were unwilling to shift their precious boxes, and moreover, that I should have to pay for those who could not or would not pay for themselves,—that is to say, for the whole party. As such a display of wealth would have been unadvisable, I dismissed the idea with a sigh. Amongst the large vessels was one freighted with Persian pilgrims, a most disagreeable race of men on a journey or a voyage. They would not land at first, because they feared the Badawin. They would not take water from the town people, because some of these were Christians. Moreover, they insisted upon making their own call to prayer, which heretical proceeding—it admits five extra words—our party, orthodox Moslems, would rather have died than have permitted. When their crier, a small wizen-faced man, began the Azan with a voice

> " in quel tenore
> Che fa il cappon quando talvolta canta,"

we received it with a shout of derision, and some, hastily

snatching up their weapons, offered him an opportunity of martyrdom. The Maghrabis, too, hearing that the Persians were Rafaz (heretics) crowded fiercely round to do a little Jihad, or Fighting for the Faith. The long-bearded men took the alarm. They were twice the number of our small party, and therefore they had been in the habit of strutting about with nonchalance, and looking at us fixedly, and otherwise demeaning themselves in an indecorous way. But when it came to the point, they showed the white feather. These Persians accompanied us to the end of our voyage. As they approached the Holy Land, visions of the "Nabbut" caused a change for the better in their manners. At Mahar they meekly endured a variety of insults, and at Yambu' they cringed to us like dogs.

CHAPTER XI.

TO YAMBU'.

ON the 11th July, 1853, about dawn, we left Tur, after a pleasant halt, with the unpleasant certainty of not touching ground for thirty-six hours. I passed the time in steadfast contemplation of the web of my umbrella, and in making the following meteorological remarks.

Morning.—The air is mild and balmy as that of an Italian spring ; thick mists roll down the valleys along the sea, and a haze like mother-o'-pearl crowns the headlands. The distant rocks show Titanic walls, lofty donjons, huge projecting bastions, and moats full of deep shade. At their base runs a sea of amethyst, and as earth receives the first touches of light, their summits, almost transparent, mingle with the jasper tints of the sky. Nothing can be more delicious than this hour. But as

> " les plus belles choses
> Ont le pire destin,"

so lovely Morning soon fades. The sun bursts up from behind the main, a fierce enemy, a foe that will force every one to crouch before him. He dyes the sky orange, and the sea " incarnadine," where its violet surface is stained by his rays, and he mercilessly puts to flight the mists and haze and the little agate-coloured masses of cloud that were before floating in the firmament. The atmosphere is so clear that now and then a planet is visible. For the two hours following sunrise the rays are endurable; after that they become a fiery ordeal.   The morning beams oppress you with a feeling of sickness; their steady glow, reflected by the glaring waters, blinds your eyes, blisters your skin, and parches your mouth : you now become a monomaniac; you do nothing but count the slow hours that must " minute by " before you can be relieved.[1]

Midday.—The wind, reverberated by the glowing hills is like the blast of a lime-kiln.   All colour melts away with the canescence from above.   The sky is a dead milk-white, and the mirror-like sea so reflects the tint that you can scarcely distinguish the line of the horizon. After noon the wind sleeps upon the reeking shore ; there is a deep stillness ; the only sound heard is the melancholy flapping of the sail.   Men are not so much sleeping as half-senseless ; they feel as if a few more degrees of heat would be death.

Sunset.—The enemy sinks behind the deep cerulean sea, under a canopy of gigantic rainbow which covers half the face of heaven.   Nearest to the horizon is an arch of tawny orange ; above it another of the brightest gold, and based upon these a semi-circle of tender sea-green blends with a score of delicate gradations into the sapphire sky.   Across the rainbow the sun throws its rays in the form of giant wheel-spokes tinged with a beautiful pink.   The Eastern sky is mantled with a purple flush that picks out the forms of the hazy Desert and the sharp-cut Hills.   Language is a thing too cold, too poor, to express the harmony and the majesty of this hour, which is as evanescent, however, as it is lovely.   Night falls rapidly, when suddenly the appearance of the Zodiacal Light[2] re-

---

1 The reader who has travelled in the East will feel that I am not exaggerating.   And to convince those who know it only by description, I will refer them to any account of our early campaigns in Sind, where many a European soldier has been taken up stone dead after sleeping an hour or two in the morning sun.

2 The Zodiacal Light on the Red Sea, and in Bombay, is far

stores the scene to what it was. Again the grey hills and
the grim rocks become rosy or golden, the palms green,
the sands saffron, and the sea wears a lilac surface of
dimpling waves. But after a quarter of an hour all fades
once more; the cliffs are naked and ghastly under the
moon, whose light falling upon this wilderness of white
crags and pinnacles is most strange—most mysterious.

Night.—The horizon is all darkness, and the sea
reflects the white visage of the night-sun as in a mirror of
steel. In the air we see giant columns of pallid light,
distinct, based upon the indigo-coloured waves, and
standing with their heads lost in endless space. The
stars glitter with exceeding brilliance.[1] At this hour are

> " — river and hill and wood,
> With all the numberless goings on of life,
> Inaudible as dreams " ;

while the planets look down upon you with the faces of
smiling friends. You feel the " sweet influence of the
Pleiades." You are bound by the "bond of Orion." Hes-
perus bears with him a thousand things. In communion
with them your hours pass swiftly by, till the heavy dews
warn you to cover up your face and sleep. And with
one look at a certain little Star in the north, under which
lies all that makes life worth living through—surely it
is a venial superstition to sleep with your eyes towards
that Kiblah!—you fall into oblivion.

Those thirty-six hours were a trial even to the hard-
headed Badawin. The Syrian and his two friends fell
ill. Omar Effendi, it is true, had the courage to say his

---

brighter than in England. I suppose this is the " after-glow "
described by Miss Martineau and other travellers : " flashes of light
like coruscations of the Aurora Borealis in pyramidal form " would
exactly describe the phenomenon. It varies, however, greatly, and
often for some days together is scarcely visible.

1 Niebuhr considers that the stars are brighter in Norway than
in the Arabian deserts ; I never saw them so bright as on the Neil-
gherry hills.

sunset prayers, but the exertion so altered him that he looked another man. Salih Shakkar in despair ate dates till threatened with a dysentery. Sa'ad the Demon had rigged out for himself a cot three feet long, which, arched over with bent bamboo, and covered with cloaks, he had slung on to the larboard side; but the loud grumbling which proceeded from his nest proved that his precaution had not been a cure. Even the boy Mohammed forgot to chatter, to scold, to smoke, and to make himself generally disagreeable. The Turkish baby appeared to be dying, and was not strong enough to wail. How the poor mother stood her trials so well, made every one wonder. The most pleasant trait in my companions' characters was the consideration they showed to her, and their attention to her children. Whenever one of the party drew forth a little delicacy—a few dates or a pomegranate—they gave away a share of it to the children, and most of them took their turns to nurse the baby. This was genuine politeness—kindness of heart. It would be well for those who sweepingly accuse Easterns of want of gallantry, to contrast this trait of character with the savage scenes of civilisation that take place among the " Overlands " at Cairo and Suez.[1] No foreigner could be present for the first time without bearing away the lasting impression that the sons of Great Britain are model barbarians.[2] On board the " Golden Wire " Salih Shakkar was the sole base exception to the general geniality of my companions.

As the sun starts towards the West, falling harmlessly upon our heads, we arise, still faint and dizzy, calling for water—which before we had not the strength

---

1 Written in the days of the vans, which preceded the Railway.

2 On one occasion I was obliged personally to exert myself to prevent a party of ladies being thrust into an old and bad transit-van ; the ruder sex having stationed itself at some distance from the starting-place in order to seize upon the best.

to drink—and pipes, and coffee, and similar luxuries. Our primitive kitchen is a square wooden box, lined with clay, and filled with sand, upon which three or four large stones are placed to form a hearth. Preparations are now made for the evening meal, which is of the simplest description. A little rice, a few dates, or an onion, will keep a man alive in our position ; a single " good dinner " would justify long odds against his seeing the next evening. Moreover, it is impossible in such cases to have an appetite—fortunately, as our store of provisions is a scanty one. Arabs consider it desirable on a journey to eat hot food once in the twenty-four hours ; so we determine to cook, despite all difficulties. The operation, however, is by no means satisfactory ; twenty expectants surround the single fire, and there is sure to be a quarrel amongst them every five minutes.

As the breeze, cooled by the dew, begins to fan our parched faces, we recover our spirits amazingly. Songs are sung; tales are told; and rough jests are bandied about till, not unfrequently, Oriental sensitiveness is sorely tried. Or, if we see the prospect of storm or calm, we draw forth, and piously peruse, a " Hizb al-Bahr." As this prayer is supposed to make all safe upon the ocean wave, I will not selfishly withhold it from the British reader. To draw forth all its virtues, the reciter should receive it from the hands of his Murshid or spiritual guide, and study it during the Chillah, or forty days of fast, of which, I venture to observe, few Sons of Bull are capable.

" O Allah, O Exalted, O Almighty, O All-pitiful, O All-powerful, Thou art my God, and sufficeth to me the knowledge of it ! Glorified be the Lord my Lord, and glorified be the Faith my Faith ! Thou givest Victory to whom Thou pleasest, and Thou art the Glorious, the Merciful ! We pray Thee for Safety in our goings forth and our standings still, in our Words and our Designs, in our

Dangers of Temptation and Doubt, and the secret Designs of our Hearts. Subject unto us this Sea, even as Thou didst subject the Deep to Musa" (Moses), "and as Thou didst subject the Fire to Ibrahim [1] " (Abraham), "and as Thou didst subject the Iron to Dáúd [2] " (David), "and as Thou didst subject the Wind and the Devils and Jinnis and Mankind to Sulayman [3] " (Solomon), "and as Thou didst subject the Moon and Al-Burak to Mohammed, upon whom be Allah's Mercy and His Blessing! And subject unto us all the Seas in Earth and Heaven, in Thy visible and in Thine invisible Worlds, the Sea of this Life, and the Sea of Futurity. O Thou who reignest over everything, and unto whom all Things return, Khyas! Khyas! Khyas [4]!"

And lastly, we lie down upon our cribs, wrapped up in thickly padded cotton coverlets; we forget the troubles of the past day, and we care nought for the discomforts of that to come.

Late on the evening of the 11th July we passed in sight of the narrow mouth of Al-'Akabah, whose *famosi rupes* are a terror to the voyagers of these latitudes. Like the Gulf of Cambay, here a tempest is said to be always brewing, and men raise their hands to pray as they cross it. We had no storm that day from without, but a fierce one was about to burst within our ship. The essence of Oriental discipline is personal respect based upon fear. Therefore it often happens that the commanding officer,

---

1 Abraham, for breaking his father's idols, was cast by Nimrod into a fiery furnace, which forthwith became a garden of roses. (See Chapter xxi. of the Koran, called " the Prophets.")

2 David worked as an armourer, but the steel was as wax in his hands.

3 Solomon reigned over the three orders of created beings: the fable of his flying carpet is well known. (See Chapter xxvii. of the Koran, called " the Ant.")

4 These are mystic words, and entirely beyond the reach of dictionaries and vocabularies.

if a mild old gentleman, is the last person whose command is obeyed,—his only privilege being that of sitting
apart from his inferiors. And such was the case with our
Rais. On the present occasion, irritated by the refusal
of the Maghrabis to stand out of the steerman's way,
and excited by the prospect of losing sight of shore for a
whole day, he threatened one of the fellows with his
slipper. It required all our exertions, even to a display
of the dreaded quarter-staves, to calm the consequent excitement. After passing Al-'Akabah, we saw nothing but
sea and sky, and we spent a weary night and day tossing
upon the waters, our only exercise ; every face brightened as, about sunset on the 12th July, we suddenly
glided into the mooring-place.

Marsá (anchorage) Damghah,[1] or rather Dumayghah,
is scarcely visible from the sea. An islet of limestone
rock defends the entrance, leaving a narrow passage to
the south. It is not before he enters that the mariner
discovers the extent and the depth of this creek, which
indents far into the land, and offers 15 to 20 feet of fine
clear anchorage which no swell can reach. Inside it
looks more like a lake, and at night its colour is gloriously
blue as Geneva itself. I could not help calling to mind,
after dinner, the old school lines—

> " Est in secessu longo locus ; insula portum
> Efficit objectu laterum ; quibus omnis ab alto
> Frangitur, inque sinus scindit sese unda reductos."

Nothing was wanted but the " atrum nemus." Where
however, shall we find such luxuries in arid Arabia ?

The Rais, as usual, attempted to deter us from landing, by romancing about the " Bedoynes and Ascopards,"
representing them to be " folke ryghte felonouse and
foule and of cursed kynde." To which we replied by
shouldering our Nabbuts and scrambling into the cock-

---

1 In Moresby's Survey, "Sherm Demerah," the creek of Demerah. Ali Bey calls it Demeg.

boat. On shore we saw a few wretched-looking beings, Juhaynah[1] or Hutaym, seated upon heaps of dried wood, which they sold to travellers; and three boat-loads of Syrian pilgrims who had preceded us. We often envied them their small swift craft, with their double latine sails disposed in " hare-ears " which, about eventide in the far distance, looked like a white gull alighting upon the purple wave; and they justified our jealousy by arriving at Yambu' two days before us. The pilgrims had bivouacked upon the beach, and were engaged in drinking their after-dinner coffee. They received us with all the rights of hospitality, as natives of Al-Madinah should everywhere be received; we sat an hour with them, ate a little fruit, satisfied our thirst, smoked their pipes, and when taking leave blessed them. Then returning to the vessel we fed, and lost no time in falling asleep.

The dawn of the next day saw our sail flapping in the idle air. And it was not without difficulty that in the course of the forenoon we entered Wijh Harbour, distant from Dumayghah but very few miles. Al-Wijh is also a natural anchorage, in no way differing from that where we passed the night, except in being smaller and shallower and less secure. From this place to Cairo the road is safe. The town is a collection of round huts meanly built of round stones, and clustering upon a piece of elevated rock on the northern side of the creek. It is

---

1 See " The Land of Midian (Revisited) " for a plan of Al-Dumayghah, and a description of Al-Wijh (al-Bahr) These men of the Beni Jahaynah, or " Juhaynah " tribe—the " Beni Kalb," as they are also called,—must not be trusted. They extend from the plains north of Yambu' into the Sinaitic Peninsula. They boast no connection with the great tribe Al-Harb; but they are of noble race, are celebrated for fighting, and, it is said, have good horses. The specimens we saw at Marsa Dumayghah were poor ones, they had few clothes, and no arms except the usual Jambiyah (crooked dagger). By their civility and their cringing style of address it was easy to see they had been corrupted by intercourse with strangers.

distant about six miles from the inland fort of the same name, which receives the Egyptian caravan, and which thrives, like its port, by selling water and provisions to pilgrims. The little bazar, almost washed by every high tide, provided us with mutton, rice, baked bread, and the other necessaries of life at a moderate rate. Luxuries also were to be found : a druggist sold me an ounce of opium at a Chinese price.

With reeling limbs we landed at Al-Wijh,[1] and finding a large coffee-house above and near the beach, we installed ourselves there. But the Persians who preceded us had occupied all the shady places outside, and were correcting their teeth with their case knives ; we were forced to content ourselves with the interior. It was a building of artless construction, consisting of little but a roof supported by wooden posts, roughly hewn from date trees : round the tamped earthen floor ran a raised bench of unbaked brick, forming a diwan for mats and sleeping-rugs. In the centre a huge square Mastabah, or platform, answered a similar purpose. Here and there appeared attempts at long and side walls, but these superfluities had been allowed to admit daylight through large gaps. In one corner stood the apparatus of the " Kahwahji," an altar-like elevation, also of earthen-work, containing a hole for a charcoal fire, upon which were three huge coffee-pots dirtily tinned. Near it were ranged the Shishas, or Egyptian hookahs, old, exceedingly unclean, and worn by age and hard work. A wooden framework, pierced with circular apertures, supported a number of porous earthen-ware *gullehs* (*gargoulettes*, or monkey jars) full of cold, sweet water ; the charge for each was, as usual in Al-Hijaz, five paras. Such was the furniture of the café, and the only relief to the barrenness of the view was a fine mellowing atmosphere composed of smoke, steam,

---

1 It is written Wish and Wejh ; by Ali Bey Vadjeh and Wadjih ; Wodjeh and Wosh by Burckhardt ; and Wedge by Moresby.

flies, and gnats in about equal proportions.   I have been diffuse in my description of the coffee-house, as it was a type of its class : from Alexandria to Aden the traveller will everywhere meet with buildings of the same kind.

Our happiness in this Paradise—for such it was to us after the "Golden Wire"—was nearly sacrificed by Sa'ad the Demon, whose abominable temper led him at once into a quarrel with the master of the café. And the latter, an ill-looking, squint-eyed, low-browed, broad-shouldered fellow, showed himself nowise unwilling to meet the Demon half way.   The two worthies, after a brief bandying of bad words, seized each other's throats leisurely, so as to give the spectators time and encouragement to interfere.   But when friends and acquaintances were hanging on to both heroes so firmly that they could not move hand or arm, their wrath, as usual, rose, till it was terrible to see.   The little village resounded with the war, and many a sturdy knave rushed in, sword or cudgel in hand, so as not to lose the sport.   During the heat of the fray, a pistol which was in Omar Effendi's hand went off—accidentally of course—and the ball passed so close to the tins containing the black and muddy Mocha, that it drew the attention of all parties. As if by magic, the storm was lulled.   A friend recognised Sa'ad the Demon, and swore that he was no black slave, but a soldier at Al-Madinah—" no waiter, but a Knight Templar."   This caused him to be looked upon as rather a distinguished man, and he proved his right to the honour by insisting that his late enemy should feed with him, and when the other decorously hung back, by dragging him to dinner with loud cries.

My *alias* that day was severely tried.   Besides the Persian pilgrims, a number of nondescripts who came in the same vessel were hanging about the coffee-house ; lying down, smoking, drinking water, bathing and picking their teeth with their daggers.   One inquisitive man

was always at my side. He called himself a Pathan
(Afghan settled in India) ; he could speak five or six
languages, he knew a number of people everywhere, and
he had travelled far and wide over Central Asia. These fellows are always good detectors of an incognito. I avoided
answering his question about my native place, and after
telling him that I had no longer name or nation, being a
Darwaysh, I asked him, when he insisted upon my having
been born somewhere, to guess for himself. To my joy
he claimed me for a brother Pathan, and in course of
conversation he declared himself to be the nephew of an
Afghan merchant, a gallant old man who had been civil
to me at Cairo. We then sat smoking together with
" effusion." Becoming confidential, he complained that
he, a Sunni, or orthodox Moslem, had been abused, mal-
treated, and beaten by his fellow-travellers, the heretical
Persian pilgrims. I naturally offered to arm my party, to
take up our cudgels, and to revenge my compatriot. This
thoroughly Sulaymanian style of doing business could not
fail to make him sure of his man. He declined, however,
wisely remembering that he had nearly a fortnight of the
Persians' society still to endure. But he promised himself the gratification, when he reached Meccah, of
sheathing his Charay[1] in the chief offender's heart.

At 8 a.m. on the 14th July we left Al-Wijh, after passing a night, tolerably comfortable by contrast, in the coffee-
house. We took with us the stores necessary, for though
our Rais had promised to anchor under Jabal Hassáni that
evening, no one believed him. We sailed among ledges of
rock, golden sands, green weeds, and in some places
through yellow lines of what appeared to me at a distance
foam after a storm. All day a sailor sat upon the mast-
head, looking at the water, which was transparent as blue
glass, and shouting out the direction. This precaution
was somewhat stultified by the roar of voices, which never

---

1 The terrible Afghan knife.

failed to mingle with the warning, but we wore every half hour, and we did not run aground. About midday we passed by Shaykh Hasan al-Marábit's tomb. It is the usual domed and whitewashed building, surrounded by the hovels of its guardians, standing upon a low flat island of yellow rock, vividly reminding me of certain scenes in Sind. Its dreary position attracts to it the attention of passing travellers; the dead saint has a prayer and a Fatihah for the good of his soul, and the live sinner wends his way with religious refreshment.

Near sunset the wind came on to blow freshly, and we cast anchor together with the Persian pilgrims upon a rock. This was one of the celebrated coral reefs of the Red Sea, and the sight justified Forskal's emphatic description—*luxus lususque naturæ*. It was a huge ledge or platform rising but little above the level of the deep; the water-side was perpendicular as the wall of a fort; and, whilst a frigate might have floated within a yard of it, every ripple dashed over the reef, replenishing the little basins and hollows in the surface. The colour of the waves near it was a vivid amethyst. In the distance the eye rested upon what appeared to be meadows of brilliant flowers resembling those of earth, only far brighter and more lovely. Nor was this Land of the Sea wholly desolate. Gulls and terns here swam the tide; there, seated upon the coral, devoured their prey. In the air, troops of birds contended noisily for a dead flying fish,[1] and in the deep water they chased a shoal, which, in fright and hurry to escape the pursuers, veiled the surface with

---

1 These the Arabs, in the vulgar tongue, call Jarad al-Bahr, " sea locusts "; as they term the shrimp Burghút al-Bahr, or the sea-flea. Such compound words, palpably derived from land objects, prove the present Ichthyophagi and the Badawin living on the coast to be a race originally from the interior. Pure and ancient Arabs still have at least one uncompounded word to express every object familiar to them, and it is in this point that the genius of the language chiefly shows itself.

spray and foam. And as night came on the scene shifted, displaying fresh beauties. Shadows clothed the background, whose features, dimly revealed, allowed full scope to the imagination. In the forepart of the picture lay the sea, shining under the rays of the moon with a metallic lustre; while its border, where the wavelets dashed upon the reef, was lit by what the Arabs call the "jewels of the deep[1]"—brilliant flashes of phosphoric light giving an idea of splendour which Art would vainly strive to imitate. Altogether it was a bit of fairyland, a spot for nymphs and sea-gods to disport upon : you might have heard, without astonishment, old Proteus calling his flocks with the writhed conch; and Aphrodite seated in her shell would have been only a fit and proper climax for its loveliness.

But—as philosophically remarked by Sir Cauline the Knyghte—

> " Every whyte must have its blacke,
> And every sweete its soure— "

this charming coral reef was nearly being the scene of an ugly accident. The breeze from seaward set us slowly but steadily towards the reef, a fact of which we soon became conscious. Our anchor was not dragging; it had not rope enough to touch the bottom, and vainly we sought for more. In fact the "Golden Wire" was as disgracefully deficient in all the appliances of safety, as any English merchantman in the nineteenth century,—a circumstance which accounts for the shipwrecks and for the terrible loss of life perpetually occurring about the Pilgrimage-season in these seas. Had she struck upon the razor-like edges of the coral-reef, she would have melted

---

1 The Arab superstition is, that these flashes of light are jewels made to adorn the necks and hair of the mermaids and mermen. When removed from their native elements the gems fade and disappear. If I remember right, there is some idea similar to this among the Scotch, and other Northern people.

away like a sugar-plum in the ripple, for the tide was rising at the time. Having nothing better to do, we began to make as much noise as possible. Fortunately for us, the Rais commanding the Persian's boat was an Arab from Jeddah; and more than once we had treated him with great civility. Guessing the cause of our distress, he sent two sailors overboard with a cable ; they swam gallantly up to us ; and in a few minutes we were safely moored to the stern of our useful neighbour. Which done, we applied ourselves to the grateful task of beating our Rais, and richly had he deserved it. Before noon, when the wind was shifting, he had not once given himself the trouble to wear ; and when the breeze was falling, he preferred dosing to taking advantage of what little wind remained. With energy we might have been moored that night comfortably under the side of Hassani Island, instead of floating about on an unquiet sea with a lee-shore of coral-reef within a few yards of our counter.

At dawn the next day (15th July) we started. We made Jabal Hassani[1] about noon, and an hour or so before sunset we glided into Marsa Mahár. Our resting-place resembled Marsa Dumayghah at an humble distance ; the sides of the cove, however, were bolder and more precipitous. The limestone rocks presented a peculiar appearance; in some parts the base and walls had crumbled away, leaving a coping to project like a canopy ; in others the wind and rain had cut deep holes, and pierced the friable material with caverns that looked like the work of art. There was a pretty opening of backwood at the bottom of the

---

1 The word Jabal will frequently occur in these pages. It is applied by the Arabs to any rising ground or heap of rocks, and, therefore, must not always be translated " Mountain." In the latter sense, it has found its way into some of the Mediterranean dialects. Gibraltar is Jabal al-Tárik, and " Mt. Ethne that men clepen Mounte Gybelle " is " Monte Gibello,"—*the* mountain, par excellence.

cove; and palm trees in the blue distance gladdened our
eyes, which pined for the sight of something green. The
Rais, as usual, would have terrified us with a description
of the Hutaym tribe that holds these parts, and I knew
from Welsted and Moresby that it is a debased race.
But forty-eight hours of cramps on board ship would
make a man think lightly of a much more imminent
danger.

Wading to shore we cut our feet with the sharp
rocks. I remember to have felt the acute pain of something running into my toe: but after looking at the place
and extracting what appeared to be a bit of thorn,[1] I dismissed the subject, little guessing the trouble it was to
give me. Having scaled the rocky side of the cove, we
found some half-naked Arabs lying in the shade; they
were unarmed, and had nothing about them except their
villainous countenances wherewith to terrify the most
timid. These men still live in limestone caves, like the
Thamud tribe of tradition ; also they are Ichthyophagi,
existing without any other subsistence but what the sea
affords. They were unable to provide us with dates, flesh,
or milk, but they sold us a kind of fish called in India
" Bui": broiled upon the embers, it proved delicious.

After we had eaten and drunk and smoked, we began
to make merry; and the Persians, who, fearing to come
on shore, had kept to their conveyance, appeared proper
butts for the wit of some of our party: one of us stood
up and pronounced the orthodox call to prayer, after which
the rest joined in a polemical hymn, exalting the virtues

---

1 It was most probably a prickle of the " egg-fruit," or *Echinus*,
so common in these seas, generally supposed to be poisonous. I
found it impossible to cure my foot in Al-Hijaz, and every remedy
seemed to make it worse. This was as much the effect of the climate
of Arabia, as of the hardships and privations of a pilgrimage. After
my return to Egypt in the autumn, the wound healed readily without medical treatment.

and dignity of the first three Caliphs.[1] Then, as general on such occasions, the matter was made personal by informing the Persians in a kind of rhyme sung by the Meccan *gamins*, that they were the " slippers of Ali and the dogs of Omar." But as they were too frightened to reply, my companions gathered up their cooking utensils, and returned to the " Golden Wire," melancholy, like disappointed candidates for the honours of Donnybrook.

Our next day was silent and weary, for we were all surly, and heartily sick of being on board ship. We should have made Yambu' in the evening but for the laziness of the Rais. Having duly beaten him, we anchored on the open coast, insufficiently protected by a reef, and almost in sight of our destination. In the distance rose Jabal Radhwah or Radhwa,[2] one of the "Mountains of Paradise[3]" in which honoured Arabia abounds. It is celebrated by poetry as well as by piety.

> " Did Radhwah strive to support my woes,
> Radhwah itself would be crushed by the weight,"

says Antar.[4] It supplies Al-Madinah with hones. I heard much of its valleys and fruits and bubbling springs, but afterwards I learned to rank these tales with the superstitious legends which are attached to it. Gazing at its bare and ghastly heights, one of our party, whose wit was soured by the want of fresh bread, surlily remarked that such a heap of ugliness deserved ejection from heaven,—an irreverence too public to escape general denunciation. We waded on shore, cooked there, and

---

1 Abu Bakr, Omar, and Osman.

2 I have found both these forms of writing the word in books; Moresby, or rather Mr. Rassam, erroneously spells it " Ridwah."

3 In a future chapter, when describing a visit to Mt. Ohod, near Al-Madinah, I shall enter into some details about these " Mountains of Paradise."

4 The translator, however, erroneously informs us, in a footnote, that Radhwah is a mountain near Meccah.

passed the night; we were short of fresh water, which, combined with other grievances, made us as surly as bears. Sa'ad the Demon was especially vicious; his eyes gazed fixedly on the ground, his lips protruded till you might have held up his face by them, his mouth was garnished with bad wrinkles, and he never opened it but he grumbled out a wicked word. He solaced himself that evening by crawling slowly on all-fours over the boy Mohammed, taking scrupulous care to place one knee upon the sleeper's face. The youth awoke in a fiery rage : we all roared with laughter ; and the sulky Negro, after savouring the success of his spite, grimly, as but half satisfied, rolled himself, like a hedgehog, into a ball ; and, resolving to be offensive even in his forgetfulness, snored violently all night.

We slept upon the sands and arose before dawn (July 17), determined to make the Rais start in time that day. A slip of land separated us from our haven, but the wind was foul, and by reason of rocks and shoals, we had to make a considerable *détour*.

It was about noon on the twelfth day after our departure from Suez, when, after slowly beating up the narrow creek leading to Yambu' harbour, we sprang into a shore-boat and felt new life when bidding an eternal adieu to the vile "Golden Wire."

I might have escaped much of this hardship and suffering by hiring a vessel to myself. There would then have been a cabin to retire into at night, and shade from the sun ; moreover, the voyage would have lasted five, not twelve, days. But I wished to witness the scenes on board a pilgrim ship,—scenes so much talked of by the Moslem palmer home-returned. Moreover, the hire was exorbitant, ranging from £40 to £50, and it would have led to a greater expenditure, as the man who can afford to take a boat must pay in proportion during his land journey.   In these countries you perforce go on as you begin: to "break one's expenditure," that is to say, to retrench expenses, is considered all but impossible.   We have now left the land of Egypt.

CHAPTER XII.

THE HALT AT YAMBU'.

THE heat of the sun, the heavy dews, and the frequent washings of the waves, had so affected my foot, that on landing at Yambu' I could scarcely place it upon the ground. But traveller's duty was to be done; so, leaning upon my "slave's" shoulder, I started at once to see the town, whilst Shaykh Hamid and the others of our party proceeded to the custom-house.

Yanbu'a al-Bahr, Yambu' or Fountain of the Sea,[1] identified, by Abyssinian Bruce, with the Iambia village of Ptolemy, is a place of considerable importance, and shares with others the title of "Gate of the Holy City." It is the third quarter of the caravan road[2] from Cairo to Meccah; and here, as well as at Al-Badr, pilgrims frequently leave behind them, in hired warehouses, goods too heavy to be transported in haste, or too valuable to risk in dangerous times. Yambu' being the port of Al-

---

1 Yanbu'a in Arabic is "a Fountain." Yanbu'a of the Sea is so called to distinguish it from "Yanbu'a of the Palm-Grounds," a village at the foot of the mountains, about 18 or 20 miles distant from the sea-port. Ali Bey places it one day's journey E. ¼ N.E. from Yanbu'a al-Bahr, and describes it as a pleasant place in a fertile valley. It is now known as Yambu'a al-Nakhil. See "The Land of Midian (Revisited)."

2 The first quarter of the Cairo caravan is Al-Akabah; the second is the Manhal Salmah (Salmah's place for watering camels); the third is Yambu'; and the fourth Meccah.

Madinah, as Jeddah is of Meccah, is supported by a considerable transport trade and extensive imports from the harbours on the Western coasts of the Red Sea; it supplies its chief town with grain, dates, and henna. Here the Sultan's dominion is supposed to begin, whilst the authority of the Pasha of Egypt ceases; there is no Nizám, or Regular Army, however, in the town,[1] and the governor is a Sharíf or Arab chief. I met him in the great bazar; he is a fine young man of light complexion and the usual high profile, handsomely dressed, with a Cashmere turband, armed to the extent of sword and dagger, and followed by two large, fierce-looking Negro slaves leaning upon enormous Nabbuts.

The town itself is in no wise remarkable. Built on the edge of a sunburnt plain that extends between the mountains and the sea, it fronts the northern extremity of a narrow winding creek. Viewed from the harbour, it is a long line of buildings, whose painful whiteness is set off by a sky-like cobalt and a sea-like indigo; behind it lies the flat, here of a bistre-brown, there of a lively tawny; whilst the background is formed by dismal Radh-wah,

> "Barren and bare, unsightly, unadorned."

Outside the walls are a few little domes and tombs, which by no means merit attention. Inside, the streets are wide; and each habitation is placed at an unsociable distance from its neighbour, except near the port and the bazars, where ground is valuable. The houses are roughly built of limestone and coralline, and their walls full of fossils crumble like almond cake; they have huge

---

1 The Nizam, as Europeans now know, is the regular Turkish infantry. In Al-Hijaz, these troops are not stationed in small towns like Yambu'. At such places a party of Irregular horse, for the purpose of escorting travellers, is deemed sufficient. The Yambu' police seems to consist of the Sharif's sturdy negroes. In Ali Bey's time Yambu' belonged to the Sharif of Meccah, and was garrisoned by him.

hanging windows, and look mean after those in the Moslem quarters of Cairo. There is a "Suk," or market-street of the usual form, a long narrow lane darkened by a covering of palm leaves, with little shops let into the walls of the houses on both sides. The cafés, which abound here, have already been described in the last chapter; they are rendered dirty in the extreme by travellers, and it is impossible to sit in them without a fan to drive away the flies. The custom-house fronts the landing-place upon the harbour; it is managed by Turkish officials,—men dressed in Tarbushes, who repose the livelong day upon the Diwans near the windows. In the case of us travellers they had a very simple way of doing business, charging each person of the party three piastres for each large box, but by no means troubling themselves to meddle with the contents.[1] Yambu' also boasts of a Hammam or hot bath, a mere date-leaf shed, tenanted by an old Turk, who, with his surly Albanian assistant, lives by "cleaning" pilgrims and travellers. Some whitewashed Mosques and Minarets of exceedingly simple form, a Wakalah or two for the reception of merchants, and a saint's tomb, complete the list of public buildings.

In one point Yambu' claims superiority over most other towns in this part of Al-Hijaz. Those who can afford the luxury drink sweet rain-water, collected amongst the hills in tanks and cisterns, and brought on camel-back to the town. Two sources are especially praised, the Ayn al-Birkat and the Ayn Ali, which suffice to supply the whole population: the brackish water of the wells is confined to coarser purposes. Some of the old people here, as at Suez, are said to prefer the drink to which

---

1 This, as far as I could learn, is the only tax which the Sultan's government derives from the northern Hijaz; the people declare it to be, as one might expect at this distance from the capital, liable to gross peculation. When the Wahhabis held Yambu', they assessed it, like all other places; for which reason their name is held in the liveliest abhorrence.

years of habit have accustomed them, and it is a standing joke that, arrived at Cairo, they salt the water of the Nile to make it palatable.

The population of Yambu'—one of the most bigoted and quarrelsome races in Al-Hijaz—strikes the eye after arriving from Egypt, as decidedly a new feature. The Shaykh or gentleman is over-armed and over-dressed, as Fashion, the Tyrant of the Desert as well as of the Court, dictates to a person of his consequence. The civilised traveller from Al-Madinah sticks in his waist-shawl a loaded pistol,[1] garnished with crimson silk cord, but he partially conceals the butt-end under the flap of his jacket. The Irregular soldier struts down the street a small armoury of weapons : one look at the man's countenance suffices to tell you what he is. Here and there stalk grim Badawin, wild as their native wastes, and in all the dignity of pride and dirt ; they also are armed to the teeth, and even the presence of the police-man's quarterstaff[2] cannot keep their swords in their scabbards. What we should call the peaceful part of the population never leave the house without the "Nabbut" over the right shoulder, and the larger, the longer, and the heavier the weapon is, the more gallantry does the bearer claim. The people of Yambu' practise the use of this implement diligently ; they become expert in delivering

---

1 Civilians usually stick one pistol in the belt ; soldiers and fighting men two, or more, with all the necessary concomitants of pouches, turnscrews, and long iron ramrods, which, opening with a screw, disclose a long thin pair of pincers, wherewith fire is put upon the chibuk.

2 The weapons with which nations are to be managed form a curious consideration. The Englishman tamely endures a staff, which would make a Frenchman mad with anger ; and a Frenchman respects a sabre, which would fill an Englishman's bosom with civilian spleen. You order the Egyptian to strip and be flogged ; he makes no objection to seeing his blood flow in this way ; but were a cutting weapon used, his friends would stop at nothing in their fury.

a head-blow so violent as to break through any guard, and with it they always decide their trivial quarrels.[1] The dress of the women differs but little from that of the Egyptians, except in the face veil,[2] which is generally white. There is an independent bearing about the Yambu' men, strange in the East; they are proud without insolence, and they look manly without blustering. Their walk partakes somewhat of the nature of a swagger, owing, perhaps, to the shape of the sandals, not a little assisted by the self-esteem of the wearer, but there is nothing offensive in it: moreover, the population has a healthy appearance, and, fresh from Egypt, I could not help noticing their freedom from ophthalmic disease. The children, too, appear vigorous, nor are they here kept in that state of filth to which fear of the Evil Eye devotes them in the Valley of the Nile.

My companions found me in a coffee-house, where I had sat down to rest from the fatigue of halting on my wounded foot through the town. They had passed their boxes through the custom-house, and were now inquiring in all directions, "Where's the Effendi?" After sitting for half an hour, we rose to depart, when an old Arab merchant, whom I had met at Suez, politely insisted

---

1 In Arabia, generally, the wound is less considered by justice and revenge, than the instrument with which it was inflicted. Sticks and stones are held to be venial weapons: guns and pistols, swords and daggers, are felonious.

2 Europeans inveigh against this article,—which represents the " loup" of Louis XIV.'s time,— for its hideousness and jealous concealment of charms made to be admired. It is, on the contrary, the most coquettish article of woman's attire, excepting, perhaps, the *Lisám* of Constantinople. It conceals coarse skins, fleshy noses, wide mouths, and vanishing chins, whilst it sets off to best advantage what in these lands is almost always lustrous and liquid—the eye. Who has not remarked this at a masquerade ball?

upon paying for my coffee, still a mark of attention in
Arabia as it was whilome in France. We then went to a
Wakalah, near the bazar, in which my companions had
secured an airy upper room on the terrace opposite the
sea, and tolerably free from Yambu's plague, the flies.
It had been tenanted by a party of travellers, who were
introduced to me as Omar Effendi's brothers; he had by
accident met them in the streets the day before their
start for Constantinople, where they were travelling to
receive the Ikram.[1] The family was, as I have said
before, from Daghistan (Circassia), and the male members still showed unequivocal signs of a northern origin,
in light yellowish skins, grey eyes fringed with dark
lashes, red lips, and a very scant beard. They were
broad-shouldered, large-limbed men, distinguished only
by a peculiar surliness of countenance; perhaps their
expression was the result of their suspecting me; for
I observed them narrowly watching every movement
during *Wuzu* and prayers. This was a good opportunity for displaying the perfect *nonchalance* of a True
Believer; and my efforts were, I believe, successful, for
afterwards they seemed to treat me as a mere stranger,
from whom they could expect nothing, and who therefore was hardly worth their notice.

On the afternoon of the day of our arrival we sent
for a *Mukharrij*,[2] (hirer of conveyance) and began to
treat for camels. One Amm Jamal, a respectable
native of Al-Madinah who was on his way home, under-
took to be the spokesman; after a long palaver (for

---

1 A certain stipend allowed by the Sultan to citizens of the Haramayn (Meccah and Al-Madinah). It will be treated of at length in a
future chapter.

2 The Shaykh, or agent of the camels, without whose assistance
it would be difficult to hire beasts. He brings the Badawin with
him; talks them over to fair terms; sees the "Arbún," or earnest-
money, delivered to them; and is answerable for their not failing in
their engagement.

the Shaykh of the camels and his attendant Badawin
were men that fought for farthings, and we were not
far inferior to them), a bargain was struck. We
agreed to pay three dollars for each beast; half in
ready money, the other half after reaching our destination, and to start on the evening of the next day
with a grain-caravan, guarded by an escort of Irregular
cavalry. I hired two animals, one for my luggage and
servant, the other for the boy Mohammed and myself,
expressly stipulating that we were to ride the better beast,
and that if it broke down on the road, its place should be
supplied by another as good. My friends could not
dissemble their uneasiness, when informed by the *Mukharrij* that the Hazimi tribe was "out," and that
travellers had to fight every day. The Daghistanis also
contributed to their alarm. "We met," said they,
"between 200 and 300 devils on a Razzia near Al-
Madinah; we gave them the Salam, but they would not
reply, although we were all on dromedaries. Then they
asked us if we were men of Al-Madinah, and we replied
'Yes;' and lastly, they wanted to know the end of our
journey; so we said Bir Abbas.[1]" The Badawin who
had accompanied the Daghistanis belonged to some tribe
unconnected with the Hazimi: the spokesman rolled his
head, as much as to say "Allah has preserved us!"
And a young Indian of the party—I shrewdly suspect
him of having stolen my pen-knife that night—displayed

---

1 The not returning "Salam" was a sign on the part of the
Badawin that they were out to fight, and not to make friends; and
the dromedary riders, who generally travel without much to rob,
thought this behaviour a declaration of desperate designs. The
Badawin asked if they were Al-Madinah men; because the former do
not like, unless when absolutely necessary, to plunder the people of
the Holy City. And the Daghistanis said their destination was Bir
Abbas, a neighbouring, instead of Yambu', a distant post, because
those who travel on a long journey, being supposed to have more
funds with them, are more likely to be molested.

the cowardice of a "*Miyan*,[1]" by looking aghast at the memory of his imminent and deadly risk. "Sir," said Shaykh Nur to me, "we must wait till all this is over." I told him to hold his tongue, and sharply reproved the boy Mohammed, upon whose manner the effect of finding himself suddenly in a fresh country had wrought a change for the worse. "Why, ye were lions at Cairo; and here, at Yambu', you are cats—hens![2]" It was not long, however, before the youth's impudence returned upon him with increased violence.

We sat through the afternoon in the little room on the terrace, whose reflected heat, together with the fiery winds from the Wilderness, seemed to incommode even my companions. After sunset we dined in the open air, a body of twenty: master, servants, children and strangers. All the procurable rugs and pillows had been seized to make a Diwan, and we squatted together round a large cauldron of boiled rice, containing square masses of mutton, the whole covered with clarified butter. Sa'ad the Demon was now in his glory. With what anecdotes the occasion supplied him! His tongue seemed to wag with a perpetual motion; for each man he had a boisterous greeting; and, to judge from his whisperings, he must have been in every one's privacy and confidence. Conversation over pipes and coffee was prolonged to ten P.M., a late hour in these lands; then we prayed the

---

1 "*Miyan*," the Hindustani word for "Sir," is known to the Badawin all over Al-Hijaz; they always address Indian Moslems with this word, which has become contemptuous, on account of the low esteem in which the race is held.

2 That is to say, sneaks and cowards. I was astonished to see our Maghrabi fellow-passengers in the bazar at Yambu' cringing and bowing to us, more like courtiers than Badawin. Such, however, is the effect of a strange place upon Orientals generally. In the Persians such humility was excusable; in no part of Al-Hijaz are they for a moment safe from abuse and blows.

Ishá[1] (or vespers), and, spreading our mats upon the terrace, slept in the open air.

The forenoon of the next day was occupied in making sundry small purchases. We laid in seven days' provisions for the journey; repacked our boxes, polished and loaded our arms, and attired ourselves appropriately for the road. By the advice of Amm Jamal[2] I dressed as an Arab, in order to avoid paying the *Jizyat*, a capitation tax[3] which, upon this road, the settled tribes extort from stranger travellers; and he warned me not to speak any language but Arabic, even to my "slave," in the vicinity of a village. I bought for my own convenience a *Shugduf* or litter[4] for which I paid two dollars. It is a

---

1 The night prayer.

2 "Amm" means literally a paternal uncle. In the Hijaz it is prefixed to the names of respectable men, who may also be addressed "Ya Amm Jamal!" (O Uncle Jamal!) To say "Ya Ammi!" (O my Uncle!) is more familiar, and would generally be used by a superior addressing an inferior.

3 Jizyat properly means the capitation tax levied on Infidels; in this land of intense pride, the Badawin, and even the town-chiefs, apply the opprobrious term to blackmail extorted from travellers, even of their own creed.

4 The Shugduf of Al-Hijaz differs greatly from that used in Syria and other countries. It is composed of two corded cots 5 feet long, slung horizontally, about half-way down, and parallel with the camel's sides. These cots have short legs, and at the halt may be used as bedsteads; the two are connected together by loose ropes, attached to the inner long sides of the framework, and these are thrown over the camel's packsaddle. Thick twigs inserted in the ends and the outer long sides of the framework, are bent over the top, bower-fashion, to support matting, carpets, and any other protection against the sun. There is an opening in this kind of wicker-work in front (towards the camel's head), through which you creep; and a similar one behind creates a draught of wind.

The Mahmil, en déshabille.

vehicle appropriated to women and children, fathers of families, married men, " Shelebis,¹ " and generally to those who are too effeminate to ride. My reason for choosing a litter was that notes are more easily taken in it than on a dromedary's back; the excuse of lameness prevented it detracting from my manhood, and I was careful when entering any populous place to borrow or hire a saddled beast.

Our party dined early that day, for the camels had been sitting at the gate since noon. We had the usual trouble in loading them : the owners of the animals vociferating about the unconscionable weight, the owners of the goods swearing that a child could carry such weight, while the beasts, taking part with their proprietors, moaned piteously, roared, made vicious attempts to bite, and started up with an agility that threw the half-secured boxes or sacks headlong to the ground. About 3 P.M. all was ready — the camels formed into Indian file were placed standing in the streets. But, as usual with Oriental travellers, all the men dispersed about the town : we did not mount before it was late in the afternoon.

I must now take the liberty of presenting to the reader an Arab Shaykh fully equipped for travelling.² Nothing can be more picturesque than the costume, and

Outside, towards the camel's tail, are pockets containing *gullehs*, or earthenware bottles, of cooled water. Inside, attached to the wicker-work, are large provision pouches, similar to those used in old-fashioned travelling chariots. At the bottom are spread the two beds. The greatest disadvantage of the Shugduf is the difficulty of keeping balance. Two men ride in it, and their weights must be made to tally. Moreover, it is liable to be caught and torn by thorn trees, to be blown off in a gale of wind ; and its awkwardness causes the camel repeated falls, which are most likely to smash it. Yet it is not necessarily an uncomfortable machine. Those for sale in the bazar are, of course, worthless, being made of badly seasoned wood. But private litters are sometimes pleasant vehicles, with turned and painted framework, silk cordage, and valuable carpets. The often described " Mahmil " is nothing but a Syrian Shugduf, royally ornamented.

1 " Exquisites."

2 It is the same rule with the Arab, on the road as at home; the

AN ARAB SHAYKH,
IN HIS TRAVELLING DRESS.

it is with regret that we see it exchanged in the towns and more civilised parts for any other. The long locks or the shaven scalps are surmounted by a white cotton skull-cap, over which is a Kúfíyah—a large square kerchief of silk and cotton mixed, and generally of a dull red colour with a bright yellow border, from which depend crimson silk twists ending in little tassels that reach the wearer's waist. Doubled into a triangle, and bound with an *Aakal*[1] or fillet of rope, a skein of yarn or a twist of wool, the kerchief fits the head close behind : it projects over the forehead, shading the eyes, and giving a fierce look to the countenance. On certain occasions one end is brought round the lower part of the face, and is fastened behind the head. This veiling the features is technically called *Lisám :* the chiefs generally fight so, and it is the usual disguise when a man fears the avenger of blood, or a woman starts to take her *Sar*.[2] In hot weather it is supposed to keep the Samun, in cold weather the catarrh, from the lungs.

more he is dressed the greater is his respectability. For this reason, you see Sharifs and other men of high family, riding or walking in their warm camel's hair robes on the hottest days. Another superstition of the Arabs is this, that thick clothes avert the evil effects of the sun's beams, by keeping out heat. To the kindness of a friend —Thomas Seddon—I owe the admirable sketch of an "Arab Shaykh in his Travelling Dress."

1 Sharifs and other great men sometimes bind a white turband or a Cashmere shawl round the kerchief, to keep it in its place. The

Aakal varies in every part of the country. Here it is a twist of dyed wool, there a bit of common rope, three or four feet long. Some of the Arab tribes use a circlet of wood, composed of little round pieces, the size of a shilling, joined side by side, and inlaid with mother-of-pearl. The Eastern Arabs wear a large circle of brown wool, almost a turband in itself. In Barbary, they twist brightcoloured cloth round a rope, and adorn it with thick golden thread.

2 Generally written "*Thár*," the blood-revenge right, acknowledged by law and custom. (See Chapter xxiv. post.)

The body dress is simply a *Kamís* or cotton shirt: tight sleeved, opening in front, and adorned round the waist and collar, and down the breast, with embroidery like net-work; it extends from neck to foot. Some wear wide trousers, but the Badawin consider such things effeminate, and they have not yet fallen into the folly of socks and stockings. Over the Kamis is thrown a long-skirted and short-sleeved cloak of camel's hair, called an Abá. It is made in many patterns, and of all materials from pure silk to coarse sheep's wool; some prefer it brown, others white, others striped: in Al-Hijaz the favourite hue is white, embroidered with gold,[1] tinsel, or yellow thread in two large triangles, capped with broad bands and other figures running down the shoulders and sides of the back. It is lined inside the shoulders and breast with handsome stuffs of silk and cotton mixed, and is tied in front by elaborate strings, and tassels or acorns of silk and gold. A sash confines the Kamis at the waist, and supports the silver-hilted *Jambíyah*[2] or crooked dagger: the picturesque Arab sandal[3] completes the costume. Finally, the

---

1 Gold, however, as well as silk, I may be excused for repeating, is a forbidden article of ornament to the Moslem.

2 The silver-hilted dagger is a sign of dignity: "I would silver my dagger," in idiomatic Hijazi, means, "I would raise myself in the world."

3 Niebuhr has accurately described this article. It is still worn in the Madras army, though long discarded from the other presidencies; the main difference between the Indian and the Arab sandal is, that the former has a ring, into which the big toe is inserted, and the latter a thong, which is clasped between the big toe and its neighbour. Both of them are equally uncomfortable, and equally injurious to soldiers, whose legs fight as much as do their arms. They abrade the skin wherever the straps touch, expose the feet to the sun, wind, and rain, and admit thorns and flints to the toes and toe-nails. In Arabia, the traveller may wear, if he pleases, slippers, but they are

Shaykh's arms are a sword and a matchlock slung behind
his back; in his right hand he carries a short javelin[1] or a
light crooked stick, about two feet and a half long, called
a *Mas'hab*,[2] used for guiding camels.

The poorer clans of Arabs twist round their waist,

---

considered townsman-like and effeminate. They must be of the
usual colours, red or yellow. Black shoes, though almost universally
worn by the Turks at Cairo and Constantinople, would most probably
excite suspicion in Al-Hijaz.

1 The *Mizrák*, as it is called, is peculiar to certain tribes, as the
Karashi and the Lahyami, and some, like the Hudayli near Meccah,
make very pretty as well as very useful darts. The head is 15 or 16
inches long, nowhere broader than an inch, and tapering gradually to
a fine point ; its shape is two shallow prisms joined at their bases,
and its socket, round like that of all lances, measures a little less
than 2 inches. The lower third of the blade only is adorned with
bars, lozenges, and cones of brass let into the iron in zig-zag and
other figures. The shaft is of hard pliant wood—I do not know of
what tree—well seasoned with grease and use; it is 23 inches long,
and strengthened and adorned at distances of half an inch apart by
bands of fine brass wire, about one inch and a half long. The heel
of the weapon is a blunt spike 14 inches long, used to stick it in
the ground, and this, as well as the lower third of the blade, is
ornamented with brass work. Being well balanced, the Mizrak is a
highly efficient weapon for throwing in hunting, and by its handsome appearance adds not a little to the bearer's dignity. But the
stranger must be careful how he so arms himself. Unless he be
undistinguishable from a Badawi, by carrying a weapon peculiar to
certain clans, he will expose himself to suspicion, or to laughter.
And to offend an Arab of Al-Hijaz mortally, you have only to say
bluntly, " Sell me thy spear." The proper style of address to the
man whose necessities compel him to break through one of his
" points d'honneur," is to say, " Give me that javelin, and I will
satisfy thee ;" after which he will haggle for each copper piece as
though you were cheapening a sheep.

2 The Mas'hab is of almond, generally brought from Syria; at
the thick end is a kind of crook, formed by cutting off a bit of the
larger branch from which the stick grows. This crook is afterwards
cut into the shape useful to seize a camel's nose-ring, or a horse's
bridle. Arabs of all degrees are fond of carrying these sticks. [It
is also called *Mághin.*]

next to the skin, a long plait of greasy leather, to support
the back; and they gird the shirt at the middle merely
with a cord, or with a coarse sash.   The dagger is stuck
in this scarf, and a bandoleer slung over the shoulders
carries the cartridge-case, powder-flask, flint and steel,
priming-horn, and other necessaries.   With the traveller,
the waist is an elaborate affair.   Next to the skin is
worn the money-pouch, concealed by the Kamis; the
latter is girt with a waist shawl, over which is strapped
a leathern belt.[1]   The latter article should always be
well garnished with a pair of long-barrelled and silver-
mounted flint pistols,[2] a large and a small dagger, and an

---

1 This article, the Silahlik of the Turks, is composed of several
oblong pieces of leather cut out to fit the front part of the body ;
between each fold there is room enough to stick a weapon ; a substantial strap fastens it round the waist, and it serves to defend the
sash or the shirt from iron mould, and the stains of gunpowder.
It is made of all kinds of material, from plain Morocco leather to
the richest velvet embroidered with gold.

2 It is as well to have a good pair of Turkish barrels and stocks,
fitted up with locks of European manufacture ; those made by
natives of these countries can never be depended upon.   The same
will apply to the gun or rifle.   Upon the whole, it is more prudent
to have flint locks.   Copper caps are now sold in the bazars of
Meccah and Al-Madinah, where a Colt's "six-shooter" might excite
attention for a day; but were the owner in a position to despise
notoriety, he might display it everywhere without danger.   One of
our guards, who was killed on the road, had a double-barrelled
English fowling-piece.   Still, when doubts must not be aroused, the
traveller will do well to avoid, even in the civilised Hijaz, suspicious
appearances in his weapons.   I carried in a secret pocket a small
pistol with a spring dagger, upon which dependence could be placed,
and I was careful never to show it, discharging it and loading it
always in the dark.   Some men wear a little dagger strapped round
the leg, below the knee.   Its use is this: when the enemy gets you
under, he can prevent you bringing your hand up to the weapon in
your waist-belt ; but before he cuts your throat, you may slip your
fingers down to the knee, and persuade him to stop by a stab in the
perineum.   This knee dagger is required only in very dangerous
places.   The article I chiefly accused myself of forgetting was a

iron ramrod with pincers inside; a little leathern pouch fastened to the waist-strap on the right side contains cartridge, wadding, and flask of priming powder. The sword hangs over the shoulder by crimson silk cords and huge tassels[1]: well-dressed men apply the same showy ornaments to their pistols. In the hand may be borne a bell-mouthed blunderbuss; or, better still, a long single-barrel gun with an ounce bore. All these weapons must shine like silver, if you wish to be respected; for the knightly care of arms is here a sign of manliness.

Pilgrims, especially those from Turkey, carry, I have said, a "Hamail," to denote their holy errand. This is a pocket Koran, in a handsome gold-embroidered crimson velvet or red morocco case, slung by red silk cords over the left shoulder. It must hang down by the right side, and should never depend below the waist-belt. For this I substituted a most useful article. To all appearance a "Hamail," it had inside three compartments; one for my watch and compass, the second for ready money, and the third contained penknife, pencils, and slips of paper, which I could hold concealed in the hollow of my hand. These were for writing and drawing: opportunities of making a "fair copy" into the diary-book,[2] are never wanting to the acute traveller. He

stout English clasp-knife, with a large handle, a blade like an "Arkansas toothpick," and possessing the other useful appliances of picker, fleam, tweezers, lancet, and punch.

1 Called "Habak": these cords are made in great quantities at Cairo, which possesses a special bazar for them, and are exported to all the neighbouring countries, where their price considerably increases. A handsome pistol-cord, with its tassels, costs about 12 shillings in Egypt; at Meccah, or Al-Madinah, the same would fetch upwards of a pound sterling.

2 My diary-book was made up for me by a Cairene; it was a long thin volume fitting into a breast-pocket, where it could be carried without being seen. I began by writing notes in the Arabic character, but as no risk appeared, my journal was afterwards kept in English. More than once, by way of experiment, I showed the

must, however, beware of sketching before the Badawin, who would certainly proceed to extreme measures, suspecting him to be a spy or a sorcerer.[1] Nothing so effectually puzzles these people as the Frankish habit of putting everything on paper; their imaginations are set at work, and then the worst may be expected from them. The only safe way of writing in presence of a Badawi would be when drawing out a horoscope or preparing a charm; he also objects not, if you can warm his heart upon the subject, to seeing you take notes in a book of genealogies. You might begin with, "And you, men of Harb, on what origin do you pride yourselves?" And while the listeners became fluent upon the, to them, all-interesting

writing on a loose slip of paper to my companions, and astonished them with the strange character derived from Solomon and Alexander, the Lord of the Two Horns, which we Afghans still use. For a short trip a pencil suffices; on long journeys ink is necessary; the latter article should be English, not Eastern, which is washed out clean the first time your luggage is thoroughly soaked with rain. The traveller may use either the Persian or the brass Egyptian inkstand; the latter, however, is preferable, being stronger and less likely to break. But, unless he be capable of writing and reading a letter correctly, it would be unadvisable to stick such an article in the waist-belt, as this gives out publicly that he is a scribe. When sketching, the pencil is the best, because the simplest and shortest mode of operation is required. Important lines should afterwards be marked with ink, as "fixing" is impossible on such journeys. For prudence sake, when my sketches were made, I cut up the paper into square pieces, numbered them for future reference, and hid them in the tin canisters that contained my medicines.

1 An accident of this kind happened not long ago, in Hazramaut, to a German traveller who shall be nameless. He had the mortification to see his sketch-book, the labour of months, summarily appropriated and destroyed by the Arabs. I was told by a Hazramaut man at Cairo, and by several at Aden, that the gentleman had at the time a narrow escape with his life; the Badawin wished to put him to death as a spy, sent by the Frank to *ensorceler* their country, but the Shaykhs forbade bloodshed, and merely deported the offender. Travellers caught sketching are not often treated with such forbearance.

theme, you could put down whatever you please upon the margin. The townspeople are more liberal, and years ago the Holy Shrines have been drawn, surveyed and even lithographed, by Eastern artists: still, if you wish to avoid all suspicion, you must rarely be seen with pen or with pencil in hand.

At 6 P.M., descending the stairs of our Wakalah, we found the camels standing loaded in the street, and shifting their ground in token of impatience.[1] My Shugduf, perched upon the back of a tall strong animal, nodded and swayed about with his every motion, impressing me with the idea that the first step would throw it over the shoulders or the crupper. The camel-man told me I must climb up the animal's neck, and so creep into the vehicle. But my foot disabling me from such exertion, I insisted upon their bringing the beast to squat, which they did grumblingly.[2] We took leave of Omar Effendi's brothers and their dependents, who insisted upon paying us the compliment of accompanying us to the gate. Then we mounted and started, which was a signal for all our party to disperse once more. Some heard the report of a vessel having arrived from Suez, with Mohammed Shiklibha and other friends on board; these hurried down to the harbour for a parting word. Others, declaring they had forgotten some necessaries for the way, ran off to spend one last hour in gossip at the coffee-house. Then the sun set, and prayers must be said. The brief twilight had almost faded away before all had mounted. With loud cries of "Wassit, ya hú!—

---

1 All Arabs assert that it pains the loaded camel's feet to stand still, and, certainly, the "fidgettiness" of the animal to start, looks as if he had some reason to prefer walking.

2 It often strains the camel to rise with a full Shugduf on his back, besides which the motion is certain to destroy the vehicle in a few days. Those who are unable to climb up the camel's neck usually carry with them a short ladder.

Go in the middle of the road, O He!" and "Jannib,
y'al Jammál[1]!—Keep to the side, O camel-man!" we
threaded our way through long, dusty, narrow streets,
flanked with white-washed habitations at considerable
intervals, and large heaps of rubbish, sometimes higher
than the houses. We were stopped at the gate to
ascertain if we were strangers, in which case, the guard
would have done his best to extract a few piastres before
allowing our luggage to pass; but he soon perceived by
my companions, accent, that they were Sons of the Holy
City,—consequently, that the case was hopeless. While
standing here, Shaykh Hamid vaunted the strong walls
and turrets of Yambu', which he said were superior to
those of Jeddah[2]: they kept Sa'ud, the Wahhabi, at bay
in A.D. 1802, but would scarcely, I should say, resist a
field battery in A.D. 1853. The moon rose fair and clear,
dazzling us with light as we emerged from the shadowy
streets; and when we launched into the Desert, the sweet
air delightfully contrasted with the close offensive atmosphere of the town. My companions, as Arabs will do
on such occasions, began to sing.

---

1 Wassit means, " go in the middle of the road " ; Jannib, " keep
clear of the sides." These words are fair specimens of how much
may be said by two Arabic syllables. Ya hu (O, he) is an address
common in Arabia as in Egypt, and Y'al Jammal (O camel-man) is
perhaps a little more civil.

2 The rivalry between the Sons of the two Holy Cities extends
even to these parts : the Madanis contending for Yambu', the Meccans for Jeddah.

CHAPTER XIII.

FROM YAMBU' TO BIR ABBAS.

On the 18th July, about 7 P.M., we passed through the gate of Yambu', and took a due Easterly course. Our route lay over the plain between the mountains of Radhwah on the left, and the sea on the right hand; the land was desert,—that is to say, a hard level plain, strewed with rounded lumps of granite and greenstone schist, with here and there a dwarf Acacia, and a tuft of rank camel grass. By the light of a glorious moon, nearly at the full, I was able to see the country tolerably well.

Our party consisted of twelve camels, and we travelled in Indian file, head tied to tail, with but one outrider, Omar Effendi, whose rank required him to mount a dromedary with showy trappings. Immediately in front of me was Amm Jamal, whom I had to reprove for asking the boy Mohammed, "Where have you picked up that Hindi, (Indian)?" "Are we, the Afghans, the Indian-slayers,[1] become Indians?" I vociferated with indignation, and brought the thing home to his feelings, by asking him how he, an Arab, would like to be called an Egyptian, —a Fellah? The rest of the party was behind, sitting or dozing upon the rough platforms made by the lids of the two huge boxes slung to the sides of their camels. Only one old woman, Al-Sitt Maryam (the lady Mary), return-

---

[1] Alluding to the celebrated mountain, the "Hindu-kush," whence the Afghans sallied forth to lay waste India.

ing to Al-Madinah, her adopted country, after a visit to a
sister at Cairo, allowed herself the luxury of a half-dollar
Shibriyah or cot, fastened crosswise over the animal's
load.   Moreover, all the party, except Omar Effendi, in
token of poverty, were dressed in the coarsest and dirtiest
of clothes,—the general suit consisting of a shirt torn in
divers places and a bit of rag wrapped round the head.
They carried short chibuks without mouth-pieces, and
tobacco-pouches of greasy leather.   Though the country
hereabouts is perfectly safe, all had their arms in readiness,
and the unusual silence that succeeded to the singing,—
even Sa'ad the Demon held his tongue,—was sufficient to
show how much they feared for their property.   After
a slow march of two hours facing the moon, we turned
somewhat towards the North-East, and began to pass
over undulating ground, in which a steady rise was perceptible.   We arrived at the halting-place at three in the
morning, after a short march of about eight hours, during
which we could not have passed over more than sixteen
miles.[1]   The camels were *nakh'd*[2]; the boxes were taken
off and piled together as a precaution against invisible
robbers ; my little tent, the only one in the party, was
pitched ; we then spread our rugs upon the ground and
lay down to sleep.

We arose at about 9 A.M. (July 19), and after congrat-
ulating one another upon being once more in the "dear
Desert," we proceeded in exhilarated mood to light the
fire for pipes and breakfast.   The meal—a biscuit, a
little rice, and a cup of milkless tea—was soon dispatched, after which I proceeded to inspect our position.

---

1 Throughout this work I have estimated the pace of a Hijazi
camel, laden and walking in caravan line, under ordinary circumstances, at two geographical miles an hour. A sandy plain or a
rocky pass might make a difference of half a mile each way, but not
more.

2 See Chap. VIII., page 152, note 1, ante.

About a mile to the westward lay the little village Al-Musahhal,[1] a group of miserable mud hovels. On the south was a strip of bright blue sea, and all around, an iron plain producing naught but stones and grasshoppers, and bounded northward by a grisly wall of blackish rock. Here and there a shrub fit only for fuel, or a tuft of coarse grass, crisp with heat, met the eye. All was sun-parched; the furious heat from above was drying up the sap and juice of the land, as the simmering and quivering atmosphere showed; moreover the heavy dews of these regions, forming in large drops upon the plants and stones, concentrate the morning rays upon them like a system of burning-glasses. After making these few observations I followed the example of my companions, and returned to sleep.

At two P.M. we were roused to a dinner as simple as the breakfast had been. Boiled rice with an abundance of the clarified butter[2] in which Easterns delight, some fragments of *Kahk* [3] or soft biscuit, and stale bread[4] and a handful of stoned and pressed date-paste, called 'Ajwah, formed the *menu*. Our potations began before dinner with a vile-tasted but wholesome drink called Akit,[5]

---

1 The reader must be warned that these little villages in Arabia, as in Sind and Baluchistan, are continually changing their names, whilst the larger settlements always retain the same. The traveller, too, must beware of writing down the first answer he receives; in one of our maps a village on the Euphrates is gravely named "M'adri," ("Don't know").

2 Here called Samn, the Indian ghee.

3 The "Kahk" in this country is a light and pleasant bread made of ground wheat, kneaded with milk, leavened with sour bean flour, and finally baked in an oven, not, as usual, in the East, upon an iron plate. The Kahk of Egypt is a kind of cake.

4 Stale unleavened bread is much relished by Easterns, who say that keeping it on journeys makes it sweet. To prevent its becoming mouldy, they cut it up into little bits, and, at the risk of hardening it to the consistence of wood, they dry it by exposure to the air.

5 This Akit has different names in all parts of Arabia; even in

dried sour milk dissolved in water ; at the meal we drank the leather-flavoured element, and ended with a large cupful of scalding tea. Enormous quantities of liquid were consumed, for the sun seemed to have got into our throats, and the perspiration trickled as after a shower of rain. Whilst we were eating, a Badawi woman passed close by the tent, leading a flock of sheep and goats, seeing which I expressed a desire to drink milk. My companions sent by one of the camel-men a bit of bread, and asked in exchange for a cupful of "laban.¹" Thus I learned that the Arabs, even in this corrupt region, still adhere to the meaningless custom of their ancestors, who chose to make the term "Labbán²" (milk-seller) an opprobrium and a disgrace. Possibly the origin of the preju-

---

Al-Hijaz it is known by the name of Mazir, as well as "Igt," (the corruption of Akit). When very sour, it is called " Saríbah," and when dried, without boiling, "Jamídah." The Arabs make it by evaporating the serous part of the milk ; the remainder is then formed into cakes or lumps with the hand, and spread upon hair cloth to dry. They eat it with clarified butter, and drink it melted in water. It is considered a cooling and refreshing beverage, but boasts few attractions to the stranger. The Baluchis and wild tribes of Sindians call this preparation of milk " Krút," and make it in the same way as the Badawin do.

1 In Arabic and Hebrew, milk ; the Maltese give the word a very different signification, and the Egyptians, like the Syrians, confine their use of it to sour milk or curds—calling sweet milk " laban halíb," or simply " halíb."

2 In a previous work (History of Sind), I have remarked that there exists some curious similarity in language and customs between the Arabs and the various races occupying the broad ranges of hills that separate India from Persia. Amongst these must be numbered the prejudice alluded to above. The lamented Dr. Stocks, of Bombay, who travelled amongst and observed the Brahui and the Baluchi nomads in the Pashin valley, informed me that, though they will give milk in exchange for other commodities, yet they consider it a disgrace to make money by it. This, methinks, is too conventional a point of honour to have sprung up spontaneously in two countries so distant, and apparently so unconnected.

dice might be the recognising of a traveller's guest-right
to call for milk gratis. However this may be, no one will
in the present day sell this article of consumption, even at
civilised Meccah, except Egyptians, a people supposed to
be utterly without honour. As a general rule in the
Hijaz, milk abounds in the spring, but at all other times
of the year it is difficult to be procured. The Badawi
woman managed, however, to send me back a cupful.

At three P.M. we were ready to start, and all saw, with
unspeakable gratification, a huge black nimbus rise from
the shoulder of Mount Radhwah, and range itself, like a
good genius, between us and our terrible foe, the sun.
We hoped that it contained rain, but presently a blast
of hot wind, like the breath of a volcano, blew over the
plain, and the air was filled with particles of sand.
This is the "dry storm" of Arabia; it appears to depend
upon some electrical phenomena which it would be desirable to investigate.[1] When we had loaded and mounted,
my camel-men, two in number, came up to the Shugduf
and demanded "Bakhshish," which, it appears, they are
now in the habit of doing each time the traveller starts.
I was at first surprised to find the word here, but after
a few days of Badawi society, my wonder diminished.
The men were Beni-Harb of the great Hijazi tribe,
which has kept its blood pure for the last thirteen centuries,—how much more we know not,—but they had
been corrupted by intercourse with pilgrims, retaining
none of their ancestral qualities but greed of gain, re-
vengefulness, pugnacity, and a frantic kind of bravery,
displayed on rare occasions. Their nobility, however,
did not prevent my quoting the Prophet's saying, "Of a
truth, the worst names among the Arabs are the Beni-

---

1 At Aden, as well as in Sind, these dry storms abound, and
there the work of meteorological investigation would be easier than
in Al-Hijaz.

Kalb and the Beni-Harb,[1]" whilst I taunted them severely with their resemblance to the Fellahs of Egypt. They would have resented this with asperity, had it proceeded from their own people, but the Turkish pilgrim—the character in which they knew me, despite my Arab dress—is a privileged person. The outer man of these Fight-Sons was contemptible; small chocolate-coloured beings, stunted and thin, with mops of course bushy hair burned brown by the sun, straggling beards, vicious eyes, frowning brows, screaming voices, and well-made, but attenuated, limbs. On their heads were Kufiyahs in the last stage of wear: a tattered shirt, indigo-dyed, and girt with a bit of common rope, composed their clothing; and their feet were protected from the stones by soles of thick leather, kept in place by narrow thongs tied to the ankle. Both were armed, one with a match-lock, and a *Shintiyan*[2] in a leathern scabbard, slung over the shoulder, the other with a Nabbut, and both showed at the waist the Arab's invariable companion, the *Jambiyah* (dagger). These ragged fellows, however, had their pride. They would eat with me, and not disdain, like certain self-styled Caballeros, to ask for more; but of work they would do none. No promise of "Bakhshish," potent as

---

1 " Beni-Kalb," (or Juhaynah, Chap. X.), would mean the "Dogs'-Sons "—" Beni-Harb," the " Sons of Fight."

2 The Shintiyan is the common sword-blade of the Badawin ; in Western Arabia, it is called Majar (from the Magyars ?), and is said to be of German manufacture. Good old weapons of the proper curve, marked like Andrew Ferraras with a certain number of lines down their length, will fetch, even in Arabia, from £7 to £8. The modern and cheap ones cost about 10s. Excellent weapons abound in this country, the reason being that there is a perpetual demand for them, and when once purchased, they become heir-looms in the family. I have heard that when the Beni Bu Ali tribe, near Ras al-Khaymah, was defeated with slaughter by Sir Lionel Smith's expedition, the victors found many valuable old European blades in the hands of the slain.

the spell of that word is, would induce them to assist in pitching my tent: they even expected Shaykh Nur to cook for them, and I had almost to use violence, for even the just excuse of a sore foot was insufficient to procure the privilege of mounting my Shugduf while the camel was sitting. It was, they said, the custom of the country from time immemorial to use a ladder when legs would not act. I agreed with them, but objected that I had no ladder. At last, wearied with their thick-headedness, I snatched the nose-string of the camel, and by main force made it kneel.

Our party was now strong enough. We had about 200 beasts carrying grain, attended by their proprietors, truculent looking as the contrabandistas of the Pyrenees. The escort was composed of seven Irregular Turkish cavalry, tolerably mounted, and supplied each with an armoury in epitome. They were privily derided by our party, who, being Arabs, had a sneaking fondness for the Badawin, however loth they might be to see them amongst the boxes.

For three hours we travelled in a south-easterly direction upon a hard plain and a sandy flat, on which several waters from the highlands find a passage to the sea westward. Gradually we were siding towards the mountains, and at sunset I observed that we had sensibly neared them. We dismounted for a short halt; and, strangers being present, my companions, before sitting down to smoke, said their prayers—a pious exercise in which they did not engage for three days afterwards, when they met certain acquaintances at Al-Hamrá. As evening came on, we emerged from a scrub of Acacia and Tamarisk and turned due East, traversing an open country with a perceptible rise. Scarcely was it dark before the cry of "Harámi" (thieves) rose loud in the rear, causing such confusion as one may see in a boat in the Bay of Naples when suddenly neared by a waterspout.   All the camel-men brandished their huge staves, and rushed back vociferating in the direction of the robbers.   They were followed by the horsemen; and truly, had the thieves possessed the usual acuteness of the profession, they might have driven off the camels in our van with safety and convenience.[1]   But these contemptible beings were only half a dozen in number, and they had lighted their matchlocks, which drew a bullet or two in their direction.   Whereupon they ran away. This incident aroused no inconsiderable excitement, for it seemed ominous of worse things about to happen to us when entangled in the hills, and the faces of my companions, perfect barometers of fair and foul tidings, fell to zero.   For nine hours we journeyed through a brilliant moonlight, and as the first grey streak appeared in the Eastern sky we entered a scanty *"Misyal,*[2]*"* or *Fiumara,* strewed with pebbles and rounded stones, about half a mile in breadth, and flanked by almost perpendicular hills of primitive formation.   I began by asking the names of peaks and other remarkable spots, when I found that a folio volume would not contain a three months' collection[3]: every hill and dale, flat, valley, and

1 The way of carrying off a camel in this country is to loosen him, and then to hang on heavily to his tail, which causes him to start at full gallop.

2 The Arabic Misyal, Masyal, Masil, or Masilah, is the Indian Nullah and the Sicilian "Fiumara," a hill water-course, which rolls a torrent during and after rain, and is either partially or wholly dry at other seasons,—the stream flowing slowly underground.   In England we want the feature, and therefore there is no single word to express it.   Our "River" is an imperfect way of conveying the idea.

3 Generalisation is not the forte of the Arabic language.   "Al-Kulzum" (the Red Sea), for instance, will be unintelligible to the native of Jeddah; call it the Sea of Jeddah, and you at once explain yourself; so the Badawin will have names for each separate part, but no single one to express the whole.   This might be explained by their ignorance of anything but details.   The same thing is observable, however, in the writings of the Arabian geographers when they come to treat of the objects near home.

water-course here has its proper name or rather names. The ingenuity shown by the Badawin in distinguishing between localities the most similar, is the result of a high organization of the perceptive faculties, perfected by the practice of observing a recurrence of landscape features few in number and varying but little amongst themselves. After travelling two hours up this torrent bed, winding in an Easterly direction, and crossing some "*Harrah*," or ridges of rock, "*Ria*," steep descents,[1] " Kitaah," patch of stony flat, and bits of " Sahil," dwarf plain, we found ourselves about eight A.M., after a march of about thirty-four miles, at Bir Sa'íd (Sa'íd's Well), our destination.

I had been led to expect at the " Well," a pastoral scene, wild flowers, flocks and flowing waters ; so I looked with a jaundiced eye upon a deep hole full of slightly brackish water dug in a tamped hollow—a kind of punch-bowl with granite walls, upon whose grim surface a few thorns of exceeding hardihood braved the sun for a season. Not a house was in sight—it was as barren and desolate a spot as the sun ever "viewed in his wide career." But this is what the Arabian traveller must expect. He is to traverse, for instance, the Wady Al-Ward—the Vale of Flowers. He indulges in sweet recollections of Indian lakes beautiful with the Lotus, and Persian plains upon which Narcissus is the meanest of grasses. He sees a plain like swish-work, where knobs of granite act daisies ; and where, at every fifty yards, some hapless bud or blossom is dying of inanition among the stones.

The sun scorched our feet as we planted the tent, and, after drinking our breakfast, we passed the usual day of perspiration and semi-lethargy. In discomfort man natur-

---

1 About the classic " Harrah," I shall have more to say at a future time. The word " Ria " in literary and in vulgar Arabic is almost synonymous with Akabah, a steep descent, a path between hills or a mountain road.

ally hails a change, even though it be one from bad to
worse.   When our enemy began slanting towards the
West, we felt ready enough to proceed on our journey. The
camels were laden shortly after 3 P.M., July 20th, and
we started, with water jars in our hands, through a storm
of Samun.

We travelled five hours in a North-Easterly course up
a diagonal valley,[1] through a country fantastic in its desolation—a mass of huge hills, barren plains, and desert
vales.   Even the sturdy Acacias here failed, and in some
places the camel grass could not find earth enough for its
root.   The road wound among mountains, rocks and
hills of granite, and over broken ground, flanked by huge
blocks and boulders piled up as if man's art had aided
Nature to disfigure herself.   Vast clefts seamed like scars
the hideous face of earth ; here they widened into dark
caves, there they were choked with glistening drift
sand.   Not a bird or a beast was to be seen or heard ;
their presence would have argued the vicinity of water;
and, though my companions opined that Badawin were
lurking among the rocks, I decided that these Badawin
were the creatures of their fears.   Above, a sky like
polished blue steel, with a tremendous blaze of yellow
light, glared upon us without the thinnest veil of mist
cloud.   Below, the brass-coloured circle scorched the face
and dazzled the eyes, mocking them the while with offers
of water that was but air.   The distant prospect was
more attractive than the near view, because it borrowed
a bright azure tinge from the intervening atmosphere ;
but the jagged peaks and the perpendicular streaks of
shadow down the flanks of the mountainous background

---

1 Valleys may be divided into three kinds.   1. Longitudinal, *i.e.*
parallel to the axis of their ridges ; 2. Transversal or perpendicular
to the same ; and, 3. Diagonal, which form an acute or an obtuse
angle with the main chain of mountains.

showed that yet in store for us was no change for the better.

Between 10 and 11 P.M., we reached human habitations—a phenomenon unseen since we left Al-Musahhal—in the shape of a long straggling village. It is called Al-Hamra, from the redness of the sands near which it is built, or Al-Wasitah, the "half-way," because it is the middle station between Yambu' and Al-Madinah. It is therefore considerably out of place in Burckhardt's map; and those who copy from him make it much nearer the sea-port than it really is. We wandered nearly an hour in search of an encamping station, for the surly villagers ordered us off every flatter bit of ground, without, however, deigning to show us where our jaded beasts might rest. At last, after long wrangling, we found the usual spot; the camels were unloaded, the boxes and baggage were disposed in a circle for greater security against the petty pilferers in which this part of the road abounds, and my companions spread their rugs so as to sleep upon their valuables. I was invited to follow the general example; but I absolutely declined the vicinity of so many steaming and snoring fellow-travellers. Some wonder was excited by the Afghan Haji's obstinacy and recklessness; but resistance to these people is sometimes *bien placé*, and a man from Kabul is allowed to say and to do strange things. In answer to their warnings of nightly peril, I placed a drawn sword by my side[1] and a cocked pistol under my pillow, the saddle-bag: a carpet spread upon the cool loose sand formed by no means an uncomfortable couch, and upon it I enjoyed a sound sleep till day-break.

Rising at dawn (July 21), I proceeded to visit the village. It is built upon a narrow shelf at the top of a precipitous hill to the North, and on the South runs a sandy

---

1 This act, by the bye, I afterwards learned to be a greater act of imprudence than the sleeping alone. Nothing renders the Arab thief so active as the chance of stealing a good weapon.

Fiumara about half a mile broad. On all sides are rocks and mountains rough and stony; so you find yourself in another of those punch-bowls which the Arabs seem to consider choice sites for settlements.[1] The Fiumara, hereabouts very winding, threads the high grounds all the way down from the plateau of Al-Madinah : during the rainy season it becomes a raging torrent, carrying westwards to the Red Sea the drainage of a hundred hills. Water of good quality is readily found in it by digging a few feet below the surface at the angles where the stream forms the deepest hollows, and in some places the stony sides give out bubbling springs.[2]

Al-Hamra itself is a collection of stunted houses or rather hovels, made of unbaked brick and mud, roofed over with palm leaves, and pierced with air-holes, which occasionally boast a bit of plank for a shutter. It appears thickly populated in the parts where the walls are standing, but, like all settlements in the Holy Land, Al-Hijaz,[3] it abounds in ruins. It is well supplied with provisions, which are here cheaper than at Al-Madinah,—a circumstance that induced Sa'ad the Demon to overload his hapless camel with a sack of wheat. In the village are a few shops where grain, huge plantains, ready-made bread, rice,

---

1 Probably, because water is usually found in such places. In the wild parts of the country, wells are generally protected by some fortified building, for men consider themselves safe from an enemy until their supply of water is cut off.

2 Near Al-Hamra, at the base of the Southern hills, within fire of the forts, there is a fine spring of sweet water. All such fountains are much prized by the people, who call them " Rock-water," and attribute to them tonic and digestive virtues.

3 As far as I could discover, the reason of the ruinous state of the country at present is the effect of the old Wahhabi and Egyptian wars in the early part of the present century, and the misrule of the Turks. In Arabia the depopulation of a village or a district is not to be remedied, as in other countries, by an influx of strangers; the land still belongs to the survivors of the tribe, and trespass would be visited with a bloody revenge.

clarified butter, and other edibles are to be purchased.
Palm orchards of considerable extent supply it with dates.
The bazar is, like the generality of such places in the
villages of Eastern Arabia, a long lane, here covered with
matting, there open to the sun, and the narrow streets—
if they may be so called—are full of dust and glare.
Near the encamping ground of caravans is a fort for the
officer commanding a troop of Albanian cavalry, whose
duty it is to defend the village,[1] to hold the country, and
to escort merchant travellers. The building consists of
an outer wall of hewn stone, loopholed for musketry, and
surmounted by "*Shararif*," "*remparts coquets*," about as
useful against artillery as the sugar gallery round a
Twelfth-cake. Nothing would be easier than to take the
place : a false attack would draw off the attention of the
defenders, who in these latitudes know nothing of sentry-
duty, whilst scaling - ladders or a bag full of powder
would command a ready entrance into the other side.
Around the Al-Hamra fort are clusters of palm-leaf huts,
where the soldiery lounge and smoke, and near it is the
usual coffee-house, a shed kept by an Albanian. These
places are frequented probably on account of the intense
heat inside the fort. We passed a comfortless day at the
"Red Village." Large flocks of sheep and goats were
being driven in and out of the place, but their surly
shepherds would give no milk, even in exchange for bread
and meat. The morning was spent in watching certain
Badawin, who, matchlock in hand, had climbed the hills
in pursuit of a troop of cranes : not one bird was hit of
the many fired at—a circumstance which did not say
much for their vaunted marksmanship. Before breakfast I bought a moderately sized sheep for a dollar.

---

1 Without these forts the Turks, at least so said my companions,
could never hold the country against the Badawin. There is a little
amour propre in the assertion, but upon the whole it is true. There
are no Mohammed Alis, Jazzárs, and Ibrahim Pachas in these days.

Shaykh Hamid "*haláled*[1]" (butchered) it, according to
rule, and my companions soon prepared a feast of boiled
mutton.   But that sheep proved a " bone of contention."
The boy Mohammed had, in a fit of economy, sold its
head to a Badawi for three piastres, and the others, disappointed in their anticipations of "haggis," lost temper.
With the "Demon's" voluble tongue and impudent
countenance in the van, they opened such a volley of
raillery and sarcasm upon the young "tripe-seller," that
he in his turn became excited—furious.   I had some
difficulty to keep the peace, for it did not suit my
interests that they should quarrel.   But to do the Arabs
justice, nothing is easier for a man who knows them
than to work upon their good feelings.   "He is a stranger
in your country—a guest!" acted as a charm;   they
listened patiently to Mohammed's gross abuse, only
promising to answer him when in *his* land, that is to
say, near Meccah.   But what especially soured our day
was the report that Sa'ad, the great robber-chief, and
his brother were in the field;   consequently that our
march would be delayed for some time :   every half-hour
some fresh tattle from the camp or the coffee-house added
fuel to the fire of our impatience.

A few particulars about this Schinderhans of Al-
Hijaz[2] may not be unacceptable.   He is the chief of the
Sumaydah and the Mahamid, two influential sub-families
of the Hamídah, the principal family of the Beni-Harb
tribe of Badawin.   He therefore aspired to rule all the
Hamidah, and through them the Beni-Harb, in which
case he would have been, *de facto*, monarch of the Holy
Land.   But the Sharif of Meccah, and Ahmad Pasha,

---

1 To "*halal*" is to kill an animal according to Moslem rites: a
word is wanted to express the act, and we cannot do better than to
borrow it from the people to whom the practice belongs.

2 He is now dead, and has been succeeded by a son worse than
himself.

the Turkish governor of the chief city, for some political reason degraded him, and raised up a rival in the
person of Shaykh Fahd, another ruffian of a similar
stamp, who calls himself chief of the Beni-Amr, the
third sub-family of the Hamidah family. Hence all kinds
of confusion. Sa'ad's people, who number it is said
5000, resent, with Arab asperity, the insult offered to
their chief, and beat Fahd's, who do not amount to 800.
Fahd, supported by the government, cuts off Sa'ad's
supplies. Both are equally wild and reckless, and—nowhere doth the glorious goddess, Liberty, show a more
brazen face than in this Eastern

"Inviolate land of the brave and the free ;"

both seize the opportunity of shooting troopers, of
plundering travellers, and of closing the roads. This
state of things continued till I left the Hijaz, when the
Sharif of Meccah proposed, it was said, to take the field
in person against the arch-robber. And, as will afterwards be seen in these pages, Sa'ad, had the audacity to
turn back the Sultan's Mahmil or litter—the ensign of
Imperial power—and to shut the road against its *cortège*,
because the Pashas of Al-Madinah and of the Damascus
caravan would not guarantee his restitution to his former
dignity. That such vermin is allowed to exist proves the
imbecility of the Turkish government. The Sultan pays
pensions in corn and cloth to the very chiefs who arm
their varlets against him ; and the Pashas, after purloin-
ing all they can, hand over to their enemies the means of
resistance. It is more than probable, that Abd al-Majid
has never heard a word of truth concerning Al-Hijaz,
and that fulsome courtiers persuade him that men there
tremble at his name. His government, however, is
desirous, if report speaks truth, of thrusting Al-Hijaz
upon the Egyptian, who on his side would willingly pay
a large sum to avert such calamity. The Holy Land
drains off Turkish gold and blood in abundance, and the

lords of the country hold in it a contemptible position. If they catch a thief, they dare not hang him. They must pay black-mail, and yet be shot at in every pass. They affect superiority over the Arabs, hate them, and are despised by them. Such in Al-Hijaz are the effects of the charter of Gulkhanah, a panacea, like Holloway's Pills, for all the evils to which Turkish, Arab, Syrian, Greek, Egyptian, Persian, Armenian, Kurd, and Albanian flesh is heir to. Such the results of the Tanzimát, the silliest copy of Europe's folly—bureaucracy and centralisation—that the pen of empirical statecraft ever traced.[1] Under a strong-handed and strong-hearted despotism, like Mohammed Ali's, Al-Hijaz, in one generation, might be purged of its pests. By a proper use of the blood feud; by vigorously supporting the weaker against the stronger classes; by regularly defeating every Badawi who earns a name for himself; and, above all, by the exercise of unsparing, unflinching justice,[2] the few thousands of half-naked bandits, who now make the land a fighting field, would soon sink into utter insignifi-

---

1 The greatest of all its errors was that of appointing to the provinces, instead of the single Pasha of the olden time, three different governors, civil, military, and fiscal, all depending upon the supreme council at Constantinople. Thus each province has three plunderers instead of one, and its affairs are referred to a body that can take no interest in it.

2 Ziyád bin Abihi was sent by Al-Mu'áwiyah, the Caliph, to reform Al-Basrah, a den of thieves; he made a speech, noticed that he meant to rule with the sword, and advised all offenders to leave the city. The inhabitants were forbidden under pain of death to appear in the streets after evening prayers, and dispositions were made to secure the execution of the penalty. Two hundred persons were put to death by the patrol during the first night, only five during the second, and not a drop of blood was shed afterwards. By similar severity, the French put an end to assassination at Naples, and the Austrians at Leghorn. We may deplore the necessity of having recourse to such means, but it is a silly practice to salve the wound which requires the knife.

cance. But to effect such end, the Turks require the old stratocracy, which, bloody as it was, worked with far less misery than the charter and the new code. What Milton calls

" The solid rule of civil government "

has done wonders for the race that nurtured and brought to perfection an idea spontaneous to their organisation. The world has yet to learn that the admirable exotic will thrive amongst the country gentlemen of Monomo-tapa or the ragged nobility of Al-Hijaz.[1] And it requires no prophetic eye to foresee the day when the Wahhabis or the Badawin, rising *en masse*, will rid the land of its feeble conquerors.[2]

Sa'ad, the Old Man of the Mountains, was described to me as a little brown Badawi; contemptible in appear-ance, but remarkable for courage and ready wit. He has for treachery a keen scent, which he requires to keep in exercise. A blood feud with Abd al-Muttalib, the present Sharif of Meccah, who slew his nephew, and the hostility of several Sultans, has rendered his life eventful. He lost all his teeth by poison, which would have killed him, had he not, after swallowing the potion, corrected it by drinking off a large pot-full of clarified butter. Since that time he has lived entirely upon fruits, which he gathers for himself, and

---

1 These remarks were written in 1853 : I see no reason to change them in 1878.

2 A weak monarch, a degenerate government, a state whose cor-ruption is evidenced by moral decay, a revenue bolstered up by a system of treasury paper, which even the public offices discount at from three to six per cent., an army accustomed to be beaten, and dis-organised provinces ; these, together with the proceedings of a ruth-less and advancing enemy, form the points of comparison between the Constantinople of the present day and the Byzantine metropolis eight hundred years ago. Fate has marked upon the Ottoman Empire in Europe "*delenda est*" : we are now witnessing the efforts of human energy and ingenuity to avert or to evade the fiat.

coffee which he prepares with his own hands. In Sultan Mahmud's time he received from Constantinople a gorgeous purse, which he was told to open, as it contained something for his private inspection. Suspecting treachery, he gave it for this purpose to a slave, bidding him carry it to some distance; the bearer was shot by a pistol cunningly fixed, like Rob Roy's, in the folds of the bag. Whether this far-known story be "true or only well found," it is certain that Shaykh Sa'ad now fears the Turks, even "when they bring gifts." The Sultan sends, or is supposed to send him, presents of fine horses, robes of honour, and a large quantity of grain. But the Shaykh, trusting to his hills rather than to steeds, sells them; he gives away the dresses to his slaves, and he distributes the grain amongst his clansmen. Of his character, men, as usual, tell two tales: some praise his charity, and call him the friend of the poor, as certainly as he is a foe to the rich. Others, on the contrary, describe him as cruel, cold-blooded, and notably, even among Arabs, revengeful and avaricious. The truth probably lies between these two extremes, but I observed that those of my companions who spoke most highly of the robber chief when at a distance seemed to be in the *sudori freddi* whilst under the shadow of his hills.

Al-Hamra is the third station from Al-Madinah in the Darb Sultani, the "Sultan's" or "High Road," the Westerly line leading to Meccah along the sea-coast. When the robbers permit, the pilgrims prefer this route on account of its superior climate, the facility of procuring water and supplies, the vicinity of the sea, and the circumstance of its passing through "Badr," the scene of the Prophet's principal military exploits (A.H. 2). After mid-day, on the 21st July, when we had made up our minds that Fate had determined we should halt at Al-Hamra, a caravan arrived from Meccah; and the new travellers had interest to procure an escort, and permission to proceed without delay towards Al-Madinah. The good news filled us with joy. A little after four p.m. we urged our panting camels over the fiery sands to join the Meccans, who were standing ready for the march, on the other side of the torrent bed. An hour afterwards we started in an Easterly direction.

My companions having found friends and relations in the Meccan caravan,—the boy Mohammed's elder brother, about whom more anon, was of the number,—were full of news and excitement. At sunset they prayed with unction : even Sa'ad and Hamid had not the face to sit their camels during the halt, when all around were washing, sanding themselves,[1] and busy with their devotions. We then ate our suppers, remounted, and started once more. Shortly after night set in, we came to a sudden halt. A dozen different reports rose to account for this circumstance, which was occasioned by a band of Badawin, who had manned a gorge, and sent forward a "parliamentary," ordering us forthwith to stop. They at first demanded money to let us pass ; but at last, hearing that we were Sons of the Holy Cities, they granted us transit on the sole condition that the military,—whom they, like Irish peasants, hate and fear,—should return to whence they came. Upon this, our escort, 200 men, wheeled their horses round and galloped back to their barracks. We moved onwards, without, however, seeing any robbers ; my camel-man pointed out their haunts, and showed me a small bird hovering over a place where he supposed water trickled from the rock. The fellow had attempted a sneer at my expense when the fray was impending. " Why don't you load your pistols, Effendi,"

---

[1] When water cannot be obtained for ablution before prayers, Moslems clap the palms of their hands upon the sand, and draw them down the face and both fore-arms. This operation, which is performed once or twice—it varies in different schools—is called Tayammum.

he cried, "and get out of your litter, and show fight?
" Because," I replied as loudly, "in my country, when
dogs run at us, we thrash them with sticks." This
stopped Mansur's mouth for a time, but he and I were
never friends. Like the lowest orders of Orientals, he
required to be ill-treated ; gentleness and condescension
he seemed to consider a proof of cowardice or of imbecility. I began with kindness, but was soon compelled
to use hard words at first, and then threats, which, though
he heard them with frowns and mutterings, produced
manifest symptoms of improvement.

> " Oignez vilain, il vous poindra!
> Poignez vilain, il vous oindra!"

says the old French proverb, and the axiom is more
valuable in the East even than in the West.

Our night's journey had no other incident. We
travelled over rising ground with the moon full in our
faces; and, about midnight, we passed through another long
straggling line of villages, called Jadaydah,[1] or Al-Khayf.[2]
The principal part of it lies on the left of the road going
to Al-Madinah; it has a fort like that of Al-Hamra,
springs of tolerable drinking water, a Nakhil or date-
ground, and a celebrated (dead) saint, Abd al-Rahim al-
Burai. A little beyond it lies the Bughaz[3] or defile,
where in A.D. 1811 Tussún Bey and his 8000 Turks were
totally defeated by 25,000 Harbi Badawin and Wahhabis.[4]

---

1 I write this word as my companions pronounced it. Burck-
hardt similarly gives it "Djedeyde," and Ali Bey "Djideïda."
Giovanni Finati wrongly calls the place "Jedeed Bughaz," which
Mr. Bankes, his editor, rightly translates the "new opening or pass."

2 Al-Khayf is a common name for places in this part of Arabia.
The word literally means a declivity or a place built upon a declivity.

3 Bughaz means in Turkish the fauces, the throat, and signifies
also here a gorge, or a mountain pass. It is the word now commonly
used in Al-Hijaz for the classical "Nakb," or "Mazik." Vincent
(Periplus) errs in deriving the word from the Italian "Bocca."

4 Giovanni Finati, who was present at this hard-fought field

This is a famous attacking-point of the Beni-Harb. In former times both Jazzar Pasha, the celebrated "butcher" of Syria, and Abdullah Pasha of Damascus, were baffled at the gorge of Jadaydah[1]; and this year the commander of the Syrian caravan, afraid of risking an attack at a place so ill-omened, avoided it by marching upon Meccah *viâ* the Desert road of Nijd. At four A.M., having travelled about twenty-four miles due East, we encamped at Bir Abbas.

---

as a soldier in Tussun's army, gives a lively description of the disastrous "day of Jadaydah" in vol. i. of his work.

1 This Abdullah, Pasha of Damascus, led the caravan in A.D. 1756. When the Shaykhs of the Harb tribe came to receive their black-mail, he cut off their heads, and sent the trophies to Stambul. During the next season the Harb were paralysed by the blow, but in the third year they levied 80,000 men, attacked the caravan, pillaged it, and slew every Turk that fell into their hands.

CHAPTER XIV.

FROM BIR ABBAS TO AL-MADINAH.

THE 22nd July was a grand trial of temper to our little party. The position of Bir Abbas exactly resembles that of Al-Hamra, except that the bulge of the hill-girt Fiumara is at this place about two miles wide. There are the usual stone-forts and palm-leaved hovels for the troopers, stationed here to hold the place and to escort travellers, with a coffee-shed, and a hut or two, called a bazar, but no village. Our encamping ground was a bed of loose sand, with which the violent Samum filled the air; not a tree or a bush was in sight; a species of hardy locust and swarms of flies were the only remnants of animal life: the scene was a caricature of Sind. Although we were now some hundred feet, to judge by the water-shed, above the level of the sea, the mid-day sun scorched even through the tent; our frail tenement was more than once blown down, and the heat of the sand made the work of repitching it painful. Again my companions, after breakfasting, hurried to the coffee-house, and returned one after the other with dispiriting reports. Then they either quarrelled desperately about nothing, or they threw themselves on their rugs, pretending to sleep in very sulkiness. The lady Maryam soundly rated her surly son for refusing to fill her chibuk for the twelfth time that morning, with the usual religious phrases, "Allah direct thee into the right way, O my son!"—meaning that he was going to the bad,—and "O my calamity, thy mother is a lone woman, O Allah!"—equivalent to the

European parental plaint about grey hairs being brought
down in sorrow to the grave. Before noon a small
caravan which followed us came in with two dead bodies,
—a trooper shot by the Badawin, and an Albanian
killed by sun-stroke, or the fiery wind.[1] Shortly after
mid-day a Caravan, travelling in an opposite direction,
passed by us; it was composed chiefly of Indian pilgrims,
habited in correct costume, and hurrying towards Meccah
in hot haste. They had been allowed to pass unmolested,
because probably a pound sterling could not have been
collected from a hundred pockets, and Sa'ad the Robber
sometimes does a cheap good deed. But our party,

---

1 The natives of Al-Hijaz assured me that in their Allah-favoured
land, the Samum never kills a man. I "doubt the fact." This
Arnaut's body was swollen and decomposing rapidly, the true
diagnostic of death by the poison-wind. (See Ibn Batuta's voyage,
" Kabul.") However, as troopers drink hard, the Arabs may still be
right, the Samum doing half the work, arrack the rest. I travelled
during the months of July, August, and September, and yet never
found myself inconvenienced by the " poison-wind " sufficiently to
make me tie my Kufiyah, Badawi-fashion, across my mouth. At
the same time I can believe that to an invalid it would be trying, and
that a man almost worn out by hunger and fatigue would receive
from it a *coup de grâce.* Niebuhr attributes the extraordinary mortality
of his companions, amongst other causes, to a want of stimulants.
Though these might doubtless be useful in the cold weather, or in the
mountains of Al-Yaman, for men habituated to them from early
youth, yet nothing, I believe, would be more fatal than strong drink
when travelling through the Desert in summer heat. The common
beverage should be water or lemonade; the strongest stimulants
coffee or tea. It is what the natives of the country do, and doubtless it is wise to take their example. The Duke of Wellington's
dictum about the healthiness of India to an abstemious man does not
require to be quoted. Were it more generally followed, we should
have less of sun-stroke and sudden death in our Indian armies, when
soldiers, fed with beef and brandy, are called out to face the violent
heat. At the same time it must be remembered, that foul and stagnant water, abounding in organic matter, is the cause of half the
diarrhœa and dysentry which prove so fatal to travellers in these
regions. To the water-drinker, therefore, a pocket-filter is indispensable.

having valuables with them, did not seem to gather heart from this event.   In the evening we all went out to see some Arab Shaykhs who were travelling to Bir Abbas in order to receive their salaries.   Without such *douceurs*, it is popularly said and believed, no stone walls could enable a Turk to hold Al-Hijaz against the hill-men. Such was our system in Afghanistan—most unwise, teaching *in limine* the subject to despise rulers subject to blackmail.   Besides which, these highly paid Shaykhs do no good.   When a fight takes place or a road is shut, they profess inability to restrain their clansmen; and the richer they are, of course the more formidable they become.   The party looked well ; they were Harb, dignified old men in the picturesque Arab costume, with erect forms, fierce thin features, and white beards, well armed, and mounted upon high-bred and handsomely equipped dromedaries from Al-Shark.[1]   Preceded by their half-naked clansmen, carrying spears twelve or thirteen feet long, garnished with single or double tufts of black ostrich feathers, and ponderous matchlocks, which were discharged on approaching the fort, they were not without a kind of barbaric pomp.

Immediately after the reception of these Shaykhs, there was a parade of the Arnaut Irregular horse.   About 500 of them rode out to the sound of the *Nakús* or little kettle-drum, whose puny notes strikingly contrasted with this really martial sight.   The men, it is true, were mounted on lean Arab and Egyptian nags, ragged-looking as their clothes; and each trooper was armed

---

1 Al-Shark, "the East," is the popular name in the Hijaz for the Western region as far as Baghdad and Bassorah, especially Nijd. The latter province supplies the Holy Land with its choicest horses and camels.   The great heats of the parts near the Red Sea appear pre-judicial to animal generation; whereas the lofty table-lands and the broad pastures of Nijd, combined with the attention paid by the people to purity of blood, have rendered it the greatest breeding country in Arabia.

in his own way, though all had swords, pistols and matchlocks, or firelocks of some kind. But they rode hard as Galway "buckeens," and there was a gallant reckless look about the fellows which prepossessed me strongly in their favour. Their animals, too, though notable "screws," were well trained, and their accoutrements were intended for use, not show. I watched their manœuvres with curiosity. They left their cantonments one by one, and, at the sound of the tom-tom, by degrees formed a "plump" or "herse"—*column*[1] it could not be called—all huddled together in confusion. Presently the little kettle-drum changed its note and the parade its aspect. All the serried body dispersed as would Light Infantry, now continuing their advance, then hanging back, then making a rush, and all the time keeping up a hot fire upon the enemy. At another signal they suddenly put their horses to full speed, and, closing upon the centre, again advanced in a dense mass. After three-quarters of an hour parading, sometimes charging singly, often in bodies, to the right, to the left, and straight in front, halting when requisite, and occasionally retreating, Parthian-like, the Arnauts turned *en masse* towards their lines. As they neared them, all broke off and galloped in, *ventre à terre*, discharging their shotted guns with much recklessness against objects assumed to denote the enemy. But ball-cartridge seemed to be plentiful hereabouts ; during the whole of this and the next day, I remarked that bullets, notched for noise, were fired away in mere fun.[2]

---

1 I mean a civilised column. "Herse" is the old military name for a column opposed to "Haye," a line. So we read that at far-famed Cressy the French fought *en battaille à haye*, the English drawn up *en herse*. This appears to have been the national predilection of that day. In later times, we and our neighbours changed style, the French preferring heavy columns, the English extending themselves into lines.

2 The Albanians, delighting in the noise of musketry, notch the ball in order to make it sing the louder. When fighting, they often

Barbarous as these movements may appear to the Cavalry Martinet of the " good old school," yet to something of the kind will the tactics of that arm of the service, I humbly opine, return, when the perfect use of the rifle, the revolver, and field artillery shall have made the present necessarily slow system fatal. Also, if we adopt the common sense opinion of a modern writer,[1] and determine that "individual prowess, skill in single combats, good horsemanship, and sharp swords render cavalry formidable," these semi-barbarians are wiser in their generation than the civilised, who never practise arms (properly so called), whose riding-drill never made a good rider, whose horses are over-weighted, and whose swords are worthless. They have yet another point of superiority over us ; they cultivate the individuality of the soldier, whilst we strive to make him a mere automaton. In the days of European chivalry, battles were a system of well-fought duels. This was succeeded by the age of discipline, when, to use the language of Rabelais, " men seemed rather a consort of organ-pipes, or mutual concord of the wheels of a clock, than an infantry and cavalry, or army of soldiers." Our aim should now be to combine the merits of both systems ; to make men individually

---

adopt the excellent plan—excellent, when rifles are not procurable— of driving a long iron nail through the bullet, and fixing its head into the cartridge. Thus the cartridge is strengthened, the bullet is rifled, and the wound which it inflicts is death. Round balls are apt to pass into and out of savages without killing them, and many an Afghan, after being shot or run through the body, has mortally wounded his English adversary before falling. It is false philanthropy, also, to suppose that in battle, especially when a campaign is commencing, it is sufficient to maim, not to kill, the enemy. Nothing encourages men to fight so much, as a good chance of escaping with a wound—especially a flesh wound. I venture to hope that the reader will not charge these sentiments with cruelty. He who renders warfare fatal to all engaged in it will be the greatest benefactor the world has yet known.

[1] The late Captain Nolan.

excellent in the use of weapons, and still train them to act naturally and habitually in concert. The French have given a model to Europe in the Chasseurs de Vincennes,—a body capable of most perfect combination, yet never more truly excellent than when each man is fighting alone. We, I suppose, shall imitate them at some future time.[1]

A distant dropping of fire-arms ushered in the evening of our first melancholy day at Bir Abbas. This, said my companions, was a sign that the troops and the hill-men were fighting. They communicated the intelligence, as if it ought to be an effectual check upon my impatience to proceed; it acted, however, in the contrary way. I supposed that the Badawin, after battling out the night, would be less warlike the next day; the others, however, by no means agreed in opinion with me. At Yambu' the whole party had boasted loudly that the people of Al-Madinah could keep their Badawin in order, and had twitted the boy Mohammed with their superiority in this respect to his townsmen, the Meccans. But now that a trial was impending, I saw none of the fearlessness so conspicuous when peril was only possible. The change was charitably to be explained by the presence of their valuables; the "*Sahharahs*," like conscience, making cowards of them all. But the young Meccan, who, having sent on his box by sea from Yambu'

---

[1] The first symptom of improvement will be a general training to the Bayonet exercise. The British is, and for years has been, the only army in Europe that does not learn the use of this weapon: how long does it intend to be the sole authority on the side of ignorance? We laughed at the Calabrese levies, who in the French war threw away their muskets and drew their stilettos ; and we cannot understand why the Indian would always prefer a sabre to a rifle. Yet we read without disgust of our men being compelled, by want of proper training, to "club their muskets" in hand-to-hand fights,— when they have in the bayonet the most formidable of offensive weapons,—and of the Kafirs and other savages wresting the piece, after drawing off its fire, from its unhappy possessor's grasp.

to Jeddah, felt merry, like the empty traveller, would not
lose the opportunity to pay off old scores.   He taunted
the Madinites till they stamped and raved with fury.   At
last, fearing some violence, and feeling answerable for the
boy's safety to his family, I seized him by the nape of his
neck and the upper posterior portion of his nether
garments, and drove him before me into the tent.

When the hubbub had subsided, and all sat after supper smoking the pipe of peace in the cool night air, I re-
joined my companions, and found them talking, as usual,
about old Shaykh Sa'ad.   The scene was appropriate for
the subject.   In the distance rose the blue peak said to be
his eyrie, and the place was pointed out with fearful meaning.   As it is inaccessible to strangers, report has converted it into another garden of Iram.   A glance, however, at its position and formation satisfied me that the
bubbling springs, the deep forests, and the orchards of
apple-trees, quinces and pomegranates, with which my
companions furnished it, were a "myth," whilst some
experience of Arab ignorance of the art of defence
suggested to me strong doubts about the existence of an
impregnable fortress on the hill-top.   The mountains,
however, looked beautiful in the moonlight, and distance
gave them a semblance of mystery well suited to the
themes which they inspired.

That night I slept within my Shugduf, for it would
have been mere madness to sleep on the open plain in a
place so infested by banditti.   The being armed is but a
poor precaution near this robbers' den.   If you wound a
man in the very act of plundering, an exorbitant sum
must be paid for blood-money.   If you kill him, even to
save your life, then adieu to any chance of escaping
destruction.   Roused three or four times during the
night by jackals and dogs prowling about our little camp,
I observed that my companions, who had agreed
amongst themselves to keep watch by turns, had all

fallen into a sound sleep. However, when we awoke in the morning, the usual inspection of goods and chattels showed that nothing was gone.

The next day (July 23rd) was a forced halt, a sore stimulant to the traveller's ill-humour; and the sun, the sand, the dust, the furious Samum, and the want of certain small supplies, aggravated our grievance. My sore foot had been inflamed by a dressing of onion skin which the lady Maryam had insisted upon applying to it.[1] Still being resolved to push forward by any conveyance that could be procured, I offered ten dollars for a fresh dromedary to take me on to Al-Madinah. Shaykh Hamid also declared he would leave his box in charge of a friend and accompany me. Sa'ad the Demon flew into a passion at the idea of any member of the party escaping the general evil; and he privily threatened Mohammed to cut off the legs of any camel that ventured into camp. This, the boy—who, like a boy of the world as he was, never lost an opportunity of making mischief—instantly communicated to me, and it brought on a furious dispute. Sa'ad was reproved and apologised for by the rest of the party; and presently he himself was pacified, principally, I believe, by the intelligence that no camel was to be hired at Bir Abbas. One of the Arnaut garrison, who had obtained leave to go to Al-Madinah, came to ask us if we could mount him, as otherwise he should be obliged to walk the whole way. With him we debated the propriety of attempting a passage through the hills by one of the many by-paths that traverse them: the project was amply discussed, and duly rejected.

We passed the day in the usual manner; all crowded

---

1 I began to treat it hydropathically with a cooling bandage, but my companions declared that the water was poisoning the wound, and truly it seemed to get worse every day. This idea is prevalent throughout Al-Hijaz; even the Badawin, after once washing a cut or a sore, never allow air or water to touch it.

together for shelter under the tent. Even Maryam joined
us, loudly informing Ali, her son, that his mother was no
longer a woman but a man; whilst our party generally,
cowering away from the fierce glances of the sun, were
either eating or occasionally smoking, or were occupied
in cooling and drinking water. About sunset-time came
a report that we were to start that night. None could
believe that such good was in store for us ; before sleeping,
however, we placed each camel's pack apart, so as to be
ready for loading at a moment's notice; and we took care
to watch that our Badawin did not drive their animals
away to any distance. At last, about 11 P.M., as the moon
was beginning to peep over the Eastern wall of rock, was
heard the glad sound of the little kettle-drum calling the
Albanian troopers to mount and march. In the shortest
possible time all made ready; and, hurriedly crossing the
sandy flat, we found ourselves in company with three or
four Caravans, forming one large body for better defence
against the dreaded Hawámid.[1] By dint of much
manœuvring, arms in hand,—Shaykh Hamid and the
" Demon " took the prominent parts,—we, though the
last comers, managed to secure places about the middle
of the line. On such occasions all push forward recklessly, as an English mob in the strife of sight-seeing ; the
rear, being left unguarded, is the place of danger, and none
seeks the honour of occupying it.

We travelled that night up the Fiumara in an Easterly
direction, and at early dawn (July 24th) found ourselves in
an ill-famed gorge called Shuab al-Hajj,[2] the " Pilgrimage
Pass." The loudest talkers became silent as we neared
it, and their countenances showed apprehension written
in legible characters. Presently from the high precipi-

---

1 Hawamid is the plural of Hamidah, Shaykh Sa'ad's tribe.

2 Shuab properly means a path through mountains, or a water-
course between hills. It is generally used in Arabia for a " Valley,"
and sometimes instead of Nakb, or the Turkish Bughaz, a " Pass."

tous cliff on our left, thin blue curls of smoke—somehow or other they caught every eye—rose in the air ; and instantly afterwards rang the sharp cracks of the hillmen's matchlocks, echoed by the rocks on the right. My Shugduf had been broken by the camel's falling during the night, so I called out to Mansur that we had better splice the framework with a bit of rope: he looked up, saw me laughing, and with an ejaculation of disgust disappeared. A number of Badawin were to be seen swarming like hornets over the crests of the hills, boys as well as men carrying huge weapons, and climbing with the agility of cats. They took up comfortable places on the cut-throat eminence, and began firing upon us with perfect convenience to themselves. The height of the hills and the glare of the rising sun prevented my seeing objects very distinctly, but my companions pointed out to me places where the rock had been scarped, and where a kind of rough stone breastwork—the Sangah of Afghanistan—had been piled up as a defence, and a rest for the long barrel of the matchlock. It was useless to challenge the Badawin to come down and fight us like men upon the plain ; they will do this on the Eastern coast of Arabia, but rarely, if ever, in Al-Hijaz. And it was equally unprofitable for our escort to fire upon a foe ensconced behind stones. Besides which, had a robber been killed, the whole country would have risen to a man; with a force of 3,000 or 4,000, they might have gained courage to overpower a Caravan, and in such a case not a soul would have escaped. As it was, the Badawin directed their fire principally against the Albanians. Some of these called for assistance to the party of Shaykhs that accompanied us from Bir Abbas; but the dignified old men, dismounting and squatting in council round their pipes, came to the conclusion that, as the robbers would probably turn a deaf ear to their words, they had better spare themselves the trouble of speaking.

We had therefore nothing to do but to blaze away as much powder, and to veil ourselves in as much smoke, as possible ; the result of the affair was that we lost twelve men, besides camels and other beasts of burden.   Though the bandits showed no symptoms of bravery, and confined themselves to slaughtering the enemy from their hill-top, my companions seemed to consider this questionable affair a most gallant exploit.

After another hour's hurried ride through the Wady Sayyalah, appeared Shuhada, to which we pushed on,

> " Like nighted swain on lonely road,
> When close behind fierce goblins tread."

Shuhada is a place which derives its name, " The Martyrs," because here are supposed to be buried forty braves that fell in one of Mohammed's many skirmishes. Some authorities consider it the cemetery of the people of Wady Sayyalah.[1] The once populous valley is now barren, and one might easily pass by the consecrated spot without observing a few ruined walls and a cluster of rude Badawin graves, each an oval of rough stones lying beneath the thorn trees on the left of and a little off the road.   Another half hour took us to a favourite halting-place, Bir al-Hindi,[2] so called from some forgotten Indian

---

[1] Others attribute these graves to the Beni Salim, or Salmah, an extinct race of Hijazi Badawin.   Near Shuhada is Jabal Warkan, one of the mountains of Paradise, also called Irk al-Zabyat, or Thread of the Winding Torrent.   The Prophet named it " Hamt," (sultriness), when he passed through it on his way to the Battle of Badr. He also called the valley " Sajasaj," (plural of Sajsaj, a temperate situation), declared it was a valley of heaven, that 70 prophets had prayed there before himself, that Moses with 70,000 Israelites had traversed it on his way to Meccah, and that, before the Resurrection day, Isa bin Maryam should pass through it with the intention of performing the Greater and the Lesser Pilgrimages. Such are the past and such the future honours of the place.

[2] The Indians sink wells in Arabia for the same reason which impels them to dig tanks at home,—" nam ke waste,"—" for the purpose of name"; thereby denoting, together with a laudable desire

who dug a well there. But we left it behind, wishing to put as much space as we could between our tents and the nests of the Hamidah. Then quitting the Fiumara, we struck Northwards into a well-trodden road running over stony rising ground. The heat became sickening; here, and in the East generally, at no time is the sun more dangerous than between eight and nine A.M. Still we hurried on. It was not before eleven A.M. that we reached our destination, a rugged plain covered with stones, coarse gravel, and thorn trees in abundance; and surrounded by inhospitable rocks, pinnacle-shaped, of granite below, and in the upper parts fine limestone. The well was at least two miles distant, and not a hovel was in sight; a few Badawi children belonging to an outcast tribe fed their starveling goats upon the hills. This place is called "Suwaykah"; it is, I was told, that celebrated in the history of the Arabs.[1] Yet not for this reason did my comrades look lovingly upon its horrors : their boxes were safe and with the eye of imagination they could now behold their homes. That night we must have travelled about twenty-two miles ; the direction of the road was due East, and the only remarkable feature in the ground was its steady rise.

---

for posthumous fame, a notable lack of ingenuity in securing it. For it generally happens that before the third generation has fallen, the well and the tank have either lost their original names, or have exchanged them for others newer and better known.

1 Suwaykah derives its name from the circumstance that in the second, or third, year of the Hijrah (Hégira), Mohammed here attacked Abu Sufiyan, who was out on a foray with 200 men. The Infidels, in their headlong flight, lightened their beasts by emptying their bags of " Sawík." This is the old and modern Arabic name for a dish of green grain, toasted, pounded, mixed with dates or sugar, and eaten on journeys when it is found difficult to cook. Such is the present signification of the word : M. C. de Perceval (vol. iii., p. 84) gives it a different and a now unknown meaning. And our popular authors erroneously call the affair the " War of the *Meal-sacks.*"

We pitched the tent under a villainous Mimosa, the tree whose shade is compared by poetic Badawin to the false friend who deserts you in your utmost need. I enlivened the hot dull day by a final affair with Sa'ad the Demon. His alacrity at Yambu' obtained for him the loan of a couple of dollars: he had bought grain at Al-Hamra, and now we were near Al-Madinah: still there was not a word about repayment. And knowing that an Oriental debtor discharges his debt as he pays his rent,—namely, with the greatest unwillingness,—and that, on the other hand, an Oriental creditor will devote the labour of a year to recovering a sixpence, I resolved to act as a native of the country, placed in my position, would; and by dint of sheer dunning and demanding pledges, to recover my property. About noon Sa'ad the Demon, after a furious rush, bare-headed, through the burning sun, flung the two dollars down upon my carpet : however, he presently recovered temper, and, as subsequent events showed, I had chosen the right part. Had he not been forced to repay his debt, he would have despised me as a "freshman," and would have coveted more. As it was, the boy Mohammed bore the brunt of unpopular feeling, my want of liberality being traced to his secret and perfidious admonitions. He supported his burden the more philosophically, because, as he notably calculated, every dollar saved at Al-Madinah would be spent under his stewardship at Meccah.

At four P.M. (July 24th) we left Suwaykah, all of us in the crossest of humours, and travelled in a N.E. direction. So "out of temper " were my companions, that at sunset, of the whole party, Omar Effendi was the only one who would eat supper. The rest sat upon the ground, pouting, grumbling, and — they had been allowed to exhaust my stock of Latakia—smoking Syrian tobacco as if it were a grievance. Such a game at naughty children, I have seldom seen played even by Oriental men. The boy Mohammed privily remarked to me that the camel-men's beards were now in his fist,—meaning that we were out of their kinsmen, the Harb's, reach. He soon found an opportunity to quarrel with them; and, because one of his questions was not answered in the shortest possible time, he proceeded to abuse them in language which sent their hands flying in the direction of their swords. Despite, however, this threatening demeanour, the youth, knowing that he now could safely go to any lengths, continued his ill words, and Mansur's face was so comically furious, that I felt too much amused to interfere. At last the camel-men disappeared, thereby punishing us most effectually for our sport. The road lay up rocky hill and down stony vale; a tripping and stumbling dromedary had been substituted for the usual *monture:* the consequence was that we had either a totter or a tumble once per mile during the whole of that long night. In vain the now fiery Mohammed called for the assistance of the camel-men with the full force of his lungs: "Where be those owls, those oxen of the oxen, those beggars, those cut-off ones, those foreigners, those Sons of Flight[1]? withered be their hands! palsied be their fingers! the foul mustachioed fellows, basest of the Arabs that ever hammered tent-peg, sneaking cats, goats of Al-Akhfash![2] Truly I will torture them the torture of the oil,[3] the mines of infamy! the cold of countenance![4]" The Badawi brotherhood of the camel-men looked at him wickedly, muttering the while,—"By Allah! and by Allah!

---

1 A popular but not a bad pun—"*H*arb" (Fight), becomes, by the alteration of the H, "Harb" (Flight).

2 The old Arabic proverb is "A greater wiseacre than the goat of Akhfash"; it is seldom intelligible to the vulgar.

3 That is to say, "I will burn them (metaphorically) as the fiery wick consumes the oil,"—a most idiomatic Hijazi threat.

4 A "cold-of-countenance" is a fool. Arabs use the word "cold" in a peculiar way. "May Allah refrigerate thy countenance!" *i.e.* may it show misery and want. "By Allah, a cold speech!" that is to say, a silly or an abusive tirade.

and by Allah! O boy, we will flog thee like a hound when we catch thee in the Desert!" All our party called upon him to desist, but his temper had got completely the upper hand over his discretion, and he expressed himself in such classic and idiomatic Hijazi, that I had not the heart to stop him. Some days after our arrival at Al-Madinah, Shaykh Hamid warned him seriously never again to go such perilous lengths, as the Beni Harb were celebrated for shooting or poniarding the man who ventured to use to them even the mild epithet "O jackass!" And in the quiet of the city the boy Mohammed, like a sobered man shuddering at dangers braved when drunk, hearkened with discomposure and penitence to his friend's words. The only immediate consequence of his abuse was that my broken Shugduf became a mere ruin, and we passed the dark hours perched like two birds upon the only entire bits of framework the cots contained.

The sun had nearly risen (July 25th) before I shook off the lethargic effects of such a night. All around me were hurrying their camels, regardless of rough ground, and not a soul spoke a word to his neighbour. " Are there robbers in sight ?" was the natural question. " No !" replied Mohammed ; " they are walking with their eyes,[1] they will presently see their homes!" Rapidly we passed the Wady al-Akik,[2] of which,

" O my friend, this is Akik, then stand by it,
Endeavouring to be distracted by love, if not really a lover," [3]

---

1 That is to say, they would use, if necessary, the dearest and noblest parts of their bodies (their eyes) to do the duty of the basest (*i.e.* their feet).

2 Writers mention two Al-Akik. The superior comprises the whole site of Al-Madinah, extending from the Western Ridge, mentioned below, to the cemetery Al-Bakia. The inferior is the Fiumara here alluded to ; it is on the Meccan road, about four miles S.W. of Al-Madinah, and its waters fall into the Al-Hamra torrent. It is called the "Blessed Valley" because the Prophet was ordered by an angel to pray in it.

3 The esoteric meaning of this couplet is, " Man ! this is a lovely

and a thousand other such pretty things, have been said by the Arab poets. It was as "dry as summer's dust," and its "beautiful trees" appeared in the shape of vegetable mummies. Half an hour after leaving the "Blessed Valley" we came to a huge flight of steps roughly cut in a long broad line of black scoriaceous basalt. This is termed the Mudarraj or flight of steps over the western ridge of the so-called Al-Harratayn.[1] It is holy ground; for the Apostle spoke well of it. Arrived at the top, we passed through a lane of dark lava, with steep banks on both sides, and after a few minutes a full view of the city suddenly opened upon us.[2]

We halted our beasts as if by word of command. All of us descended, in imitation of the pious of old, and sat down, jaded and hungry as we were, to feast our eyes with a view of the Holy City.

"O Allah! this is the Harim (sanctuary) of Thy Apostle; make it to us a Protection from Hell Fire, and a Refuge from Eternal Punishment! O open the Gates of Thy Mercy, and let us pass through them to the Land of Joy!" and "O Allah, bless the last of Prophets, the Seal of Prophecy, with Blessings in number

---

portion of God's creation: then stand by it, and here learn to love the perfections of thy Supreme Friend."

1 Al-Harratayn for Al-Harratani, the oblique case of the dual and plural noun being universally used for the nominative in colloquial Arabic. The other one of the Two Ridges will be described in a future part of this Book.

2 The city is first seen from the top of the valley called Nakb, or Shuab Ali, close to the Wady al-Akik, a long narrow pass, about five miles from Al-Madinah. Here, according to some, was the Mosque Zu'l Halifah, where the Prophet put on the Pilgrim's garb when travelling to Meccah. It is also called "The Mosque of the Tree," because near it grew a fruit tree under which the Prophet twice sat. Ibn Jubayr considers that the Harim (or sacred precincts of Al-Madinah) is the space enclosed by three points, Zu'l Halifah, Mount Ohod, and the Mosque of Kuba. To the present day pilgrims doff their worldly garments at Zu'l Halifah.

as the Stars of Heaven, and the Waves of the Sea, and
the Sands of the Waste—bless him, O Lord of Might
and Majesty, as long as the Corn-field and the Date-
grove continue to feed Mankind[1]!" And again, "Live
for ever, O Most Excellent of Prophets!—live in the
Shadow of Happiness during the Hours of Night and the
Times of Day, whilst the Bird of the Tamarisk (the dove)
moaneth like the childless Mother, whilst the West-wind
bloweth gently over the Hills of Nijd, and the Lightning
flasheth bright in the Firmament of Al-Hijaz!"

Such were the poetical exclamations that rose all
around me, showing how deeply tinged with imagination
becomes the language of the Arab under the influence
of strong passion or religious enthusiasm. I now understood the full value of a phrase in the Moslem ritual,
"And when his" (the pilgrim's) "eyes shall *fall upon
the Trees of Al-Madinah*, let him raise his Voice and bless
the Apostle with the choicest of Blessings." In al
the fair view before us nothing was more striking, after
the desolation through which we had passed, than
the gardens and orchards about the town. It was
impossible not to enter into the spirit of my companions, and truly I believe that for some minutes my
enthusiasm rose as high as theirs. But presently when
we remounted,[2] the traveller returned strong upon me:
I made a rough sketch of the town, put questions about
the principal buildings, and in fact collected materials for
the next chapter.

---

1 That is to say, "throughout all ages and all nations." The
Arabs divide the world into two great bodies: first themselves, and,
secondly, "'Ajami," *i.e.* all that are not Arabs. Similar bi-partitions
are the Hindus and Mlenchhas, the Jews and Gentiles, the Greeks
and Barbarians, &c., &c.

2 Robust religious men, especially those belonging to the school
of Al-Málik, enter into Al-Madinah, after the example of Ali, on
foot, reverently, as the pilgrims approach Meccah.

The distance traversed that night was about twenty-
two miles in a direction varying from easterly to north-
easterly. We reached Al-Madinah on the 25th July, thus
taking nearly eight days to travel over little more than
130 miles. This journey is performed with camels in four
days, and a good dromedary will do it without difficulty
in half that time.[1]

---

1 Barbosa makes three days' journey from Yambu' to Al-
Madinah, D'Herbelot eight, and Ovington six. The usual time is
from four to five days. A fertile source of error to home geographers, computing distances in Arabia, is their neglecting the
difference between the slow camel travelling and the fast dromedary
riding.

The following is a synopsis of our stations:—

		Miles.	
1.	From Yambu', 18th July, to Musahhal, N.E. . . .	16	⎫
2.	From Musahhal, 19th July, to Bir Sa'id, S. and E. .	34	⎬ 64 miles
3.	From Bir Sa'id, 20th July, to Al-Hamra, N.E. . . .	14	⎭
4.	From Al-Hamra, 21st July, to Bir Abbas, E. . . .	24	⎫
5.	From Bir Abbas, 23rd July, to Suwaykah, E. . . .	22	⎬ 68 miles
6.	From Suwaykah, 24th July, to Al-Madinah, N. and E.	22	⎭

Total English miles . . 132

PART II.

———

AL-MADINAH.

L.Burton, delt.

C.F. Kell, Lith.

VIEW OF AL-MADINAH.

Taken from the Harrah (or ridge) west of the Town.

CHAPTER XV.

THROUGH THE SUBURB OF AL-MADINAH TO HAMID'S HOUSE.

As we looked Eastward, the sun arose out of the horizon of low hill, blurred and dotted with small tufted trees, which gained from the morning mists a giant stature, and the earth was stained with purple and gold. Before us lay a spacious plain, bounded in front by the undulating ground of Nijd : on the left was a grim pile of rocks, the celebrated Mount Ohod, with a clump of verdure and a white dome or two nestling at its base. Rightwards, broad streaks of lilac-coloured mists, here thick with gathered dew, there pierced and thinned by the morning rays, stretched over the date groves and the gardens of Kuba, which stood out in emerald green from the dull tawny surface of the plain. Below, distant about two miles, lay Al-Madinah ; at first sight it appeared a large place, but a closer inspection proved the impression to be erroneous. A tortuous road from the Harrah to the city wound across the plain, and led to a tall rectangular gateway, pierced in the ruinous mud-wall which surrounds the suburb. This is the "Ambari" entrance. It is flanked on the left (speaking as a sketcher) by the domes and minarets of a pretty Turkish building, a " Takiyah," erected by the late Mo-hammed Ali for the reception of Darwaysh travellers ; on the right by a long low line of white-washed buildings garnished with ugly square windows, an imitation of civilised barracks. Beginning from the left hand, as we sat upon the ridge, the remarkable features of the town thus presented themselves in succession. Outside, among the palm trees to the north of the city, were the picturesque ruins of a large old *Sabíl*, or public fountain; and, between this and the enceinte, stood a conspicuous building, in the Turkish pavilion style—the Governor's palace. On the north-west angle of the town-wall is a tall white-washed fort, partly built upon an outcropping mass of rock: its ramparts and embrasures give it a modern and European appearance, which contrasts strangely with its truly Oriental history.[1] In the suburb "Al-Manakhah," the "kneeling-place of camels," the bran-new domes and minarets of the Five Mosques stand brightly out from the dull grey mass of house and ground. And behind, in the most Easterly part of the city, remarkable from afar, is the gem of Al-Madinah,—the four tall substantial towers, and the flashing green Dome under which the Apostle's remains rest.[2] Half concealed by this mass of buildings and by the houses of the town, are certain white specks upon a green surface, the tombs that adorn the venerable cemetery, Al-Bakia. From that point southwards begins the mass of palm groves celebrated in Al-Islam as the "Trees of Al-

1 In the East, wherever there is a compound of fort and city, that place has certainly been in the habit of being divided against itself. Surat in Western India is a well-known instance. I must refer the reader to Burckhardt (Travels in Arabia, vol. ii., page 281, and onwards) for a detailed account of the feuds and affrays between the "Agha of the Castle" and the "Agha of the Town." Their day has now gone by,—for the moment.

2 Sir John Mandeville, writing in the 14th century, informed Europe that "Machomet lyeth in the Cytee of Methone." In the 19th century, Mr. Halliwell, his editor, teaches us in a foot-note that "Methone" is Meccah! It is strange how often this gross mistake is still made by respectable authors in France as well as in England.

Madinah." The foreground is well fitted to set off such
a view; fields of black basaltic scoriæ showing clear signs
of a volcanic origin, are broken up into huge blocks and
boulders, through which a descent, tolerably steep for
camels, winds down into the plain.

After a few minutes' rest I remounted, and slowly
rode on towards the gate. Even at this early hour the
way was crowded with an eager multitude coming out to
meet the Caravan. My companions preferred walking,
apparently for the better convenience of kissing, embracing, and skaking hands with relations and friends.
Truly the Arabs show more heart on these occasions
than any Oriental people I know; they are of a more
affectionate nature than the Persians, and their manners
are far more demonstrative than those of the Indians.
The respectable Maryam's younger son, a pleasant contrast to her surly elder, was weeping aloud for joy as he
ran round his mother's camel, he standing on tiptoe, she
bending double in vain attempts to exchange a kiss; and,
generally, when near relatives or intimates, or school
companions, met, the fountains of their eyes were
opened. Friends and comrades greeted one another,
regardless of rank or fortune, with affectionate embraces,
and an abundance of queries, which neither party seemed
to think of answering. The general mode of saluting
was to throw one arm over the shoulder and the other
round the side, placing the chin first upon the left and
then upon the right collar-bone, and rapidly shifting till
a *"jam satis"* suggested itself to both parties. Inferiors
recognized their superiors by attempting to kiss hands,
which were violently snatched away; whilst mere acquaintances gave each other a cordial *"poignée de mains,"* and
then raising the finger tips to their lips, kissed them
with apparent relish.

Passing through the Bab Ambari we defiled slowly
down a broad dusty street, and traversed the *Harat*

(Quarter), Al-Ambariyah, the principal in the Manakhah suburb. The thoroughfare is by no means remarkable after Cairo; only it is rather wider and more regular than the traveller is accustomed to in Asiatic cities. I was astonished to see on both sides of the way, in so small a place, so large a number of houses too ruinous to be occupied. Then we crossed a bridge, a single little round arch of roughly hewn stone, built over the bed of a torrent, Al-Sayh,[1] which in some parts appeared about fifty feet broad, with banks showing a high and deeply indented water-mark. Here the road abuts upon an open space called the " Barr al-Manakhah,[2]" or more concisely Al-Barr, " the Plain." Straightforward a line leads directly into the Bab al-Misri, the Egyptian gate of the city. But we turned off to the right; and, after advancing a few yards, we found ourselves at the entrance of our friend Hamid's house.

The Shaykh had preceded us early that morning, in order to prepare an apartment for his guests, and to receive the first loud congratulations and embraces of his mother and the "daughter of his uncle.[3]" Apparently he had not concluded this pleasing duty when we arrived, for the camels were kneeling at least five minutes at his door, before he came out to offer the usual hospitable salutation. I stared to see the difference of his appearance this morning. The razor had passed over his head

---

1 This torrent is called Al-Sayh,—" the Running Water,"—which, properly speaking, is the name of a well-wooded Wady outside the town, in the direction of Kuba.

2 " Manakhah " is a place where camels kneel down; it is a derivation from the better known root to "Nakh," or cause the animal to kneel.

3 Arabs, and, indeed, most Orientals, are generally received after returning from a journey, with shrill cries of joy by all the fair part of the household, and they do not like strangers to hear this demonstration.

and face[1]; the former was now surmounted by a muslin
turband of goodly size, wound round a new embroidered
cap; and the latter, besides being clean, boasted of neat
little moustaches turned up like two commas, whilst a
well-trimmed goat's beard narrowed until it resembled
what our grammars call an "exclamation point." The
dirty, torn shirt, with the bits of rope round the loins, had
been exchanged for a *Jubbah* or outer cloak of light pink
merinos, a long-sleeved *Caftan* of rich flowered stuff, a fine
shirt of *Halaili*,[2] silk and cotton, and a sash of plaid pattern,
elaborately fringed at both ends, and, for better display,
wound round two-thirds of his body. His pantaloons
were also of *Halaili*, with tasteful edgings about the ankles
like a "pantilette's," while his bare and sun-burnt feet
had undergone a thorough purification before being
encased in new *Mizz*[3] (inner slippers), and *Papush* (outer
slippers), of bright lemon-coloured leather of the newest
and most fashionable Constantinopolitan cut. In one
of his now delicate hands the Shaykh bore a mother-
of-pearl rosary, token of piety ; in the other a handsome pipe with a jasmine stick, and an expensive
amber mouth-piece ; his tobacco pouch, dangling
from his waist, like the little purse in the bosom
pocket of his coat, was of broadcloth richly embroidered with gold. In course of time I saw that all

---

1 An Eastern Barber is not content to pass the razor over hairy
spots : he must scrape the forehead, trim the eyebrows, clean the
cheeks, run the blade rapidly over the nose, correct the upper and
under lines of the mustaches, parting them in the centre, and so on.

2 *Halaili* is a cotton stuff, with long stripes of white silk, a
favourite material amongst the city Arabs. At Constantinople,
where the best is sold, the piece, which will cut into two shirts,
costs about thirty shillings.

3 The "*Mizz*" (in colloquial Arabic *Misd*) are the tight-fitting
inner slippers of soft Cordovan leather, worn as stockings inside the
slipper ; they are always clean, so they may be retained in the Mosque
or on the Diwan (divan or sofa).

my companions had metamorphosed themselves in an equally remarkable manner. As men of sense they appeared in tatters where they were, or when they wished to be, unknown, and in fine linen where and when the world judged their prosperity by their attire. Their grand suits of clothes, therefore, were worn only for a few days after returning from the journey, by way of proof that the wearer had wandered to some purpose ; they were afterwards laid up in lavender, and reserved for choice occasions, as old ladies in Europe store up their state dresses.

The Shaykh, whose manners had changed with his garments, from the vulgar and boisterous to a certain staid courtesy, took my hand, and led me up to the Majlis[1] (parlour), which was swept and garnished, with all due apparatus, for the forthcoming reception-ceremony. And behind us followed the boy Mohammed, looking more downcast and ashamed of himself than I can possibly describe ; he was still in his rags, and he felt keenly that every visitor staring at him would mentally inquire,—

"Who may that snob be?"

With the deepest dejectedness he squeezed himself into a corner, and Shaykh Nur, who was foully dirty, as an Indian *en voyage* always is, would have joined him in his shame, had I not ordered the "slave" to make himself generally useful.

It is customary for all relations and friends to call upon the traveller the very day he returns, that is to say, if amity is to endure. The pipes therefore stood ready filled, the Diwans were duly spread, and the coffee[2] was being boiled upon a brazier in the passage.

---

1 The *Majlis* (" the Place of Sitting ") is the drawing or reception room ; it is usually in the first story of the house, below the apartments of the women.

2 The coffee drank at Al-Madinah is generally of a good quality. In Egypt that beverage in the common coffee-shops is,—as required to be by the people who frequent those places,—" bitter as death, black as Satan, and hot as Jahannam." To effect this desideratum,

Scarcely had I taken my place at the cool window-sill,—it was the best in the room,—when the visitors began to pour in, and the Shaykh rose to welcome and embrace them. They sat down, smoked, chatted politics, asked all manner of questions about the other wayfarers and absent friends; drank coffee; and, after half an hour's visit, rose abruptly, and, exchanging embraces, took leave. The little men entered the assembly, after an accolade at the door, noiselessly, squatted upon the worst seats with polite *congés* to the rest of the assembly; smoked, took their coffee, as it were, under protest, and glided out of the room as quietly as they crept in.

The great people, generally busy and consequential individuals, upon whose countenances were writ large the words "well to do in the world," appeared with a noise that made each person in the room rise reverentially upon his feet; sat down with importance, monopolised the conversation; and, departing in a dignified manner, expected all to stand on the occasion.

The Jihad (Holy War), as usual, was the grand topic of conversation. The Sultan had ordered the Czar to become a Moslem. The Czar had sued for peace, and offered tribute and fealty. But the Sultan had exclaimed—

"No, by Allah! Al-Islam!"

---

therefore, they toast the grain to blackness, boil it to bitterness, and then drink scalding stuff of the consistency of water-gruel. At Al-Madinah, on the contrary,—as indeed in the houses of the better classes even in Egypt,—the grain is carefully picked, and that the flavour may be preserved, it is never put upon the fire until required. It is toasted too till it becomes yellow, not black; and afterwards is bruised, not pounded to powder. The water into which it is thrown is allowed to boil up three times, after which a cold sprinkling is administered to clear it, and then the fine light-dun infusion is poured off into another pot. Those who admire the "Kaimak," or froth, do not use a second vessel. The Arabs seldom drink more than one cup of coffee at a time, but with many the time is every half-hour of the day. The coffee-husk or "Kishr" of Al-Yaman is here unknown.

The Czar could not be expected to take such a step
without a little hesitation, but "Allah smites the faces of
the Infidels!" Abd al-Majid would dispose of the
"Moskow[1]" in a short time ; after which he would turn
his victorious army against all the idolaters of Feringistan,
beginning with the English, the French, and the Arwam
or Greeks.[2] Amongst much of this nonsense,—when
applied to for my opinion, I was careful to make it
popular,—I heard news foreboding no good to my journey
towards Maskat. The Badawin had decided that there
was to be an "Arab contingent," and had been looking
forward to the spoils of Europe : this caused quarrels, as
all the men wanted to go, and not a ten-year-old would
be left behind. The consequence was, that this amiable
people was fighting in all directions. At least so said
the visitors, and I afterwards found out that they were
not far wrong.

The Samman is a great family, in numbers as in
dignity ; from 8 A.M. till mid-day therefore the Majlis was
crowded with people, and politeness delayed our break-
fasts until an unconscionable hour.

To the plague of strangers succeeded that of children.
No sooner did the parlour become, comparatively speaking,
vacant than they rushed in *en masse*, treading upon our
toes, making the noise of a nursery of madlings, pulling
to pieces everything they could lay their hands upon, and
using language that would have alarmed an old man-o'-
war's-man.[3] In fact, no one can conceive the plague but

---

1 The common name for the Russians in Egypt and Al-Hijaz.

2 The Greeks are well known at Al-Madinah, and several of the
historians complain that some of the minor holy places had fallen
into the hands of this race, (Moslems, or pretended Moslems, I presume), who prevented people visiting them. It is curious that the
impostor Cagliostro should have hit upon the truth when he located
Greeks at Al-Madinah

3 Parents and full-grown men amuse themselves with grossly

those who have studied the "*enfans terribles*" which India sends home in cargoes.

One urchin, scarcely three years old, told me, because I objected to his perching upon my wounded foot, that his father had a sword at home with which he would cut my throat from ear to ear, suiting the action to the word. By a few taunts, I made the little wretch furious with rage; he shook his infant fist at me, and then opening his enormous round black eyes to their utmost stretch, he looked at me, and licked his knee with portentous meaning. Shaykh Hamid, happening to come in at the moment, stood aghast at the doorway, chin in hand, to see the Effendi subject to such indignity; and it was not without trouble that I saved the offender from summary nursery discipline. Another scamp caught up one of my loaded pistols before I could snatch it out of his hand, and clapped it to his neighbour's head; fortunately, it was on half-cock, and the trigger was stiff. Then a serious and majestic boy about six years old, with an ink-stand in his belt, in token of his receiving a literary education, seized my pipe and began to smoke it with huge puffs. I ventured laughingly to institute a comparison between the length of his person and the pipe-stick, when he threw it upon the ground, and stared at me fixedly with flaming eyes and features distorted by anger. The cause of this "bouldness" soon appeared. The boys, instead of being well beaten, were scolded with fierce faces, a mode of punishment which only made them laugh.

They had their redeeming points, however; they were manly angry boys, who punched one another like Anglo-Saxons in the house, whilst abroad they were always

---

abusing children, almost as soon as they can speak, in order to excite their rage, and to judge of their dispositions. This supplies the infant population with a large stock-in-trade of ribaldry. They literally lisp in bad language.

fighting with sticks and stones. And they examined our weapons,—before deigning to look at anything else,—as if eighteen instead of five had been the general age.

At last I so far broke through the laws of Arab politeness as to inform my host in plain words—how inconceivably wretched the boy Mohammed was thereby rendered ! —that I was hungry, thirsty, and sleepy, and that I wanted to be alone before visiting the Harim. The good-natured Shaykh, who was preparing to go out at once in order to pray before his father's grave, immediately brought me breakfast; lighted a pipe, spread a bed, darkened the room, turned out the children, and left me to the society I most desired—my own. I then overheard him summon his mother, wife, and other female relatives into the store-room, where his treasures had been carefully stowed away. During the forenoon, in the presence of the visitors, one of Hamid's uncles had urged him, half jocularly, to bring out the Sahharah. The Shaykh did not care to do anything of the kind. Every time a new box is opened in this part of the world, the owner's generosity is appealed to by those whom a refusal offends, and he must allow himself to be plundered with the best possible grace. Hamid therefore prudently suffered all to depart before exhibiting his spoils; which, to judge by the exclamations of delight which they elicited from feminine lips, proved highly satisfactory to those most concerned.

After sleeping, we all set out in a body to the Harim, as this is a duty which must not be delayed by the pious. The boy Mohammed was in better spirits,—the effect of having borrowed from Hamid, amongst other articles of clothing, an exceedingly gaudy embroidered coat. As for Shaykh Nur, he had brushed up his Tarbush, and, by means of some cast-off dresses of mine, had made himself look like a respectable Abyssinian slave, in a nondescript toilette, half Turkish, half Indian. I propose to reserve

the ceremony of Ziyárat, or Visitation, for another chapter, and to conclude this with a short account of our style
of living at the Shaykh's hospitable house.

Hamid's abode is a small corner building, open on
the North and East to the Barr al-Manakhah : the ground
floor shows only a kind of vestibule, in which coarse
articles, like old Shugdufs, mats and bits of sacking, are
lying about ; the rest are devoted to purposes of sewer-
age.   Ascending dark winding steps of ragged stone
covered with hard black earth, you come to the first floor,
where the men live.   It consists of two rooms to the front
of the house, one a Majlis, and another converted into a
store.   Behind them is a dark passage, into which the
doors open ; and the back part of the first story is a long
windowless room, containing a Hanafiyah,[1] or large copper
water-pot, and other conveniences for purification.   On
the second floor is the kitchen, which I did not inspect,
it being as usual occupied by the " Harim."

The Majlis has dwarf windows, or rather apertures
in the northern and eastern walls, with rude wooden
shutters and reed blinds ; the embrasures being garnished
with cushions, where you sit, morning and evening, to
enjoy the cool air.   The ceiling is of date-sticks laid across
palm-rafters stained red, and the walls are of rough
scoriæ, burnt bricks, and wood-work cemented with lime.
The only signs of furniture in the sitting-room are a
Diwan[2] round the sides and a carpet in the centre.   A

---

1 The Hanafiyah is a large vessel of copper, sometimes tinned,
with a cock in the lower part, and, generally, an ewer, or a basin, to
receive the water.

2 It is wonderful that this most comfortable, inexpensive, and
ornamental style of furnishing a room, has not been oftener imitated
in India and the hot countries of Europe. The Diwan—it must not
be confounded with the leathern perversion which obtains that name
in our club smoking-rooms—is a line of flat cushions ranged round
the room, either placed upon the ground, or on wooden benches, or
on a step of masonry, varying in height according to the fashion of

huge wooden box, like a seaman's chest, occupies one of the corners. In the southern wall there is a Suffah, or little shelf of common stone, sunk under a single arch; upon this are placed articles in hourly use, perfume-bottles, coffee-cups, a stray book or two, and sometimes a turband, to be out of the children's way. Two hooks on the western wall, hung jealously high up, hold a pair of pistols with handsome crimson cords and tassels, and half a dozen cherry-stick pipes. The centre of the room is never without one or more Shishas[1] (water pipes), and in the corner is a large copper brazier containing fire, with all the utensils for making coffee either disposed upon its broad brim or lying about the floor. The passage, like the stairs, is spread over with hard black earth, and is regularly watered twice a day during the hot weather.

The household consisted of Hamid's mother, wife, some nephews and nieces, small children who ran about in a half-wild and more than half-nude state, and two African slave girls. When the Damascus Caravan came

the day. When such foundation is used, it should be about a yard in breadth, and slope very gently from the outer edge towards the wall, for the greater convenience of reclining. Cotton-stuffed pillows, covered with chintz for summer, and silk for winter, are placed against the wall, and can be moved to make a luxurious heap; their covers are generally all of the same colour, except those at the end. The seat of honour is denoted by a small square cotton-stuffed silk coverlet, placed in one of the corners, which the position of the windows determines, the place of distinction being on the left of the host. Thus in Egypt you have a neatly-furnished room for £5 or £6.

1 The Madinah *Shisha* is a large cocoa-nut, with a tall wooden stem, both garnished with brass ornaments; some trifling differences in the latter distinguish it from the Meccah pipe. Both are inconveniently mounted upon small brass tripods, and are easily overturned, scattering fire and water over the carpets. The "lay," or snakes, are the substantial manufacture of Al-Yaman. Some grandees at Al-Madinah have glass Turkish *Shishas* and Constantinople snakes, which are of admirable elegance, compared with the clumsy and unsightly Arab inventions. (See page 80, ante.)

in, it was further reinforced by the arrival of his three younger brothers.

Though the house was not grand, it was made lively by the varied views out of the Majlis' windows. From the East, you looked upon the square Al-Barr, the town walls and houses beyond it, the Egyptian gate, the lofty minarets of the Harim, and the distant outlines of Jabal Ohod.[1] The north commanded a prospect of Mohammed's Mosque, one of the Khamsah Masajid,[2] or the five suburban Mosques[3]; of part of the fort-wall; and, when the Damascus Caravan came in, of the gay scene of the " Prado " beneath. The Majlis was tolerably cool during the early part of the day : in the afternoon the sun shone fiercely upon it. I have described the establishment at some length as a specimen of how the middle classes are lodged at Al-Madinah. The upper ranks affect Turkish and Egyptian luxuries in their homes, as I had an opportunity of seeing at Omar Effendi's house in the " Barr ;" and in these countries the abodes of the poor are everywhere very similar.

Our life in Shaykh Hamid's house was quiet, but not disagreeable. I never once set eyes upon the face of woman, unless the African slave girls be allowed the title. Even these at first attempted to draw their ragged veils over their sable charms, and would not answer the simplest question ; by degrees they allowed me to see them, and they ventured their voices to reply to me ; still they never threw off a certain appearance of shame.[4]

---

1 From this window I sketched the walls and the Egyptian gate of Al-Madinah.

2 " Five mosques."

3 This Mosque must not be confounded with the Harim. It is described in Chapter XV.

4 Their voices are strangely soft and delicate, considering the appearance of the organs from which they proceed. Possibly this may be a characteristic of the African races; it is remarkable amongst the Somali women.

I never saw, nor even heard, the youthful mistress of the household, who stayed all day in the upper rooms. The old lady, Hamid's mother, would stand upon the stairs, and converse aloud with her son, and, when few people were about the house, with me. She never, however, as afterwards happened to an ancient dame at Meccah, came and sat by my side.

When lying during mid-day in the gallery, I often saw parties of women mount the stairs to the Gynæconitis, and sometimes an individual would stand to shake a muffled hand[1] with Hamid, to gossip awhile, and to put some questions concerning absent friends ; but they were most decorously wrapped up, nor did they ever deign to *déroger*, even by exposing an inch of cheek.

At dawn we arose, washed, prayed, and broke our fast[2] upon a crust of stale bread, before smoking a pipe, and drinking a cup of coffee.[3] Then it was time to dress, to mount, and to visit the Harim or one of the Holy Places outside the city. Returning before the sun became intolerable, we sat together, and with conversation, Shishas and Chibuks,[4] coffee, and cold water perfumed with mastich-smoke,[5] we whiled away the time till our

---

1 After touching the skin of a strange woman, it is not lawful in Al-Islam to pray without ablution. For this reason, when a fair dame shakes hands with you, she wraps up her fingers in a kerchief, or in the end of her veil.

2 Nafukku'r rik, literally, "Let us open the saliva," is most idiomatic Hijazi for the first morsel eaten in the morning. Hence it is called Fakkur' rik, also Gura and Tasbih : the Egyptians call it "Al-Fatúr."

3 Orientals invariably begin by eating an "akratisma" in the morning before they will smoke a pipe, or drink a cup of coffee ; they have also an insuperable prejudice against the internal use of cold water at this hour.

4 The tobacco generally smoked here is Syrian, which is brought down in large quantities by the Damascus caravan. Latakia is more expensive, and generally too dry to retain its flavour.

5 The interior of the water jar is here perfumed with the smoke

" Ariston," a dinner which appeared at the primitive hour of 11 A.M. The meal, here called Al-Ghada, was served in the Majlis on a large copper tray, sent from the upper apartments. Ejaculating " Bismillah"—the Moslem "grace"—we all sat round it, and dipped equal hands in the dishes set before us. We had usually unleavened bread, different kinds of meat and vegetable stews ; and, at the end of the first course, plain boiled rice eaten with spoons ; then came the fruits, fresh dates, grapes, and pomegranates.

After dinner I used invariably to find some excuse— such as the habit of a " Kaylúlah[1]" (mid-day siesta) or the being a " Saúdawí[2] "—a person of melancholy tempera- ment—to have a rug spread in the dark passage behind

---

of mastich, exactly as described by Lane, (*Mod. Egyptians*, vol. i. ch. 5). I found at Al-Madinah the prejudice alluded to by Sonnini, namely, that the fumes of the gum are prejudicial, and sometimes fatal to invalids.

1 Kaylulah is the half hour's siesta about noon. It is a Sunnat, and the Prophet said of it, " Kilu, fa inna 'sh' Shayátina lá Takil,"— " Take the mid-day siesta, for, verily, the demons sleep not at this hour." "Aylúlah" is slumbering after morning prayers (our " beauty sleep"), which causes heaviness and inability to work. Ghaylúlah is the sleeping about 9 A.M., the effect of which is poverty and wretched- ness. *K*aylúlah (with the guttural kaf) is sleeping before evening prayers, a practice reprobated in every part of the East. And, finally, Faylúlah is sleeping immediately after sunset,—also considered highly detrimental.

2 The Arabs, who suffer greatly from melancholia, are kind to people afflicted with this complaint ; it is supposed to cause a distaste for society, and a longing for solitude, an unsettled habit of mind, and a neglect of worldly affairs. Probably it is the effect of over- working the brain, in a hot dry atmosphere. I have remarked, that in Arabia students are subject to it, and that amongst their philoso- phers and literary men, there is scarcely an individual who was not spoken of as a " Saudawi." My friend Omar Effendi used to com- plain, that at times his temperament drove him out of the house,— so much did he dislike the sound of the human voice,—to pass the day seated upon some eminence in the vicinity of the city.

the Majlis ; and there to lie reading, dozing, smoking, or writing, *en cachette*, in complete *déshabille*, all through the worst part of the day, from noon to sunset.

Then came the hour for receiving or paying visits. We still kept up an intimacy with Omar Effendi and Sa'ad the Demon, although Salih Skakkar and Amm Jamal, either disliking our society, or perhaps thinking our sphere of life too humble for their dignity, did not appear once in Hamid's house. The evening prayers ensued, either at home, or in the Harim, followed by our Asha or " deipnon," another substantial meal like the dinner, but more plentiful, of bread, meat, vegetables, plain rice and fruits, concluding with the invariable pipes and coffee.

To pass our *soirée*, we occasionally dressed in common clothes, shouldered a Nabbut,[1] and went to the *café;* sometimes on festive occasions we indulged in a Taatumah (or Itmiyah), a late supper of sweetmeats, pomegranates, and dried fruits. Usually we sat upon mattresses spread upon the ground in the open air at the Shaykh's door ; receiving . evening visits, chatting, telling stories, and making merry, till each, as he felt the approach of the drowsy god, sank down into his proper place, and fell asleep.

Whatever may be the heat of the day, the night at Al-Madinah, owing, I suppose, to its elevated position, is cool and pleasant. In order to allay the dust, the ground before the Shaykh's door was watered every evening, and the evaporation was almost too great to be safe,—the boy Mohammed suffered from a smart attack of lumbago,

---

1 This habit of going out at night in common clothes, with a Nabbut upon one's shoulders, is, as far as I could discover, popular at Al-Madinah, but confined to the lowest classes at Meccah. The boy Mohammed always spoke of it with undisguised disapprobation. During my stay at Meccah, I saw no such costume amongst respectable people there; though oftentimes there was a suspicion of a disguise.

which, however, yielded readily to frictions of olive oil in which ginger had been boiled.

Our greatest inconvenience at night-time was the pugnacity of the animal creation. The horses of the troopers tethered in the Barr were sure to break loose once in twelve hours. Some hobbled old nag, having slipped the headstall, would advance with kangaroo-leaps towards a neighbour against whom it had a private grudge. Their heads would touch for a moment ; then came a snort and a whinny, a furious kick, and, lastly, a second horse loose and dashing about with head and tail viciously cocked. This was the signal for a general breaking of halters and heel-ropes ; after which, a " stampede " scoured the plain, galloping, rearing, kicking, biting, snorting, pawing, and screaming, with the dogs barking sympathetically, and the horse-keepers shouting in hot pursuit.

It was a strange sight to see by moonlight the forms of these " demon steeds " exaggerated by the shades ; and, on more than one occasion, we had all to start up precipitately from our beds, and yield them to a couple of combatants who were determined to fight out their quarrel *à l'outrance*, wherever the battle-field might be.

The dogs at Al-Madinah are not less pugnacious than the horses.[1] They are stronger and braver than those that haunt the streets at Cairo ; like the Egyptians, they have amongst themselves a system of police regulations, which brings down all the *posse comitatus* upon the unhappy straggler who ventures into a strange quarter of the town. They certainly met in Al-Barr upon common

---

[1] Burckhardt (Travels in Arabia, vol. ii., p. 268) remarks that Al-Madinah is the only town in the East from which dogs are excluded. This was probably as much a relic of Wahhabi-ism, (that sect hating even to look at a dog), as arising from apprehension of the Mosque being polluted by canine intrusion. I have seen one or two of these animals in the town, but I was told, that when they enter it in any numbers, the police-magistrate issues orders to have them ejected.

ground, to decide the differences which must arise in so
artificial a state of canine society.

Having had many opportunities of watching them, I
can positively assert that they were divided into two
parties, which fought with a skill and an *acharnement* that
astounded me. Sometimes when one side gave way, and
as the retreat was degenerating into a *sauve qui peut*, some
proud warrior, a dog-hero, would sacrifice himself for the
public weal, and with gnashing teeth and howls of rage
encounter the assaults of the insolent victors until his
flying friends had time to recover heart. Such an one my
companions called "Mubariz.[1]" At other times, some
huge animal, an Ajax of his kind, would plunge into
the ring with frantic yells, roll over one dog, snap at a
second, worry a third for a minute or two, and then dash
off to a distant part, where a thicker field required his
presence. This uncommon sagacity has been remarked
by the Arabs, who look on amused at their battles.
Current in Al-Hijaz are also certain superstitions about
the dog resembling ours ; only, as usual, more poetical
and less grotesque. Most people believe that when the
animal howls without apparent cause in the neighbourhood of a house, it forbodes death to one of the inmates ;
for the dog they say can distinguish the awful form of
Azrail, the Angel of Death, hovering over the doomed
abode, whereas man's spiritual sight is dull and dim by
reason of his sins.

When the Damascus Caravan entered Al-Madinah,
our day became a little more amusing. From the windows
of Shaykh Hamid's house there was a perpetual succession
of strange scenes. A Persian nobleman, also, had pitched
his tents so near the door, that the whole course of his
private life became public and patent to the boy Moham-

---

1 The "Mubariz" is the single combatant, the champion of the
Arabian classical and chivalrous times.

med, who amused his companions by reporting all manner of ludicrous scenes. The Persian's wife was rather a pretty woman, and she excited the youth's fierce indignation, by not veiling her face when he gazed at her,—thereby showing that, as his beard was not grown, she considered him a mere boy.

" I will ask her to marry me," said Mohammed, " and thereby rouse her shame ! "

He did so, but, unhappy youth! the fair Persian never even ceased fanning herself.

The boy Mohammed was for once confounded.

CHAPTER XVI.

A VISIT TO THE PROPHET'S TOMB.

Having performed the greater ablution, and used the toothstick as directed, and dressed ourselves in white clothes, which the Apostle loved, we were ready to start upon our holy errand. As my foot still gave me great pain, Shaykh Hamid sent for a donkey. A wretched animal appeared, raw-backed, lame of one leg, and wanting an ear, with accoutrements to match, a pack-saddle without stirrups, and a halter instead of a bridle. Such as the brute was, however, I had to mount it, and to ride through the Misri gate, to the wonder of certain Badawin, who, like the Indians, despise the ass.

> " Honourable is the riding of a horse to the rider,
> But the mule is a dishonour, and the donkey a disgrace,"

says their song. The Turkish pilgrims, however, who appear to take a pride in ignoring all Arab points of prejudice, generally mount donkeys when they cannot walk. The Badawin therefore settled among themselves, audibly enough, that I was an Osmanli, who of course could not understand Arabic, and they put the question generally,

" By what curse of Allah had they been subjected to ass-riders ? "

But Shaykh Hamid is lecturing me upon the subject of the Mosque.

The Masjid Al-Nabawi, or the Prophet's Mosque, is one of the Haramayn, or the " two sanctuaries " of Al-

Islam, and is the second of the three[1] most venerable places of worship in the world; the other two being the Masjid al-Harim at Meccah (connected with Abraham) and the Masjid al-Aksa of Jerusalem (the peculiar place of Solomon). A Hadís or traditional saying of Mohammed asserts, "One prayer in this my Mosque is more efficacious than a thousand in other places, save only the Masjid al-Harim.[2]" It is therefore the visitor's duty, as long as he stays at Al-Madinah, to pray there *the five times per diem*, to pass the day in it reading the Koran, and the night, if possible, in watching and devotion.

A visit to the Masjid al-Nabawi, and the holy spots within it, is technically called "Ziyárat" or Visitation.[3] An essential difference is made between this rite and Hajj or pilgrimage. The latter is obligatory by Koranic order upon every Moslem once in his life: the former is only a meritorious action. "Tawáf," or circumambulation of the House of Allah at Meccah, must never be performed at the Apostle's tomb. This should not be visited in the Ihram or pilgrim dress; men should not kiss it, touch it with the hand, or press the bosom against it, as at the Ka'abah; or rub the face with dust collected near the sepulchre; and those who prostrate themselves before it, like certain ignorant Indians, are held to be

---

1 Others add a fourth, namely, the Masjid al-Takwa, at Kuba.

2 The Moslem divines, however, naïvely remind their readers, that they are not to pray once in the Al-Madinah Mosque, and neglect the other 999, as if absolved from the necessity of them. The passage in the text merely promises 1000 blessings upon that man's devotion who prays at the Prophet's Mosque.

3 The visitor, who approaches the Sepulchre as a matter of religious ceremony, is called "Záir," his conductor "Muzawwir," whereas the pilgrim at Meccah becomes a "Haji." The Imam Malik disapproved of a Moslem's saying, "I have visited the Prophet's tomb," preferring him to express himself thus—"I have visited the Prophet." Others again dislike the latter formula, declaring the Prophet too venerable to be so visited by Amr and Zayd.

guilty of deadly sin. On the other hand, to spit upon any part of the Mosque, or to treat it with contempt, is held to be the act of an Infidel.

Thus the learned and religious have settled, one would have thought, accurately enough the spiritual rank and dignity of the Masjid al-Nabawi. But mankind, especially in the East, must always be in extremes. The orthodox school of Al-Malik holds Al-Madinah, on account of the sanctity of, and the religious benefits to be derived from, Mohammed's tomb, more honourable than Meccah. Some declare that the Apostle preferred his place of refuge, blessing it as Abraham did Meccah. Moreover, as a tradition declares that every man's body is drawn from the ground in which he is buried, Al-Madinah evidently had the honour of supplying materials for the Apostle's person. Others, like Omar, were uncertain which to prefer. The Wahhabis, on the other hand, rejecting the Intercession of the Apostle on the Day of Judgment, considering the grave of a mere mortal unworthy of notice, and highly disgusted by the idolatrous respect paid to it by certain foolish Moslems, plundered the sacred building with sacrilegious violence, and forbade visitors from distant countries to enter Al-Madinah.[1]

The general consensus of Al-Islam admits the superiority of the *Bayt Allah* (" House of God ") at Meccah to the whole world ; and declares Al-Madinah to be more venerable than every part of Meccah, and consequently all the earth, except only the Bayt Allah. This last is a *juste milieu* view by no means in favour with the inhabitants of either place. In the meanwhile the Meccans claim unlimited superiority over the Madani : the Madani over the Meccans.

---

1 In A.D. 1807, they prevented Ali Bey (the Spaniard Badia) from entering Al-Madinah, and it appears that he had reason to congratulate himself upon escaping without severe punishment.

Passing through muddy streets,—they had been freshly watered before evening time,—I came suddenly upon the Mosque. Like that at Meccah, the approach is choked up by ignoble buildings, some actually touching the holy " enceinte," others separated by a lane compared with which the road round St. Paul's is a Vatican Square.[1] There is no outer front, no general prospect of the Prophet's Mosque; consequently, as a building, it has neither beauty nor dignity.

And entering the Bab al-Rahmah[2]—the Gate of Pity, —by a diminutive flight of steps, I was astonished at the mean and tawdry appearance of a place so universally venerated in the Moslem world. It is not, like the Meccan Temple, grand and simple, the expression of a single sublime idea : the longer I looked at it, the more it suggested the resemblance of a museum of second-rate art, an old Curiosity-shop, full of ornaments that are not accessories, and decorated with pauper splendour.

The Masjid al-Nabi is a parallelogram about four hundred and twenty feet in length by three hundred and forty broad, the direction of the long walls being nearly north and south. As usual in Al-Islam, it is a hypæthral building with a spacious central area, called Al-Sahn, Al-Hosh, Al-Haswah, or Al-Ramlah,[3] surrounded by a peristyle with numerous rows of pillars like the colonnades of an Italian cloister. The arcades or porticoes are flat-ceilinged, domed above with the small *Media*

---

1 Nothing in the Spanish cathedrals suggests their Oriental origin and the taste of the people, more than the way in which they are hedged in by secular buildings.

2 The ceremony of Ziyarat, however, begins at the Bab al-Salam. We rode up to this gate only in order to avoid the sun.

3 Haswah is a place covered with gravel : Ramlah, one which is sanded over. Both are equally applicable, and applied to the areas of Mosques. Al-Sahn is the general word; Al-Hosh is occasionally used, but is more properly applied to the court-yard of a dwelling-house.

Naranja, or half-orange cupola of Spain, and divided into four parts by narrow passages, three or four steps below the level of the pavement. Along the whole inner length of the Northern short wall runs the Majidi Riwak, so called from the then reigning Sultan.[1] The Western long wall is occupied by the Riwak of the Rahmah Gate ; the Eastern by that of the Bab al-Nisa, the " Women's Entrance.[2]"

Embracing the inner length of the Southern short wall, and deeper by nearly treble the amount of columns than the other porticoes, is the main colonnade, called *Al-Rauzah*[3] (the Garden), the adytum containing all that is venerable in the building. These four Riwaks, arched externally, are supported internally by pillars of different shape and material, varying from fine porphyry to dirty plaster. The Southern, where the sepulchre or cenotaph stands, is paved with handsome slabs of white marble and marquetry work, here and there covered with coarse matting, and above this by unclean carpets, well worn by faithful feet.[4]

But this is not the time for *Tafarruj* or lionising.

---

1 This Riwak was begun about five or six years ago by Abd al-Majid. To judge from the size of the columns, and the other preparations which encumber the ground, this part of the building will surpass all the rest. But the people of Al-Madinah assured me that it will not be finished for some time,—a prophecy likely to be fulfilled by the present state of Turkish finance.

2 This gate derives its peculiar name from its vicinity to the Lady Fatimah's tomb; women, when they do visit the Mosque, enter it through all the doors indifferently.

3 It is so called by the figure synecdoche: it contains the Rauzah or the Prophet's Garden, and therefore the whole portico enjoys that honoured name.

4 These carpets are swept by the eunuchs, who let out the office for a certain fee to pilgrims, every morning, immediately after sunrise. Their diligence, however, does by no means prevent the presence of certain little parasites, concerning which politeness is dumb

N.

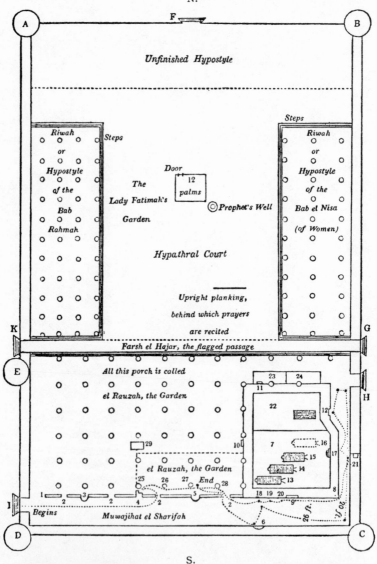

S.

The long walls are 420 feet.
The short walls 340.
The Hujrah is an irregular square of 55 feet.
The space marked with dots and called Al-Rauzah is about 80 feet long.
Between the Hujrah and the Eastern wall 20 feet.
Between the Hujrah and the Southern wall 25 or 26 feet.

A Shikayliyah Minaret, being now rebuilt.
B Sulaymaniyah Minaret.
C Raisiyah Minaret.
D Minaret of Salam Gate.
E Minaret of Rahmah Gate.
F New Gate Al-Majidi.
G Bab al-Nisa (of women).
H Bab Jibrail (of Gabriel).
I Bab Salam (of Safety).
K Bab Rahmah (of Pity).

1 Dwarf wall.
2 Passages through wall.
3 Mihrab al-Sulaymani (Niche of Sultan Sulayman).
4 The Prophet's pulpit.
5 The Prophet's niche.
6 Osman's niche.
7 Al-Hujrah, the chamber in which the Prophet died and was buried. An irregular square of 50 or 55 feet.
8 The passage encircling the tombs.
9 The door in the grating called Bab al-Muwajihah.
10 The Bab al-Taubah (of Repentance).
11 The Bab al-Shami (Syrian).
12 The Gate of our Lady Fatimah.
13 The Prophet's Tomb.
14 Abu Bakr's Tomb.
15 Omar's Tomb.
16 Vacant place intended for the sepulture of Isa bin Maryam.
17 The Makam Sayyidna Isa (Place of our Lord Isa).
18 The Shubak al-Naby (Prophet's window).
19 Abu Bakr's window.
20 Omar's window.
21 The Mahbat Jibrail, or place where Gabriel used to descend, vulgarly called Gabriel's Gate.
22 Fatimah's Tomb, supposed to be in her house.
23 The Dakkat al-Aghawah, a low enclosure where the eunuchs sit.
24 The place where the Koran is constantly read.

The dotted lines denote the visitor's course : the larger points denote the stations of prayer.

25 The Weeping Post.
26 Ayishah's Pillar.
27 The Pillar of the Fugitives.
28 The Pillar of Repentance, or of Abu Lubabah.
29 The Mukabbariyah, consisting of a stone seat supported by four columns. Here the Muballigh, (who is to the interior of the Mosque what the Mu'ezzin is to the exterior,) warns people five times a day to prayer.

Shaykh Hamid warns me, with a nudge, that other things
are expected of a Zair (visitor). He leads me to the Bab
al-Salam, fighting his way through a troop of beggars,
and inquires markedly if I am religiously pure.[1] Then,
placing our hands a little below and on the left of the
waist, the palm of the right covering the back of the left,
in the position of prayer, and beginning with the dexter
feet,[2] we pace slowly forwards down the line called the
Muwajihat al-Sharifah, or "the Illustrous Fronting,"
which, divided off like an aisle, runs parallel with the
Southern wall of the Mosque. On my right hand walks
the Shaykh, who recites aloud the following prayer,
making me repeat it after him.[3] It is literally rendered,
as, indeed, are all the formulæ, and the reader is requested
to excuse the barbarous fidelity of the translation.

"In the Name of Allah and in the faith of Allah's
Apostle! O Lord, cause me to enter the Entering of
Truth, and cause me to issue forth the Issuing of Truth,
and permit me to draw near to Thee, and make me a
Sultan Victorious[4]!" Then follow blessings upon the
Apostle, and afterwards: "O Allah! open to me the
Doors of Thy Mercy, and grant me Entrance into it, and
protect me from the Stoned Devil!"

During this preliminary prayer we had passed down
two-thirds of the Muwajihat al-Sharifah. On the left
hand is a dwarf wall, about the height of a man, painted
with arabesques, and pierced with four small doors which

---

1 Because if not pure, ablution is performed at the well in the
centre of the hypæthra. Zairs are ordered to visit the Mosque perfumed, and in their best clothes, and the Hanafi school deems it
lawful on this occasion only to wear dresses of pure silk.

2 In this Mosque, as in all others, it is proper to enter with the
right foot, and to retire with the left.

3 I must warn the reader that almost every Muzawwir has his
own litany, which descends from father to son: moreover, all the
books differ at least as much as do the oral authorities.

4 That is to say, "over the world, the flesh, and the devil."

open into the Muwajihat. In this barrier are sundry small erections, the niche called the Mihráb Sulaymani,[1] the Mambar, or pulpit, and the Mihrab al-Nabawi.[2]

The two niches are of beautiful mosaic, richly worked with various coloured marbles, and the pulpit is a graceful collection of slender columns, elegant tracery, and inscriptions admirably carved. Arrived at the Western small door in the dwarf wall, we entered the celebrated spot called Al-Rauzah, after a saying of the Apostle's, "Between my Tomb and my Pulpit is a Garden of the Gardens of Paradise.[3]" On the North and West sides it is

---

1 This by strangers is called the Masalla Shafe'i, or the Place of Prayer of the Shafe'i school. It was sent from Constantinople about 100 years ago, by Sultan Sulayman the Magnificent. He built the Sulaymaniyah minaret, and has immortalised his name at Al-Madinah, as well as at Meccah, by the number of his donations to the shrine.

2 Here is supposed to have been one of the Prophet's favourite stations of prayer. It is commonly called the Musalla Hanafi, because now appropriated by that school.

3 This tradition, like most others referring to events posterior to the Prophet's death, is differently given, and so important are the variations, that I only admire how all Al-Islam does not follow Wahhabi example, and summarily consign them to oblivion. Some read "Between my dwelling-house (in the Mosque) and my place of Prayer (in the Barr al-Manakhah) is a Garden of the Gardens of Paradise." Others again, "Between my house and my pulpit is a Garden of the Gardens of Paradise." A third tradition—"Between my tomb and my pulpit is a Garden of the Gardens of Paradise, and verily my pulpit is in my Full Cistern," or "upon a Full Cistern of the Cisterns of Paradise," has given rise to a new superstition. "Tara," according to some commentators, alludes especially to the cistern Al-Kausar; consequently this Rauzah is, like the black stone at Meccah, *bonâ fide*, a bit of Paradise, and on the day of resurrection, it shall return bodily to the place whence it came. Be this as it may, all Moslems are warned that the Rauzah is a most holy spot. None but the Prophet and his son-in-law Ali ever entered it, when ceremonially impure, without being guilty of deadly sin. The Mohammedan of the present day is especially informed that on no account must he here tell lies, or even perjure himself. Thus

not divided from the rest of the portico ; on the South
runs the dwarf wall, and on the East it is limited by the
west end of the lattice-work containing the tomb.

Accompanied by my Muzawwir I entered the Rauzah,
and was placed by him with the Mukabbariyah[1] behind
me, fronting Meccah, with my right shoulder opposite to,
and about twenty feet distant from, the dexter pillar of
the Apostle's Pulpit.[2] There, after saying the afternoon
prayers,[3] I performed the usual two bows in honour of the
temple,[4] and at the end of them recited the hundred and
ninth and the hundred and twelfth chapters of the Koran—
the "Kul, ya ayyuha'l-Kafiruna," and the "Surat al-
Ikhlas," called also the "Kul, Huw' Allah," or the
Declaration of Unity ; and may be thus translated :

"Say, He is the one God!

"The eternal God!

"He begets not, nor is He begot !

the Rauzah must be respected as much as the interior of the Bayt
Allah at Meccah.

1 This is a stone desk on four pillars, where the *Muballighs* (or
clerks) recite the *Ikámah*, the call to divine service. It was presented
to the Mosque by Kaid-Bey, the Mamluk Sultan of Egypt.

2 I shall have something to say about this pulpit when entering
into the history of the Harim.

3 The afternoon prayers being *Farz*, or obligatory, were recited,
because we feared that evening might come on before the ceremony
of *Ziyarat* (visitation) concluded, and thus the time for Al-Asr (afternoon prayers) might pass away. The reader may think this rather
a curious forethought in a man who, like Hamid, never prayed except
when he found the case urgent. Such, however, is the strict order,
and my Muzawwir was right to see it executed.

4 This two-bow prayer, which generally is recited in honour
of the Mosque, is here, say divines, addressed especially to the
Deity by the visitor who intends to beg the intercession of his
Prophet. It is only just to confess that the Moslems have done
their best by all means in human power, here as well as elsewhere, to
inculcate the doctrine of eternal distinction between the creature
and the Creator. Many of the Maliki school, however, make the
ceremony of Ziyarat to precede the prayer to the Deity.

"And unto Him the like is not."

After which was performed a single Sujdah (Prostration) of Thanks,[1] in gratitude to Allah for making it my fate to visit so holy a spot.

This being the recognised time to give alms, I was besieged by beggars, who spread their napkins before us on the ground, sprinkled with a few coppers to excite generosity. But not wishing to be distracted by them, before leaving Hamid's house I had changed two dollars, and had given the coin to the boy Mohammed, who accompanied me, strictly charging him to make that sum last through the Mosque.

My answer to the beggars was a reference to my attendant, backed by the simple action of turning my pockets inside out ; and, whilst he was battling with the beggars, I proceeded to cast my first *coup-d'œil* upon the Rauzah.

The "Garden" is the most elaborate part of the Mosque. Little can be said in its praise by day, when it bears the same relation to a second-rate church in Rome as an English chapel-of-ease to Westminster Abbey. It is a space of about eighty feet in length, tawdrily decorated so as to resemble a garden. The carpets are flowered, and the pediments of the columns are cased with bright green tiles, and adorned to the height of a man with gaudy and unnatural vegetation in arabesque. It is disfigured by handsome branched candelabras of cut crystal, the work, I believe, of a London house, and presented to the shrine by the late Abbas Pasha of Egypt.[2]

The only admirable feature of the view is the light

---

1 The *Sujdah* is a single "prostration" with the forehead touching the ground. It is performed from a sitting position, after the *Dua* or supplication that concludes the two-bow prayer. Some of the Olema, especially those of the Shafe'i school, permit this "Sujdah of thanks" to be performed before the two-bow prayer if the visitor have any notable reason to be grateful.

2 The candles are still sent from Cairo.

cast by the windows of stained glass[1] in the Southern wall. Its peculiar background, the railing of the tomb, a splendid filigree-work of green and polished brass, gilt or made to resemble gold, looks more picturesque near than at a distance, when it suggests the idea of a gigantic bird-cage. But at night the eye, dazzled by oil-lamps[2] suspended from the roof, by huge wax candles, and by smaller illuminations falling upon crowds of visitors in handsome attire, with the richest and the noblest of the city sitting in congregation when service is performed,[3] becomes less critical. Still the scene must be viewed with Moslem bias, and until a man is thoroughly imbued with the spirit of the East, the last place the Rauzah will remind him of, is that which the architect primarily intended it to resemble—a garden.

Then with Hamid, professionally solemn, I reassumed the position of prayer, and retraced my steps. After passing through another small door in the dwarf wall that bounds the Muwajihah, we did not turn to the right, which would have led us to the Bab al-Salam; our course was in an opposite direction, towards the Eastern wall of the temple. Meanwhile we repeated, " Verily Allah and His Angels[4] bless the Apostle! O ye who believe, bless him,

---

1 These windows are a present from Kaid-Bey, the Mamluk Sultan of Egypt.

2 These oil lamps are a present from the Sultan.

3 The five daily liturgies are here recited by Imams, and every one presses to the spot on account of its peculiar sanctity.

4 In Moslem theology "Salat" from Allah means mercy, from the angels intercession for pardon, and from mankind blessing. The act of blessing the Prophet is one of peculiar efficacy in a religious point of view. Cases are quoted of sinners being actually snatched from hell by a glorious figure, the personification of the blessings which had been called down by them upon Mohammed's head. This most poetical idea is borrowed, I believe, from the ancient Guebres, who fabled that a man's good works assumed a beautiful female shape, which stood to meet his soul when winding its way to judgment. Also when a Moslem blesses Mohammed at Al-Madinah, his

and salute Him with Honour!" At the end of this prayer, we arrived at the Mausoleum, which requires some description before the reader can understand the nature of our proceedings there.

The Hujrah[1] or " Chamber " as it is called, from the circumstance of its having been Áyishah's room, is an irregular square of from fifty to fifty-five feet in the South-East corner of the building, and separated on all sides from the walls of the Mosque by a passage about twenty-six feet broad on the South side, and twenty on the East. The reason of this isolation has been before explained, and there is a saying of Mohammed's, " O Allah, cause not my Tomb to become an Object of Idolatrous Adoration! May Allah's Wrath fall heavy upon the People who make the Tombs of their Prophets Places of Prayer[2]!"

---

sins are not written down for three days,—thus allowing ample margin for repentance,—by the recording angel. Al-Malakayn (the two Angels), or Kiram al-Katibín (the Generous Writers), are mere personifications of the good principle and the evil principle of man's nature; they are fabled to occupy each a shoulder, and to keep a list of words and deeds. This is certainly borrowed from a more ancient faith. In Hermas II. (command. 6), we are told that "every man has two angels, one of godliness, the other of iniquity," who endeavour to secure his allegiance,—a superstition seemingly founded upon the dualism of the old Persians. Mediæval Europe, which borrowed so much from the East at the time of the Crusades, degraded these angels into good and bad fairies for children's stories.

1 Burckhardt writes this word Hedjra (which means "flight"). Nor is M. Caussin de Perceval's "El Hadjarat" less erroneous. At Madinah it is invariably called Al-Hujrah—the chamber. The chief difficulty in distinguishing the two words, meaning "chamber" and "flight," arises from our only having one *h* to represent the hard and soft *h* of Arabic, حجرة and حجرة. In the case of common saints, the screen or railing round the cenotaph is called a "Maksurah."

2 Yet Mohammed enjoined his followers to frequent graveyards. "Visit graves; of a verity they shall make you think of futurity!"

Inside there are, or are supposed to be, three tombs facing the South, surrounded by stone walls without any aperture, or, as others say, by strong planking.[1] Whatever this material may be, it is hung outside with a curtain, somewhat like a large four-post bed. The external railing is separated by a dark narrow passage from the inner, which it surrounds ; and is of iron filigree painted of a vivid grass green,—with a view to the garden. Here carefully inserted in the verdure, and doubly bright by contrast, is the gilt or burnished brass work forming the long and graceful letters of the Suls character, and disposed into the Moslem creed, the Profession of Unity, and similar religious sentences.

On the South side, for greater honour, the railing is plated over with silver, and silver letters are interlaced with it. This fence, which connects the columns and forbids passage to all men, may be compared to the baldacchino of Roman churches. It has four gates : that to the South is the Bab al-Muwajihah ; Eastward is the gate of our Lady Fátimah ; westward the Bab al-Taubah (of Repentance), opening into the Rauzah or garden ; and to the North, the Bab al-Shami or Syrian gate. They are constantly kept closed, except the fourth, which admits, into the dark narrow passage above alluded to, the officers who have charge of the treasures there deposited ; and the eunuchs who sweep the floor, light

---

And again, "Whoso visiteth his two parents' grave, or one of the two, every Friday, he shall be written a pious child, even though he might have been in the world, before that, a disobedient."

1 The truth is no one knows what is there. I have even heard a learned Persian declare that there is no wall behind the curtain, which hangs so loosely that, when the wind blows against it, it defines the form of a block of marble, or a built-up tomb. I believe this to be wholly apocryphal, for reasons which will presently be offered.

the lamps, and carry away the presents sometimes thrown
in here by devotees.[1]

In the Southern side of the fence are three windows,
holes about half a foot square, and placed from four to
five feet above the ground ; they are said to be between
three and four cubits distant from the Apostle's head.
The most Westerly of these is supposed to front Mohammed's tomb, wherefore it is called the Shubak al-Nabi, or
the Prophet's window.   The next, on the right as you
front it, is Abu Bakr's, and the most Easterly of the three
is Omar's.

Above the Hujrah is the Green Dome, surmounted
outside by a large gilt crescent springing from a series of
globes.   The glowing imaginations of the Moslems crown
this gem of the building with a pillar of heavenly light,
which directs from three days' distance the pilgrims' steps
towards Al-Madinah.   But alas ! none save holy men
(and perhaps, odylic sensitives), whose material organs
are piercing as their spiritual vision, may be allowed the
privilege of beholding this poetic splendour.

Arrived at the Shubak al-Nabi, Hamid took his stand
about six feet or so out of reach of the railing, and at that
respectful distance from, and facing[2] the Hazirah (or pre-

---

1 The peculiar place where the guardians of the tomb sit and
confabulate is the Dakkat al-Ágháwát (eunuch's bench) or Al-Mayda
—the table—a raised bench of stone and wood, on the North side of
the Hujrah.   The remaining part of this side is partitioned off from
the body of the Mosque by a dwarf wall, inclosing the "Khasafat al-
Sultan," the place where *Fakihs* are perpetually engaged in *Khitmahs*,
or perusals of the Koran, on behalf of the reigning Sultan.

2 The ancient practice of Al-Islam during the recitation of the
following benedictions was to face Meccah, the back being turned
towards the tomb, and to form a mental image of the Prophet, supposing him to be in front.   Al-Kirmani and other doctors prefer this
as the more venerable custom, but in these days it is completely ex-
ploded, and the purist would probably be soundly bastinadoed by
the eunuchs for attempting it.

sence), with hands raised as in prayer, he recited the following supplication in a low voice, telling me in a stage whisper to repeat it after him with awe, and fear, and love :—

"Peace be upon Thee, O Apostle of Allah, and the Mercy of Allah and his Blessings ! Peace be upon Thee, O Apostle of Allah ! Peace be upon Thee, O Friend of Allah ! Peace be upon Thee, O best of Allah's Creation ! Peace be upon Thee, O pure Creature of Allah ! Peace be upon Thee, O Chief of Prophets ! Peace be upon

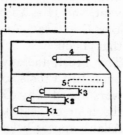

1. Mohammed.
2. Abu Bakr.
3. Omar.
4. Fatimah's Tomb.
5. The dotted space left empty for Isa.

Thee, O Seal of the Prophets ! Peace be upon Thee, O Prince of the Pious ! Peace be upon Thee, O Apostle of the Lord of the (three) Worlds ! Peace be upon Thee, and upon Thy Family, and upon Thy pure Wives ! Peace be upon Thee, and upon all Thy Companions ! Peace be upon Thee, and upon all the Prophets, and upon those sent to preach Allah's Word ! Peace be upon Thee, and upon all Allah's righteous Worshippers ! Peace be upon Thee, O thou Bringer of Glad Tidings ! Peace be upon Thee, O Bearer of Threats ! Peace be upon Thee, O thou bright Lamp ! Peace be upon Thee, O thou Apostle of Mercy ! Peace be upon Thee, O Ruler of Thy Faith ! Peace be upon Thee, O Opener of Grief ! Peace be upon Thee ! and Allah bless Thee ! and Allah repay Thee for us, O Thou Apostle of Allah ! the choicest of Blessings with which He ever blessed Prophet ! Allah bless Thee as often as Mentioners have mentioned Thee, and Forgetters have forgotten Thee ! And Allah bless Thee among the First and the Last, with the best, the highest, and the fullest of Blessings ever bestowed on Man ; even as we escaped Error by means of Thee, and were made to see after Blindness, and after Ignorance were directed into the Right Way. I bear Witness that there is no god but *the* God (Allah), and I testify that Thou art His Servant, and His Apostle, and His Faithful Follower, and Best Creature. And I bear Witness, O Apostle of Allah! that Thou hast delivered thy Message, and discharged Thy Trust, and advised Thy Faith, and opened Grief, and published Proofs, and fought valiantly for Thy Lord, and worshipped Thy God till Certainty came to Thee (*i.e.* to the hour of death). And we Thy Friends, O Apostle of Allah! appear before Thee, Travellers from distant lands and far Countries, through Dangers and Difficulties, in the Times of Darkness, and in the Hours of Day, longing to give Thee Thy Rights (*i.e.* to honour Thee by benediction and visitation), and to obtain the Blessings of Thine Intercession, for our Sins have broken our Backs, and Thou intercedest with the Healer. And Allah said,[1] 'And though they have injured themselves, they came to Thee, and begged Thee to secure their Pardon, and they found God an Acceptor of Penitence, and full of Compassion.' O Apostle of Allah, Intercession! Intercession! Intercession[2]! O Allah, bless Mohammed and Mohammed's Family, and give Him Superiority and high Rank, even as Thou didst promise Him, and graciously allow us to conclude this Visitation. I deposit on this spot, and near Thee, O Apostle of God, my everlasting Profession (of faith) from this our Day, to the Day of Judgment, that there is no god but Allah, and that our Lord Mohammed is His Servant and His Apostle.[3] Amen! O Lord of the (three) Worlds![4]"

1 This is the usual introduction to a quotation from the Koran.

2 It may easily be conceived how offensive this must be to the Wahhabis, who consider it blasphemy to assert that a mere man can stand between the Creator and the creature on the last day.

3 This is called the Testification. Like the Fatihah, it is repeated at every holy place and tomb visited at Al-Madinah.

4 Burckhardt mentions that in his day, among other favours

After which, performing Ziyarat[1] for ourselves, we repeated the Fatihah or "opening" chapter of the Koran.

"In the name of Allah, the Merciful, the Compassionate!

"Praise be to Allah, who the (three) Worlds made.

"The Merciful, the Compassionate.

"The King of the Day of Faith.

"Thee (alone) do we worship, and of Thee (alone) do we ask Aid.

"Guide us to the Path that is straight—

"The Path of those for whom thy Love is great, not those on whom is Hate, nor they that deviate.

"Amen! O Lord of Angels, Jinnis, and Men![2]"

After reciting this mentally with upraised hands, the forefinger of the right hand being extended to its full length, we drew our palms down our faces and did alms-deeds, a vital part of the ceremony. Thus concludes the first part of the ceremony of visitation at the Apostle's tomb.

---

supplicated in prayer to the Deity, the following request was made,— "Destroy our enemies, and may the torments of hell-fire be their lot!" I never heard it at the Prophet's tomb. As the above benediction is rather a long one, the Zair is allowed to shorten it *à discrétion*, but on no account to say less than "Peace be upon Thee, O Apostle of Allah"—this being the gist of the ceremony.

1 Though performing Ziyarat for myself, I had promised my old Shaykh at Cairo to recite a Fatihah in his name at the Prophet's tomb; so a double recitation fell to my lot. If acting Zair for another person (a common custom, we read, even in the days of Al-Walid, the Caliph of Damascus), you are bound to mention your principal's name at the beginning of the benediction, thus: "Peace be upon Thee, O Apostle of Allah from such an one, the son of such an one, who wants Thine Intercession, and begs for Pardon and Mercy." Most Zairs recite Fatihahs for all their friends and relations at the tomb.

2 I have endeavoured in this translation to imitate the imperfect rhyme of the original Arabic. Such an attempt, however, is full of difficulties : the Arabic is a language in which, like Italian, it is almost impossible not to rhyme.

Hamid then stepped about a foot and half to the right, and I followed his example, so as to place myself exactly opposite the second aperture in the grating called Abu Bakr's window.   There, making a sign towards the mausoleum, we addressed its inmate, as follows :—

" Peace be upon Thee, O Abu Bakr, O Thou Truthful One !   Peace be upon Thee, O Caliph of Allah's Apostle over his People !   Peace be upon Thee, O Companion of the Cave, and Friend in Travel !   Peace be upon Thee, O Thou Banner of the Fugitives and the Auxiliaries !   I testify Thou didst ever stand firm in the right Way, and wast a Smiter of the Infidel, and a Benefactor to Thine own people.   Allah grant Thee through His Apostle Weal !   We pray Almighty God to cause us to die in Thy Friendship, and to raise us up in Company with His Apostle and Thyself, even as He hath mercifully vouchsafed to us this Visitation.[1]"

After which we closed one more step to the right, and standing opposite Omar's window, the most easterly of the three, after making a sign with our hands, we addressed the just Caliph in these words :—

" Peace be upon Thee, O Omar !   O Thou Just One ! Thou Prince of True Believers !   Peace be upon Thee, who spakest with Truth, and who madest Thy Word agree with the Strong Book! (the Koran): O Thou Faruk! (the Separator).[2]   O Thou Faithful One !   who girdedst thy Loins with the Apostle, and the First Believers, and with them didst make up the full Number forty,[3] and thus causedst to be accomplished the Apostle's Prayer,[4] and

---

1 It will not be necessary to inform the reader more than once that all these several divisions of prayer ended with the Testification and the Fatihah.

2 Faruk,—the separator,—a title of Omar.

3 When the number of the *Ashab* or " Companions " was thirty-nine, they were suddenly joined by Omar, who thus became the fortieth.

4 It is said that Mohammed prayed long for the conversion of

then didst return to Thy God a Martyr leaving the World
with Praise! Allah grant Thee, through his Apostle
and his Caliph and his Followers, the best of Good, and
may Allah feel in Thee plenary Satisfaction!"

Shaykh Hamid, after wrenching a beggar or two
from my shoulders, then permitted me to draw near to
the little window, called the Apostle's, and to look in.
Here my proceedings were watched with suspicious
eyes. The Persians have sometimes managed to pollute the
part near Abu Bakr's and Omar's graves by tossing through
the aperture what is externally a handsome shawl intended as a present for the tomb.[1] After straining my
eyes for a time, I saw a curtain,[2] or rather hangings, with

---

Omar to Al-Islam, knowing his sterling qualities, and the aid he
would lend to the establishment of the faith.

1 This foolish fanaticism has lost many an innocent life, for the
Arabs on these occasions seize their sabres, and cut down every Persian they meet. Still, bigoted Shi'ahs persist in practising and applaud-
ing it, and the man who can boast at Shiraz of having defiled
Abu Bakr's, Omar's, or Osman's tomb becomes at once a lion and a
hero. I suspect that on some occasions when the people of Al-
Madinah are anxious for an " avanie," they get up some charge of
the kind against the Persians. So the Meccans have sometimes
found these people guilty of defiling the house of Allah—at which Infidel act a Shi'ah would shudder as much as a Sunni. This style of
sacrilege is, we read, of ancient date in Arabia. Nafil, the Hijazi,
polluted the Kilis (Christian church) erected by Abrahah of Sanaa to
outshine the Ka'abah, and draw off worshippers from Meccah. The
outrage caused the celebrated " affair of the Elephant." (See
D'Herbelot, *Bibl. Or.*, v. " Abrahah.")

2 Burckhardt, with his usual accuracy, asserts that a new curtain
is sent when the old one is decayed, or when a new Sultan ascends
the throne, and those authors err who, like Maundrell, declare the
curtain to be removed every year. The Damascus Caravan conveys,
together with its Mahmil or emblem of royalty, the new Kiswah (or
" garment ") when required for the tomb. It is put on by the eunuchs,
who enter the baldaquin by its Northern gate at night time, and there
is a superstitious story amongst the people that they guard their eyes
with veils against the supernatural splendours which pour from the

three inscriptions in long gold letters, informing readers
that behind them lie Allah's Apostle and the first two
Caliphs.

The exact place of Mohammed's tomb is moreover
distinguished by a large pearl rosary, and a peculiar ornament, the celebrated *Kaukab-al-Durri*, or constellation of
pearls, suspended to the curtain breast-high.[1] This is
described to be a "brilliant star set in diamonds and
pearls," placed in the dark that man's eye may be able
to bear its splendours: the vulgar believe it to be a "jewel
of the jewels of Paradise." To me it greatly resembled
the round glass stoppers used for the humbler sort of
decanters; but I thought the same of the Koh-i-Nur.
Moreover I never saw it quite near enough to judge fairly,
and I did not think fit to pay an exorbitant sum for the
privilege of entering the inner passage of the baldaquin.[2]

---

tomb.   The Kiswah is a black, purple, or green brocade, embroidered with white or with silver letters.   A piece in my possession,
the gift of Omar Effendi, is a handsome silk and cotton Damascus
brocade, with white letters worked in it — manifestly the produce of
manual labour, not the poor dull work of machinery.   It contains the
formula of the Moslem faith in the cursive style of the Suls character, seventy-two varieties of which are enumerated by calligraphists.
Nothing can be more elegant or appropriate than its appearance.
The old curtain is usually distributed amongst the officers of the
Mosque, and sold in bits to pilgrims; in some distant Moslem countries, the possessor of such a relic would be considered a saint.   When
treating of the history of the Mosque, some remarks will be offered
about the origin of the curtain.

1 The place of the Prophet's head is, I was told, marked by a fine
Koran hung up to the curtain   This volume is probably a successor
to the relic formerly kept there, the Cufic Koran belonging to Osman,
the fourth Caliph, which Burckhardt supposes to have perished in
the conflagration which destroyed the Mosque.

2 The eunuchs of the tomb have the privilege of admitting
strangers.   In this passage are preserved the treasures of the place;
they are a "Bayt Mal al-Muslimin," or public treasury of the Moslems;
therefore to be employed by the Caliph (*i.e.* the reigning Sultan) for
the exigencies of the faith.   The amount is said to be enormous,
which I doubt.

Altogether the *coup-d'œil* had nothing to recommend it by day. At night, when the lamps, hung in this passage, shed a dim light upon the mosaic-work of the marble floors, upon the glittering inscriptions, and the massive hangings, the scene is more impressive.

Never having seen the Tomb,[1] I must depict it from books,—by no means an easy task. Most of the historians are silent after describing the inner walls of the Hujrah. Al-Kalkashandi declares *in eo lapidem nobilem continere sepulchra Apostoli, Abubecr et Omar, circumcinctum peribole in modum conclavis fere usque ad tectum assurgente, quæ velo serico nigro obligatur.* This author, then, agrees with my Persian friends, who declare the sepulchre to be a marble slab. Ibn Jubayr, who travelled in A.H. 580, relates that the Apostle's coffin is a box of ebony (*abnus*) covered with sandal-wood, and plated with silver ; it is placed, he says, behind a curtain, and surrounded by an iron grating. Al-Samanhudi,[1] quoted by Burckhardt, declares that the curtain covers a square building of black stones, in the interior of which are the tombs of Mohammed and of his two immediate successors. He adds that the tombs are

---

1 And I might add, never having seen one who has seen it. Niebuhr is utterly incorrect in his hearsay description of it. It is not "enclosed within iron railings for fear lest the people might surreptitiously offer worship to the ashes of the Prophet." The tomb is not "of plain mason-work in the form of a chest," nor does any one believe that it is "placed within or between two other tombs, in which rest the ashes of the first two Caliphs." The traveller appears to have lent a credulous ear to the eminent Arab merchant, who told him that a guard was placed over the tomb to prevent the populace scraping dirt from about it, and preserving it as a relic.

2 Burckhardt writes this author's name El Samhoudy, and in this he is followed by all our popular book-makers. Moslems have three ways of spelling it : 1. Al-Samhudi, 2. Al-Samahnudi, and 3. Al-Samanhudi. I prefer the latter, believing that the learned Shaykh, Nur al-Din Ali bin Abdullah al-Hasini (or Al-Husayni) was originally from Samanhud in Egypt, the ancient Sebennitis. He died in A.H. 911, and was buried in the Bakia cemetery.

deep holes ; and that the coffin which contains the Apostle is cased with silver, and has on the top a marble slab inscribed "Bismillah! Allahumma salli alayh!" (" In the name of Allah! Allah have Mercy upon Him[1]!")

The Apostle's body, it should be remembered, lies, or is supposed to lie, stretched at full length on the right side, with the right palm supporting the right cheek, the face fronting Meccah, as Moslems are always buried, and consequently the body lies with the head almost due West and the feet due East. Close behind him is placed Abu Bakr, whose face fronts the Apostle's shoulder[2]; and, lastly, Omar holds the same position with respect to his predecessor.

The places they are usually supposed to occupy, then, would be thus disposed. But Moslem historians are not agreed even upon so simple a point as this.

---

1 Burckhardt, however, must be in error when he says "The tombs are also covered with precious stuffs, and in the shape of cata-falques, like that of Ibrahim in the great Mosque of Meccah." The eunuchs positively declare that no one ever approaches the tomb, and that he who ventured to do so would at once be blinded by the super-natural light. Moreover the historians of Al-Madinah all quote tales of certain visions of the Apostle, directing his tomb to be cleared of dust that had fallen upon it from above, in which case some man cele-brated for piety and purity was *let through a hole in the roof*, by cords, down to the tomb, with directions to wipe it with his beard. This style of ingress is explained by another assertion of Al-Samanhudi, quoted by Burckhardt. "In A.H. 892, when Kaid-Bey rebuilt the Mosque, which had been destroyed by lightning, three deep graves were found in the inside, full of rubbish, but the author of this his-tory, who himself entered it, saw no traces of tombs. The original place of Mohammed's tomb was ascertained with great difficulty ; the walls of the Hujrah *were then rebuilt*, and the iron railing placed round it, which is now there."

2 Upon this point authors greatly disagree. Ibn Jubayr, for in-stance, says that Abu Bakr's head is opposite the Apostle's feet, and that Omar's face is on a level with Abu Bakr's shoulder.

Many prefer this position, in line 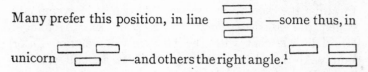 —some thus, in

unicorn —and others the right angle.[1]

It is popularly asserted that in the Hujrah there is now spare place for only a single grave, reserved for Isa bin Maryam after his second coming. The historians of Al-Islam are full of tales proving that though many of their earlier saints, as Osman the Caliph and Hasan the Imam, were desirous of being buried there; and that although Ayishah, to whom the room belonged, willingly acceded to their wishes, son of man has as yet been unable to occupy it.

After the Fatihah pronounced at Omar's tomb, and the short inspection of the Hujrah, Shaykh Hamid led me round the south-east corner of the baldaquin.[2] Turning

---

1 The vulgar story of the suspended coffin has been explained in two ways. Niebuhr supposes it to have arisen from the rude drawings sold to strangers. Mr. William Bankes (Giovanni Finati, vol. ii., p. 289) believes that the mass of rock popularly described as hanging unsupported in the Mosque of Omar at Jerusalem was confounded by Christians, who could not have seen either of these Moslem shrines, with the Apostle's Tomb at Al-Madinah.

2 Some Moslems end their Ziyarat at the Apostle's Tomb; others, instead of advancing, as I did, return to the Apostle's window, pray, and beg pardon for their parents and themselves, and ask all they desire, concluding with prayers to the Almighty. Thence they repair to the Rauzah or Garden, and standing at the column called after Abu Lubabah, pray a two-bow prayer there; concluding with the " Dua," or benediction upon the Apostle, and there repeat these words: " O Allah, Thou hast said, and Thy word is true, ' Say, O Lord, pardon and show Mercy; for Thou art the best of the Merciful,' (chap. 23). O God, verily we have heard Thy Word, and we come for Intercession to Thy Apostle from our own Sins, repenting our Errors, and confessing our Shortcomings and Transgressions! O Allah, pity us, and by the Dignity of Thy Apostle raise our Place, (in the Heavenly Kingdom)! O Allah, pardon our Brothers who have preceded us in the Faith!" Then the Zair prays for himself, and his parents, and for those he loves. He should repeat, " Allah have mercy upon

towards the north, we stopped at what is commonly
called the *Mahbat Jibrail* ("Place of the Archangel
Gabriel's Descent with the Heavenly Revelations"), or
simply Al-Malaikah—the Angels.   It is a small window
in the Eastern wall of the Mosque ; we turned our backs
upon it, and fronting the Hujrah, recited the following
prayer :—

"Peace be upon You, O Angels of Allah, the Mukar-
rabin (cherubs), and the Musharrifin (seraphs), the pure,
the holy, honored by the Dwellers in Heaven, and by
those who abide upon the Earth.   O beneficent Lord!
O Long-suffering! O Almighty! O Pitier! O thou Compassionate One! perfect our Light, and pardon our Sins,
and accept Penitence for our Offences, and cause us to die
among the Holy! Peace be upon Ye, Angels of the
Merciful, one and all! And the Mercy of God and His
Blessings be upon You !"   After which I was shown the
spot in the Hujrah where Sayyidna Isa shall be buried[1] by
Mohammed's side.

Thee, O Apostle of Allah ! " seventy times, when an angel will reply,
" Allah bless thee, O thou blesser."   Then he should sit before the
Pulpit, and mentally conceive in it the Apostle surrounded by the
Fugitives and the Auxiliaries.   Some place the right hand upon the
pulpit, even as Mohammed used to do.   The Zair then returns to
the column of Abu Lubabah, and repents his sins there.   Secondly,
he stands in prayer at Ali's Pillar in front of the form.   And, lastly,
he repairs to the Ustuwanat al-Ashab (the Companions' Column) the
fourth distant from the Pulpit on the right, and the third from the
Hujrah on the left ; here he prays and meditates, and blesses Allah
and the Apostle.   After which, he proceeds to visit the rest of the
holy places.

1 It is almost unnecessary to inform the reader that all Moslems
deny the personal suffering of Christ, cleaving to the heresy of the
Christian Docetes,—certain " beasts in the shape of men," as they are
called in the Epistles of Ignatius to the Smyrneans,—who believed
that a phantom was crucified in our Saviour's place.   They also hold
to the second coming of the Lord in the flesh, as a forerunner to
Mohammed, who shall reappear shortly before the day of judgment.
Bartema (Appendix 2) relates a story concerning the Saviour's
future tomb.

Then turning towards the West, at a point where there is a break in the symmetry of the Hujrah, we arrived at the sixth station, the sepulchre or cenotaph of the Lady Fatimah. Her grave is outside the enceinte and the curtain which surrounds her father's remains; so strict is Moslem decorum, and so exalted its opinion of the "Virgin's"[1] delicacy. The Eastern side of the Hujrah, here turning a little Westward, interrupts the shape of the square, in order to give this spot the appearance of disconnection with the rest of the building. The tomb, seen through a square aperture like those above described, is a long catafalque, covered with a black pall. Though there is great doubt whether the Lady be not buried with her son Hassan in the Bakia cemetery, this place is always visited by the pious Moslem. The following is the prayer opposite the grave of the amiable Fatimah :—

"Peace be upon Thee, Daughter of the Apostle of Allah! Peace be upon Thee, Daughter of the Prophet of Allah ! Peace be upon Thee, thou Daughter of Mustafa! Peace be upon Thee, thou Mother of the Shurafa![2] (seed of Mohammed.) Peace be upon Thee, O Lady amongst Women ! Peace be upon Thee, O fifth of the Ahl al-Kisa![3] Peace be upon Thee, O Zahra and Batúl![4] (Pure and Vir-

---

1 This epithet will be explained below. The reader must bear in mind, that this part of the Harim was formerly the house of Ali and Fatimah; it was separated from the Hujrah—the abode of Mohammed and Ayishah—only by a narrow brick wall, with a window in it, which was never shut. Omar Bin Abd al-Aziz enclosed it in the mosque, by order of Al-Walid, A.H. 90.

2 Plural of Sharif, a descendant of Mohammed.

3 The "people of the garment," so called, because on one occasion the Apostle wrapped his cloak around himself, his daughter, his son-in-law, and his two grandsons, thereby separating them in dignity from other Moslems.

4 Burckhardt translates "Zahra" "bright blooming Fatimah." This I believe to be the literal meaning of the epithet. When thus applied, however, it denotes "virginem τα καταμηνια nescientem,"

gin). Peace be upon Thee, O Daughter of the Apostle! Peace be upon Thee, O Spouse of our Lord Ali al-Murtaza! Peace be upon Thee, O Mother of Hasan and Husayn, the two Moons, the two Lights, the two Pearls, the two Princes of the Youth of Heaven, and Coolness of the Eyes[1] (*i.e.* joy and gladness) of true Believers! Peace be upon Thee, and upon Thy Sire, Al-Mustafa, and Thy Husband, our Lord Ali! Allah honour his Face, and Thy Face, and Thy Father's Face in Paradise, and Thy two Sons, the Hasanayn! And the Mercy of Allah and His Blessings!"

We then broke away as we best could from the crowd of female "askers," who have established their Lares and Penates under the shadow of the Lady's wing; and, advancing a few paces, we fronted to the North, and recited a prayer in honour of Hamzah, and of the martyrs who lie buried at the foot of Mount Ohod.[2] We then turned to the right, and, fronting the Easterly wall, prayed for the souls of the blessed whose mortal spirits repose within Al-Bakia's hallowed circuit.[3]

After this we returned to the Southern wall of the Mosque, and, facing towards Meccah, we recited the following supplication:—"O Allah! (three times repeated) O Compassionate! O Beneficent! O Requiter (of good and

---

in which state of purity the daughter of the Apostle is supposed to have lived. For the same reason she is called Al-Batul, the Virgin, —a title given by Eastern Christians to the Mother of our Lord. The perpetual virginity of Fatimah, even after the motherhood, is a point of orthodoxy in Al-Islam.

1 Meaning "joy and gladness in the sight of true believers."

2 The prayer is now omitted, in order to avoid the repetition of it when describing a visit to Mount Ohod.

3 The prayers usually recited here are especially in honour of Abbas, Hasan, (Ali, called) Zayn al-Abidin, Osman, the Lady Halimah, the Martyrs, and the Mothers of the Moslems, (*i.e.* the Apostle's wives), buried in the holy cemetery. When describing a visit to Al-Bakia, they will be translated at full length.

evil)! O Prince! O Ruler! O ancient of Benefits! O Omniscient! O Thou who givest when asked, and who aidest when Aid is required, accept this our Visitation, and preserve us from Dangers, and make easy our Affairs, and broaden our Breasts, (gladden our hearts), and receive our Prostration, and requite us according to our good Deeds, and turn not against us our evil Deeds, and place not over us one who feareth not Thee, and one who pitieth not us, and write Safety and Health upon us and upon Thy Slaves, the Hujjaj (pilgrims), and the Ghuzzat (fighters for the faith), and the Zawwar[1] (visitors to the tomb), and the Home-dwellers and the Wayfarers of the Moslems, by Land and by Sea, and pardon those of the Faith of our Lord Mohammed One and All!"

From the Southern wall we returned to the "Apostle's Window," where we recited the following tetrastich and prayer:—

"O Mustafa! verily, I stand at Thy door,
A man, weak and fearful, by reason of my sins :
If Thou aid me not, O Apostle of Allah!
I die—for, in the world there is none generous as Thou art!"

" Of a Truth, Allah and His Angels bless the Apostle! O Ye who believe, bless Him and salute Him with salutation![2] O Allah ! verily I implore Thy Pardon and supplicate Thine Aid in this World as in the next ! O Allah! O Allah ! abandon us not in this Holy Place to the consequences of our Sins without pardoning them, or to our Griefs without consoling them, or to our Fears, O Allah! without removing them. And Blessings and Salutation to Thee, O Prince of Apostles, Commissioned (to preach the word), and laud be to Allah, the Lord of the (three) Worlds !"

We turned away from the Hujrah, and after gratifying

---

1 Hujjaj is the plural of Hajj—pilgrims; Ghuzzat, of Ghazi—crusaders ; and Zawwar of Zair—visitors to Mohammed's tomb.

2 " Taslím " is " to say Salám " to a person.

a meek-looking but exceedingly importunate Hindi beggar, who insisted on stunning me with the Chapter Y, S.,[1] we fronted Southwards, and taking care that our backs should not be in a line with the Apostle's face, stood opposite the niche called Mihrab Osman. There Hamid proceeded with another supplication. "O Allah! (three times repeated), O Safeguard of the Fearful, and Defender of those who trust in Thee, and Pitier of the Weak, the Poor, and the Destitute! accept us, O Beneficent! and pardon us, O Merciful! and receive our Penitence, O Compassionate! and have Mercy upon us, O Forgiver! —for verily none but Thou canst remit Sin! Of a Truth Thou alone knowest the hidden, and veilest Man's Transgressions : veil, then, our Offences, and pardon our Sins, and broaden our Breasts, and cause our last Words at the Supreme Hour of Life to be the Words, ' There is no god but Allah,[2] and our Lord Mohammed is the Apostle of Allah ! ' O Allah ! cause us to live according to this Saying, O thou Giver of life ; and make us to die in this Faith, O thou Ruler of Death ! And the best of Blessings and the completest of Salutations upon the sole Lord of Intercession, our Lord Mohammed and His Family, and His Companions One and All !"

Lastly, we returned to the Garden,[3] and prayed another two-bow prayer, ending, as we began, with the worship of the Creator.

✻   ✻   ✻   ✻   ✻   ✻

1 The Yá Sín (Y, S), the 36th chapter of the Koran, frequently recited by those whose profession it is to say such masses for the benefit of living, as well as of dead, sinners. Most educated Moslems commit it to memory.

2 Or more correctly, "There is no Iláh but Allah," that is, "There is no god but *the* God."

3 Some Zairs, after praying at the Caliph Osman's niche, leave the Mosque, especially when the "Jamá'at," or public worship, is not being performed in the Rauzah. Others, as we did, pray alone in the Garden, and many authors prefer this conclusion to Visitation, for the reason above given.

Unfortunately for me, the boy Mohammed had donned that grand embroidered coat. At the end of the ceremony the Ághás, or eunuchs of the Mosque, a race of men considered respectable by their office, and prone to make themselves respected by the freest administration of club-law, assembled in Al-Rauzah to offer me the congratulation *Ziyaratak Mubárak*—" Blessed be thy Visitation,"—and to demand fees. Then came the Sakká, or water-carrier of the Mosque well, Zemzem,[1] offering a tinned saucer filled from the holy source. And lastly I was beset by beggars.

Some were mild beggars and picturesque, who sat upon the ground immersed in the contemplation of their napkins; others, angry beggars who cursed if they were not gratified; and others noisy and petulant beggars, especially the feminine party near the Lady's tomb, who captured me by the skirt of my garment, compelling me to ransom myself. There were, besides, pretty beggars, boys who held out the right hand on the score of good looks ; ugly beggars, emaciated rascals whose long hair, dirt, and leanness entitled them to charity; and lastly, the blind, the halt, and the diseased, who, as Sons of the Holy City, demanded from the Faithful that support with which they could not provide themselves. Having been compelled by my companions, highly against my inclination, to become a man of rank, I was obliged to pay in proportion, and my almoner in the handsome coat, as usual, took a kind of pride in being profuse. This first visit cost me double what I had intended—four dollars—nearly one pound sterling, and never afterwards could I pay less than half that sum.[2]

---

1 This has become a generic name for a Well situated within the walls of a Mosque.

2 As might be expected, the more a man pays, the higher he estimates his own dignity. Some Indians have spent as much as 500 dollars during a first visit. Others have "made Maulids," *i. e.*, feasted all the poor connected with the temple with rice, meat,

Having now performed all the duties of a good Zair, I was permitted by Shaykh Hamid to wander about and see the sights. We began our circumambulation at the Bab al-Salam,[1] the Gate of Salvation, the South-Western entrance pierced in the long wall of the Mosque. It is a fine archway handsomely encrusted with marble and glazed tiles ; the many gilt inscriptions on its sides give it, especially at night-time, an appearance of considerable splendour. The portcullis-like doors are of wood, strengthened with brass plates, and nails of the same metal. Outside this gate is a little Sabil, or public fountain, where those who will not pay for the water, kept ready in large earthen jars by the "Sakka" of the Mosque, perform their ablutions gratis. Here all the mendicants congregate in force, sitting on the outer steps and at the entrance of the Mosque, up and through which the visitors must pass.

About the centre of the Western wall is the Bab al-Rahmah, the Gate of Pity, which admits the dead bodies of the Faithful when carried to be prayed over in the Mosque. There is nothing remarkable in its appearance ; in common with the other gates it has huge folding doors, iron-bound, an external flight of steps, and a few modern inscriptions.

The Bab Majídi, or Gate of the Sultan Abd al-Majid, stands in the centre of the Northern wall ; like its portico, it is unfinished, but its present appearance promises that it will eclipse all except the Bab al-Salam.

The Bab al-Nisa, or Gate of Women, is in the Eastern wall opposite the Bab al-Rahmah, with which it is connected by the "Farsh al-Hajar," a broad band of stone, two or three steps below the level of the portico,

&c., whilst others brought rare and expensive presents for the officials. Such generosity, however, is becoming rare in these unworthy days.

1 This gate was anciently called the Bab al-Atákah, "of Deliverance."

and slightly raised above the Sahn or the hypæthral portion of the Mosque. And lastly, in the Southern portion
of the same Eastern wall is the Bab Jibrail, the Gate of
the Archangel Gabriel.[1]

All these entrances are arrived at by short external
flights of steps leading from the streets, as the base of the
temple, unlike that of Meccah, is a little higher than the
foundation of the buildings around it. The doors are
closed by the attendant eunuchs immediately after the
night prayers, except during the blessed month Al-
Ramazan and in the pilgrimage season, when pious
visitors pay considerable fees there to pass the night in
meditation and prayer.

The minarets are five in number ; but one, the
Shikayliyah, at the North-West angle of the building, has
been levelled, and is still in process of being rebuilt. The
Munar Bab al-Salam stands by the gate of that name : it
is a tall, handsome tower, surmounted by a large ball or
cone[2] of brass gilt or burnished. The Munar Bab al-
Rahmah, about the centre of the Western wall, is of more
simple form than the others : it has two galleries, with
the superior portion circular, and surmounted by the
conical "extinguisher"-roof so common in Turkey and
Egypt. On the North-East angle of the Mosque stands
the Sulaymaniyah Munar, so named after its founder,
Sultan Sulayman the Magnificent. It is a well-built and
substantial stone-tower divided into three stages ; the two

---

1 Most of these entrances have been named and renamed. The
Bab Jibrail, for instance, which derives its present appellation
from the general belief that the archangel once passed through it, is
generally called in books Bab al-Jabr, the Gate of Repairing (the
broken fortunes of a friend or follower). It must not be confounded
with the Mahbat Jibrail, or the window near it in the Eastern wall,
where the archangel usually descended from heaven with the Wahy
or Inspiration.

2 By some wonderful process the " Printer's Devil " converted,
in the first edition, this " ball or cone " into " bull or cow."

lower portions are polygonal, the upper cylindrical, and each terminates in a platform with a railed gallery carried all round for the protection of those who ascend.

And lastly, from the South-East angle of the Mosque, supposed to be upon the spot where Belal, the Apostle's loud-lunged crier, called the first Moslems to prayer,[1] springs the Munar Raisiyah, so called because it is appropriated to the Ruasa or chiefs of the Mu'ezzins. Like the Sulaymaniyah, it consists of three parts : the first and second stages are polygonal ; and the third, a cylinder, is furnished like the lower two with a railed gallery. Both the latter minarets end in solid ovals of masonry, from which project a number of wooden triangles. To these and to the galleries on all festive occasions, such as the arrival of the Damascus caravan, are hung oil-lamps—a poor attempt at illumination, which may rationally explain the origin of the Madinite superstition concerning the column of light which crowns the Prophet's tomb. There is no uniformity in the shape or the size of these four minarets, and at first sight, despite their beauty and grandeur, they appear somewhat *bizarre* and misplaced. But after a few days I found that my eye grew accustomed to them, and I had no difficulty in appreciating their massive proportions and lofty forms.

Equally irregular are the Riwaks, or porches, surrounding the hypæthral court. Along the Northern wall there will be, when finished, a fine colonnade of granite, paved with marble. The Eastern Riwak has three rows of pillars, the Western four, and the Southern, under which stands the tomb, of course has its columns ranged deeper than all the others. These supports of the building are of different material ; some of fine marble, others of

---

[1] Belal, the loud-lunged crier, stood, we are informed, by Moslem historians, upon a part of the roof on one of the walls of the Mosque. The minaret, as the next chapter will show, was the invention of a more tasteful age.

rough stone, plastered over and painted with the most vulgar of arabesques,—vermilion and black in irregular patches and broad streaks, like the stage-face of a London clown.[1] Their size, moreover, is different, the Southern colonnade being composed of pillars palpably larger than those in the other parts of the Mosque. Scarcely any two shafts own similar capitals; many have no pedestal, and some of them are cut with a painful ignorance of art. I cannot extend my admiration of the minarets to the columns—in *their* " architectural lawlessness " there is not a redeeming point.

Of these unpraisable pillars three are celebrated in the annals of Al-Islam, for which reason their names are painted upon them, and five others enjoy the honour of distinctive appellations. The first is called Al-Mukhallak, because, on some occasion of impurity, it was anointed with a perfume called Khaluk. It is near the Mihrab al-Nabawi, on the right of the place where the Imam prays; and it notes the spot where, before the invention of the Pulpit, the Apostle, leaning upon the Ustuwanat al-Hannanah—the Weeping Pillar[2]—used to recite the Khutbah or Friday sermon.

The second stands third from the Pulpit, and third from the Hujrah. It is called the Pillar of Ayishah, also the Ustuwanat al-Kurah, or the Column of Lots, because the Apostle, according to the testimony of his favourite wife, declared that if men knew the value of the place, they would cast lots to pray there: in some books it is known as the Pillar of the Muhájirín or Fugitives, and others mention it as Al-Mukhallak—the Perfumed.

Twenty cubits distant from Ayishah's Pillar, and the

---

1 This abomination may be seen in Egypt on many of the tombs, —those outside the Bal al-Nasr at Cairo, for instance.

2 The tale of this Weeping Pillar is well known. Some suppose it to have been buried beneath the pulpit: others—they are few in number—declare that it was inserted in the body of the pulpit.

second from the Hujrah, and the fourth from the Pulpit, is the Pillar of Repentance, or of Abu Lubabah. It derives its name from the following circumstance. Abu Lubabah was a native of Al-Madinah, one of the Auxiliaries and a companion of Mohammed, originally it is said a Jew, according to others of the Beni Amr bin Auf of the Aus tribe. Being sent for by his kinsmen or his allies, the Benú Kurayzah, at that time capitulating to Mohammed, he was consulted by the distracted men, women, and children, who threw themselves at his feet, and begged of him to intercede for them with the offended Apostle. Abu Lubabah swore he would do so: at the same time, he drew his hand across his throat, as much as to say, "Defend yourselves to the last, for if you yield, such is your doom." Afterwards repenting, he bound himself with a huge chain to the date-tree in whose place the column now stands, vowing to continue there until Allah and the Apostle accepted his penitence—a circumstance which did not take place till the tenth day, when his hearing was gone and he had almost lost his sight.

The less celebrated pillars are the Ustuwanat al-Sarír, or Column of the Cot, where the Apostle was wont to sit meditating on his humble couch-frame of date-sticks. The Ustuwanat Ali notes the spot where the fourth Caliph used to pray and watch near his father-in-law at night. At the Ustuwanat al-Wufud, as its name denotes, the Apostle received envoys, couriers, and emissaries from foreign places. The Ustuwanat al-Tahajjud now stands where Mohammed, sitting upon his mat, passed the night in prayer. And lastly is the Makam Jibrail (Gabriel's place), for whose other name, Mirbaat al-Bair, "the Pole of the Beast of Burden," I have been unable to find an explanation.

The four Riwaks, or porches, of the Madinah Mosque open upon a hypæthral court of parallelogramic shape.

The only remarkable object in it[1] is a square of wooden railing enclosing a place full of well-watered earth, called the Garden of our Lady Fatimah.[2] It now contains a dozen date-trees—in Ibn Jubayr's time there were fifteen. Their fruit is sent by the eunuchs as presents to the Sultan and the great men of Al-Islam; it is highly valued by the vulgar, but the Olema do not think much of its claims to importance. Among the palms are the venerable remains of a Sidr, or Lote tree,[3] whose produce is sold for inordinate sums. The enclosure is entered by a dwarf gate in the South-Eastern portion of the railing, near the well, and one of the eunuchs is generally to be seen in it: it is under the charge of the Mudir, or chief treasurer. These gardens are not uncommon in Mosques, as the traveller who passes through Cairo can convince himself. They form a pretty and an appropriate feature in a building erected for the worship of Him "Who spread the Earth with Carpets of Flowers and drew shady Trees from the dead Ground." A tradition of the Apostle also declares that "Acceptable is Devotion in the Garden and in the Orchard."

---

1 The little domed building which figures in the native sketches, and in all our prints of the Al-Madinah Mosque, was taken down three or four years ago. It occupied part of the centre of the square, and was called Kubbat al-Zayt—Dome of Oil; or Kubbat al-Shama—Dome of Candles,—from its use as a store-room for lamps and wax candles.

2 This is its name among the illiterate, who firmly believe the palms to be descendants of trees planted there by the hands of the Prophet's daughter. As far as I could discover, the tradition has no foundation, and in old times there was no garden in the hypæthral court. The vulgar are in the habit of eating a certain kind of date, "Al-Sayhani," in the Mosque, and of throwing the stones about; this practice is violently denounced by the Olema.

3 Rhamnus Nabeca, Forsk. The fruit, called Nabak, is eaten, and the leaves are used for the purpose of washing dead bodies. The visitor is not forbidden to take fruit or water as presents from Al-Madinah, but it is unlawful for him to carry away earth, or stones, or cakes of dust, made for sale to the ignorant.

At the South-East angle of this enclosure, under a wooden roof supported by pillars of the same material, stands the Zemzem, generally called the Bir al-Nabi, or " the Apostle's well." My predecessor declares that the brackishness of its produce has stood in the way of its reputation for holiness. Yet a well-educated man told me that it was as "light" (wholesome) water[1] as any in Al-Madinah,—a fact which he accounted for by supposing a subterraneous passage[2] which connects it with the great Zemzem at Meccah. Others, again, believe that it is filled by a vein of water springing directly under the Apostle's grave : generally, however, among the learned it is not more revered than our Lady's Garden, nor is it ranked in books among the holy wells of Al-Madinah.

Between this Zemzem well and the Eastern Riwak is the Stoa, or Academia, of the Prophet's city. In the cool mornings and evenings the ground is strewed with professors, who teach the young idea, as an eminent orientalist hath it, to shout rather than to shoot.[3] A few feet to the South of the palm garden is a moveable wooden planking painted green, and about three feet high ; it serves to separate the congregation from the Imam when he prays here ; and at the North-Eastern angle of the enclosure is a

---

1 The Arabs, who, like all Orientals, are exceedingly curious about water, take the trouble to weigh the produce of their wells; the lighter the water, the more digestible and wholesome it is considered.

2 The common phenomenon of rivers flowing underground in Arabia has, doubtless, suggested to the people these subterraneous passages, with which they connect the most distant places. At Al-Madinah, amongst other tales of short cuts known only to certain Badawi families, a man told me of a shaft leading from his native city to Hazramaut : according to him, it existed in the times of the Prophet, and was a journey of only three days!

3 The Mosque Library is kept in large chests near the Bab al-Salam ; the only MS. of any value here is a Koran written in the Sulsi hand. It is nearly four feet long, bound in a wooden cover, and padlocked, so as to require from the curious a " silver key.'

Shajar Kanadil, a large brass chandelier, which completes the furniture of the court.

After this inspection, the shadows of evening began to gather round us. We left the Mosque, reverently taking care to issue forth with the left foot, and not to back out of it as is the Sunnat or practice derived from the Apostle, when taking leave of the Meccan Temple.

To conclude this long chapter. Although every Moslem, learned and simple, firmly believes that Mohammed's remains are interred in the Hujrah at Al-Madinah, I cannot help suspecting that the place is doubtful as that of the Holy Sepulchre at Jerusalem. It must be remembered that a tumult followed the announcement of the Apostle's death, when the people, as often happens, believing him to be immortal,[1] refused to credit the report, and even Omar threatened destruction to any one that asserted it.

Moreover the body was scarcely cold when the contest about the succession arose between the fugitives of Meccah and the auxiliaries of Al-Madinah : in the ardour of which, according to the Shi'ahs, the house of Ali and Fatimah— within a few feet of the spot where the tomb of the Apostle is now placed—was threatened with fire, and Abu Bakr was elected Caliph that same evening. If anyone find cause to wonder that the last resting-place of a personage so important was not fixed for ever, he may find many a parallel case in Al-Madinah. To quote no other, three several localities claim the honour of containing the Lady Fatimah's mortal spoils, although one might suppose that the daughter of the Apostle and the mother of the Imams would not be laid in an unknown grave. My reasons for incredulity are the following :

---

1 So the peasants in Brittany believe that Napoleon the First is not yet dead; the Prussians expect Frederick the Second; the Swiss, William Tell; the older English, King Arthur; and certain modern fanatics look forward to the re-appearance of Joanna Southcote. Why multiply instances in so well known a branch of the history of popular superstitions?

From the earliest days the shape of the Apostle's tomb has never been generally known in Al-Islam. For this reason it is that graves are made convex in some countries, and flat in others. Had there been a Sunnat,[1] such would not have been the case.

The accounts of the learned are discrepant. Al-Samanhudi, perhaps the highest authority, contradicts himself. In one place he describes the coffin ; in another he expressly declares that he entered the Hujrah when it was being repaired by Kaid-Bey, and saw in the inside three deep graves, but no traces of tombs.[2] Either, then, the mortal remains of the Apostle had, despite Moslem superstition,[3] mingled with the dust, (a probable circum-

---

1 The Sunnat is the custom or practice of the Apostle, rigidly conformed to by every good and orthodox Moslem.

2 The reader will bear in mind that I am quoting from Burckhardt. When in Al-Hijaz and at Cairo, I vainly endeavoured to buy a copy of Al-Samanhudi. One was shown to me at Al-Madinah; unhappily, it bore the word Wakf (bequeathed), and belonged to the Mosque. I was scarcely allowed time to read it. (See p. 102, ante.)

3 In Moslem law, prophets, martyrs, and saints, are not supposed to be dead; their property, therefore, remains their own. The Olema have confounded themselves in the consideration of the prophetic state after death. Many declare that prophets live and pray for forty days in the tomb; at the expiration of which time, they are taken to the presence of their Maker, where they remain till the blast of Israfil's trumpet. The common belief, however, leaves the bodies in the graves, but no one would dare to assert that the holy ones are suffered to undergo corruption. On the contrary, their faces are blooming, their eyes bright, and blood would issue from their bodies if wounded. Al-Islam, as will afterwards appear, abounds in traditions of the ancient tombs of saints and martyrs, when accidentally opened, exposing to view corpses apparently freshly buried. And it has come to pass that this fact, the result of sanctity, has now become an unerring indication of it. A remarkable case in point is that of the late Sharif Ghalib, the father of the present Prince of Meccah. In his lifetime he was reviled as a wicked tyrant. But some years after his death, his body was found undecomposed ; he then became a saint, and men now pray at his tomb Perhaps his tyranny was no drawback to his holy reputation. La

stance after nearly nine hundred years' interment), or, what is more likely, they had been removed by the Shi'ah schismatics who for centuries had charge of the sepulchre.[1]

And lastly, I cannot but look upon the tale of the blinding light which surrounds the Apostle's tomb, current for ages past and still universally believed upon the authority of the attendant eunuchs, who must know its falsehood, as a priestly gloss intended to conceal a defect.

I here conclude the subject, committing it to some future and more favoured investigator. In offering the above remarks, I am far from wishing to throw a doubt upon an established point of history. But where a suspicion of fable arises from popular " facts," a knowledge of man and of his manners teaches us to regard it with favouring eye.[2]

Brinvilliers was declared after execution, by her confessor and the people generally, a saint;—simply, I presume, because of the enormity of her crimes.

1 NOTE TO THIRD EDITION.—I have lately been assured by Mohammed al-Halabi, Shaykh al-Olema of Damascus, that he was permitted by the Aghawat to pass through the gold-plated door leading into the Hujrah, and that he saw no trace of a sepulchre.

2 I was careful to make a ground-plan of the Prophet's Mosque, as Burckhardt was prevented by severe illness from so doing. It will give the reader a fair idea of the main point, though, in certain minor details, it is not to be trusted. Some of my papers and sketches, which by precaution I had placed among my medicines, after cutting them into squares, numbering them, and rolling them carefully up, were damaged by the breaking of a bottle. The plan of Al-Madinah is slightly altered from Burckhardt's. Nothing can be more ludicrous than the views of the Holy City, as printed in our popular works. They are of the style " bird's-eye," and present a curious perspective. They despise distance like the Chinese,— pictorially audacious; the Harrah, or ridge in the foreground appears to be 200 yards, instead of three or four miles, distant from the town. They strip the place of its suburb Al-Manakhah, in order to show the enceinte, omit the fort, and the gardens north and south of the city, enlarge the Mosque twenty-fold for dignity, and make it occupy the whole centre of the city, instead of a small corner in the south-

east quarter. They place, for symmetry, towers only at the angles
of the walls, instead of all along the curtain, and gather up and press
into the same field all the venerable and interesting features of the
country, those behind the artist's back, and at his sides, as well as
what appears in front.   Such are the Turkish lithographs.   At
Meccah, some Indians support themselves by depicting the holy
shrines ; their works are a truly Oriental mixture of ground plan and
elevation, drawn with pen and ink, and brightened with the most
vivid colours—grotesque enough, but less unintelligible than the
more ambitious imitations of European art.

CHAPTER XVII.

AN ESSAY TOWARDS THE HISTORY OF THE PROPHET'S MOSQUE.

Ibn Abbas has informed the world that when the eighty individuals composing Noah's family issued from the ark, they settled at a place distant ten marches and twelve parasangs[1] (thirty-six to forty-eight miles) from Babel or Babylon. There they increased and multiplied, and spread into a mighty empire. At length under the rule of Namrud (Nimrod), son of Kanaan (Canaan), son of Ham, they lapsed from the worship of the true God : a miracle dispersed them into distant parts of the earth, and they were further broken up by the one primæval language being divided into seventy-two dialects.

A tribe called Aulad Sam bin Nuh (the children of Shem), or Amalikah and Amalik,[2] from their ancestor Amlak bin Arfakhshad bin Sam bin Nuh, was inspired

[1] In Oriental geography the parasang still, as in the days of Pliny, greatly varies, from 1500 to 6000 yards. Captain Francklin, whose opinion is generally taken, makes it (in his Tour to Persia) a measure of about four miles (Preface to Ibn Haukal, by Sir Gore Ouseley).

[2] M. C. de Perceval (*Essai sur l'Histoire des Arabes avant l'Islamisme*), makes Amlak son of Laoud (Lud), son of Shem, or, according to others, son of Ham. That learned writer identifies the Amalik with the Phœnicians, the Amalekites, the Canaanites, and the Hyksos. He alludes, also, to an ancient tradition which makes them to have colonised Barbary in Africa.

with a knowledge of the Arabic tongue[1] : it settled at Al-Madinah, and was the first to cultivate the ground and to plant palm-trees.   In course of time these people extended over the whole tract between the seas of Al-Hijaz (the Red Sea) and Al-Oman, (north-western part of the Indian Ocean), and they became the progenitors of the Jabábirah[2] (tyrants or " giants ") of Syria, as well as the Farainah (Pharaohs) of Egypt.[3]   Under these Amalik such

---

1 The Dabistan al-Mazahib relates a tradition that the Almighty, when addressing the angels in command, uses the Arabic tongue, but when speaking in mercy or beneficence, the Deri dialect of Persian.

2 These were the giants who fought against Israel in Palestine.

3 In this wild tradition we find a confirmation of the sound geographical opinion which makes Arabia " Une des pépinières du genre humain " (M. Jomard).   It must be remembered that the theatre of all earliest civilisation has been a fertile valley with a navigable stream, like Sind, Egypt, and Mesopotamia.   The existence of such a spot in Arabia would have altered every page of her history ; she would then have become a centre, not a source, of civilisation.   Strabo's Malothes river in Al-Yaman is therefore a myth. As it is, the immense population of the peninsula—still thick, even in the deserts—has, from the earliest ages, been impelled by drought, famine, or desire of conquest, to emigrate into happier regions.   All history mentions two main streams which took their rise in the wilds. The first set to the North-East, through Persia, Mekran, Baluchistan, Sind, and the Afghan Mountains, as far as Samarkand, Bokhara, and Tibet ; the other, flowing towards the North-West, passed through Egypt and Barbary into Etruria, Spain, the Isles of the Mediterranean, and Southern France.   There are two minor emigrations chronicled in history, and written in the indelible characters of physiognomy and philology.   One of these set in an exiguous but perennial stream towards India, especially Malabar, where, mixing with the people of the country, the Arab merchants became the progenitors of the Moplah race.   The other was a partial emigration, also for commercial purposes, to the coast of Berberah, in Eastern Africa, where, mixing with the Galla tribes, the people of Hazramaut became the sires of the extensive Somali and Sawahil nations.   Thus we have from Arabia four different lines of emigration, tending N.E. and S.E., N.W. and S.W.   At some future time I hope to develop this curious but somewhat obscure portion of Arabian history.   It bears upon a most interesting subject, and serves to explain, by the consanguinity of races, the marvellous celerity with

was the age of man that during the space of four hundred years a bier would not be seen, nor " keening " be heard, in their cities.

The last king of the Amalik, "Arkam bin al-Arkam,[1]" was, according to most authors, slain by an army of the children of Israel sent by Moses after the Exodus,[2] with orders thoroughly to purge Meccah and Al-Madinah of their Infidel inhabitants. All the tribe was destroyed, with the exception of the women, the children, and a youth of the royal family, whose extraordinary beauty persuaded the invaders to spare him pending a reference to the Prophet. When the army returned, they found that Moses had died during the expedition, and they were received with reproaches by the people for having violated his express command. The soldiers, unwilling to live with their own nation under this reproach, returned to Al-Hijaz, and settled there.

Moslem authors are agreed that after the Amalik the Benu Israel ruled in the Holy Land of Arabia, but the learned in history are not agreed upon the cause of their emigration. According to some, when Moses was returning from a pilgrimage to Meccah, a multitude of his followers, seeing in Al-Madinah the signs of the city which, according to the Taurat, or Pentateuch, should hear the preaching of the last Prophet, settled there, and were joined by many Badawin of the neighbourhood who

---

which the faith of Al-Islam spread from the Pillars of Hercules to the confines of China—embracing part of Southern Europe, the whole of Northern and a portion of Central Africa, and at least three-fourths of the continent of Asia.

1 Of this name M. C. de Perceval remarks, " Le mot Arcam était une désignation commune à tous ces rois." He identifies it with Rekem (Numbers xxxi. 8), one of the kings of the Midianites ; and recognises in the preservation of the royal youth the history of Agag and Samuel.

2 And some most ignorantly add, " after the entrance of Moses into the Promised Land."

conformed to the law of Moses. Ibn Shaybah also informs us that when Moses and Aaron were wending northwards from Meccah, they, being in fear of certain Jews settled at Al-Madinah, did not enter the city,[1] but pitched their tents on Mount Ohod. Aaron being about to die, Moses dug his tomb, and said, " Brother, thine hour is come! turn thy face to the next world!" Aaron entered the grave, lay at full length, and immediately expired; upon which the Jewish lawgiver covered him with earth, and went his way towards the Promised Land.[2]

Abu Hurayrah asserted that the Benu Israel, after long searching, settled in Al-Madinah, because, when driven from Palestine by the invasion of Bukht al-Nasr (Nebuchadnezzar), they found in their books that the last Prophet would manifest himself in a town of the towns of Arabiyah,[3] called Zat Nakhl, or the "Place of Palm trees." Some of the sons of Aaron occupied the city; other tribes settled at Khaybar,[4] and in the neigh-

---

1 In those days, we are told, the Jews, abandoning their original settlement in Al-Ghabbah or the low lands to the N. of the town, migrated to the highest portions of the Madinah plain on the S. and E., and the lands of the neighbourhood of the Kuba Mosque.

2 When describing Ohod, I shall have occasion to allude to Aaron's dome, which occupies the highest part. Few authorities, however, believe that Aaron was buried there; his grave, under a small stone cupola, is shown over the summit of Mount Hor, in the Sinaitic Peninsula, and is much visited by devotees.

3 It must be remembered that many of the Moslem geographers derive the word " Arabia " from a tract of land in the neighbourhood of Al-Madinah.

4 Khaybar in Hebrew is supposed to signify a castle. D'Herbelot makes it to mean a pact or association of the Jews against the Moslems. This fort appears to be one of the latest as well as the earliest of the Hebrew settlements in Al-Hijaz. Benjamin of Tudela asserts that there were 50,000 Jews resident at their old colony, Bartema in A.D. 1703 found remnants of the people there, but his account of them is disfigured by fable. In Niebuhr's time the Beni Khaybar had inde-

bourhood, building "Utum," or square, flat-roofed, stone
castles for habitation and defence. They left an order to
their descendants that Mohammed should be favourably
received, but Allah hardened their hearts unto their own
destruction. Like asses they turned their backs upon
Allah's mercy,[1] and the consequence is, that they have
been rooted out of the land.

The Tarikh Tabari declares that when Bukht al-
Nasr,[2] after destroying Jerusalem, attacked and slew the
king of Egypt, who had given an asylum to a remnant of
the house of Israel, the persecuted fugitives made their
way into Al-Hijaz, settled near Yasrib (Al-Madinah),
where they founded several towns, Khaybar, Fadak,
Wady al-Subu, Wady al-Kura, Kurayzah, and many
others. It appears, then, by the concurrence of historians,
that the Jews at an early time either colonised, or sup-
planted the Amalik at, Al-Madinah.

At length the Israelites fell away from the worship of
the one God, who raised up against them the Arab tribes
of Aus and Khazraj, the progenitors of modern Ansar.
Both these tribes claimed a kindred origin, and

---

pendent Shaykhs, and were divided into three tribes, viz., the Benu
Masad, the Benu Shahan, and the Benu Anizah (this latter, however,
is a Moslem name), who were isolated and hated by the other Jews,
and therefore the traveller supposes them to have been Karaites.
In Burckhardt's day the race seems to have been entirely rooted out.
I made many inquiries, and all assured me that there is not a single
Jewish family now in Khaybar. It is indeed the popular boast in Al-
Hijaz, that, with the exception of Jeddah (and perhaps Yambu',
where the Prophet never set his foot), there is not a town in the country
harbouring an Infidel. This has now become a point of fanatic
honour ; but if history may be trusted, it has become so only lately.

1 When the Arabs see the ass turn tail to the wind and rain, they
exclaim, "Lo ! he turneth his back upon the mercy of Allah !"

2. M. C. de Perceval quotes Judith, ii. 13, 26, and Jeremiah,
xlix. 28, to prove that Holofernes, the general of Nebuchadnezzar
the First, laid waste the land of Midian and other parts of Northern
Arabia.

Al-Yaman as the land of their nativity. The circumstances of their emigration are thus described. The descendants of Yarab bin Kahtan bin Shalik bin Arkfakhshad bin Sam bin Nuh, kinsmen to the Amalik, inhabited in prosperity the land of Saba.[1] Their sway extended two months' journey from the dyke of Mareb,[2] near the modern capital of Al-Yaman, as far as Syria, and incredible tales are told of their hospitality and of the fertility of their land. As usual, their hearts were perverted by prosperity. They begged Allah to relieve them from the troubles of extended empire and the duties of hospitality by diminishing their possessions. The consequence of their impious supplications was the well-known Flood of Iram.

The chief of the descendants of Kahtan bin Saba, one of the ruling families in Al-Yaman, was one Amru bin Amin Má al-Sama,[3] called "Al-Muzaykayh" from his rending in pieces every garment once worn. His wife Tarikah Himyariah, being skilled in divination, foresaw the fatal event, and warned her husband, who, unwilling to break from his tribe without an excuse, contrived the following stratagem. He privily ordered his adopted son, an orphan,

---

1 Saba in Southern Arabia.

2 The erection of this dyke is variously attributed to Lukman the Elder (of the tribe of Ad) and to Saba bin Yashjab. It burst according to some, beneath the weight of a flood; according to others, it was miraculously undermined by rats. A learned Indian Shaykh has mistaken the Arabic word "Jurád," a large kind of mouse or rat, for "Jarad," a locust, and he makes the wall to have sunk under a "bár i Malakh," or weight of locusts! No event is more celebrated in the history of pagan Arabia than this, or more trustworthy, despite the exaggeration of the details — the dyke is said to have been four miles long by four broad — and the fantastic marvels which are said to have accompanied its bursting. The ruins have lately been visited by M. Arnaud, a French traveller, who communicated his discovery to the French Asiatic Society in 1845.

3 Ma al-Sama, "the water (or "the splendour") of heaven," is, generally speaking, a feminine name amongst the pagan Arabs; possibly it is here intended as a matronymic.

to dispute with him, and to strike him in the face at a feast composed of the principal persons in the kingdom. The disgrace of such a scene afforded him a pretext for selling off his property, and, followed by his thirteen sons,—all borne to him by his wife Tarikah,—and others of the tribe, Amru emigrated Northwards. The little party, thus preserved from the Yamanian Deluge, was destined by Allah to become the forefathers of the Auxiliaries of his chosen Apostle.

All the children of Amru thus dispersed into different parts of Arabia. His eldest son, Salabah bin Amru, chose Al-Hijaz, settled at Al-Madinah, then in the hands of the impious Benu Israel, and became the father of the Aus and Khazraj. In course of time, the new comers were made by Allah an instrument of vengeance against the disobedient Jews. Of the latter people, the two tribes Kurayzah and Nazir claimed certain feudal rights (well known to Europe) upon all occasions of Arab marriages. The Aus and the Khazraj, after enduring this indignity for a time, at length had recourse to one of their kinsmen who, when the family dispersed, had settled in Syria. Abu Jubaylah, thus summoned, marched an army to Al-Madinah, avenged the honour of his blood, and destroyed the power of the Jews, who from that moment became Mawali, or clients to the Arabs.

For a time the tribes of Aus and Khazraj, freed from the common enemy, lived in peace and harmony. At last they fell into feuds and fought with fratricidal strife, until the coming of the Prophet effected a reconciliation between them. This did not take place, however, before the Khazraj received, at the battle of Buas (about A.D. 615), a decided defeat from the Aus.

It is also related, to prove how Al-Madinah was pre-destined to a high fate, that nearly three centuries before the siege of the town by Abu Jubaylah, the Tobba al-

Asghar[1] marched Northward, at the requisition of the Aus and Khazraj tribes, in order to punish the Jews; or, according to others, at the request of the Jews to revenge them upon the Aus and Khazraj. After capturing the town, he left one of his sons to govern it, and marched onwards to conquer Syria and Al-Irák.

Suddenly informed that the people of Al-Madinah had treacherously murdered their new prince, the exasperated Tobba returned and attacked the place; and, when his horse was killed under him, he swore that he would never decamp before razing it to the ground. Whereupon two Jewish priests, Ka'ab and Assayd, went over to him and informed him that it was not in the power of man to destroy the town, it being preserved by Allah, as their books proved, for the refuge of His Prophet, the descendant of Ishmael.[2]

The Tobba Judaized. Taking four hundred of the priests with him, he departed from Al-Madinah, performed pilgrimage to the Ka'abah of Meccah, which he invested with a splendid covering[3]; and, after erecting a house

1 This expedition to Al-Madinah is mentioned by all the pre-Islamatic historians, but persons and dates are involved in the greatest confusion. Some authors mention two different expeditions by different Tobbas; others only one, attributing it differently, however, to two Tobbas,—Abu Karb in the 3rd century of the Christian era, and Tobba al-Asghar, the last of that dynasty, who reigned, according to some, in A.D. 300, according to others in A.D. 448. M. C. de Perceval places the event about A. D. 206, and asserts that the Aus and Khazraj did not emigrate to Al-Madinah before A.D. 300. The word Tobba or Tubba, I have been informed by some of the modern Arabs, is still used in the Himyaritic dialect of Arabic to signify "the Great" or "the Chief."

2 Nothing is more remarkable in the annals of the Arabs than their efforts to prove the Ishmaelitic descent of Mohammed; at the same time no historic question is more open to doubt.

3 If this be true it proves that the Jews of Al-Hijaz had in those days superstitious reverence for the Ka'abah; otherwise the Tobba, after conforming to the law of Moses, would not have shown it this

for the expected Prophet, he returned to his capital in Al-Yaman, where he abolished idolatry by the ordeal of fire. He treated his priestly guests with particular attention, and on his death-bed he wrote the following tetrastich :—

> " I testify of Ahmad that he of a truth
> Is a prophet from Allah, the Maker of souls.
> Be my age extended into his age,
> I would be to him a Wazír and a cousin."

Then sealing the paper he committed it to the charge of the High Priest, with a solemn injunction to deliver the letter, should an opportunity offer, into the hands of the great Prophet ; and that, if the day be distant, the missive should be handed down from generation to generation till it reached the person to whom it was addressed. The house founded by him at Al-Madinah was committed to a priest of whose descendants was Abu Ayyúb the Ansari, the first person over whose threshold the Apostle passed when he ended the Flight. Abu Ayyub had also charge of the Tobba's letter, so that after three or four centuries, it arrived at its destination.

Al-Madinah was ever well inclined to Mohammed. In[1]

---

mark of respect. Moreover there is a legend that the same Rabbis dissuaded the Tobba from plundering the sacred place when he was treacherously advised so to do by the Benu Hudayl Arabs. I have lately perused " The Worship of Ba'alim in Israel," based upon the work of Dr. R. Dozy, " The Israelites in Mecca." By Dr. H. Oort. Translated from the Dutch, and enlarged, with Notes and Appendices, by the Right Rev. John William Colenso, D.D. (Longmans.) I see no reason why Meccah or Beccah should be made to mean "A Slaughter"; why the Ka'abah should be founded by the Simeonites ; why the Hajj should be the Feast of Trumpets ; and other assertions in which everything seems to be taken for granted except etymology, which is tortured into confession. If Meccah had been founded by the Simeonites, why did the Persians and the Hindus respect it ?

[1] It is curious that Abdullah, Mohammed's father, died and was buried at Al-Madinah, and that his mother Áminah's tomb is at Abwa, on the Madinah road. Here, too, his great-grandfather Hashim married Salma Al-Mutadalliyah, before him espoused to Uhayhah, of the Aus tribe. Shaybah, generally called Abd al-Muttalib, the

the early part of his career, the emissaries of a tribe called the Benu Abd al-Ashhal came from that town to Meccah, in order to make a treaty with the Kuraysh, and the Apostle seized the opportunity of preaching Al-Islam to them. His words were seconded by Ayyâs bin Ma'az, a youth of the tribe, and opposed by the chiefs of the embassy ; who, however, returned home without pledging themselves to either party.[1] Shortly afterwards a body of the Aus and the Khazraj came to the pilgrimage of Meccah : when Mohammed began preaching to them, they recognised the person so long expected by the Jews, and swore to him an oath which is called in Moslem history the " First Fealty of the Steep.[2]"

After the six individuals who had thus pledged themselves returned to their native city, the event being duly bruited abroad caused such an effect that, when the next pilgrimage season came, twelve, or according to others forty persons, led by As'ad bin Zarahah, accompanied the original converts, and in the same place swore the " Second Fealty of the Steep." The Prophet dismissed them in company with one Musab bin Umayr, a Meccan, charged to teach them the Koran and their religious duties, which in those times consisted only of prayer and the Profession of Unity. They arrived at Al-Madinah on a Friday, and this was the first day on which the city witnessed the public devotions of the Moslems.

After some persecutions, Musab had the fortune to convert a cousin of As'ad bin Zararah, a chief of the Aus, Sa'ad bin Ma'az, whose opposition had been of the fiercest. He persuaded his tribe, the Benu Abd al-Ashhal, to break

---

Prophet's grandfather, was the son of Salma, and was bred at Al-Madinah.

1 Ayyas bin Ma'az died, it is said, a Moslem.

2 " Bayat al-Akabat al-úlá." It is so called because this oath was sworn at a place called Al-Akabah (the Mountain-road), near Muna. A Mosque was afterwards built there to commemorate the event.

their idols and openly to profess Al-Islam. The next season, Musab having made many converts, some say seventy, others three hundred, marched from Al-Madinah to Meccah for their pilgrimage ; and there induced his followers to meet the Prophet at midnight upon the Steep near Muna. Mohammed preached to them their duties towards Allah and himself, especially insisting upon the necessity of warring down infidelity. They pleaded ancient treaties with the Jews of Al-Madinah, and showed apprehension lest the Apostle, after bringing them into disgrace with their fellows, should desert them and return to the faith of his kinsmen, the Kuraysh. Mohammed, smiling, comforted them with the assurance that he was with them, body and soul, for ever. Upon this they asked him what would be their reward if slain. He re-plied, "Gardens 'neath which the streams flow,"—that is to say, Paradise.

Then, in spite of the advice of Al-Abbas, Mohammed's uncle, who was loud in his denunciations, they bade the Preacher stretch out his hand, and upon it swore the oath known as the " Great Fealty of the Steep." After com-forting them with an Áyát, or Koranic verse, which pro-mised heaven, the Apostle divided his followers into twelve bodies ; and placing a chief at the head of each,[1] dismissed them to their homes. He rejected the offer made by one of the party—namely, to slay all the idolaters present at the pilgrimage—saying that Allah had favoured him with no such order. For the same reason he refused their invitation to visit Al-Madinah, which was the prin-cipal object of their mission ; and he then took an affec-tionate leave of them.

---

1 Some Moslem writers suppose that Mohammed singled out twelve men as apostles, and called them Nakil, in imitation of the example of our Saviour. Other Moslems ignore both the fact and the intention. M. C. de Perceval gives the names of these Nakils in vol. iii. p. 8.

Two months and a half after the events above detailed, Mohammed received the inspired tidings that Al-Madinah of the Hijaz was his predestined asylum. In anticipation of the order, for as yet the time had not been revealed, he sent forward his friends, among whom were Omar, Talhah, and Hamzah, retaining with him Abu Bakr[1] and Ali. The particulars of the Flight, that eventful accident to Al-Islam, are too well known to require mention here ; besides which they belong rather to the category of general than of Madinite history.

Mohammed was escorted into Al-Madinah by one Buraydat al-Aslami and eighty men of the same tribe, who had been offered by the Kuraysh a hundred camels for the capture of the fugitives. But Buraydat, after listening to their terms, accidentally entered into conversation with Mohammed ; and no sooner did he hear the name of his interlocutor, than he professed the faith of Al-Islam. He then prepared for the Apostle a standard by attaching his turband to a spear, and anxiously inquired what house was to be honoured by the presence of Allah's chosen servant. " Whichever," replied Mohammed, " this she-camel[2] is ordered to show me." At the last

---

1 Orthodox Moslems do not fail to quote this circumstance in honour of the first Caliph, upon whom moreover they bestow the title of " Friend of the Cave." The Shi'ahs, on the other hand, hating Abu Bakr, see in it a symptom of treachery, and declare that the Prophet feared to let the " Old Hyena," as they opprobriously term the venerable successor, out of his sight for fear lest he should act as spy to the Kuraysh. The voice of history and of common sense is against the Shi'ahs. M. C. de Perceval justly remarks, that Abu Bakr and Omar were men truly worthy of their great predecessor.

2 This animal's name, according to some, was Al-Kaswa ("the tips of whose ears are cropped ") ; according to others Al-Jada'a ("one mutilated in the ear, hand, nose, or lip"). The Prophet bought her for 800 dirhams, on the day before his flight, from Abu Bakr, who had fattened two fine animals of his own breeding. The camel was offered as a gift, but Mohammed insisted upon paying its price, because, say the Moslem casuists, he being engaged in the work of

halting-place, he accidentally met some of his disciples returning from a trading voyage to Syria ; they dressed him and his companion Abu Bakr in white clothing which, it is said, caused the people of Kuba to pay a mistaken reverence to the latter. The Moslems of Al-Madinah were in the habit of repairing every morning to the heights near the city, looking out for the Apostle ; and, when the sun waxed hot, they returned home. One day, about noon, a Jew, who discovered the retinue from afar, suddenly warned the nearest party of Ansar, or Auxiliaries of Al-Madinah, that the fugitive was come. They snatched up their arms and hurried from their houses to meet him.

Mohammed's she-camel advanced to the centre of the then flourishing town of Kuba. There she suddenly knelt upon a place which is now consecrated ground ; at that time it was an open space, belonging, they say, to Abu Ayyub the Ansari, who had a house there near the abodes of the Benu Amr bin Auf. This event happened on the first day of the week, the twelfth of the month Rabia al-Awwal[1] (June 28, A. D. 622), in the first year of the Flight: for which reason Monday, which also witnessed the birth, the mission, and the death of the Prophet, is an auspicious day to Al-Islam.

After halting two days in the house of Kulsum bin Hadmah at Kuba, and there laying the foundation of the

---

God would receive no aid from man. According to M. C. de Perceval, the Prophet preached from the back of Al-Kaswa the celebrated pilgrimage sermon at Arafat on the 8th March, A.D. 632.

1 The Prophet is generally supposed to have started from Meccah on the first of the same month, on a Friday or a Monday. This discrepancy is supposed to arise from the fact that Mohammed fled his house in Meccah on a Friday, passed three days in the cave on Jabal Saur, and finally left it for Al-Madinah on Monday, which therefore, according to Moslem divines, was the first day of the " Hijrah." But the æra now commences on the 1st of the previous Muharram, an arrangement made seventeen years after the date of the flight by Omar the Caliph, with the concurrence of Ali.

first Mosque upon the lines where his she-camel trod, the
Apostle was joined by Ali, who had remained at Meccah,
for the purpose of returning certain trusts and deposits
committed to Mohammed's charge.   He waited three days
longer ; on Friday morning (the 16th Rabia al-Awwal,
A.H. 1,=2nd July, A.D. 622), about sunrise he mounted Al-
Kaswa, and, accompanied by a throng of armed Ansar
on foot and on horseback, he took the way to the city.   At
the hour of public prayer,[1] he halted in the Wady or valley
near Kuba, upon the spot where the Masjid al-Jum'ah now
stands, performed his devotions, and preached an eloquent
sermon.   He then remounted.   Numbers pressed forward
to offer him hospitality ; he blessed them, and bade them
stand out of the way, declaring that Al-Kaswa would halt
of her own accord at the predestined spot.   He then
advanced to where the Apostle's pulpit now stands.   There
the she-camel knelt, and the rider exclaimed, as one
inspired, "This is our place, if Almighty Allah please!"

Descending from Al-Kaswa, he recited, "O Lord,
cause me to alight a good Alighting, and Thou art the
Best of those who cause to alight!"   Presently the camel
rose unaided, advanced a few steps, and then, according
to some, returning, sat down upon her former seat ;
according to others, she knelt at the door of Abu Ayyub
al-Ansari, whose abode in those days was the nearest to
the halting-place.   The descendant of the Jewish High
Priest in the time of the Tobbas, with the Apostle's permission, took the baggage off the camel, and carried it
into his house.   Then ensued great rejoicings.   The
Abyssinians came and played with their spears.   The

---

1 The distance from Kuba to Al-Madinah is little more than
three miles, for which six hours—Friday prayers being about noon—
may be considered an inordinately long time.   But our author
might urge as a reason that the multitude of people upon a narrow
road rendered the Prophet's advance a slow one, and some historians
relate that he spent several hours in conversation with the Benu
Salim

maidens of the Benu Najjar tribe sang and beat their
kettle-drums. And all the wives of the Ansar celebrated
with shrill cries of joy the auspicious event; whilst the
males, young and old, freemen and slaves, shouted with
effusion, "Allah's Messenger is come! Allah's Messenger
is here!"

Mohammed caused Abu Ayyub and his wife to
remove into the upper story, contenting himself with the
humbler lower rooms. This was done for the greater
convenience of receiving visitors without troubling the
family; but the master of the house was thereby rendered
uncomfortable in mind. His various remarks about the
Apostle's diet and domestic habits, especially his avoiding
leeks, onions, and garlic,[1] are gravely chronicled by Moslem
authors.

After spending seven months, more or less, at the
house of Abu Ayyub, Mohammed, now surrounded by his
wives and family, built, close to the Mosque, huts for
their reception. The ground was sold to him by Sahal
and Suhayl, two orphans of the Benu Najjar,[2] a noble
family of the Khazraj. Some time afterwards one Harisat
bin al-Nu'umán presented to the Prophet all his houses in
the vicinity of the temple. In those days the habitations
of the Arabs were made of a framework of Jaríd or palm
sticks, covered over with a cloth of camel's hair, a curtain
of similar stuff forming the door. The more splendid had
walls of unbaked brick, and roofs of palm fronds plastered

---

1 Mohammed never would eat these strong smelling vegetables on
account of his converse with the angels, even as modern "Spirit-
ualists" refuse to smoke tobacco; at the same time he allowed his
followers to do so, except when appearing in his presence, entering
a Mosque, or joining in public prayers. The pious Moslem still eats
his onions with these limitations. Some sects, however, as the Wahhabis, considering them abominable, avoid them on all occasions.

2 The name of the tribe literally means "sons of a carpenter";
hence the error of the learned and violent Humphrey Prideaux, corrected by Sale.

over with mud or clay. Of this description were the abodes of Mohammed's family. Most of them were built on the North and East of the Mosque, which had open ground on the Western side; and the doors looked towards the place of prayer. In course of time, all, except Abu Bakr[1] and Ali, were ordered to close their doors, and even Omar was refused the favour of having a window opening into the temple.

Presently the Jews of Al-Madinah, offended by the conduct of Abdullah bin Salam, their most learned priest and a descendant from the Patriarch Joseph, who had become a convert to the Moslem dispensation, began to plot against Mohammed.[2] They were headed by Hajj bin Akhtah, and his brother Yasir bin Akhtah, and were joined by many of the Aus and the Khazraj. The events that followed this combination of the Munáfikun, or Hypocrites, under their chief, Abdullah, belong to the domain of Arabian history.[3]

Mohammed spent the last ten years of his life at Al-Madinah. He died on Monday, some say at nine A.M., others at noon, others a little after, on the twelfth of Rabia al-Awwal in the eleventh year of the Hijrah. When his family and companions debated where he should be buried, Ali advised Al-Madinah, and Abu Bakr, Ayishah's cham-

---

1 Some say that Abu Bakr had no abode near the Mosque. But it is generally agreed upon, that he had many houses, one in Al-Bakia, another in the higher parts of Al-Madinah, and among them a hut on the spot between the present gates called Salam and Rahmah.

2 It is clear from the fact above stated, that in those days the Jews of Arabia were in a state of excitement, hourly expecting the advent of their Messiah, and that Mohammed believed himself to be the person appointed to complete the law of Moses.

3 In many minor details the above differs from the received accounts of Pre-Islamitic and early Mohammedan history. Let the blame be borne by the learned Shaykh Abd al-Hakk al-Muhaddis of Delhi, and his compilation, the " Jazb al-Kulúb ila Diyar al-Mahhúb (the "Drawing of Hearts towards the Holy Parts"). From the multitude of versions at last comes correctness.

ber, quoting a saying of the deceased that prophets and martyrs are always interred where they happen to die. The Apostle was placed, it is said, under the bed where he had given up the ghost, by Ali and the two sons of Abbas, who dug the grave. With the life of Mohammed the interest of Al-Madinah ceases, or rather is concentrated in the history of its temple. Since then the city has passed through the hands of the Caliphs, the Sharifs of Meccah, the Sultans of Constantinople, the Wahhabis, and the Egyptians. It has now reverted to the Sultan, whose government is beginning to believe that, in these days when religious prestige is of little value, the great Khan's title, " Servant of the Holy Shrines," is purchased at too high a price. As has before been observed, the Turks now struggle for existence in Al-Hijaz with a soldier ever in arrears, and officers unequal to the task of managing an unruly people. The pensions are but partly paid,[1] and they are not likely to increase with years. It is probably a mere consideration of interest that prevents the people rising *en masse*,

---

1 A Firman from the Porte, dated 13th February, 1841, provides for the paying of these pensions regularly. " It being customary to send every year from Egypt provisions in kind to the two Holy Cities, the provisions and other articles, whatever they may be, which have up to this time been sent to this place, shall continue to be sent thither." Formerly the Holy Land had immense property in Egypt, and indeed in all parts of Al-Islam. About thirty years ago, Mohammed Ali Pasha bought up all the Wakf (church property), agreeing to pay for its produce, which he rated at five piastres the ardeb, when it was worth three times as much. Even that was not regularly paid. The Sultan has taken advantage of the present crisis to put down Wakf in Turkey. The Holy Land, therefore, will gradually lose all its land and house property, and will soon be compelled to depend entirely upon the presents of the pilgrims, and the Sadakah, or alms, which are still sent to it by the pious Moslems of distant regions. As might be supposed, both the Meccans and the Madani loudly bewail their hard fates, and by no means approve of the Ikram, the modern succedaneum for an extensive and regularly paid revenue. At a future time, I shall recur to this subject.

and re-asserting the liberties of their country. And I have heard from authentic sources that the Wahhabis look forward to the day when a fresh crusade will enable them to purge the land of its abominations in the shape of silver and gold.

The Masjid al-Nabi, or Prophet's Mosque, is the second in Al-Islam in point of seniority, and the second, or, according to others, the first in dignity, ranking with the Ka'abah itself. It is erected around the spot where the she-camel, Al-Kaswa, knelt down by the order of Heaven. At that time the land was a palm grove and a Mirbad, or place where dates are dried. Mohammed, ordered to erect a place of worship there, sent for the youths to whom it belonged, and certain Ansar, or Auxiliaries, their guardians; the ground was offered to him in free gift, but he insisted upon purchasing it, paying more than its value. Having caused the soil to be levelled and the trees to be felled, he laid the foundation of the first Mosque.

In those times of primitive simplicity its walls were made of rough stone and unbaked bricks: trunks of date-trees supported a palm-stick roof, concerning which the Archangel Gabriel delivered an order that it should not be higher than seven cubits, the elevation of Moses's temple. All ornament was strictly forbidden. The Ansar, or men of Al-Madinah, and the Muhajirin, or Fugitives from Meccah, carried the building materials in their arms from the cemetery Al-Bakia, near the well of Ayyub, north of the spot where Ibrahim's Mosque now stands, and the Apostle was to be seen aiding them in their labours, and reciting for their encouragement,

"O Allah! there is no good but the good of futurity,
Then have mercy upon my Ansar and Muhajirin!"

The length of this Mosque was fifty-four cubits from North to South, and sixty-three in breadth, and it was hemmed in by houses on all sides save the Western. Till the seventeenth month of the new æra the congregation faced towards the Northern wall.   After that time a fresh revelation turned them in the direction of Meccah, Southwards : on which occasion the Archangel Gabriel descended and miraculously opened through the hills and wilds a view of the Ka'abah, that there might be no difficulty in ascertaining its true position.

After the capture of Khaybar in A.H. 7, the Prophet and his first three successors restored the Mosque, but Moslem historians do not consider this a second foundation.   Mohammed laid the first brick, and Abu Hurayrah declares that he saw him carry heaps of building materials piled up to his breast.   The Caliphs, each in the turn of his succession, placed a brick close to that laid by the Prophet, and aided him in raising the walls.   Al-Tabrani relates that one of the Ansar had a house adjacent which Mohammed wished to make part of the place of prayer ; the proprietor was promised in exchange for it a home in Paradise, which he gently rejected, pleading poverty. His excuse was admitted, and Osman, after purchasing the place for ten thousand dirhams, gave it to the Apostle on the long credit originally offered.

This Mosque was a square of a hundred cubits. Like the former building, it had three doors : one on the South side, where the Mihrab al-Nabawi, or the "Prophet's Niche," now is; another in the place of the present Bab al-Rahmah; and the third at the Bab Osman, now called the Gate of Gabriel.   Instead of a Mihrab or prayer-niche,[1] a large block of stone directed the congregation; at first it was placed against the Northern wall

---

[1] The prayer-niche and the minaret both date their existence from the days of Al-Walid, the builder of the third Mosque.   At this age of their empire, the Moslems had travelled far and had seen art in various lands ; it is therefore not without a shadow of reason that the Hindus charge them with having borrowed their two favourite symbols, and transformed them into an arch and a tower.

of the Mosque, and it was removed to the Southern when Meccah became the Kiblah.

In the beginning the Prophet, whilst preaching the Khutbah or Friday sermon, leaned when fatigued against a post.[1] The Mambar,[2] or pulpit, was the invention of a Madinah man, of the Benu Najjar. It was a wooden frame, two cubits long by one broad, with three steps, each one span high; on the topmost of these the Prophet sat when he required rest. The pulpit assumed its present form about A.H. 90, during the artistic reign of Al-Walid.

In this Mosque Mohammed spent the greater part of the day[3] with his companions, conversing, instructing, and

---

1 The Ustawanat al-Hannanah, or "Weeping-Post." See page 335, chapter XVI., ante.

2 As usual, there are doubts about the invention of this article. It was covered with cloth by the Caliph Osman, or, as others say, by Al-Mu'áwiyah, who, deterred by a solar eclipse from carrying out his project of removing it to Damascus, placed it upon a new framework, elevated six steps above the ground. Al-Mahdi wished to raise the Mambar six steps higher, but was forbidden so to do by the Imam Malik. The Abbasides changed the pulpit, and converted the Prophet's original seat into combs, which were preserved as relics. Some historians declare that the original Mambar was burnt with the Mosque in A.H. 654. In Ibn Jubayr's time (A.H. 580), it was customary for visitors to place their right hands upon a bit of old wood, inserted into one of the pillars of the pulpit ; this was supposed to be a remnant of the "weeping-post." Every Sultan added some ornament to the Mambar, and at one time it was made of white marble, covered over with a dome of the "eight metals." It is now a handsome structure, apparently of wood, painted and gilt of the usual elegant form, which has been compared by some travellers with the *suggesta* of Roman Catholic churches. I have been explicit about this pulpit, hoping that, next time the knotty question of Apostolic seats comes upon the *tapis*, our popular authors will not confound a Curule chair with a Moslem Mambar. Of the latter article, Lane (Mod. Egyptians, chap. iii.) gave a sketch in the "Interior of a Mosque."

3 The Prophet is said to have had a dwelling-house in the Ambariyah, or the Western quarter of the Manakhah suburb, and

comforting the poor. Hard by were the abodes of his wives, his family, and his principal friends. Here he prayed, at the call of the Azan, or devotion-cry, from the roof. Here he received worldly envoys and embassies, and the heavenly messages conveyed by the Archangel Gabriel. And within a few yards of the hallowed spot, he died, and found a grave.

The theatre of events so important to Al-Islam could not be allowed—especially as no divine decree forbade the change—to remain in its pristine lowliness. The first Caliph contented himself with merely restoring some of the palm pillars, which had fallen to the ground: Omar, the second successor, surrounded the Hujrah, or Ayishah's chamber, in which the Prophet was buried, with a mud wall; and in A.H. 17, he enlarged the Mosque to 140 cubits by 120, taking in ground on all sides except the Eastern, where stood the abodes of the "Mothers of the Moslems.[1]" Outside the Northern wall he erected a Suffah, called Al-Batha—a raised bench of wood, earth, or stone, upon which the people might recreate themselves with conversation and quoting poetry, for the Mosque was now becoming place of peculiar reverence to men.[2]

The second Masjid was erected A.H. 29, by the third Caliph, Osman, who, regardless of the clamours of the people, overthrew the old walls and extended the building

---

here, according to some, he lodged Mariyah, the Coptic girl. As pilgrims do not usually visit the place, and nothing of the original building can be now remaining, I did not trouble myself about it.

1 Meaning the Prophet's fifteen to twenty-five wives. Their number is not settled. He left nine wives and two concubines. It was this title after the Koranic order (chap, xxxiii. *v.* 53) which rendered their widowhood eternal ; no Arab would willingly marry a woman whom he has called mother or sister.

2 Authors mention a place outside the Northern wall called Al-Suffah, which was assigned by Mohammed as a habitation to houseless believers ; from which circumstance these paupers derived the title of Ashab al-Suffah, "Companions of the Sofa."

greatly towards the North, and a little towards the West; but he did not remove the Eastern limit on account of the private houses.   He made the roof of Indian teak,[1] and the walls of hewn and carved stone.   These innovations caused some excitement, which he allayed by quoting a tradition of the Prophet, with one of which he appears perpetually to have been prepared.   The saying in question was, according to some, " Were this my Mosque extended to Safa "—a hill in Meccah—" it verily would still be my Mosque "; according to others, " Were the Prophet's Mosque extended to Zu'l Halifah[2] it would still be his."   But Osman's skill in the quotation of tradition did not prevent the new building being in part a cause of his death. It was finished on the first Muharram, A.H. 30.

At length, Al-Islam, grown splendid and powerful, determined to surpass other nations in the magnificence of its public buildings.[3]   In A.H. 88, Al-Walid[4] the First, twelfth Caliph of the Benu Ummayah race, after building, or rather restoring, the noble " Jami' al-Ammawi " (cathedral of the Ommiades) at Damascus, determined to

---

1 So I translate the Arabicised word "Sáj."

2 A place about five miles from Al-Madinah, on the Meccan way. See Chap. XIV.

3 And curious to say Al-Islam still has the largest cathedral in the world—St. Sophia's at Constantinople.   Next to this ranks St. Peter's at Rome; thirdly, I believe, the " Jumma Masjid," or cathedral of the old Moslem city Bijapur in India ; the fourth is St. Paul's, London,

4 It is to this monarch that the Saracenic Mosque-architecture mainly owes its present form.   As will be seen, he had every advantage of borrowing from Christian, Persian, and even Indian art. From the first he took the dome, from the second the cloister—it might have been naturalised in Arabia before his time—and possibly from the third the minaret and the prayer-niche.   The latter appears to be a peculiarly Hindu feature in sacred buildings, intended to contain the idol, and to support the lamps, flowers, and other offerings placed before it.

display his liberality at Al-Madinah. The governer of the place, Umar bin Abd Al-Aziz, was directed to buy for seven thousand Dinárs (ducats) all the hovels of raw brick that hedged in the Eastern side of the old Mosque. They were inhabited by descendants of the Prophet and of the early Caliphs, and in more than one case, the ejection of the holy tenantry was effected with considerable difficulty. Some of the women—ever the most obstinate on such occasions—refused to take money, and Omar was forced to the objectionable measure of turning them out of doors with exposed faces[1] in full day. The Greek Emperor, applied to by the magnificent Caliph, sent immense presents, silver lamp chains, valuable curiosities,[2] forty loads of small cut stones for *pietra-dura*, and a sum of eighty thousand Dinars, or, as others say, forty thousand Miskáls of gold. He also despatched forty Coptic and forty Greek artists to carve the marble pillars and the casings of the walls, and to superintend the gilding and the mosaic work. One of these Christians was beheaded for sculpturing a hog on the Kiblah wall; and another, in an attempt to defile the roof, fell to the ground, and his brains were dashed out. The remainder Islamized, but this did not prevent the older Arabs murmuring that their Mosque had been turned into a Kanísah, a Christian idol-house.

The Hujrah, or chamber, where, by Mohammed's permission, Azrail, the Angel of Death, separated his

---

1 The reader will remember that in the sixth year of the Hijrah, after Mohammed's marriage with Zaynab, his wives were secluded behind the Hijab, Pardáh, or curtain. A verse of the Koran directed the Moslems to converse with them behind this veil. Hence the general practice of Al-Islam: now it is considered highly disgraceful in any Moslem to make a Moslemah expose her face, and she will frequently found a threat upon the prejudice. A battle has been prevented by this means, and occasionally an insurrection has been caused by it.

2 Amongst which some authors enumerate the goblet and the mirror of Kisra.

soul from his body, whilst his head was lying in the lap of Ayishah, his favourite wife, was now for the first time taken into the Mosque. The raw-brick enceinte [1] which surrounded the three graves was exchanged for one of carved stone, enclosed by an outer precinct with a narrow passage between.[2] These double walls were either without a door, or had only a small blocked-up wicket on the Northern side, and from that day (A.H. 90), no one, says Al-Samanhudi, has been able to approach the sepulchre.[3] A minaret was erected at each corner of the Mosque.[4] The building was enlarged to 200 cubits by 167, and was finished in A.H. 91. When Al-Walid, the Caliph, visited it in state, he inquired of his lieutenant why greater magnificence had not been displayed in the erection ; upon which Omar, the governor, informed him,

---

1 The outer wall, built by Al-Walid, remained till A.H. 550, when Jamal al-Din of Isafahan, Wazir to Nur al-Din Shahid Mahmud bin Zangi, supplied its place by a grating of open sandal woodwork, or, as others say, of iron. About the same time, Sayyid Abu 'l Hayja sent from Egypt a sheet of white brocade, embroidered in red silk with the chapter Y. S., in order to cover the inner wall. This was mounted on the accession of Al-Mustazi bi'lláh, the Caliph, after which it became the custom for every Sultan to renew the offering. And in A.H. 688, Kalaun of Egypt built the outer network of brass as it now is, and surmounted it with the Green Dome.

2 The inner wall, erected by Al-Walid, seems to have resisted the fire which in A.H. 654 burnt the Mosque to the ground. Also, in A.H. 886, when the building was consumed by lightning, the Hujrah was spared by the devouring element.

3 After the Prophet's death and burial, Ayishah continued to occupy the same room, without even a curtain between her and the tomb. At last, vexed by the crowds of visitors, she partitioned off the hallowed spot with a wall. She visited the grave unveiled as long as her father Abu Bakr only was placed behind the Prophet ; but when Omar's corpse was added, she always covered her face.

4 One of these, the minaret at the Bab-al-Salam, was soon afterwards overthrown by Al-Walid's brother Sulayman, because it shaded the house of Marwán, where he lodged during his visit to Al-Madinah in the cold season.

to his astonishment, that the walls alone had cost forty-five thousand ducats.[1]

The fourth Mosque was erected in A.H. 191, by Al-Mahdi, third prince of the Benu Abbas or Baghdad Caliphs—celebrated in history only for spending enormous sums upon a pilgrimage. He enlarged the building by adding ten handsome pillars of carved marble, with gilt capitals, on the Northern side. In A.H. 202, Al-Ma'amún made further additions to this Mosque. It was from Al-Mahdi's Masjid that Al-Hákim bi 'Amri 'llah, the third Fatimite Caliph of Egypt, and the deity of the Druze sect, determined to steal the bodies of the Prophet and his two companions. About A.H. 412, he sent emissaries to Al-Madinah: the attempt, however, failed, and the would-be violators of the tomb lost their lives. It is generally supposed that Al-Hakim's object was to transfer the Visitation to his own capital; but in one so manifestly insane it is difficult to discover the spring of action. Two Christians, habited like Maghrabi pilgrims, in A.H. 550, dug a mine from a neighbouring house into the temple. They were discovered, beheaded, and burned to ashes. In relating these events the Moslem historians mix up many foolish preternaturalisms with credible matter. At last, to prevent a recurrence of such sacrilegious attempts, Al-Malik al-Ádil Nur al-Din of the Baharite Mamluk Sultans, or, according to others, Sultan Nur al-Din Shahid Mahmud bin Zangi, who, warned by a vision of the Apostle, had started for Al-Madinah only in time to discover the two Christians, surrounded the holy place with a deep trench filled with molten lead. By this means Abu Bakr and Omar, who had run considerable risks of their own, have ever since been enabled to occupy their last homes undisturbed.

In A.H. 654, the fifth Mosque was erected in consequence of a fire, which some authors attribute to a

---

1 The dinar (denarius) was a gold piece, a ducat, a sequin.

volcano that broke out close to the town in terrible eruption[1]; others, with more fanaticism and less probability, to the schismatic Benu Husayn, then the guardians of the tomb. On this occasion the Hujrah was saved, together with the old and venerable copies of the Koran there deposited, especially the Cufic MSS., written by Osman, the third Caliph. The piety of three sovereigns, Al-Mustasim (last Caliph of Baghdad), Al-Muzaffar Shems al-Din Yusuf, chief of Al-Yaman, and Al-Zahir Beybars, Baharite Sultan of Egypt, completed the work in A.H. 688. This building was enlarged and beautified by the princes of Egypt, and lasted upwards of two hundred years.

The sixth Mosque was built, almost as it now stands, by Kaid-Bey, nineteenth Sultan of the Circassian Mamluk kings of Egypt, in A.H. 888: it is now therefore more than four centuries old. Al-Mustasim's Mosque had been struck by lightning during a storm; thirteen men were killed at prayers, and the destroying element spared nothing but the interior of the Hujrah.[2] The railing and dome were restored; niches and a pulpit were sent from Cairo, and the gates and minarets were distributed as they are now. Not content with this, Kaid-Bey established "Wakf" (bequests) and pensions, and introduced order among the attendants on the tomb. In the tenth century, Sultan Sulayman the Magnificent paved with fine white marble the Rauzah or garden, which Kaid-Bey, not daring to alter, had left of earth, and erected the fine minaret that bears his name.

---

1 I purpose to touch upon this event in a future chapter, when describing my route from Al-Madinah to Meccah.

2 "On this occasion," says Al-Samanhudi, quoted by Burckhardt, "the interior of the Hujrah was cleared, and three deep graves were found in the inside, full of rubbish, but the author of this history, who himself entered it, saw no traces of tombs." Yet in another place he, an eye-witness, had declared that the coffin containing the dust of Mohammed was cased with silver. I repeat these details.

During the dominion of the later Sultans, and of Mohammed Ali, a few trifling presents, of lamps, carpets, wax candles and chandeliers, and a few immaterial alterations, have been made. The present head of Al-Islam is, as I have before said, rebuilding one of the minarets and the Northern colonnade of the temple.

Such is the history of the Mosque's prosperity.

During the siege of Al-Madinah by the Wahhabis,[1] the principal people seized and divided amongst themselves the treasures of the tomb, which must have been considerable. When the town surrendered, Sa'ud, accompanied by his principal officers, entered the Hujrah, but, terrified by dreams, he did not penetrate behind the curtain, or attempt to see the tomb. He plundered, however, the treasures in the passage, the "Kaukab al-Durri[2]" (or pearl star), and the ornaments sent as presents from every part of Al-Islam. Part of these he sold, it is said, for 150,000 Riyals (dollars), to Ghalib, Sharif of Meccah, and the rest he carried with him to Daraiyah, his capital.[3] An accident prevented any further desecration of the building. The greedy Wahhabis, allured by the appearance of the golden or gilt globes and crescents surmounting the green dome, attempted to throw down the latter. Two of their number, it is said, were killed by falling

---

1 Burckhardt has given a full account of this event in his history of the Wahhabis.

2 See Chapter XVI., ante.

3 My predecessor estimates the whole treasury in those days to have been worth 300,000 Riyals,—a small sum, if we consider the length of time during which it was accumulating. The chiefs of the town appropriated 1 cwt. of golden vessels, worth at most 50,000 dollars, and Sa'ud sold part of the plunder to Ghalib for 100,000 (I was told one-third more), reserving for himself about the same amount of pearls and corals. Burckhardt supposes that the governors of Al-Madinah, who were often independent chiefs, and sometimes guardians of the tombs, made occasional draughts upon the generosity of the Faithful.

from the slippery roof,[1] and the rest, struck by superstitious fears, abandoned the work of destruction. They injured, however, the prosperity of the place by taxing the inhabitants, by interrupting the annual remittances, and by forbidding visitors to approach the tomb. They are spoken of with abhorrence by the people, who quote a peculiarly bad trait in their characters, namely, that in return for any small religious assistance of prayer or recitation, they were in the habit of giving a few grains of gunpowder, or something equally valuable, instead of " stone-dollars.[2] "

When Abdullah, son of Sa'ud, had concluded in A.D. 1815 a treaty of peace with Tussun Pasha, the Egyptian General bought back from the townspeople, for 10,000 Riyals, all the golden vessels that had not been melted down, and restored the treasure to its original place. This I have heard denied ; at the same time it rests upon credible evidence. Amongst Orientals the events of the last generation are, usually speaking, imperfectly remembered, and the Olema are well acquainted with the history of vicissitudes which took place 1200 years ago, when profoundly ignorant of what their grandfathers witnessed. Many incredible tales also I heard concerning the present wealth of the Al-Madinah Mosque : this must be expected when the exaggeration is considered likely to confer honour upon the exaggerator.

The establishment attached to the Al-Madinah Mosque is greatly altered since Burckhardt's time,[3] the result of the increasing influence of the Turkish half-

---

1 I inquired in vain about the substance that covered the dome. Some told me it was tinfoil ; others supposed it to be rivetted with green tiles.

2 The Badawi calls a sound dollar " Kirsh Hajar," or " Riyal Hajar," a " stone dollar."

3 At the same time his account is still carefully copied by our popular and general authors, who, it is presumed, could easily become better informed.

breeds. It is still extensive, because in the first place the principle of divided labour is a favourite throughout the East, and secondly because the Sons of the Holy Cities naturally desire to extract as much as they can from the Sons of other cities with the least amount of work. The substance of the following account was given to me by Omar Effendi, and I compared it with the information of others upon whom I could rely.

The principal of the Mosque, or Shaykh al-Harim, is no longer a neuter.[1] The present is a Turkish Pasha, Osman, appointed from Constantinople with a salary of about 30,000 piastres a month. His Naib or deputy is a black eunuch, the chief of the Aghawat,[2] upon a pay of 5000 piastres. The present principal of this college is one Tayfur Agha, a slave of Esma Sultanah, sister to the late Sultan Mahmud. The chief treasurer is called the Mudir al-Harim ; he keeps an eye upon the Khaznadar, or treasurer, whose salary is 2000 piastres. The Mustaslim is the chief of the Katibs, or writers who settle the

---

1 The Persians in remote times, as we learn from Herodotus (lib. 6), were waited upon by eunuchs, and some attribute to them the invention. Ammianus Marcellinus (lib. 14) ascribes the origin to Semiramis. In Al-Islam, the employment of such persons about the Mosque is a " Bida'ah " or custom unknown in the time of the Prophet. It is said to have arisen from the following three considerations : 1. These people are concentrated in their professions ; 2. They must see and touch strange women at the shrines; and 3. The shrines are " Harim," or sacred, having adyta which are kept secret from the prying eyes of men, and, therefore, should be served by eunuchs. It is strange that the Roman Catholic church, as well as the Moslem Mosque, should have admitted such an abomination.

2 One of these gentry, if called " Tawáshi,"—his generic name,— would certainly insult a stranger. The polite form of address to one of them is " Agha "—Master,—in the plural " Aghawat." *In partibus,* they exact the greatest respect from men, and the title of the Eunuch of the Tomb is worth a considerable sum to them. The eunuchs of Al-Madinah are more numerous and better paid than those of Meccah : they are generally the slaves of rich men at Constantinople, and prefer this city on account of its climate.

accounts of the Mosque; his pay is 1500, and under him
is a Nakib or assistant upon 1000 piastres.   There are
three Shaykhs of the eunuchs who receive from 700
to 1000 piastres a month each.   The eunuchs, about
a hundred and twenty in number, are divided into
three orders.   The Bawwabin, or porters, open the
doors of the Mosque.   The Khubziyah sweep the purer
parts of the temple, and the lowest order, popularly
called "Battalin," clean away all impurities, beat
those found sleeping, and act as beadles, a duty here
which involves considerable use of the cane.   These men
receive as perquisites presents from each visitor when
they offer him the usual congratulation, and for other
small favours, such as permitting strangers to light the
lamps,[1] or to sweep the floor.   Their pay varies from 250
to 500 piastres a month: they are looked upon as honourable men, and are, generally speaking, married, some of
them indulging in three or four wives,—which would have
aroused Juvenal's bile.   The Agha's character is curious
and exceptional as his outward conformation.   Discon-
nected with humanity, he is cruel, fierce, brave, and
capable of any villany.   His frame is unnaturally long
and lean, especially the arms and legs, with high
shoulders, protruding joints, and a face by contrast
extraordinarily large ; he is unusually expert in the use
of weapons, and sitting well " home," he rides to admiration, his hoarse, thick voice investing him with all the
circumstances of command.

Besides the eunuchs, there are a number of free servants, called Farrashin, attached to the Mosque ; almost
all the middle and lower class of citizens belong to this
order.   They are divided into parties of thirty each, and
are changed every week, those on duty receiving a Ghazi
or twenty-two piastres for their services.   Their business

---

1 The " Sons of the City," however, are always allowed to do
such service gratis; if, indeed, they are not paid for it.

is to dust, and to spread the carpets, to put oil and wicks into the lamps which the eunuchs let down from the ceiling, and, generally speaking, diligently to do nothing.

Finally, the menial establishment of the Mosque consists of a Shaykh al-Sakka (chief of the water-carriers), under whom are from forty-five to fifty men who sprinkle the floors, water the garden, and, for a consideration, supply a cupful of brackish liquid to visitors.

The literary establishment is even more extensive than the executive and the menial. There is a Kazi, or chief judge, sent every year from Constantinople. After twelve months at Al-Madinah, he passes on to Meccah, and returns home after a similar term of service in the second Holy City. Under him are three Muftis,[1] of the Hanafi, the Shafe'i, and the Maliki schools ; the fourth, or Hanbali, is not represented here or at Cairo.[2] Each of these officers receives as pay about two hundred and fifty piastres a month. The Ruasa,[3] as the Mu'ezzins (prayer-callers) here call themselves, are extensively represented ; there are forty-eight or forty-nine of the lowest order, presided over by six Kubar or Masters, and these again are under the Shaykh al-Ruasa, who alone has the privilege of calling to prayers from the Raisiyah minaret. The Shaykh receives a hundred and fifty piastres, the chiefs about a hundred, and the common criers sixty ; there are

---

1 Others told me that there were only two muftis at Al-Madinah, namely, those of the Hanafi and Shafe'i schools. If this be true, it proves the insignificance of the followers of Malik, which personage, like others, is less known in his own town than elsewhere.

2 The Hanbali school is nowhere common except in Nijd, and the lands Eastward as far as Al-Hasa. At present it labours under a sort of imputation, being supposed to have thrown out a bad offshoot, the Wahhabis.

3 " Ruasa " is the plural of Rais, a chief or president. It is the term generally applied in Arabia to the captain of a vessel, and in Al-Yaman it often means a barber, in virtue, I presume, of its root—Ras, the head.

forty-five Khatibs, who preach and pray before the congregation on Fridays for a hundred and twenty piastres a
month ; they are under the Shaykh al-Khutaba.   About
the same sum is given to seventy-five Imams, who recite
the five ordinary prayers of every day in the Mosque ; the
Shaykh al-Aimmat is their superior.[1]

Almost all the citizens of Al-Madinah who have not
some official charge about the temple qualify themselves
to act as Muzawwirs. They begin as boys to learn the
formula of prayer, and the conducting of visitors ; and
partly by begging, partly by boldness, they often pick up
a tolerable livelihood at an early age. The Muzawwir will
often receive strangers into his house, as was done to me,
and direct their devotions during the whole time of their
stay. For such service he requires a sum of money pro-
portioned to his guests' circumstances, but this fee does
not end the connexion. If the Muzawwir visit the home
of his Zair, he expects to be treated with the utmost hospitality, and to depart with a handsome present. A religious visitor will often transmit to his cicerone at Meccah
and at Al-Madinah yearly sums to purchase for himself a
prayer at the Ka'abah and the Prophet's Tomb. The
remittance is usually wrapped up in paper, and placed in
a sealed leathern bag, somewhat like a portfolio, upon
which is worked the name of the person entitled to receive
it. It is then given in charge either to a trustworthy
pilgrim, or to the public treasurer, who accompanies the
principal caravans.

I could procure no exact information about the amount
of money forwarded every year from Constantinople and
Cairo to Al-Madinah ; the only point upon which men
seemed to agree was that they were defrauded of half their
dues. When the Sadaka and Aukaf (the alms and bequests)
arrive at the town, they are committed by the Surrah, or

---

[1] Some say that the Egyptian distinction between the Imam
Khatib and the Imam Ratib does not obtain at Al-Madinah.

financier of the caravan, to the Muftis, the chief of the Khatibs, and the Kazi's clerk. These officers form a committee, and after reckoning the total of the families entitled to pensions, divide the money amongst them, according to the number in each household, and the rank of the pensioners. They are divided into five orders :—

The Olema, or learned, and the Mudarrisin, who profess, lecture, or teach adults in the Harim.

The Imams and Khatibs.

The descendants of the Prophet.

The Fukaha, poor divines, pedadogues, gerund-grinders, who teach boys to read the Koran.

The Awam, or *nobile vulgus* of the Holy City, including the Ahali, or burghers of the town, and the Mujawirin, or those settled in the place.

Omar Effendi belonged to the second order, and he informed me that his share varied from three to fifteen Riyals per annum.

CHAPTER XVIII.

AL-MADINAH.

It is equally difficult to define, politically and geographically, the limits of Al-Hijaz. Whilst some authors,
as Abulfeda,[1] fix its Northern frontier at Aylah (Fort Al-
'Akabah) and the Desert, making Al-Yaman its Southern
limit, others include in it only the tract of land lying
between Meccah and Al-Madinah. The country has no
natural boundaries, and its political limits change with
every generation ; perhaps, therefore, the best distribution
of its frontier would be that which includes all the property
called Holy Land, making Yambu' the Northern, and Jeddah the Southern extremes, while a line drawn through Al-
Madinah, Suwayrkiyah, and Jabal Kora—the mountain of
Taif—might represent its Eastern boundary. Thus Al-
Hijaz would be an irregular parallelogram, about two
hundred and fifty miles in length, with a maximum
breadth of one hundred and fifty miles.

Two meanings are assigned to the name of this
venerated region. Most authorities make it mean the
" Separator," the " Barrier," between Nijd and Tahamah,[2]
or between Al-Yaman and Syria. According to others, it
signifies the " colligated," *i.e.* by mountains. It is to be
observed that the people of the country, especially the
Badawin, distinguish the lowlands from the high regions

---

1 To the East he limits Al-Hijaz by Yamamah (which some include
in it), Nijd, and the Syrian desert, and to the West by the Red Sea.
The Greeks, not without reason, included it in their Arabia Petræa.
Niebuhr places the Southern boundary at Hali, a little town south
of Kunfudah (Gonfoda). Captain Head *(Journey from India to Europe)*
makes the village Al-Kasr, opposite the Island of Kotambul, the limit
of Al-Hijaz to the South.

2 Or, according to others, between Al-Yaman and Syria.

R. Burton, delt.

C.F. Kell, Lith.

VIEW OF AL-MADINAH, THE BURIAL PLACE OF THE PROPHET.

by different names ; the former are called Tahamat al-Hijaz—the sea coast of Al-Hijaz, as we should say in India, "below the Ghauts;" the latter is known peculiarly as Al-Hijaz.[1]

Madinat al-Nabi,[2] the Prophet's City, or, as it is

---

1 If you ask a Badawi near Meccah, whence his fruit comes, he will reply "min Al-Hijaz," "from the Hijaz," meaning from the mountainous part of the country about Taif. This would be an argument in favour of those who make the word to signify a "place tied together," (by mountains). It is notorious that the Badawin are the people who best preserve the use of old and disputed words ; for which reason they were constantly referred to by the learned in the palmy days of Moslem philology. "Al-Hijaz," also, in this signification, well describes the country, a succession of ridges and mountain chains ; whereas such a name as "the barrier" would appear to be rather the work of some geographer in his study. Thus Al-Nijd was so called from its high and open lands, and, briefly, in this part of the world, names are most frequently derived from some physical and material peculiarity of soil or climate.

2 Amongst a people, who, like the Arabs or the Spaniards, hold a plurality of names to be a sign of dignity, so illustrious a spot as Al-Madinah could not fail to be rich in nomenclature. A Hadis declares, "to Al-Madinah belong ten names": books, however, enumerate nearly a hundred, of which a few will suffice as a specimen. Tabah, Tibah, Taibah, Tayyibah, and Mutayyibah, (from the root "Tib," "*good*," "*sweet*," or "*lawful*,") allude to the physical excellencies of Al-Madinah as regards climate—the perfume of the Prophet's tomb, and of the red rose, which was a thorn before it blossomed by the sweat of his brow—and to its being free from all moral impurity, such as the presence of Infidels, or worshippers of idols. Mohammed declared that he was ordered by Allah to change the name of the place to Tabah, from Yasrib or Asrib. The latter, according to some, was a proper name of a son of Noah ; others apply it originally to a place west of Mount Ohod, not to Al-Madinah itself ; and quote the plural form of the word, "Asarib," ("spots abounding in palms and fountains,") as a proof that it does not belong exclusively to a person. However this may be, the inauspicious signification of Yasrib, whose root is "Sarab," (destruction,) and the notorious use of the name by the Pagan Arabs, have combined to make it, like the other heathen designation, Al-Ghalabah, obsolete, and the pious Moslem who pronounces the word is careful to purify his mouth by repeating ten times the name "Al-Madinah." Barah and Barrah allude to its

usually called for brevity, Al-Madinah, *the* City, is situated
on the borders of Nijd, upon the vast plateau of high land

obedience and purity; Hasunah to its beauty; Khayrah and Khay-
yarah to its goodness; Mahabbah, Habibah and Mahbubah, to the
favour it found in the eyes of the Prophet; whilst Jabirah, Jabbarah,
and Jabarah, (from the root Jabr, joining or breaking), at once denote
its good influence upon the fortunes of the Faithful and its evil effects
upon the Infidel. " Al-Iman," (the Faith,) is the name under which
it is hinted at in the Koran. It is called Shafiyah (the Healer), on
account of the curative effects of earth found in its neighbourhood;
Nasirah, the Saving, and Asimah, the Preserving, because Mohammed and his companions were there secure from the fury of their
foes; Fazihah, the Detector, from its exposing the Infidel and the
hypocrite; Muslimah and Muminah, the Faithful City; Mubarakah,
the Blessed; Mahburah, the Happy; and Mahturah, the Gifted.
Mahrusah, the Guarded; and Mahfuzah, the Preserved, allude to the
belief that an angel sits in each of its ten main streets, to watch over
the town, and to prevent " Antichrist " entering therein. " Al-
Dajjal," as this personage is called, will arise in the East and will
peregrinate the earth; but he will be unable to penetrate into Meccah;
and on approaching Jabal Ohod, in sight of Al-Madinah, he will turn
off towards his death-place, Al-Sham (Damascus). In the Taurat or
Pentateuch, the town is called Mukaddasah, the Holy, or Marhumah
the Pitied, in allusion to the mission of Mohammed; Marzukah, the
Fed, is a favourable augury of plenty to it, and Miskinah, the Poor,
hints that it is independent of treasure of gold or store of silver to
keep up its dignity. Al-Makarr, means the Residence or the Place
of Quiet; Makinat, the Firmly-fixed, (in the right faith); Al-Harim,
the Sacred or Inviolable; and, finally, Al-Balad, *the* Town, and Al-
Madinah, *the* City by excellence. So an inhabitant calls himself Al-
Madani, whilst the natives of other and less-favoured " Madinahs "
affix Madini to their names. Its titles are Arz-Allah, Allah's Land;
Arz al-Hijrah, the Land of Exile; Akkalat al-Buldan, the Eater of
Towns; and Akkalat al-Kura, the Eater of Villages, on account of
its superiority, even as Meccah is entitled Umm al-Kura, the Mother
of Villages; Bayt Rasul Allah, House of Allah's Prophet; Jazirat al-
Arab, Isle of the Arab; and Harim Rasul Allah, the Sanctuary of
Allah's Prophet. In books and letters it has sometimes the title of
Madinah Musharrafah, the Exalted; more often that of Madinah
Munawwarah, the Enlightened—*scil.* by the lamp of faith and the
column of light supposed to be based upon the Prophet's tomb. The
Moslems are not the only people who lay claim to Al-Madinah.
According to some authors—and the legend is more credible than at

which forms central Arabia. The limits of the sanctuary called the Hudúd al-Harim, as defined by the Apostle, may still serve to mark out the city's plain. Northwards, at a distance of about three miles, is Jabal Ohod, or, according to others, Jabal Saur, a hill somewhat beyond Ohod ; these are the last ribs of the vast tertiary and primitive chine[1] which, extending from Taurus to near Aden, and from Aden again to Maskat, fringes the Arabian trapezium. To the South-west the plain is bounded by ridges of scoriaceous basalt, and by a buttress of rock called Jabal Ayr, like Ohod, about three miles distant from the town. Westward, according to some authors, is the Mosque Zu'l-Halifah. On the East there are no natural landmarks, nor even artificial, like the " Alamayn " at Meccah ; an imaginary line, therefore, is drawn, forming an irregular circle of which the town is the centre, with a diameter from ten to twelve miles. Such is the sanctuary.[2] Geographically considered, the

first sight it would appear—the old Guebres had in Arabia and Persia seven large fire temples, each dedicated to a planet. At " Mahdinah," as they pervert the word, was an image of the Moon, wherefore the place was originally called the " Religion of the Moon." These Guebres, amongst other sacred spots. claim Meccah, where they say Saturn and the Moon were conjointly venerated ; Jerusalem, the Tomb of Ali at Najaf, that of Hosayn at Kerbela, and others. These pretensions of course the Moslems deny with insistance, which does not prevent certain symptoms of old and decayed faith peeping out in localities where their presence, if duly understood, would be considered an abomination. This curious fact is abundantly evident in Sind, and I have already alluded to it (*History of Sind*).

1 Such is its formation in Al-Hijaz.

2 Within the sanctuary all Muharramat, or sins, are forbidden ; but the several schools advocate different degrees of strictness. The Imam Malik, for instance, allows no *latrinæ* nearer to Al-Madinah than Jabal Ayr, a distance of about three miles. He also forbids slaying wild animals, but at the same time he specifies no punishment for the offence. Some do not allow the felling of trees, alleging that the Prophet enjoined their preservation as an ornament to the city, and a pleasure to visitors. Al-Khattabi, on the contrary, permits people to cut wood, and this is certainly the general practice.

plain is bounded, on the East, with a thin line of low
dark hills, traversed by the Darb al-Sharki, or the " Eastern road," through Al-Nijd to Meccah: Southwards, the
plateau is open, and almost perfectly level as far as the
eye can see.

Al-Madinah dates its origin doubtless from ancient
times, and the cause of its prosperity is evident in the
abundant supply of water, a necessary generally scarce in
Arabia.   The formation of the plateau is in some places
salt sand, but usually a white chalk, and a loamy clay,
which even by the roughest manipulation makes tolerable
bricks.   Lime also abounds.   The town is situated upon a
gently-shelving part of the plain, the lowest portion of
which, to judge from the versant, is at the southern base
of Mount Ohod, hence called Al-Safilah, and the highest
at the Awali, or plains about Kuba, and the East.

The Southern and South-Eastern walls of the suburb
are sometimes carried away by violent " Sayl," or torrents, which, after rain, sweep down from the Western as

---

All authors strenuously forbid within the boundaries slaying man
(except invaders, infidels, and the sacrilegious), drinking spirits, and
leading an immoral life.   As regards the dignity of the sanctuary,
there is but one opinion ; a number of Hadis testify to its honour,
praise its people, and threaten dreadful things to those who injure it
or them.   It is certain that on the last day, the Prophet will intercede for, and aid, all those who die, and are buried, at Al-Madinah.
Therefore, the Imam Malik made but one pilgrimage to Meccah,
fearing to leave his bones in any other cemetery but Al-Bakia.
There is, however, much debate concerning the comparative sanctity
of Al-Madinah and Meccah.   Some say Mohammed preferred the
former, blessing it as Abraham did Meccah.   Moreover, as a tradition
declares that every man's body is drawn from the dust of the ground
in which he is buried, Al-Madinah, it is evident, had the honour of
supplying materials for the Prophet's person.   Others, like Omar,
were uncertain in favour of which city to decide.   Others openly
assert the pre-eminence of Meccah ; the general *consensus* of Al-Islam
preferring Al-Madinah to Meccah, save only the Bayt Allah in the
latter city.   This last is a *juste-milieu* view, by no means in favour with
the inhabitants of either place.   In the meanwhile the Meccans claim
unlimited superiority over the Madani ; the Madani over the Meccans.

well as from the Eastern highlands. The water-flow is towards Al-Ghabbah, lowlands in the Northern and Western hills, a little beyond Mount Ohod. This basin receives the drainage of the mountains and the plain ; according to some absorbing it, according to others col-lecting it till of sufficient volume to flow off to the sea. Water, though abundant, is rarely of good quality. In the days of the Prophet, the Madani consumed the produce of wells, seven of which are still celebrated by the people.[1] Historians relate that Omar, the second Caliph, provided the town with drinking-water from the Northern parts of the plains by means of an aqueduct. The modern city is supplied by a source called the Ayn al-Zarka or Azure Spring,[2] which arises some say at the foot of Mount Ayr, others, with greater probability, in the date-groves of Kuba. Its waters were first brought to Al-Madinah by Marwan, governor in Al-Mu'awiyah's day. It now flows down a subterraneous canal, about thirty feet below the surface ; in places the water is exposed to the air, and

---

1 These seven wells will be noticed in Chapter XIX., post.

2 I translate Al-Zarka "azure," although Sir G. Wilkinson remarks, *àpropos* of the Bahr al-Azrak, generally translated by us the "Blue Nile," that, "when the Arabs wish to say dark or jet black, they use the word 'Azrak.'" It is true that Azrak is often applied to indeterminate dark hues, but "Aswad," not Azrak, is the opposite to Abyaz, "white." Moreover, Al-*Zarka* in the feminine is applied to women with light blue eyes ; this would be no distinctive appellation if it signified black eyes, the almost universal colour. Zarka of Yamamah is the name of a celebrated heroine in Arab story, and the curious reader, who wishes to see how much the West is indebted to the East, even for the materials of legend, will do well to peruse her short history in Major Price's "Essay," or M. C. de Perceval's "Essai," &c., vol. i., p. 101. Both of these writers, however, assert that Zarka's eyes, when cut out, were found to contain fibres blackened by the use of Kohl, and they attribute to her the invention of this pigment. I have often heard the legend from the Arabs, who declare that she painted her eyes with "Ismid," a yellow metal, of what kind I have never been able to determine, although its name is everywhere known.

steps lead to it for the convenience of the inhabitants: this was the work of Sultan Sulayman the Magnificent. After passing through the town it turns to the North-west, its course being marked by a line of circular walls breast high, like the Kariz of Afghanistan, placed at unequal distances, and resembling wells : it then loses itself in the Nakhil or palm-groves.   During my stay at Al-Madinah, I always drank this water, which appeared to me, as the citizens declared it to be, sweet and wholesome.[1] There are many wells in the town, as water is found at about twenty feet below the surface of the soil : few produce anything fit for drinking, some being salt and others bitter.   As usual in the hilly countries of the East, the wide beds and Fiumaras, even in the dry season, will supply travellers for a day or two with an abundance of water, filtrated through, and, in some cases, flowing beneath the sand.

The climate of the plain is celebrated for a long, and, comparatively speaking, a rigorous winter ; a popular saying records the opinion of the Apostle "that he who patiently endures the cold of Al-Madinah and the heat of Meccah, merits a reward in Paradise."   Ice is not seen in the town, but may frequently be met with, it is said, on Jabal Ohod ;   fires are lighted in the houses during winter, and palsies attack those who at this season imprudently bathe in unwarmed water.   The fair complexions of the people prove that this account of the brumal rigours is not exaggerated.   Chilly and violent winds from the Eastern Desert are much dreaded, and though Ohod screens the town on the North and North-East, a gap in the mountains to the North-West fills the

---

1 Burckhardt confounds the Ayn al-Zarka with the Bir al-Khatim, or Kuba well, of whose produce the surplus only mixes with it, and he complains loudly of the "detestable water of Madinah."   But he was ill at the time, otherwise he would not have condemned it so strongly after eulogising the salt-bitter produce of the Meccan Zemzem.

air at times with raw and comfortless blasts. The rains begin in October, and last with considerable intervals through six months; the clouds, gathered by the hill-tops and the trees near the town, discharge themselves with violence, and about the equinoxes, thunder-storms are common. At such times the Barr al-Manakhah, or the open space between the town and the suburbs, is a sheet of water, and the land near the Southern and the South-Eastern wall of the faubourg becomes a pool. Rain, however, is not considered unhealthy here; and the people, unlike the Meccans and the Cairenes, expect it with pleasure, because it improves their date-trees and fruit plantations.[1] In winter it usually rains at night, in spring during the morning, and in summer about evening time. This is the case throughout Al-Hijaz, as explained by the poet Labíd in these lines, which describe the desolate site of an old encampment :—

"It (the place) hath been fertilised by the first spring showers of the constellations, and hath been swept by
The incessant torrents of the thunder-clouds, falling in heavy and in gentle rains,
From each night-cloud, and heavily dropping morning-cloud,
And the even-cloud, whose crashings are re-echoed from around."

And the European reader will observe that the Arabs generally reckon three seasons, including our autumn, in their summer. The hot weather at Al-Madinah appeared to me as extreme as the hibernal cold is described to be, but the air was dry, and the open plain prevented the faint and stagnant sultriness which distinguishes Meccah. Moreover, though the afternoons were close, the nights and the mornings were cool and dewy. At this season the citizens sleep on the house-tops, or on the ground

---

1 The people of Nijd, as Wallin informs us, believe that the more the palms are watered, the more syrup will the fruit produce; they therefore inundate the ground, as often as possible. At Al-Jauf, where the date is peculiarly good, the trees are watered regularly every third or fourth day.

outside their doors.   Strangers must follow this example
with considerable circumspection ; the open air is safe
in the Desert, but in cities it causes, to the unaccustomed,
violent catarrhs and febrile affections.

I collect the following notes upon the diseases and
medical treatment of the Northern Hijaz.   Al-Madinah
has been visited four times by the Rih al-Asfar[1] (yellow
wind), or Asiatic Cholera, which is said to have committed great ravages, sometimes carrying off whole households.   In the Rahmat al-Kabirah, the " Great Mercy,"
as the worst attack is piously called, whenever a man
vomited, he was abandoned to his fate ; before that, he
was treated with mint, lime-juice, and copious draughts of
coffee.   It is still the boast of Al-Madinah, that the Taun,
or plague, has never passed her frontier.[2]   The Judari, or
smallpox, appears to be indigenous to the countries
bordering upon the Red Sea ; we read of it there in the
earliest works of the Arabs,[3] and even to the present
time it sometimes sweeps through Arabia and the Somali

---

1 Properly meaning the Yellow Wind or Air.   The antiquity of the
word and its origin are still disputed.

2 Burckhardt *(Travels in Arabia*, vol. ii.) informs us, that in
A.D. 1815, when Meccah, Yambu', and Jeddah suffered severely from
the plague, Al-Madinah and the open country between the two sea-
ports escaped.

3 Conjecture, however, goes a little too far when it discovers
small-pox in the Tayr Ababil, the " swallow birds," which, according
to the Koran, destroyed the host of Abrahat al-Ashram.   Major
Price (Essay) may be right in making Ababil the plural of Abilah, a
vesicle ; but it appears to me that the former is an Arabic and the
latter a Persian word, which have no connection whatever.   M. C. de
Perceval, quoting the Sirat al-Rasul, which says that at that time
small-pox first appeared in Arabia, ascribes the destruction of the
host of Al-Yaman to an epidemic and a violent tempest.   The strangest
part of the story is, that although it occurred at Meccah, about two
months before Mohammed's birth, and, therefore, within the memory
of many living at the time, the Prophet alludes to it in the Koran as
a miracle.

country with desolating violence. In the town of Al-Madinah it is fatal to children, many of whom, however, are in these days inoculated[1]: amongst the Badawin, old men die of it, but adults are rarely victims, either in the City or in the Desert. The nurse closes up the room whilst the sun is up, and carefully excludes the night air, believing that, as the disease is "hot,[2]" a breath of wind will kill the patient. During the hours of darkness, a lighted candle or lamp is always placed by the side of the bed, or the sufferer would die of madness, brought on by evil spirits or fright. Sheep's wool is burnt in the sick-room, as death would follow the inhaling of any perfume. The only remedy I have heard of is pounded Kohl (antimony) drunk in water, and the same is drawn along the breadth of the eyelid, to prevent blindness. The diet is Adas (lentils),[3] and a peculiar kind of date, called Tamr al-Birni. On the twenty-first day the patient is washed with salt and tepid water.

Ophthalmia is rare.[4] In the summer, quotidian and

---

1 In Al-Yaman, we are told by Niebuhr, a rude form of inoculation—the mother pricking the child's arm with a thorn—has been known from time immemorial. My Madinah friend assured me that only during the last generation, this practice has been introduced amongst the Badawin of Al-Hijaz.

2 Orientals divide their diseases, as they do remedies and articles of diet, into hot, cold, and temperate.

3 This grain is cheaper than rice on the banks of the Nile—a fact which enlightened England, now paying a hundred times its value for "Revalenta Arabica," apparently ignores.

4 Herodotus (Euterpe) has two allusions to eye disease, which seems to have afflicted the Egyptians from the most ancient times. Sesostris the Great died stone-blind; his successor lost his sight for ten years, and the Hermaic books had reason to devote a whole volume to ophthalmic disease. But in the old days of idolatry, the hygienic and prophylactic practices alluded to by Herodotus, the greater cleanliness of the people, and the attention paid to the canals and drainage, probably prevented this malarious disease becoming the scourge which it is now. The similarity of the soil and the climate of Egypt to those of

tertian fevers (Hummah Salis) are not uncommon, and
if accompanied by emetism, they are frequently fatal.

Upper Sind, and the prevalence of the complaint in both countries,
assist us in investigating the predisposing causes. These are, the nitrous
and pungent nature of the soil—what the old Greek calls "acrid
matter exuding from the earth,"—and the sudden transition from
extreme dryness to excessive damp checking the invisible perspiration
of the circumorbital parts, and flying to an organ which is already
weakened by the fierce glare of the sun, and the fine dust raised by
the Khamsin or the Chaliho. Glare and dust alone, seldom cause eye
disease. Every one knows that ophthalmia is unknown in the Desert,
and the people of Al-Hijaz, who live in an atmosphere of blaze and
sand, seldom lose their sight. The Egyptian usually catches ophthalmia in his childhood. It begins with simple conjunctivitis, caused
by constitutional predisposition, exposure, diet, and allowing the eye
to be covered with swarms of flies. He neglects the early symptoms,
and cares the less for being a Cyclops, as the infirmity will most
probably exempt him from military service. Presently the sane
organ becomes affected sympathetically. As before, simple disease of
the conjunctiva passes into purulent ophthalmia. The man, after
waiting a while, will go to the doctor and show a large cicatrix in
each eye, the result of an ulcerated cornea. Physic can do nothing
for him ; he remains blind for life. He is now provided for, either
by living with his friends, who seldom refuse him a loaf of bread, or
if industriously inclined, by begging, by acting Mu'ezzin, or by en-
gaging himself as "Yamaniyah," or chaunter, at funerals. His
children are thus predisposed to the paternal complaint, and gradually
the race becomes tender-eyed. Most travellers have observed that
imported African slaves seldom become blind either in Egypt or in
Sind. Few Englishmen settled in Egypt lose their sight, except they
be medical men, who cannot afford time to nurse the early symptoms.
The use of coffee and of water as beverages has much to do with this.
In the days of hard drinking our Egyptian army suffered severely,
and the Austrian army in Tuscany showed how often blindness is
caused by importing Northern habits into Southern countries. Many
Europeans in Egypt wash their eyes with cold water, especially after
walking, and some use once a day a mildly astringent or cooling wash,
as Goulard's lotion or vinegar and water. They avoid letting flies
settle upon their eyes, and are of opinion that the evening dews are
prejudicial, and that sleeping with open windows lays the foundation
of disease. Generally when leaving a hot room, especially a Nile-
boat cabin, for the cold damp night air, the more prudent are careful

The attack generally begins with the Naffazah, or cold fit, and is followed by Al-Hummah, the hot stage. The principal remedies are cooling drinks, such as Sikanjabin (oxymel) and syrups. After the fever the face and body frequently swell, and indurated lumps appear on the legs and stomach. There are also low fevers, called simply Hummah ; they are usually treated by burning charms in the patient's room. Jaundice and bilious complaints are common, and the former is popularly cured in a peculiar way. The sick man looks into a pot full of water, whilst the exorciser, reciting a certain spell, draws the heads of two needles from the patient's ears along his eyes, down his face, lastly dipping them into water, which at once becomes yellow. Others have " Mirayat," magic mirrors,[1] on which the patient looks, and looses the com-

---

to bathe and to wipe the eyes and forehead as a preparation for change of atmosphere. During my short practice in Egypt I found the greatest advantage from the employment of counter-irritants,—blisters and Pommade Emétisé,—applied to the temples and behind the ears. Native practitioners greatly err by confining their patients in dark rooms, thereby injuring the general health and laying the foundation of chronic disease. They are ignorant that, unless the optic nerve be affected, the stimulus of light is beneficial to the eye. And the people by their dress favour the effects of glare and dust. The Tarbush, no longer surrounded as of old by a huge turband, is the least efficient of protectors, and the comparative rarity of ophthalmic disease among the women, who wear veils, proves that the exposure is one of its co-efficient causes.

1 This invention dates from the most ancient times, and both in the East and in the West has been used by the weird brotherhood to produce the appearances of the absent and the dead, to discover treasure, to detect thieves, to cure disease, and to learn the secrets of the unknown world. The Hindus called it Anjan, and formed it by applying lamp-black, made of a certain root, and mixed with oil to the palm of a footling child, male or female. The Greeks used oil poured into a boy's hand. Cornelius Agrippa had a crystal mirror, which material also served the Counts de Saint Germain and Cagliostro. Dr. Dee's " show-stone " was a bit of cannel coal. The modern Sindians know the art by the name of Gahno or Vinyano; there, as in Southern Persia, ink is rubbed upon the seer's thumb-nail. The people of Northern Africa are considered skilful in this science, and I

plaint.   Dysenteries frequently occur in the fruit season, when the greedy Arabs devour all manner of unripe

---

have a Maghrabi magic formula for inking the hand of a " boy, a black slave girl, a virgin, or a pregnant woman," which differs materially from those generally known.   The modern Egyptians call it Zarb al Mandal, and there is scarcely a man in Cairo who does not know something about it.   In selecting subjects to hold the ink, they observe the right hand, and reject all who have not what is called in palmistry the "linea media naturalis" straight and deeply cut. Even the barbarous Finns look into a glass of brandy, and the natives of Australia gaze at a kind of shining stone.   Lady Blessington's crystal ball is fresh in the memory of the present generation, and most men have heard of Electro-Biology and the Cairo magician.   Upon this latter subject, a vexed one, I must venture a few remarks.   In the first account of the magician by Mr. Lane, we have a fair and dispassionate recital of certain magical, mystical, or mesmeric phenomena, which "excited considerable curiosity and interest thoughout the civilised world."   As usual in such matters, the civilised world was wholly ignorant of what was going on at home ; otherwise, in London, Paris, and New York, they might have found dozens studying the science. But a few years before, Dr. Herklots had described the same practice in India, filling three goodly pages ; but he called his work " Qanoon-i-Islam," and, consequently, despite its excellencies, it fell still-born from the press.   Lady H. Stanhope frequently declared "the spell by which the face of an absent person is thrown upon a mirror to be within the reach of the humblest and most contemptible of magicians ; " but the civilised world did not care to believe a prophetess. All, however, were aroused by Mr. Lane's discovery, and determined to decide the question by the ordeal of reason.   Accordingly, in A.D. 1844, Mr. Lane, aided by Lord Nugent and others, discovered that a "coarse and stupid fraud " had been perpetrated upon him by Osman Effendi, the Scotchman.   In 1845, Sir G. Wilkinson remarked of this rationalism, " The explanation lately offered, that Osman Effendi was in collusion with the magician, is neither fair on him nor satisfactory, as he was not present when those cases occurred which were made so much of in Europe," and he proposed "leading questions and accidents " as the word of the riddle.   Eothen attributed the whole affair to "shots," as schoolboys call them, and ranked success under the head of Paley's "tentative miracles."   A writer in the Quarterly explained them by suggesting the probability of divers (impossible) optical combinations, and, lest the part of belief should have been left unrepresented, Miss Martineau was enabled to see clear signs of mesmeric action, and by the decisive experiment of self, discovered the

peaches, grapes, and pomegranates. The popular treatment is by the actual cautery ; the scientific affect the
use of drastics and astringent simples, and the Bizr
al-Kutn (cotton-seed), toasted, pounded, and drunk in
warm water. Almost every one here, as in Egypt,
suffers more or less from hæmorrhoids ; they are treated
by dietetics—eggs and leeks—and by a variety of drugs,
Myrobalans, Lisan-al-Hamal (*Arnoglossum*), etc. But the
patient looks with horror at the scissors and the knife, so
that they seldom succeed in obtaining a radical cure. The
Filaria Medinensis, locally called " Farantit," is no longer
common at the place which gave it its European name.
At Yambu', however, the people suffer much from the Vena
appearing in the legs. The complaint is treated here as
in India and in Abyssinia : when the tumour bursts, and
the worm shows, it is extracted by being gradually
wound round a splinter of wood. Hydrophobia is rare,
and the people have many superstitions about it. They
suppose that a bit of meat falls from the sky, and that a
dog eating it becomes mad. I was assured by respectable
persons, that when a man is bitten, they shut him up
with food, in a solitary chamber, for four days, and that
if at the end of that time he still howls like a dog, they
expel the Ghúl (demon) from him, by pouring over him
boiling water mixed with ashes—a certain cure I can
easily believe. The only description of leprosy known in
Al-Hijaz is that called "Al-Baras": it appears in white
patches on the skin, seldom attacks any but the poorer
classes, and is considered incurable. Wounds are treated
by Marham, or ointments, especially by the "Balesan,"
or Balm of Meccah; a cloth is tied round the limb, and

---

magic to be an " affair of mesmerism." Melancholy to relate,
after all this philosophy, the herd of travellers at Cairo is still divided
in opinion about the magician, some holding his performance to be
" all humbug," others darkly hinting that " there may be something
in it."

not removed till the wound heals, which amongst this
people of simple life, generally takes place by first intention.   Ulcers are common in Al-Hijaz, as indeed all over
Arabia.   We read of them in ancient times.   In A.D.
504, the poet and warrior, Amr al-Kays, died of this
dreadful disease, and it is related that when Mohammed
Abu Si Mohammed, in A.H. 132, conquered Al-Yaman with
an army from Al-Hijaz, he found the people suffering
from sloughing and mortifying sores, so terrible to look
upon that he ordered the sufferers to be burnt alive.
Fortunately for the patients, the conqueror died suddenly
before his inhuman mandate was executed.   These sores
here, as in Al-Yaman,[1] are worst when upon the shin
bones; they eat deep into the leg, and the patient dies
of fever and gangrene.   They are treated on first appearance by the actual cautery, and, when practicable,
by cutting off the joint; the drugs popularly applied are
Tutiya (tutty) and verdigris.   There is no cure but rest,
a generous diet, and change of air.

By the above short account it will be seen that the
Arabs are no longer the most skilful physicians in the
world.   They have, however, one great advantage in their
practice, and they are sensible enough to make free use
of it.   As the children of almost all the respectable
citizens are brought up in the Desert, the camp becomes
to them a native village.   In cases of severe wounds or
chronic diseases, the patient is ordered off to the Black
Tents, where he lives as a Badawi, drinking camels'
milk (a diet for the first three or four days highly cathartic),
and doing nothing.   This has been the practice from time
immemorial in Arabia, whereas Europe is only beginning
to systematise the adhibition of air, exercise, and simple
living.   And even now we are obliged to veil it under the
garb of charlatanry—to call it a "milk-cure" in Switzer-

---

1 They distinguish, however, between the Hijaz "Násur" and
the "Jurh al-Yamani," or the "Yaman Ulcer."

land, a "water-cure" in Silesia, a "grape-cure" in France, a "hunger-cure" in Germany, and other sensible names which act as dust in the public eyes.

Al-Madinah consists of three parts,—a town, a fort, and a suburb little smaller than the body of the place. The town itself is about one-third larger than Suez, or nearly half the size of Meccah. It is a walled enclosure forming an irregular oval with four gates. The Bab al-Shami, or "Syrian Gate," in the North-West side of the enceinte, leads towards Jabal Ohod, Hamzah's burial-place, and the mountains. In the Eastern wall, the Bab al-Jum'ah, or Friday Gate, opens upon the Nijd road and the cemetery, Al-Bakia. Between the Shami and the Jum'ah gates, towards the North, is the Bab al-Ziyafah (of Hospitality); and Westwards the Bab al-Misri (Egyptian) opens upon the plain called the Barr al-Manakhah. The Eastern and the Egyptian gates are fine massive buildings, with double towers close together, painted with broad bands of red, yellow, and other colors, not unlike that old entrance of the Cairo citadel which opens upon the Ramayliyah plain. They may be compared with the gateway towers of the old Norman castles — Arques, for instance. In their shady and well-watered interiors, soldiers keep guard, camel-men dispute, and numerous idlers congregate, to enjoy the luxuries of coolness and of companionship. Beyond this gate, in the street leading to the Mosque, is the great bazar. Outside it lie the Suk al-Khuzayriyah, or greengrocers' market, and the Suk al-Habbabah, or the grain bazar, with a fair sprinkling of coffee-houses. These markets are long masses of palm-leaf huts, blackened in the sun and wind, of a mean and squalid appearance, detracting greatly from the appearance of the gates. Amongst them there is a little domed and whitewashed building, which I was told is a Sabil or public fountain. In the days of the Prophet the town

was not walled. Even in Al-Idrisi's time (twelfth century), and as late as Bartema's (eighteenth century), the
fortifications were mounds of earth, made by order of
Kasim al-Daulat al-Ghori, who re-populated the town
and provided for its inhabitants. Now, the enceinte is
in excellent condition. The walls are well built of granite
and lava blocks, in regular layers, cemented with lime;
they are provided with "Mazghal" (or "Matras") long
loopholes, and "Shararif" or trefoil-shaped crenelles:
in order to secure a flanking fire, semicircular towers, also
loopholed and crenellated, are disposed in the curtain at
short and irregular intervals. Inside, the streets are what
they always should be in these torrid lands, deep, dark,
and narrow, in few places paved—a thing to be deprecated
—and generally covered with black earth well watered
and trodden to hardness. The most considerable lines
radiate towards the Mosque. There are few public buildings. The principal Wakalahs are four in number;
one is the Wakalat Bab Salam near the Harim, another
the Wakalat Jabarti, and two are inside the Misri gate;
they all belong to Arab citizens. These Caravanserais
are used principally as stores, rarely for dwelling-places
like those of Cairo; travellers, therefore, must hire houses
at a considerable expense, or pitch tents to the detriment
of health and to their extreme discomfort. The other
public buildings are a few mean coffee-houses and an
excellent bath in the Harat Zarawan, inside the town:
far superior to the unclean establishments of Cairo, it
borrows something from the luxury of Stambul. The
houses are, for the East, well built, flat-roofed and double-
storied; the materials generally used are a basaltic scoria,
burnt brick, and palm wood. The best enclose spacious
courtyards and small gardens with wells, where water
basins and date trees gladden the owners' eyes. The
latticed balconies, first seen by the overland European
traveller at Malta, are here common, and the windows are

R. Burton, delt.

C. F. Kell. Lith.

SKETCH OF AL-MADINAH, BY A NATIVE ARTIST.

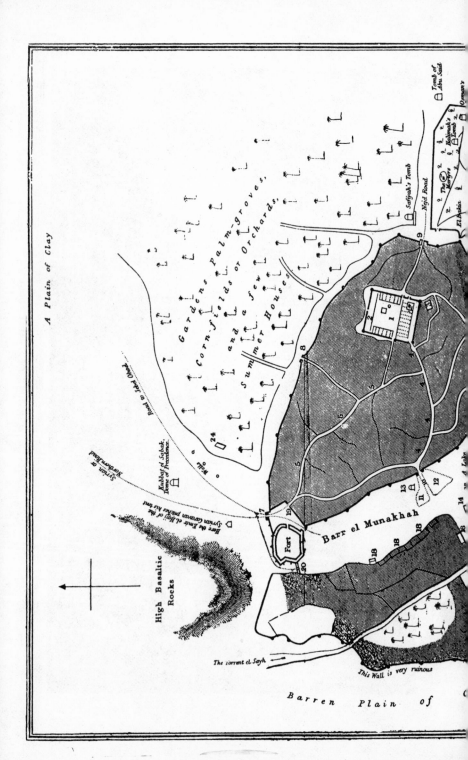

A Plain of Clay

Gardens Palm-groves, Corn-fields or Orchards, and a few Summer Houses

High Basaltic Rocks

Syrian or Northern Road

Road to Jabal Ohod

Kubbat el Sabak. Dome of Prostration.

Bare de Emír el Hájj of the Syrian caravan pitches his tent

Road

Fort

Barr el Munakhah

The torrent el Sayh

This Wall is very ruinous

Barren Plain of

Tomb of Abu Said

Ommán's

Sáfiyah's Tomb

Nejd Road

Halímah's Tomb

Tomb

Margès

El Batin

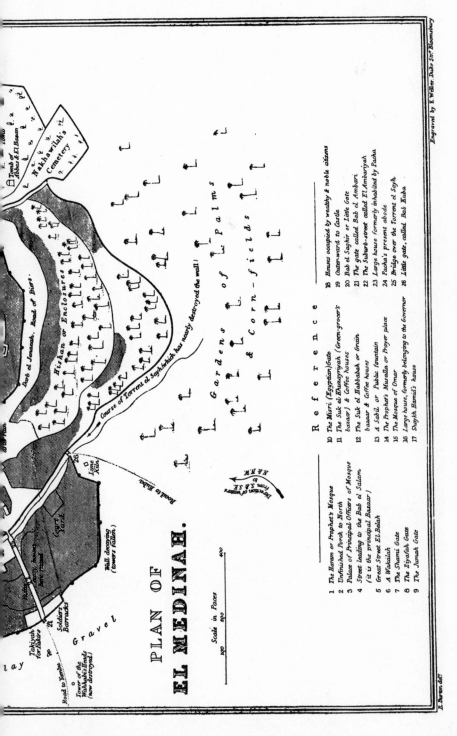

PLAN OF EL MEDINAH.

Scale in Paces
100   200   300   400

Reference

1 The Haram or Prophet's Mosque
2 Unfinished Portek to North
3 Palace of Principal Officers of Mosque
4 Street leading to the Bab el Salam (it is the principal Bazaar)
5 Great Street El Belah
6 A Wakalah
7 The Shami Gate
8 The Ziyafah Gate
9 The Jumah Gate
10 The Misri (Egyptian) Gate
11 The Suk el Khuzayriyah (Green-grocer's bazaar) & Coffee houses
12 The Suk el Habbabah or Grain bazaar & Coffee house
13 A Sabil or Public fountain
14 The Prophet's Musalla or Prayer place
15 The Mosque of Omar
16 Large house, formerly belonging to the Governor
17 Shaykh Hamid's house
18 Houses occupied by wealthy & noble citizens
19 Outer-ward to Castle
20 Bab el Saghir or Little Gate
21 The gate called Bab el Ambari
22 The Suburb-street called El Ambariyah
23 Large house formerly inhabited by Pasha
24 Pasha's present abode
25 Bridge over the Torrent el Sayh
26 Little gate, called Bab Kuba

Deviation of watter's from S.S.E. to N.N.W.

Engraved by E. Weller, Duke St.ⁿ Bloomsbury
R. Burton del.ᵗ

mere apertures in the wall, garnished, as usual in Arab
cities, with a shutter of planking. Al-Madinah fell rapidly
under the Wahhabis, but after their retreat, it soon rose
again, and now it is probably as comfortable and flourishing a little city as any to be found in the East. It contains
between fifty and sixty streets, including the alleys and
culs-de-sac. There is about the same number of Harat or
quarters; but I have nothing to relate of them save their
names. Within the town few houses are in a dilapidated
condition. The best authorities estimate the number of
habitations at about 1500 within the enceinte, and those
in the suburb at 1000. I consider both accounts exaggerated; the former might contain 800, and the Manakhah
perhaps 500; at the same time I must confess not to have
counted them, and Captain Sadlier (in A.D. 1819) declares that the Turks, who had just made a kind of
census, reckoned 6000 houses and a population of 18,000
souls. Assuming the population to be 16,000 (Burckhardt raises it as high as 20,000), of which 9000 occupy
the city, and 7000 the suburbs and the fort, this would
give a little more than twelve inhabitants to each house, a
fair estimate for an Arab town, where the abodes are large
and slaves abound.[1]

The castle joins on to the North-West angle of the city
enceinte, and the wall of its Eastern outwork is pierced for

---

1 I afterwards received the following information from Mr. Charles
Cole, H.B.M. Vice-Consul at Jeddah, a gentleman well acquainted with
Western Arabia, and having access to official information : " The population of Al-Madinah is from 16,000 to 18,000, and the Nizam troops
in garrison 400. Meccah contains about 45,000 inhabitants, Yambu'
from 6000 to 7000, Jeddah about 2500 (this I think is too low), and
Taif 8000. Most of the troops are stationed at Meccah and at Jeddah.
In Al-Hijaz there is a total force of five battalions, each of which
ought to contain 800 men ; they may amount to 3500, with 500 artillery, and 4500 irregulars, though the muster rolls bear 6000. The
Government pays in paper for all supplies, (even for water for the
troops,) and the paper sells at the rate of forty piastres per cent."

a communication through a court strewed with guns and
warlike apparatus, between the Manakhah Suburb and
the Bab al-Shami, or the Syrian Gate. Having been
refused entrance into the fort, I can describe only its
exterior. The outer wall resembles that of the city, only
its towers are more solid, and the curtain appears better
calculated for work. Inside, a donjon, built upon a rock,
bears proudly enough the banner of the Crescent and the
Star ; its whitewashed walls make it a conspicuous object,
and guns pointed in all directions, especially upon the
town, project from their embrasures. The castle is said
to contain wells, bomb-proofs, provisions, and munitions
of war ; if so, it must be a kind of Gibraltar to the Badawin and the Wahhabis. The garrison consisted of a Nisf
Urtah,[1] or half battalion (four hundred men) of Nizam
infantry, commanded by a Pasha ; his authority also
extends to a Sanjak, or about five hundred Kurdish and
Albanian Bash-Buzuks, whose duty it is to escort
caravans, to convey treasures, and to be shot at in the
Passes. The Madani, who, as usual with Orientals,
take a personal pride in their castle, speak of it with
much exaggeration. Commanded by a high line of rocks
on the North-West, and built as it is in most places without moat, glacis, earthwork, or outworks, a few shells
and a single battery of siege guns would soon render it
untenable. In ancient times it has more than once been
held by a party at feud with the town, for whose mimic
battles the Barr al-Manakhah was a fitting field. Northward from the fort, on the road to Ohod, but still within
fire, is a long many-windowed building, formerly Da'ud
Pasha's palace. In my time it had been bought by
Abbas Pasha of Egypt.

---

1 The Urtah or battalion here varies from 800 to 1000 men. Of
these, four form one Alai or regiment, and thirty-six Alai an Urdu or
camp. This word Urdu, pronounced " Ordoo," is the origin of our
" horde."

The suburbs lie to the South and West of the town.
Southwards they are separated from the enceinte by a
wide road, called the Darb al-Janazah, the Road of Biers,
so called because the corpses of certain schismatics, who
may not pass through the city, are carried this way to
their own cemetery near the Bab al-Jumah, or Eastern
Gate. Westwards, between Al-Madinah and its faubourg,
lies the plain of Al-Manakhah, about three-quarters of a
mile long, by three hundred yards broad. The straggling
suburbs occupy more ground than the city : fronting the
enceinte they are without walls ; towards the West, where
open country lies, they are enclosed by mud or raw brick
ramparts, with little round towers, all falling to decay.
A number of small gates lead from the suburb into the
country. The only large one, a poor copy of the Bab
al-Nasr at Cairo, is the Ambari or Western entrance,
through which we passed into Al-Madinah. The suburb
contains no buildings of any consequence, except the
Khaskiyah, or official residence of the Muhafiz (governor),
a plain building near the Barr al-Manakhah, and the
Khamsah Masajid, or the Five Mosques, which every
Zair is expected to visit. They are

The Prophet's Mosque in the Manakhah.

Abu Bakr's near the Ayn al-Zarka.

Ali's Mosque in the Zukak al-Tayyar of the
Manakhah. Some authors call this the " Musalla al-Íd,"
because the Prophet here prayed the Festival Prayer.

Omar's Mosque, near the Bab Kuba of the Manakhah, and close to the little torrent called Al-Sayh.

Belal's Mosque, celebrated in books ; I did not see
it, and some Madani assured me that it no longer exists.

A description of one of these buildings will suffice,
for they are all similar. Mohammed's Mosque in the
Manakhah stands upon a spot formerly occupied, some
say, by the Jami Ghamamah. Others believe it to be
founded upon the Musalla al-Nabi, a place where the

Apostle recited the first Festival prayers after his arrival at
Al-Madinah, and used frequently to pray, and to address
those of his followers who lived far from the Harim,[1]
or Sanctuary.   It is a trim modern building of cut stone
and lime in regular layers, of parallelogramic shape,
surmounted by one large and four small cupolas.   These
are all whitewashed; and the principal is capped with a
large crescent, or rather a trident, rising from a series of
gilt globes: the other domes crown the several corners.
The minaret is of the usual Turkish shape, with a conical
roof, and a single gallery for the Mu'ezzin.   An Acacia-
tree or two on the Eastern side, and behind it a wall-like
line of mud houses, finish the *coup-d'œil;* the interior of
this building is as simple as is the exterior.   And here I
may remark that the Arabs have little idea of splendour,
either in their public or in their private architecture.
Whatever strikes the traveller's eye in Al-Hijaz is always
either an importation or the work of foreign artists.   This
arises from the simple tastes of the people, combined,
doubtless, with their notable thriftiness.   If strangers
will build for them, they argue, why should they build
for themselves?   Moreover, they have scant inducement
to lavish money upon grand edifices.   Whenever a disturbance takes place, domestic or from without, the
principal buildings are sure to suffer.   And the climate is
inimical to their enduring.   Both ground and air at Al-
Madinah, as well as at Meccah, are damp and nitrous in
winter, in summer dry and torrid: the lime is poor; palm-
timber soon decays: even foreign wood-work suffers, and
a few years of neglect suffice to level the proudest pile
with the dust.

The suburbs to the South of Al-Madinah are a collection

---

1 One of the traditions, "Between my house and my place of
prayers is a Garden of the Gardens of Paradise," has led divines to
measure the distance: it is said to be 1000 cubits from the Bab Salam
of the Harim to this Musalla.

R. Burton, delt.

C.F. Kell, Lith.

MUSALLA AL—NABI, THE PROPHET'S PLACE OF PRAYER.

of walled villages, with plantations and gardens between. They are laid out in the form, called here, as in Egypt, Hosh—court-yards, with single-storied tenements opening into them. These enclosures contain the cattle of the inhabitants; they have strong wooden doors, shut at night to prevent "lifting," and they are capable of being stoutly defended. The inhabitants of the suburb are for the most part Badawi settlers, and a race of schismatics who will be noticed in another chapter. Beyond these suburbs, to the South, as well as to the North and North-east, lie gardens and extensive plantations of palm-trees.

CHAPTER XIX.

THE principal places of pious visitation in the vicinity of Al-Madinah are the Mosques of Kuba, the Cemetery Al-Bakia, and the martyr Hamzah's tomb, at the foot of Mount Ohod. These the Zair is directed by all the Olema to visit, and on the holy ground to pray Allah for a blessing upon himself, and upon his brethren of the faith.

Early one Saturday morning, I started for Kuba with a motley crowd of devotees. Shaykh Hamid, my Muzaw-wir, was by my side, mounted upon an ass more miserable than I had yet seen. The boy Mohammed had procured for me a Meccan dromedary, with splendid trappings, a saddle with burnished metal peaks before and behind, covered with a huge sheepskin died crimson, and girthed over fine saddle-bags, whose enormous tassels hung almost to the ground. The youth himself, being too grand to ride a donkey, and unable to borrow a horse, preferred walking. He was proud as a peacock, being habited in a style somewhat resembling the plume of that gorgeous bird, in the coat of many colours—yellow, red, and golden flowers, apparently sewed on a field of bright green silk—which cost me so dear in the Harim. He was armed, as indeed all of us were, in readiness for the Badawin, and he anxiously awaited opportunities of dis-charging his pistol. Our course lay from Shaykh Hamid's house in the Manakhah, along and up the

Fiumara, "Al-Sayh," and through the Bab Kuba, a little
gate in the suburb wall, where, by-the-bye, my mounted
companion was nearly trampled down by a rush of half-
wild camels. Outside the town, in this direction, South-
ward, is a plain of clay, mixed with chalk, and here and
there with sand, whence protrude blocks and little ridges
of basalt. As far as Kuba, and the Harrah ridge to the
West, the earth is sweet and makes excellent gugglets.[1]
Immediately outside the gate I saw a kiln, where they
were burning tolerable bricks. Shortly after leaving the
suburb, an Indian, who joined our party upon the road,
pointed out on the left of the way what he declared was
the place of the celebrated Khandak, or Moat, the Torres
Vedras of Arabian History.[2]

Presently the Nakhil, or palm plantations, began.
Nothing lovelier to the eye, weary with hot red glare,
than the rich green waving crops and the cool shade, the
"food of vision," as the Arabs call it, and "pure water to
the parched throat." For hours I could have sat and
looked at it. The air was soft and balmy; a perfumed
breeze, strange luxury in Al-Hijaz, wandered amongst
the date fronds; there were fresh flowers and bright foliage;
in fact, at Midsummer, every beautiful feature of Spring.
Nothing more delightful to the ear than the warbling of
the small birds, that sweet familiar sound; the splashing
of tiny cascades from the wells into the wooden troughs,

---

1 The Baradiyah or gugglets of Al-Madinah are large and heavy,
of a reddish-grey colour, and celebrated for cooling water, a property
not possessed by those of Meccan fabric.

2 I afterwards found reason to doubt this location. Ibn Jubayr
(12th century), places it an arrow-shot from the Westward wall of Al-
Madinah, and seems to have seen it. M. C. de Perceval states, I
know not upon whose authority, that it was dug to protect the North-
west, the North, and the North-eastern sides of the town: this is
rendered highly improbable by the features of the ground. The
learned are generally agreed that all traces of the moat had disappeared before our 15th century.

and the musical song of the water-wheels. Travellers—
young travellers—in the East talk of the "dismal grating,"
the "mournful monotony," and the "melancholy creaking
of these dismal machines." To the veteran wanderer
their sound is delightful from association, reminding him
of fields and water-courses, and hospitable villages, and
plentiful crops. The expatriated Nubian, for instance,
listens to the water-wheel with as deep emotion as the
Ranz des Vaches ever excited in the hearts of Switzer
mercenary at Naples, or "Lochaber no more," among a
regiment of Highlanders in the West Indies.

The date-trees of Al-Madinah merit their celebrity.
Their stately columnar stems, here, seems higher than in
other lands, and their lower fronds are allowed to tremble
in the breeze without mutilation.[1] These enormous
palms were loaded with ripening fruits; and the clusters,
carefully tied up, must often have weighed upwards of
eighty pounds. They hung down between the lower
branches by a bright yellow stem, as thick as a man's
ankle. Books enumerate a hundred and thirty-nine varieties of trees; of these between sixty and seventy are well
known, and each is distinguished, as usual among Arabs,
by its peculiar name. The best kind is Al-Shelebi; it is
packed in skins, or in flat round boxes covered with paper,
somewhat in the manner of French prunes, and sent as
presents to the remotest parts of the Moslem world.[2]
The fruit is about two inches long, with a small stone,

---

1 In Egypt, the lower branches of the date are lopped off about
Christmas time to increase the flavour of the fruit; and the people
believe that without this "Taklim," as it is called, the tree would die.
In Upper Egypt, however, as at Al-Madinah, the fronds are left un-
touched.

2 The visitor from Al-Madinah would be badly received by the
women of his family, if he did not present them on his return with a
few boxes of dates, some strings of the same fruit, and skins full of
henna powder. Even the Olema allow such articles to be carried
away, although they strictly forbid keepsakes of earth or stone.

and has a peculiar aromatic flavour and smell; it is seldom eaten by the citizens on account of the price, which varies from two to ten piastres the pound. The tree, moreover, is rare, and is said to be not so productive as the other species. The Ajwah[1] date is eaten, but not sold, because a tradition of the Prophet declares, that whoso breaketh his fast every day with six or seven of these fruits, need fear neither poison nor magic. The third kind, Al-Hilwah, also a large date, derives a name from its exceeding sweetness : of this palm the Moslems relate that the Prophet planted a stone, which in a few minutes grew up and bore fruit. Next comes Al-Birni, of which was said, " It causeth sickness to depart, and there is no sickness in it." The Wahshi on one occasion bent its head, and "salamed" to Mohammed as he ate its fruit, for which reason even now its lofty tuft turns earthwards. The Sayhani (Crier) is so called, because when the founder of Al-Islam, holding Ali's hand, happened to pass beneath, it cried, " This is Mohammed the Prince of Prophets, and this is Ali the Prince of the Pious, and the Progenitor of the Immaculate Imams.[2] " Of course the descendants of so intelligent a vegetable hold high rank in the kingdom of palms, and the vulgar were in the habit of eating the Sayhani and of throwing the stones about the Harim. The Khuzayriyah is thus named because it preserves its green colour, even when ripe ; it is dried and preserved as a curiosity. The Jabali is the common fruit : the poorest kinds are the Laun and

1 This fruit must not be confounded with the enucleated conserve of dates, which in Arabia, as in Egypt, is known by the name of Ajwah. The Arabs infinitely despise the stuff sold at Alexandria and Cairo, declaring that it is fit only for cows. The Ajwah of the Oases, particularly of Siwah, is of excellent quality.

2 So in A.D. 1272 the Crucifix spoke to St. Thomas Aquinas. Superstitions are of no age or country.

the Hilayah, costing from four to seven piastres per mudd.[1]

I cannot say that the dates of Al-Madinah are finer than those of Meccah, although it is highly heretical to hold such tenet. The produce of the former city was the favourite food of the Prophet, who invariably broke his fast with it : a circumstance which invests it with a certain degree of relic-sanctity. The citizens delight in speaking of dates as an Irishman does of potatoes, with a manner of familiar fondness : they eat them for medicine as well as for food ; " Rutab," or wet dates, being held to be the most saving, as it is doubtless the most savoury, of remedies. The fruit is prepared in a great variety of ways : the favourite dish is a broil with clarified butter, extremely distasteful to the European palate. The date is also left upon the tree to dry, and then called " Balah " : this is eaten at dessert as the " Nukliyat "—the *quatre mendiants* of Persia. Amongst peculiar preparations must be mentioned the " Kulladat al-Sham[2] " (necklace of Sham). The unripe fruit is dipped in boiling water to preserve its gamboge colour, strung upon a thick thread and hung out in the air to dry. These strings are worn all over Al-Hijaz as necklaces by children, who seldom fail to munch the ornament when not in fear of slappings ; and they are sent as presents to distant countries.

---

1 At Al-Madinah—

12 Dirhams	(drams)	make 1	Wukkiyah (ounce).
20 Wukkiyah		,, 1	Ratl (pound).
33 Wukkiyah and 3	(drams)	,, 1	Wukkah (less than 2 lbs).
4 Wukkah		,, 1	Mudd.
24 Mudd		,, 1	Ardeb.

This Ratl, or pound, is the larger one applied to particular articles of commerce—such as meat, vegetables, and clarified butter ; coffee, rice, soap, &c., are sold by the smaller Ratl of Meccah, equal to 140 dirhams. In Egypt, the Ratl is 144 Dirhams or 12 Wukkiyahs,—about 1 lb. 2 oz. and 8 dwts. troy.

2 " Necklace of Syria." I was told they derive this name from the place where they are made. " Al-Safra " (on the Meccah road) being also called Al-Sham (Damascus).

January and February are the time for the mascula-
tion[1] of the palm. The "Nakhwali," as he is called, opens
the female flower, and having inserted the inverted male
blossom, binds them together : this operation is performed,
as in Egypt, upon each cluster.[2] The fruit is ripe about
the middle of May, and the gathering of it forms the
Arabs' "vendemmia." The people make merry the more
readily because their favourite diet is liable to a variety
of accidents : droughts injure the tree, locusts destroy the
produce, and the date crop, like most productions which
men are imprudent enough to adopt singly as the staff of
life, is often subject to complete failure.

One of the reasons for the excellence of Madinah
dates is the quantity of water they obtain : each garden
or field has its well ; and even in the hottest weather the
Persian wheel floods the soil every third day. It has
been observed that the date-tree can live in dry and
barren spots ; but it loves the beds of streams and places
where moisture is procurable. The palms scattered over
the other parts of the plain, and depending solely upon
rain water, produce less fruit, and that too of an inferior
quality.

Verdure is not usually wholesome in Arabia, yet
invalids leave the close atmosphere of Al-Madinah to seek
health under the cool shades of Kuba. The gardens are
divided by what might almost be called lanes, long narrow
lines with tall reed fences on both sides. The graceful
branches of the Tamarisk, pearled with manna, and cot-
toned over with dew, and the broad leaves of the castor
plant, glistening in the sun, protected us from the morning

---

1 This is a translation of the Arab word " Tazkir," which is certainly more appropriate than our " caprification " applied to dates.

2 The male tree is known by its sterility. In some countries
only the fecundating pollen is scattered over the female flower, and
this doubtless must have been Nature's method of impregnating the
date.

rays. The ground on both sides of the way was sunken, the earth being disposed in heaps at the foot of the fences, an arrangement which facilitates irrigation, by giving a fall to the water, and in some cases affords a richer soil than the surface. This part of the Madinah plain, however, being higher than the rest, is less subject to the disease of salt and nitre. On the way here and there the earth crumbles and looks dark under the dew of morning ; but nowhere has it broken out into that glittering efflorescence which denotes the last stage of the attack. The fields and gardens are divided into small oblongs, separated from one another by little ridges of mould which form diminutive water-courses. Of the cereals there are luxuriant maize, wheat, and barley, but the latter two are n small quantities. Here and there patches of "Barsim," or Egyptian clover, glitter brightly in the sunbeams. The principal vegetables are Badanjan (Egg-plant), the Bamiyah (a kind of esculent *hibiscus,* called Bhendi in India), and Mulukhiyah *(Corchoris olitorius),* a mucilaginous spinage common throughout this part of the East. These three are eaten by citizens of every rank ; they are, in fact, the potatoes and the greens of Arabia. I remarked also onions and leeks in fair quantities, a few beds of carrots and beans ; some Fijl (radishes), Lift (turnips), gourds, cucumbers, and similar plants. Fruit trees abound. There are five descriptions of vines, the best of which is Al-Sharifi, a long white grape of a flavour somewhat resembling the produce of Tuscany.[1] Next to it, and very similar, is Al-Birni. The Hijazi is a round fruit, sweet, but insipid, which is also the reproach of the Sawadi, or black grape. And lastly, the Raziki is a small white fruit, with a diminutive stone. The Nebek, Lote,

1 The resemblance is probably produced by the similarity of treatment. At Al-Madinah, as in Italy, the vine is "married" to some tall tree, which, selfish as a husband, appropriates to itself the best of everything,—sun, breeze, and rain.

or Jujube, is here a fine large tree with a dark green leaf, roundish and polished like the olive ; it is armed with a short, curved, and sharp thorn,[1] and bears a pale straw-coloured berry, about the size of the gooseberry, with red streaks on the side next the sun. Little can be said in favour of the fruit, which has been compared successively by disappointed " Lotus eaters[2]" to a bad plum, an unripe cherry, and an insipid apple. It is, however, a favourite with the people of Al-Madinah, who have reckoned many varieties of the fruit : Hindi (Indian), Baladi ("native"), Tamri (date-like), and others. There are a few peaches, hard like the Egyptian, and almost tasteless, fit only for stewing, but greedily eaten in a half-ripe state ; large coarse bananas, lime trees, a few water-melons, figs, and apples, but neither apricots nor pears.[3] There are three kinds of pomegranates : the best is the Shami (Syrian) : it is red outside, very sweet, and costs one piastre : the Turki is large, and of a white colour : and the Misri has a greenish rind, and a somewhat sub-acid and harsh flavour ; the latter are sold at one-fourth the price of the best. I never saw in the East, except at Meccah, finer fruits than the Shami : almost stoneless like those of Maskat, they are delicately perfumed, and as large as an infant's head. Al-Madinah is celebrated, like Taif, for its " Rubb Rumman," a thick pomegranate syrup, drunk

---

1 This thorn (the Rhamnus Nabeca, or Zizyphus Spina Christi) is supposed to be that which crowned the Saviour's head. There are Mimosas in Syria ; but no tree, save the fabled Zakhum, could produce the terrible apparatus with which certain French painters of the modern school have attempted to heighten the terrors of the scene.

2 For what reason I am entirely unable to guess, our dictionaries translate the word Sidr (the literary name of the tree that bears the Nebek) " Lote-tree." No wonder that believers in " Homeric writ " feel their anger aroused by so poor a realisation of the beautiful myth.

3 The only pears in Al-Hijaz, I believe, are to be found at Taif, to which place they were transplanted from Egypt.

with water during the hot weather, and esteemed cooling
and wholesome.

After threading our way through the gardens, an
operation requiring less time than to describe them, we
saw, peeping through the groves, Kuba's simple minaret.
Then we came in sight of a confused heap of huts and
dwelling-houses, chapels and towers with trees between,
and foul lanes, heaps of rubbish, and barking dogs,—the
usual material of a Hijazi village. Having dismounted, we
gave our animals in charge of a dozen infant Badawin,
the produce of the peasant gardeners, who shouted
" Bakhshish" the moment they saw us. To this they
were urged by their mothers, and I willingly parted with
a few paras for the purpose of establishing an intercourse
with fellow-creatures so fearfully and wonderfully resembling the tailless baboon. Their bodies, unlike those
of Egyptian children, were slim[1] and straight, but their
ribs stood out with curious distinctness; the colour of the
skin was that oily lamp-black seen upon the face of a
European sweep; and the elf-locks, thatching the cocoa-
nut heads, had been stained by the sun, wind, and rain to
that reddish-brown hue which Hindu romances have
appropriated to their Rakshasas or demons. Each anatomy
carried in his arms a stark-naked miniature of himself,
fierce-looking babies with faces all eyes, and the strong
little wretches were still able to extend the right hand
and exert their lungs with direful clamour. Their mothers
were fit progenitors for such progeny: long, gaunt, with
emaciated limbs, wall-sided, high-shouldered, and straight-
backed, with pendulous bosoms, spider-like arms, and
splay feet. Their long elf-locks, wrinkled faces, and high
cheek-bones, their lips darker than the epidermis, hollow
staring eyes, sparkling as if to light up the extreme

---

1 Travellers always remark the curious pot-bellied children on
the banks of the Nile. This conformation is admired by the Egyptians,
who consider it a sign of strength and a promise of fine growth.

ugliness around, and voices screaming as though in a
perennial rage, invested them with all the "charms of
Sycorax." These "Houris of Jahannam" were habited
in long night-gowns dyed blue to conceal want of washing,
and the squalid children had about a yard of the same
material wrapped round their waists for all toilette. This
is not an overdrawn portrait of the farmer race of Arabs,
the most despised by their fellow-countrymen, and the
most hard-favoured, morally as well as physically, of all the
breed.

Before entering the Mosque of Al-Kuba[1] it will be
necessary to call to mind some passages of its past history. When the Apostle's she-camel, Al-Kaswa, as he
was approaching Al-Madinah after the flight from Meccah,
knelt down here, he desired his companions to mount the
animal. Abu Bakr and Omar[2] did so ; still she sat upon
the ground; but when Ali obeyed the order, she arose.
The Apostle bade him loose her halter, for she was
directed by Allah, and the Mosque walls were built upon
the line over which she trod. It was the first place of
public prayer in Al-Islam. Mohammed laid the first
brick, and with an "Anzah," or iron-shod javelin, marked
out the direction of prayer[3]: each of his successors followed his example. According to most historians, the

1 I believe Kuba to be about three miles S. S. E. of Al-Madinah ;
but Al-Idrisi, Ibn Haukal, and Ibn Jubayr all agree in saying two
miles.

2 Osman, the fourth Companion, was absent at this time, not
having returned from the first or Little Flight to Abyssinia.

3 Some believe that in this Mosque the direction of prayer was
altered from Jerusalem to Meccah, and they declare, as will presently
be seen, that the Archangel Gabriel himself pointed out the new line.
M. C. de Perceval forgets his usual accuracy when he asserts " le
Mihrab de la Mosquée de Médine, qui fut d'abord placé au Nord, fut
transféré au Midi: et la Mosquée prit le nom de ' Masjid-el-Kiblatayn,'
Mosquée des deux Kiblah." In the first place, the Mihrab is the invention of a later date, about ninety years ; and, secondly, the title of
Al-Kiblatyn is never now given to the Mosque of Al-Madinah.

land belonged to Abu Ayyub the Ansari, the Apostle's host; for which reason the "Bayt Ayyub," his descendants, still perform the service of the Mosque, keep the key, and share with the Bawwabs, or porters, the alms and fees here offered by the Faithful. Others declared that the ground was the property of one Linah, a woman who was in the habit of tethering her ass there.[1] The Apostle used to visit it every Saturday[2] on foot, and always made a point of praying the dawn-prayer there on the 17th Ramazan.[3] A number of traditions testify to its dignity: of these, two are especially significant. The first assures all Moslems that a prayer at Kuba is equal to a Lesser Pilgrimage at Meccah in religious efficacy; and the second declares that such devotion is more acceptable to the Deity than prostrations at the Bayt al-Mukuddas (Jerusalem). Moreover, sundry miracles took place here, and a verset of the Koran descended from heaven. For which reasons the Mosque was much respected by Omar, who, once finding it empty, swept it himself with a broom of thorns, and expressed his wonder at the lukewarmness of Moslem piety. It was originally a square building of very small size; Osman enlarged it in the direction of the minaret, making it sixty-six cubits each way. It is no longer "mean and decayed" as in Burckhardt's time: the Sultan Abd al-Hamid, father of

---

1 This degrading report caused certain hypocrites to build a kind of rival chapel called the Mosque Zarar. It was burnt to the ground shortly after its erection, and all known of it is, that it stood near Kuba.

2 Some say on Monday, probably because on that day Mohammed alighted at Kuba. But the present practice of Al-Islam, handed down from generation to generation, is to visit it on the Saturday.

3 There is on this day at Kuba a regular Ziyarat or visitation. The people pray in the Harim of Al-Madinah, after which they repair to the Kuba Mosque, and go through the ceremonies which in religious efficacy equal an Umrah or Lesser pilgrimage. In books I have read that the 15th of Ramazan is the proper day.

the Sultan Mahmud, erected a minaret of Turkish shape and a neat structure of cut stone, whose crenelles make it look more like a place of defence than of prayer. It has, however, no pretentions to grandeur. To the South a small and narrow Riwak (porch), with unpretending columns, looks out Northwards upon a little open area simply sanded over; and this is the whole building.

The large Mastabah or stone bench at the entrance of the Mosque was crowded with sitting people : we therefore lost no time, after ablution and the Niyat ("the Intention") peculiar to this Visitation, in ascending the steps, in pulling off our slippers, and in entering the sacred building. We stood upon the Musalla al-Nabi (the Prophet's place of Prayer)[1] : after Shaykh Nur and Hamid had forcibly cleared that auspicious spot of a devout Indian, and had spread a rug upon the dirty matting, we performed a two-bow prayer, in front of a pillar into which a diminutive marble Mihrab or niche had been inserted by way of memento. Then came the Dua, or supplication, which was as follows :

" O Allah ! bless and preserve, and increase, and perpetuate, and benefit, and be propitous to, our Lord Mohammed, and to his Family, and to his Companions, and be Thou their Preserver ! O Allah! this is the Mosque Kuba, and the Place of the Prophet's Prayers. O Allah ! pardon our Sins, and veil our Faults, and place not over us one who feareth not Thee, and who pitieth not us, and pardon us, and the true Believers, Men and Women, the Quick of them and the Dead : for verily Thou, O Lord, art the Hearer, the near to us, the Answerer of our Supplications." After which we recited the Testification and the Fatihah, and we drew our palms as usual down our faces.

We then moved away to the South-Eastern corner of the edifice, and stood before a Mihrab in the Southern wall.

---

[1] This is believed to be the spot where the Prophet performed his first Rukat, or prayer-bow.

It is called " Takat al-Kashf " or " Niche of Disclosure,"
by those who believe that as the Prophet was standing
undecided about the direction of Meccah, the Archangel
Gabriel removed all obstructions to his vision.   There
again we went through the two-bow prayer, the Supplication, the Testification, and the Fatihah, under difficulties,
for people mobbed us excessively.   During our devotions,
I vainly attempted to decipher a Cufic inscription fixed in
the wall above and on the right of the Mihrab,—my regret
however, at this failure was transitory, the character not
being of an ancient date.   Then we left the Riwak, and
despite the morning sun which shone fiercely with a sickly
heat, we went to the open area where stands the " Mabrak
al-Nakah," or the " Place of kneeling of the she-Dromedary.[1]"   This, the exact spot where Al-Kaswa sat down,
is covered with a diminutive dome of cut stone, supported
by four stone pillars : the building is about eight feet high
and a little less in length and in breadth.   It has the
appearance of being modern.   On the floor, which was
raised by steps above the level of the ground, lay, as usual,
a bit of dirty matting, upon which we again went through
the ceremonies above detailed.

Then issuing from the canopy into the sun, a little outside the Riwak and close to the Mabrak, we prayed upon
the " Makan al-Ayat,[2]" or the " Place of Signs."   Here
was revealed to Mohammed a passage in the Koran
especially alluding to the purity of the place and of the
people of Kuba, " a Temple founded in Purity from its
first Day ; " and again : " there live Men who love to be

---

1 " Mabrak " is the locative noun from the triliteral root
" Baraka—he blessed, or he (the camel) knelt upon the ground."
Perhaps this philological connection may have determined Mohammed to consider the kneeling of the dromedary a sign that Allah had
blessed the spot.

2 " Ayat " here means a verset of the Koran.   Some authors
apply the above quoted lines to the Prophet's Mosque at Al-Madinah
exclusively, others to both buildings.

cleansed, and verily Allah delights in the Clean." The Prophet exclaimed in admiration, "O ye Sons of Amr! what have ye done to deserve all this Praise and Beneficence?" when the people offered him an explanation of their personal cleanliness which I do not care to repeat. The temple of Kuba from that day took a fresh title— Masjid al-Takwa, or the " Mosque of Piety."

Having finished our prayers and ceremonies at the Mosque of Piety, we fought our way out through a crowd of importunate beggars, and turning a few paces to the left, halted near a small chapel adjoining the South-West angle of the larger temple. We there stood at a grated window in the Western wall, and recited a Supplication, looking the while reverently at a dark dwarf archway under which the Lady Fatimah used to sit grinding grain in a hand-mill. The Mosque in consequence bears the name of Sittna Fatimah. A surly-looking Khadim, or guardian stood at the door demanding a dollar in the most authoritative Arab tone—we therefore did not enter.

At Al-Madinah and at Meccah the traveller's hand must be perpetually in his pouch: no stranger in Paris or in London is more surely or more severely taken in. Already I began to fear that my eighty pounds would not suffice for all the expenses of sight-seeing, and the apprehension was justified by the sequel. My only friend was the boy Mohammed, who displayed a fiery economy that brought him into considerable disrepute with his countrymen. They saw with emotion that he was preaching parsimony to me solely that I might have more money to spend at Meccah under his auspices. This being palpably the case, I threw all the blame of penuriousness upon the young Machiavel's shoulders, and resolved, as he had taken charge of my finances at Al-Madinah, so at Meccah to administer them myself.

After praying at the window, to the great disgust of the Khadim, who openly asserted that we were " low fellows," we passed through some lanes lined with beggars and Badawi children, till we came to a third little Mosque situated due South of the larger one. This is called the Masjid Arafat, and is erected upon a mound also named Tall Arafat, because on one occasion the Prophet, being unable to visit the Holy Mountain at the pilgrimage season, stood there, saw through the intervening space, and in spirit performed the ceremony. Here also we looked into a window instead of opening the door with a silver key, and the mesquin appearance of all within prevented my regretting the necessity of economy. In India or in Sind every village would have a better Mosque. Our last visit was to a fourth chapel, the Masjid Ali, so termed because the Apostle's son-in-law had a house upon this spot.[1] After praying there—and terribly hot the little hole was !—we repaired to the last place of visitation at Kuba—a large deep well called the Bir al-Aris, in a garden to the West of the Mosque of Piety, with a little oratory adjoining it. A Persian wheel was going drowsily round, and the cool water fell into a tiny pool, whence it whirled and bubbled away in childish mimicry of a river. The music sounded sweet in my ears ; I stubbornly refused to do any more praying—though Shaykh Hamid, for form's sake, reiterated with parental emphasis, " how very wrong it was,"—and I sat down, as the Prophet himself did not disdain to do, with the resolution of enjoying on the brink of the well a few moments of unwonted " Kayf." The heat was over-powering, though it was only nine o'clock, the sound of the stream was soothing, that water-wheel was creaking a lullaby, and the limes and pomegranates, gently rustling, shed voluptuous fragrance through the morning air. I fell asleep, and—wondrous the contrast !—dreamed that I was once more standing

" By the wall whereon hangeth the crucified vine,"

---

1 Ibn Jubayr informs us that Abu Bakr, Ayishah, and Omar had habitations at Kuba.

looking upon the valley of the Lianne, with its glaucous seas and grey skies, and banks here and there white with snow.

The Bir al-Aris,[1] so called after a Jew of Al-Madinah, is one which the Apostle delighted to visit. He would sit upon its brink with his bare legs hanging over the side, and his companions used to imitate his example. This practice caused a sad disaster. In the sixth year of his caliphate, Osman, according to Abulfeda and Yakut, dropped from his finger the prophetie ring which, engraved in three lines with " Mohammed—Apostle—(of) Allah," had served to seal the letters sent to neighbouring kings, and had descended to the first three successors.[2] The precious article was not recovered after three days' search, and the well was thenceforward called Bir al-Khatim—of the Seal Ring. It is also called the Bir al-Taflat—of Saliva[3]—because the Prophet honoured it by expectoration, as, by-the-bye, he seems to have done to almost all the wells in Al-Madinah. The effect of the operation upon the Bir al-Aris, says the historians, was to sweeten the water, which before was salt. Their testimony, however, did not prevent my detecting a pronounced medicinal taste in the lukewarm draught drawn for me by Shaykh Hamid. In Mohammed's days the total number of wells is recorded to

---

1 Some authors mention a second Bir al-Aris, belonging in part to the Caliph Osman. According to Yakut, "Aris" is the Hebrew or Syriac word for a peasant; he quotes the plural form Arísún and Arárisah.

2 Others assert, with less probability, that the article in question was lost by one Ma'akah, a favourite of Osman. As that ill-fated Caliph's troubles began at the time of this accident, the ring is generally compared to Solomon's. Our popular authors, who assert that Mohammed himself lost the ring, are greatly in error.

3 According to some authors, Mohammed drew a bucket of water, drank part of the contents, spat into the rest, and poured it back into the well, which instantly became sweet. Ibn Jubayr applies the epithet Bir Al-Taflat peculiarly to the Aris well: many other authors are not so exact.

have been twenty : most of them have long since disappeared ; but there still remain seven, whose waters were drunk by the Prophet, and which, in consequence, the Zair is directed to visit.[1]   They are known by the classical title of Saba Abar, or the seven wells, and their names are included in this couplet :

> " Aris and Ghars, and Rumah and Buza'at
> And Busat, with Bayruha and Ihn."[2]

---

[1] The pious perform the Lesser Ablution upon the brink of the seven wells, and drink of the remnant of the water in " Tabarruk " or to secure the blessings of God.

[2] Some alter the 3rd, the 5th, and the 7th names to Bir al-Nabi, a well in the Kuba gardens, Bir al-Ghurbal, and Bir al-Fukayyir, where the Prophet, together with Salman the Persian and others of his companions, planted date trees.   The Bir al-Aris has already been described.   The Bir al-Ghars, Gharas or Ghurs, so called, it is said, from the place where it was sunk, about half a mile N.E. of the Kuba Mosque, is a large well with an abundance of water.   Mohammed used to perform ablution on its brink, and directed Ali to wash his corpse with seven skins full of the water.   The Bir Rumah is a large well with a spring at the bottom, dug in the Wady al-Akik, to the north of the Mosque Al-Kiblatayn.   It is called " Kalib Mazni " (the old well of Mazni), in this tradition ; " the best of old wells is the old well of Mazni."   And ancient it must be if the legend say true, that when Abu Karb besieged Al-Madinah (A.D. 495), he was relieved of sickness by drinking its produce.   Some assert that it afforded the only sweet water in Al-Madinah when the Prophet arrived there. The town becoming crowded by an influx of visitors, this water was sold by its owner, a man of the Benu Ghaffar tribe, or according to others, by one Mazni, a Jew.   Osman at last bought it by paying upwards of 100 camels.   The Bir Buza'at, or Biza'at, or Bisa'at, is in the Nakhil or palm plantations, outside the Bab al-Shami or Northwestern gate of Al-Madinah on the right of the road leading to Ohod.   Whoever washes in its waters three times shall be healed.   The Bir Busat is near the Bakia cemetery, on the left of the road leading to Kuba.   The Prophet used to bathe in the water, and he declared it healthy to the skin.   The Bir Bayruha, under whose trees the Prophet was fond of sitting, lies outside the Bab Dar al-Ziyafah, leading to Mount Ohod.   The Kamus gives the word " Bayruha upon the measure of Fayluha."   Some authorities upon the subject of Ziyarat, write Bayruha, " Bir Ha,"—the well of Ha, and variously suppose

After my sleep, which was allowed to last until a pipe or two of Latakia had gone round the party, we remounted our animals. Returning towards Al-Madinah, my companions pointed out to me, on the left of the village, a garden called Al-Madshuniyah. It contains a quarry of the yellow loam or bole-earth, called by the Arabs, Tafl, by the Persians, Gil-i-Sarshui, and by the Sindians, Metu. It is used as soap in many parts of the East, and, mixed with oil, it is supposed to cool the body, and to render the skin fresh and supple. It is related that the Prophet cured a Badawi of the Benu Haris tribe, of fever, by washing him with a pot of Tafl dissolved in water, and hence the earth of Al-Madinah derived its healing fame. As far as I could learn from the Madani, this clay is no longer valued by them, either medicinally or cosmetically: the only use they could mention was its being eaten by the fair sex, when in the peculiar state described by "chlorosis."

" Ha " to be the name of a man, a woman, or a place. Yahut mentions other pronunciations : "Barihá," "Baríhá," "Bayrihá," &c. The Bir Ihn is in a large garden E. of Kuba. Little is said in books about this well, and the people of Al-Madinah do not know the name.

CHAPTER XX.

THE VISITATION OF HAMZAH'S TOMB.

On the morning of Sunday, the twenty-third Zu'l Ka'adah (28th August, 1853), arrived from Al-Sham, or Damascus,[1] the great Caravan popularly called Hajj al-Shami, the "Damascus pilgrimage," as the Egyptian Cafila is Al-Misri,[2] or the Cairo pilgrimage. It is the main stream which carries off all the small currents that, at this season of general movement, flow from Central Asia towards the great centre of the Islamitic world, and in 1853 it amounted to about seven thousand souls. The arrival was anxiously expected by the people for several reasons. In the first place, it brought with it a new curtain for the Prophet's Hujrah, the old one being in a tattered condition; secondly, it had charge of the annual stipends and pensions of the citizens; and thirdly, many families expected members returning under its escort to their homes. The popular anxiety was greatly increased by the disordered state of the country round about; and, moreover, the great caravan had been one day late, generally arriving on the morning of the twenty-second Zu'l Ka'adah.[3]

---

1 This city derives its names, the "Great Gate of Pilgrimage," and the "Key of the Prophet's Tomb" from its being the gathering-place of this caravan.

2 The Egyptians corruptly pronounce "Al-Misr," *i.e.* Cairo, as "Al-Masr."

3 NOTE TO FOURTH EDITION.—I reprint the following from the *Illustrated News* in proof that the literati of England have still something

During the night three of Shaykh Hamid's brothers, who had entered as Muzawwirs with the Hajj, came suddenly to the house : they leaped off their camels, and lost not a moment in going through the usual scene of kissing, embracing, and weeping bitterly for joy. I arose in the morning, and looked out from the windows of the Majlis. The Barr al-Manakhah, from a dusty waste dotted with a few Badawi hair-tents, had assumed all the various shapes and the colours of a kaleidoscope. The eye was bewildered by the shifting of innumerable details, in all parts totally different from one another, thrown confusedly together in one small field ; and, however jaded with sight-seeing, it dwelt with delight upon the variety, the vivacity, and the intense picturesqueness of the scene. In one night had sprung up a town of tents of every size, colour, and shape ; round, square, and oblong ; open and closed,—from the shawl-lined and gilt-topped pavilion of the Pasha, with all the luxurious appurtenances of the Harim, to its neighbour the little dirty green "rowtie" of the tobacco-seller. They were pitched in admirable order : here ranged in a long line,

---

to learn :—" On the 1st instant the annual ceremony of the departure of the Suré-emini with the Imperial gifts for the *Prophet's tomb at Mecca* took place in front of the palace at Constantinople. The *Levant Herald* states that the presents, which consist, beside the large money donation, of rich shawls and gold-woven stuffs, were brought out of the Imperial apartments and packed in presence of the Sultan, on two beautiful camels, which, after the delivery of the usual prayers, were then led in grand procession, accompanied by all the high officers of state, to the landing-place at Cabatash, where the Sure-emini and camels were embarked on a Government steamer and ferried over to Scutari. There the holy functionary will remain some days, till the ' faithful' of the capital and those who have come from the interior have joined him, when the caravan will start for Damascus. At this latter city the grand rendezvous takes place, and, that accomplished, the great caravan sets out for Mecca under the Emir-el-Hadj of the year. The Imperial presents on this occasion cost more than £20,000."

where a street was required ; there packed in dense masses, where thoroughfares were unnecessary. But how describe the utter confusion in the crowding, the bustling, and the vast variety and volume of sound ? Huge white Syrian dromedaries, compared with which those of Al-Hijaz appeared mere pony-camels, jingling large bells, and bearing Shugdufs[1] (litters) like miniature green tents, swaying and tossing upon their backs ; gorgeous Takht-rawán, or litters carried between camels or mules with scarlet and brass trappings ; Badawin bestriding naked-backed "Daluls[2]" (dromedaries), and clinging like apes to the hairy humps ; Arnaut, Kurd, and Turkish Irregular Cavalry, fiercer looking in their mirth than Roman peasants in their rage ; fainting Persian pilgrims, forcing their stubborn camels to kneel, or dismounted grumbling from jaded donkeys ; Kahwajis, sherbet sellers, and ambulant tobacconists crying their goods ; country-people driving flocks of sheep and goats with infinite clamour through lines of horses fiercely snorting and biting and kicking and rearing ; towns-people seeking their friends ; returned travellers exchanging affectionate salutes ; devout Hajis jostling one another, running under the legs of camels, and tumbling over the tents' ropes in their hurry to reach the Harim ; cannon roaring from the citadel ; shopmen, water-carriers, and fruit vendors fighting over their bargains ; boys with loud screams bullying heretics ; a well-mounted

---

1 The Syrian Shugduf differs entirely from that of Al-Hijaz. It is composed of two solid wooden cots about four feet in length, slung along the camel's sides and covered over with cloth, in the shape of a tent. They are nearly twice as heavy as the Hijazi litter, and yet a Syrian camel-man would as surely refuse to put one of the latter upon his beast's back, as the Hijazi to carry a Syrian litter. See p. 223, ante.

2 This is the Arabic modern word, synonymous with the Egyptian Hajin, namely, a she-dromedary. The word "Nakah," at present popular in Al-Hijaz, means a she-dromedary kept for breeding as well as for riding.

R. Burton delt.

C. E. Keil, Lith.

THE TAKHT-RAWÁN, OR GRANDEE'S LITTER.

party of fine old Arab Shaykhs of the Hamidah clan,
preceded by their varlets, performing the Arzah or war
dance,—compared with which the Pyrenean bear's performance is grace itself,—firing their duck-guns upwards,
or blowing the powder into the calves of those before
them, brandishing their swords, leaping frantically the
while, with their bright coloured rags floating in the wind,
tossing their long spears tufted with ostrich feathers high
in the air, reckless where they fall ; servants seeking
their masters, and masters their tents, with vain cries of
Ya Mohammed[1] ; grandees riding mules or stalking on
foot, preceded by their crowd-beaters, shouting to clear
the way ; here the loud shrieks of women and children,
whose litters are bumping and rasping against one
another ; there the low moaning of some poor wretch
that is seeking a shady corner to die in : add a thick
dust which blurs the outlines like a London fog, with a
flaming sun that draws sparkles of fire from the burnished
weapons of the crowd, and the brass balls of tent and
litter ; and—I doubt, gentle reader, that even the length,
the jar, and the confusion of this description is adequate
to its subject, or that any " word-painting " of mine can
convey a just idea of the scene.

This was the day appointed for our visiting the
martyrs of Ohod. After praying the dawn prayers as
directed at the Harim, we mounted our donkeys; and,
armed with pistols and knives, we set out from the city.
Our party was large. Sa'ad the Demon had offered to
accompany us, and the bustle around kept him in the best
of humours ; Omar Effendi was also there, quiet-looking
and humble as usual, leading his ass to avoid the trouble
of dismounting every second minute.[2] I had the boy

---

1 One might as sensibly cry out " John " in an English theatre.

2 Respectable men in Al-Hijaz, when they meet friends, acquaintances, or superiors, consider it only polite to dismount from a
donkey.

Mohammed and my "slave," and Shaykh Hamid was attended by half a dozen relations. To avoid the crush of the Barr al-Manakhah, we made a *détour* Westwards, over the bridge and down the course of the torrent-bed "Al-Sayh." We then passed along the Southern wall of the castle, traversed its Eastern outwork, and issued from the Bab al-Shami. During the greater part of the time we were struggling through a living tide; and among dromedaries and chargers a donkey is by no means a pleasant *monture*. With some difficulty, but without any more serious accident than a fall or two, we found ourselves in the space beyond and northward of the city. This also was covered with travellers and tents, amongst which on an eminence to the left of the road, rose conspicuous the bright green pavilion of the Emir Al-Hajj, the commandant of the Caravan.[1] Hard by, half its height surrounded by a Kanat or tent wall, stood the Syrian or Sultan's Mahmil (litter), all glittering with green and gilding and gold, and around it were pitched the handsome habitations of the principal officers and grandees of the pilgrimage. On the right hand lay extensive palm plantations, and on the left, strewed over the plain, were signs of wells and tanks, built to supply the Hajj with water. We pass two small buildings, one the Kubbat Al-Sabak, or Dome of Precedence, where the Prophet's warrior friends used to display their horseman-

---

1 The title of the Pasha who has the privilege of conducting the Caravan. It is a lucrative as well as an honourable employment, for the Emir enjoys the *droit d'aubaine*, becoming heir to the personal property of all pilgrims who die in the Holy Cities or on the line of march. And no Persian, even of the poorest, would think of undertaking a pilgrimage by this line of country, without having at least £80 in ready money with him. The first person who bore the title of Emir Al-Hajj was Abu Bakr, who, in the ninth year of the Hijrah, led 300 Moslems from Al-Madinah to the Meccah pilgrimage. On this occasion idolaters and infidels were for the first time expelled the Holy City.

ship; the second the Makan, or burial-place of Sayyidna Zaki al-Din, one of Mohammed's multitudinous descendants. Then we fall into a plain, resembling that of Kuba, but less fertile. While we are jogging over it, a few words concerning Mount Ohod may not be misplaced. A popular distich says,

> " Verily there is healing to the eye that looks
> Unto Ohod and the two Harrahs[1] (ridges) near."

And of this holy hill the Apostle declared, " Ohod is a Mountain which loves Us and which We love : it is upon the Gate of Heaven[2];" adding,

---

1 " Harrah" from Harr (heat) is the generic name of lava, porous basalt, scoriæ, greenstone, schiste, and others supposed to be of igneous origin. It is also used to denote a ridge or hill of such formation. One Harrah has already been mentioned in Chapter XV. The second is on the road to Ohod. There is a third Harrah, called Al-Wakin or Al-Zahrah, about one mile Eastward of Al-Madinah. Here the Prophet wept, predicting that the last men of his faith would be foully slain. The prophecy was fulfilled in the days of Yazid, when the people of Al-Madinah filled their assembly with slippers and turbands to show that on account of his abominations they had cast off their allegiance as a garment. The "Accursed" sent an aged sinner, Muslim bin Akbah al-Marai, who, though a cripple, defeated the Madani in a battle called the " Affair of the Ridge," slaying of them 10,000 citizens, 1700 learned and great men, 700 teachers of the Koran, and 97 Karashi nobles. This happened in the month of Zu'l Hijjah, A.H. 63. For three days the city was plundered, the streets ran blood, dogs ate human flesh in the Mosque, and no fewer than 1000 women were insulted. It was long before Al-Madinah recovered from this fatal blow, which old Muslim declared would open to him the gates of Paradise. The occurrence is now forgotten at Al-Madinah, though it will live in history. The people know not the place, and even the books are doubtful whether this Harrah be not upon the spot where the Khandak or moat was.

2 Meaning that on the Day of Resurrection it shall be so treated. Many, however, suppose Ohod to be one of the four hills of Paradise. The other three, according to Al-Tabrani from Amr bin Auf, are Sinai, Lebanon, and Mount Warkan on the Meccan road. Others suppose Ohod to be one of the six mountains which afforded materials for the Kaabah, viz., Abu Kubays, Sinai, Kuds (at Jerusalem), Warkan and

"And Ayr[1] is a Place which hates Us and which We
hate: it is upon the Gate of Hell." The former
sheltered Mohammed in the time of danger; therefore, on Resurrection Day it will be raised to Paradise: whereas Jabal Ayr, its neighbour, having been
so ill-judged as to refuse the Prophet water on an
occasion while he thirsted, will be cast incontinently into
Jahannam. Moslem divines, be it observed, ascribe to
Mohammed miraculous authority over animals, vegetables,
and minerals, as well as over men, angels, and jinnis.
Hence the speaking wolf, the weeping post, the oil-stone,
and the love and hate of these two mountains. It is
probably one of the many remains of ancient paganism
pulled down and afterwards used to build up the edifice
of Al-Islam. According to the old Persians, the sphere
has an active soul. Some sects of Hindus believe "mother
earth," upon whose bosom we little parasites crawl, to be
a living being. This was a dogma also amongst the
ancient Egyptians, who denoted it by a peculiar symbol,
—the globe with human legs. Hence the " Makrokos-
mos " of the plagiaristic Greeks, the animal on a large
scale, whose diminutive was the " Mikrokosmos "—man.
Tota natura, repeats Malpighi, *existit in minimis*. Amongst
the Romans, Tellus or Terra was a female deity,
anthropomorphised according to their syncretic system,
which furnished with strange gods their Pantheon, but
forgot to append the scroll explaining the inner sense of

Radhwah near Yambu'. Also it is said that when the Lord con-
versed with Moses on Sinai, the mountain burst into six pieces,
three of which flew to Al-Madinah, Ohod, Warkan and Radhwah,
and three to Meccah, Hira (now popularly called Jabal Nur), Sabir,
(the old name for Jabal Muna), and Saur.

1 " Ayr " means a " wild ass," whereas Ohod is derived from
Ahad, " one,"—so called because fated to be the place of victory to
those who worship *one* God. The very names, say Moslem divines,
make it abundantly evident that even as the men of Al-Madinah were
of two parties, friendly and hostile to the Prophet, so were these
mountains.

the symbol. And some modern philosophers, Kepler, Blackmore, and others, have not scrupled to own their belief in a doctrine which as long as "Life" is a mere word on man's tongue, can neither be proved nor disproved. The Mohammedans, as usual, exaggerate the dogma,— a Hadis related by Abu Hurayrah casts on the day of judgment the sun and the moon into hell fire.

Jabal Ohod owes its present reputation to a cave which sheltered the Apostle when pursued by his enemies[1]; to certain springs of which he drank,[2] and especially to its being the scene of a battle celebrated in Al-Islam. On Saturday, the 11th Shawwal, in the third year of the Hijrah (26th January, A.D. 625), Mohammed with seven hundred men engaged three thousand Infidels under the command of Abu Sufiyan; ran great personal danger, and lost his uncle Hamzah, the "Lord of Martyrs." On the topmost pinnacle, also, is the Kubbat Harun, the dome erected over Aaron's remains. It is now, I was told, in a ruinous condition, and is placed upon the "pinnacle of seven hills[3]" in a position somewhat like that of certain buildings on St. Angelo in the Bay of Naples. Alluding to the toil of reaching it, the Madani quote a facetious rhyme inscribed upon the wall by one of their number who had wasted his breath:—

> "Malun ibn Malun
> Man tala'a Kubbat Harun!"

Anglicè, "The man must be a ruffian who climbs up to Aaron's dome." Devout Moslems visit Ohod every Thursday morning after the dawn devotions in the

---

1 This Cave is a Place of Visitation, but I did not go there, as it is on the Northern flank of the hill, and all assured me that it contained nothing worth seeing. Many ignore it altogether.

2 Ohod, it is said, sent forth in the Prophet's day 360 springs, of which ten or twelve now remain.

3 Meaning that the visitor must ascend several smaller eminences. The time occupied is from eight to nine hours, but I should not advise my successor to attempt it in the hot weather.

Harim; pray for the Martyrs; and, after going through the ceremonies, return to the Harim in time for mid-day worship. On the 12th of Rajab, Zairs come out in large bodies from the city, encamp on the plain for three or four days, and pass the time in feasting, jollity, and devotion, as is usual at pilgrimages and at saints' festivals in general.

After half an hour's ride we came to the Mustarah or resting-place, so called because the Prophet sat here for a few minutes on his way to the battle of Ohod. It is a newly-built square enclosure of dwarf whitewashed walls, within which devotees pray. On the outside fronting Al-Madinah is a seat like a chair of rough stones. Here I was placed by my Muzawwir, who recited an insignificant supplication to be repeated after him. At its end with the Fatihah and accompaniments, we remounted our asses and resumed our way. Travelling onwards, we came in sight of the second Harrah or ridge. It lies to the right and left of the road, and resembles lines of lava, but I had not an opportunity to examine it narrowly.[1] Then we reached the gardens of Ohod, which reflect in miniature those of Kuba; and presently we arrived at what explained the presence of verdure and vegetable life,—a deep Fiumara full of loose sand and large stones denoting an impetuous stream. It flows along the Southern base of Ohod, said to be part of the plain of Al-Madinah, and it collects the drainage of the high lands lying to the South and South-east. The bed becomes impassable after rain, and sometimes the torrents overflow the neighbouring gardens. By the direction of this Fiumara I judged that it must supply the Ghabbah or "basin" in the hills north of the plain. Good authori-

---

1 When engaged in such a holy errand as this, to have ridden away for the purpose of inspecting a line of black stone, would have been certain to arouse the suspicions of an Arab. Either, he would argue, you recognise the place of some treasure described in your books, or you are a magician seeking a talisman.

ties, however, informed me that a large volume of water will not stand there, but flows down the beds that wind through the Ghats westward of Al-Madinah, and falls into the sea near the harbour of Wijh. To the south of the Fiumara is a village on an eminence, containing some large brick houses now in a ruinous state; these are the villas of opulent and religious citizens who visited the place for change of air, recreation, and worship at Hamzah's tomb. Our donkeys presently sank fetlock-deep in the loose sand of the torrent-bed. Then reaching the Northern side, and ascending a gentle slope, we found ourselves upon the battle-field.

This spot, so celebrated in the annals of Al-Islam, is a shelving strip of land, close to the Southern base of Mount Ohod. The army of the Infidels advanced from the Fiumara in crescent shape, with Abu Sufiyan, the general, and his idols in the centre. It is distant about three miles from Al-Madinah, in a Northerly direction.[1] All the visitor sees is hard gravelly ground, covered with little heaps of various coloured granite, red sandstone, and bits of porphyry, to denote the different places where the martyrs fell, and were buried.[2] Seen from this point, there is something appalling in the look of the Holy Mountain. Its seared and jagged flanks rise like masses of iron from the plain, and the crevice into which the Moslem host retired, when the disobedience of the archers in hastening to plunder enabled Khalid bin Walid to fall upon Mohammed's rear, is the only break in the grim wall. Reeking with heat, its surface pro-

---

1 Most Arab authors place Ohod about two miles N. of Al-Madinah. Al-Idrisi calls it the nearest hill, and calculates the distance at 6000 paces. Golius gives two leagues to Ohod and Ayr, which is much too far. In our popular accounts, "Mohammed posted himself *upon* the hill of Ohod, about *six* miles from Al-Madinah," two mistakes.

2 They are said to be seventy, but the heaps appeared to me at least three times more numerous.

duces not one green shrub or stunted tree; neither bird
nor beast appeared upon its inhospitable sides, and the
bright blue sky glaring above its bald and sullen brow,
made it look only the more repulsive. I was glad to turn
away my eyes from it.

To the left of the road North of the Fiumara, and leading to the mountains, stands Hamzah's Mosque, which,
like the Harim of Al-Madinah, is a Mausoleum as well as
a fane. It is a small strongly built square of hewn stone,

1. Mastabah.
2. Entrance.
3. Passage leading to Minaret.
4. Hypæthra.
5. Hypostyle.
6. Hamzah's Tomb.
7. The Zawiyah and palm trees.

with a dome covering the solitary hypostyle
to the South, and the usual minaret. The
Westward wing is a Zawiyah or oratory,[1]
frequented by the celebrated Sufi and
Saint, Mohammed al-Samman, the
"Clarified Butter-Seller," one of whose
blood, the reader will remember, stood by
my side in the person of Shaykh Hamid.
On the Eastern side of the building a half
wing projects; and a small door opens to
the South, upon a Mastabah or stone
bench five or six feet high: this completes the square of
the edifice. On the right of the road opposite Hamzah's
Mosque, is a large erection, now in ruins, containing a
deep hole leading to a well, with huge platforms for the
accommodation of travellers. Beyond, towards the mountains, are the small edifices presently to be described.

Some Turkish women were sitting veiled upon the
shady platform opposite the Martyrs' Mosque. At a
little distance their husbands, and the servants holding
horses and asses, lay upon the ground, and a large crowd
of Badawin, boys, girls, and old women, had gathered
around to beg, draw water, and sell dry dates. They

---

1 A Zawiyah in Northern Africa resembles the Takiyah of India,
Persia, and Egypt, being a monastery for Darwayshes who reside there
singly or in numbers. A Mosque, and sometimes, according to the
excellent practice of Al-Islam, a school, are attached to it.

were awaiting the guardian, who had not yet acknowledged the summons. After half an hour's vain patience,
we determined to proceed with the ceremonies. Ascending
by its steps the Mastabah subtending half the Eastern
wall, Shaykh Hamid placed me so as to front the tomb.
There standing in the burning sun, we repeated the
following prayer: " Peace be upon Thee, O our Lord
Hamzah! O Paternal Uncle of Allah's Apostle! O
Paternal Uncle of Allah's Prophet! Peace be upon Thee,
O Paternal Uncle of Mustafa! Peace be upon Thee, O
Prince of the Martyrs! O Prince of the Happy! Peace
be upon Thee, O Lion of Allah! O Lion of His Prophet!"
After which, we asked Hamzah and his companions to
lend us their aid in obtaining for us and ours pardon,
worldly prosperity and future happiness. Scarcely had
we finished, when, mounted on a high-trotting dromedary,
appeared the emissary of Mohammed Kalifah, descendant of Al-Abbas, who keeps the key of the Mosque, and
who receives the fees and donations of the devout. It
was to be opened for the Turkish pilgrims. I waited to
see the interior. The Arab drew forth from his pouch,
with abundant solemnity, a bunch of curiously made
keys, and sharply directed me to stand away from and
out of sight of the door. When I obeyed, grumblingly,
he began to rattle the locks, and to snap the padlocks,
opening them slowly, shaking them, and making as much
noise as possible. The reason of the precaution—it
sounded like poetry if not sense—is this. It is believed
that the souls of martyrs, leaving the habitations of their
senseless clay,[1] are fond of sitting together in spiritual

---

1 Some historians relate that forty-six years after the battle of
Ohod, the tombs were laid bare by a torrent, when the corpses appeared in their winding-sheets as if buried the day before. Some
had their hands upon their death wounds, from which fresh blood
trickled when the pressure was forcibly removed. In opposition to
this Moslem theory, we have that of the modern Greeks, namely,

converse, and profane eye must not fall upon the scene.
What grand pictures these imaginative Arabs see! Conceive the majestic figures of the saints—for the soul with
Mohammedans is like the old European spirit, a something immaterial in the shape of the body—with long
grey beards, earnest faces, and solemn eyes, reposing
beneath the palms, and discussing events now buried in
the gloom of a thousand years. I would fain be hard
upon this superstition, but shame prevents. When in
Nottingham, eggs may not be carried out after sunset;
when Ireland hears Banshees, or apparitional old women,
with streaming hair, and dressed in blue mantles; when
Scotland sees a shroud about a person, showing his
approaching death; when France has her *loup-garous*,
revenants, and *poules du Vendredi Saint* (*i.e.* hens
hatched on Good Friday supposed to change colour
every year): as long as the Holy Coat cures devotees at
Trèves, Madonnas wink at Rimini, San Januario melts
at Naples, and Addolorate and Estatiche make converts
to hysteria at Rome: whilst the Virgin manifests herself
to children on the Alps and in France, whilst Germany
sends forth Psychography, whilst Europe, the civilised,
the enlightened, the sceptical, dotes over clairvoyance
and table-turning, and whilst even hard-headed America
believes in " mediums," in " snail-telegraphs," and
" spirit-rappings,"[1]— I must hold the men of Al-
Madinah to be as wise, and their superstition to
be as respectable, as that of others. But the reali-
ties of Hamzah's Mosque have little to recommend them. The building is like that of Kuba, only
smaller: and the hypostyle is hung with oil lamps and
ostrich eggs, the usual paltry furniture of an Arab

---

that if the body be not decomposed within a year, it shows that the
soul is not where it should be.

  1 In fairness I must confess to believing in the reality of these
phenomena, but not in their " spiritual " origin.

mausoleum. On the walls are a few modern inscriptions and framed poetry, written in a calligraphic hand. Beneath the Riwak lies Hamzah, under a mass of black basaltic stone,[1] resembling that of Aden, only more porous and scoriaceous, convex at the top, like a heap of earth, without the Kiswah,[2] or cover of a saint's tomb, and railed round with wooden bars. At his head, or westward, lies Abdullah bin Jaysh, a name little known to fame, under a plain whitewashed tomb, also convex ; and in the courtyard is a similar pile, erected over the remains of Shammas bin Osman, another obscure Companion.[3] We then passed through a door in the Northern part of the Western wall, and saw a diminutive palm plantation and a well. After which we left the Mosque, and I was under the " fatal necessity " of paying a dollar for the honour of entering it. But the guardian promised that the chapters Y. S. and Al-Ikhlas should be recited for my benefit, the latter forty times ; and if their efficacy be one-twentieth part of what men say it is, the reader cannot quote against me a certain popular proverb concerning an order of men easily parted from their money.

Issuing from the Mosque, we advanced a few paces towards the mountain. On our left we passed by—at a respectful distance, for the Turkish Hajis cried out that their women were engaged in ablution—a large Sahrij or tank, built of cut stone with steps, and intended to detain

---

1 In Ibn Jubayr's time the tomb was red.

2 In the common tombs of martyrs, saints, and holy men, this covering is usually of green cloth, with long white letters sewn upon it. I forgot to ask whether it was temporarily absent from Hamzah's grave.

3 All these erections are new. In Burckhardt's time they were mere heaps of earth, with a few loose stones placed around them. I do not know what has become of the third martyr, said to have been interred near Hamzah. Possibly some day he may reappear : meanwhile the people of Al-Madinah are so wealthy in saints, that they can well afford to lose sight of one.

the overflowing waters of the torrent. The next place we prayed at was a small square, enclosed with dwarf whitewashed walls, containing a few graves denoted by ovals of loose stones thinly spread upon the ground. This is primitive Arab simplicity. The Badawin still mark the places of their dead with four stones planted at the head, the feet, and the sides; in the centre the earth is either heaped up Musannam (*i.e.* like the hump of a camel), or more generally left Musattah (level). I therefore suppose that the latter was the original shape of the Prophet's tomb. Within the enclosure certain martyrs of the holy army were buried. After praying there, we repaired to a small building still nearer to the foot of the mountain. It is the usual cupola springing from four square walls, not in the best preservation. Here the Prophet prayed, and it is called the Kubbat al-Sanaya, " Dome of the Front Teeth," from the following circumstance. Five Infidels were bound by oath to slay Mohammed at the battle of Ohod: one of these, Ibn Kumayyah, threw so many stones, and with such goodwill, that two rings of the Prophet's helmet were driven into his cheek, and blood poured from his brow down his mustachios, which he wiped with a cloak to prevent the drops falling to the ground. Then Utbah bin Abi Wakkas hurled a stone at him, which, splitting his lower lip, knocked out one of his front teeth.[1] On the left of the Mihrab, inserted low down in the wall, is a square stone, upon which Shaykh Hamid showed me the impression of a tooth[2]: he kissed it with peculiar reverence, and so did I. But the boy Mohammed being by me objurgated—for I

---

1 Formerly in this place was shown a slab with the mark of a man's head—like St. Peter's at Rome—where the Prophet had rested. Now it seems to have disappeared, and the tooth has succeeded to its honours.

2 Some historians say that four teeth were knocked out by this stone. This appears an exaggeration.

remarked in him a jaunty demeanour combined with neg-
lectfulness of ceremonies — saluted it sulkily, muttering
the while hints about the holiness of his birthplace
exempting him from the trouble of stooping. Already
he had appeared at the Harim without his Jubbah, and
with ungirt loins—in waistcoat and shirt-sleeves. Moreover, he had conducted himself indecorously by nudging
Shaykh Hamid's sides during divine service. Feeling
that the youth's "moral man" was, like his physical,
under my charge, and determined to arrest a course of
conduct which must have ended in obtaining for me,
the master, the reputation of a "son of Belial," I insisted upon his joining us in the customary two-
bow prayers. And Sa'ad the Demon, taking my side of
the question with his usual alacrity when a disturbance
was in prospect, the youth found it necessary to yield.
After this little scene, Shaykh Hamid pointed out a
sprawling inscription blessing the Companions of the
Prophet. The unhappy Abu Bakr's name had been half
effaced by some fanatic Shi'ah, a circumstance which
seemed to arouse all the evil in my companion's nature;
and, looking close at the wall I found a line of Persian
verse to this effect:

"I am weary of my life (Umr), because it bears the name of
   Umar."[1]

We English wanderers are beginning to be shamed out
of our "vulgar" habit of scribbling names and nonsense
in noted spots. Yet the practice is both classical and
oriental. The Greeks and Persians left their marks
everywhere, as Egypt shows; and the paws of the Sphinx
bears scratches which, being interpreted, are found to be
the same manner of trash as that written upon the remains
of Thebes in A.D. 1879. And Easterns appear never to

---

[1] In Persian characters the word Umr, life, and Umar, the name
of the hated caliph, are written in the same way; which explains the
pun.

enter a building with a white wall without inditing upon it
platitudes in verse and prose.   Influenced by these considerations, I drew forth a pencil and inscribed in the
Kubbat al-Sanaya,

"Abdullah, the servant of Allah."
(A.H.) 1269.

Issuing from the dome, we turned a few paces to the
left, passed northwards, and thus blessed the Martyrs of
Ohod :

"Peace be upon Ye, O Martyrs !   Peace be upon
Ye, O Blessed !   ye Pious !   ye Pure !   who fought upon
Allah's Path the good Fight, who worshipped your Lord
until He brought you to Certainty.[1]   Peace be upon You
of whom Allah said (viz., in the Koran), 'Verily repute
not them slain on God's Path (*i.e.*, warring with Infidels);
nay, rather they are alive, and there is no Fear upon
them, nor are they sorrowful !'   Peace be upon Ye, O
Martyrs of Ohod !   One and All, and the Mercy of Allah
and His Blessings."

Then again we moved a few paces forward and went
through a similar ceremony, supposing ourselves to be in
the cave that sheltered the Apostle.   After which, returning towards the torrent-bed by the way we came, we
stood a small distance from a cupola called Kubbat al-
Masra.   It resembles that of the "Front-teeth," and
notes, as its name proves, the place where the gallant

---

1 That is to say, " to the hour of death."

Hamzah fell by the spear of Wahshi the slave.[1] We faced towards it and finished the ceremonies of this Ziyarat by a Supplication, the Testification, and the Fatihah.

In the evening I went with my friends to the Harim. The minaret galleries were hung with lamps, and the inside of the temple was illuminated. It was

---

1 When Jubayr bin Mutim was marching to Ohod, according to the Rauzat al-Safa, in revenge for the death of his uncle Taymah, he offered manumission to his slave Wahshi, who was noted for the use of the Abyssinian spear, if he slew Hamzah. The slave sat in ambush behind a rock, and when the hero had despatched one Siba'a bin Abd al-Ayiz, of Meccah, he threw a javelin which pierced his navel and came out of his back. The wounded man advanced towards his assassin, who escaped. Hamzah then fell, and his friends coming up, found him dead. Wahshi waited till he saw an opportunity, drew the javelin from the body, and mutilated it, in order to present trophies to the ferocious Hinda (mother of Mu'awiyah), whose father Utbah had been slain by Hamzah. The amazon insisted upon seeing the corpse : having presented her necklace and bracelets to Wahshi, she supplied their place with the nose, the ears, and other parts of the dead hero. After mangling the body in a disgusting manner, she ended by tearing open the stomach and biting the liver, whence she was called " Akkalat al-Akbad." When Mohammed saw the state of his father's brother, he was sadly moved. Presently comforted by the inspirations brought by Gabriel, he cried, " It is written among the people of the seven Heavens, Hamzah, son of Muttalib, is the Lion of Allah, and the Lion of his Prophet," and ordered him to be shrouded and prayed over him, beginning, says the Jazb al-Kulub, with seventy repetitions of " Allah Akbar." Ali had brought in his shield some water for Mohammed, from a Mahras or stone trough, which stood near the scene of action (M. C. de Perceval translates it " un creux de rocher formant un bassin naturel "). But the Prophet refused to drink it, and washed with it the blood from the face of him " martyred by the side of the Mahras." It was of the Moslems slain at Ohod, according to Abu Da'ud, that the Prophet declared that their souls should be carried in the crops of green birds, that they might drink of the waters and taste the fruits of Paradise, and nestle beneath the golden lamps that hang from the celestial ceiling. He also forbade, on this occasion, the still popular practice of mutilating an enemy's corpse.

crowded with Hajis, amongst whom were many women, a circumstance which struck me from its being unusual.[1] Some pious pilgrims, who had duly paid for the privilege, were perched upon ladders trimming wax candles of vast dimensions, others were laying up for themselves rewards in Paradise, by performing the same office to the lamps; many were going through the ceremonies of Ziyarat, and not a few were sitting in different parts of the Mosque apparently overwhelmed with emotion. The boys and the beggars were inspired with fresh energy, the Aghawat were gruffer and surlier than I had ever seen them, and the young men about town walked and talked with a freer and an easier demeanour than usual. My old friends the Persians—there were about 1200 of them in the Hajj Caravan—attracted my attention. The door-keepers stopped them with curses as they were about to enter, and all claimed from each the sum of five piastres, whilst other Moslems were allowed to enter the Mosque free. Unhappy men! they had lost all the Shiraz swagger, their mustachios dropped pitiably, their eyes would not look any one in the face, and not a head bore a cap stuck upon it crookedly. Whenever an "'Ajami," whatever might be his rank, stood in the way of an Arab or a Turk, he was rudely thrust aside, with abuse muttered loud enough to be heard by all around. All eyes followed them as they went through the ceremonies of Ziyarat, especially as they approached the tombs of Abu Bakr and Omar,—which every man is bound to defile if he can,—and the supposed place of Fatimah's burial. Here they stood in parties, after praying before the Prophet's window: one read from a book the pathetic tale of the Lady's life, sorrows, and

---

1 The Prophet preferred women and young boys to pray privately, and in some parts of Al-Islam they are not allowed to join a congregation. At Al-Madinah, however, it is no longer, as in Burckhardt's time, "thought very indecorous in women to enter the Mosque."

mourning death, whilst the others listened to him with breathless attention. Sometimes their emotion was too strong to be repressed. " Ay Fatimah! Ay Muzlumah! Way! way!—O Fatimah! O thou injured one! Alas! alas!" burst involuntarily from their lips, despite the danger of such exclamations; tears trickled down their hairy cheeks, and their brawny bosoms heaved with sobs. A strange sight it was to see rugged fellows, mountaineers perhaps, or the fierce Iliyat of the plains, sometimes weeping silently like children, sometimes shrieking like hysteric girls, and utterly careless to conceal a grief so coarse and grisly, at the same time so true and real, that I knew not how to behold it. Then the Satanic scowls with which they passed by, or pretended to pray at, the hated Omar's tomb! With what curses their hearts are belying those mouths full of blessings! How they are internally canonising Fayruz—the Persian slave who stabbed Omar in the Mosque—and praying for his eternal happiness in the presence of the murdered man! Sticks and stones, however, and not unfrequently the knife and the sabre, have taught them the hard lesson of disciplining their feelings; and nothing but a furious contraction of the brow, a roll of the eye, intensely vicious, and a twitching of the muscles about the region of the mouth, denote the wild storm of wrath within. They generally, too, manage to discharge some part of their passion in words. " Hail Omar, thou hog!" exclaims some fanatic Madani as he passes by the heretic—a demand more outraging than requiring a red-hot, black-north Protestant to bless the Pope. " O Allah! *hell* him!" meekly responds the Persian, changing the benediction to a curse most intelligible to, and most delicious in, his fellows' ears.[1]

---

1 I have heard of a Persian being beaten to death, because instead of saying "Peace be with thee, Ya Omar," he insisted upon saying "Peace be with thee, Ya Humár (O ass!)" A favourite trick is to change "Razi Allahu anhu—may Allah be satisfied with him!"—

An evening hour in the steamy heat of the Harim was equal to half a dozen afternoons; and I left it resolved never to revisit it till the Hajj departed from Al-Madinah. It was only prudent not to see much of the 'Ajamis; and as I did so somewhat ostentatiously, my companions discovered that the Shaykh Abdullah, having slain many of those heretics in some war or other, was avoiding them to escape retaliation. In proof of my generalistic qualities, the rolling down of the water jar upon the heads of the Maghribi Pilgrims in the " Golden Thread " was quoted, and all offered to fight for me *à l'outrance*. I took care not to contradict the report.

---

to " Razi Allahu Aan." This last word is not to be found in Richardson, but any "Luti" from Shiraz or Isfahan can make it intelligible to the curious linguist.

END OF VOLUME I.